D1329433

Diamond in the Dark

Leaving the Shadow of Abuse

Phyllis Hain

After-Book Professional Commentary by Bryan Glazier, Ph.D. L.M.H.C.

bancroft press

Published by Bancroft Press "Books that Enlighten"
P.O. Box 65360, Baltimore, MD 21209
800-637-7377
(410) 764-1967 (fax)
www.bancroftpress.com

Cover design: Steve Parke
Interior design: Tracy Copes; Daft Generation
Author photo: Robert Hain

Hardcover / ISBN 978-1-61088-100-5 / $25.00
Printed in the United States of America
First Edition

bancroft
press

To my husband, Robert Hain, for standing by me, loving me, encouraging me to end my lifelong pattern of silence, and rejoicing with me as I found my voice and shed my burden of shame.

Table of Contents

Preface

Photo by: Robert Hain

Like so many other victims I have worked with, I find the letting go of my closely-held secrets the hardest thing I have ever done. An unanticipated life event was the catalyst for disclosure. It pushed me to mentally go back in time and make an attempt to document my life's journey. I thought I'd been doing so well getting my life together, staying busy, experiencing life's pleasures, and enjoying the security of my marriage, job, and family. Yet, it turns out, I had simply managed to suppress and hide the unsavory bits of my life, but they were always there, waiting patiently for a time and place to escape.

I have now attained what is somewhat magical for me—the ripe old age of 60. There's no getting away from accepting my advanced lifeline when I have celebrated my youngest child's 40th birthday and my grand-daughter's eighteenth. Recognition of these milestones in my life, and theirs, reminds me I no longer have to protect and shield my children from my weaknesses and mistakes. In fact, they want to know the truth about the family, relationships, and events that shaped their lives.

Having never written a book before, I found the task daunting and anxiety-filled. In my first attempt, I tried to tackle head-on the mid-life events that suggest my need to validate my feelings and to defend myself. I found, though, that none of my explanations made sense without exposing those hidden wounds, going back in time to look not only at the genetic part of who I am, but my family's struggles and the environment that helped shape who I am today.

In writing my story, I changed many of the names in order to protect innocent individuals, as well as the names of some family members who really didn't want to be "involved" with me or my story. Inevitably, some changes will end up protecting the guilty. As a matter of public record, key names are true to their characters, and are included to cover all facets of my story. Everything here is true, from my perspective, at the time the events were taking place, and to the best of my memory. Some events will also be addressed in retrospect, as additional information was learned after the fact.

The silence of shame

empowers the abuser.

Chapter 1
May Day!

Jamie, Jake, and Sugarboy, her beloved Shetland pony.

For me, the weekend seems to start like all the others. I begin every Saturday and Sunday struggling with painful slowness. But this weekend is different. Only a person who has suffered through an unbearable relationship can understand how the impending end of a marriage can make a life devoid of pleasure. I ask myself, how is it that spring, a time that should normally bring joy and a sense of renewal, can harbor such emptiness and usher in the acceptance of defeat?

It's May 31, 1980. The day is beautiful, with blue skies and a gentle breeze. I look out my kitchen window. The white café curtain is pulled back so I can view the entire back pasture, but now I watch a calamity in the making. My bulldog, Jake, is running full speed, the hair on his back standing straight up. He's growling and barking at Sugarboy, my daughter Jamie's poor pony. The pony is running for its life. Sugarboy's eyes are wide with fear, his whites clearly visible around their hazel center, as he is about to crash into the fence. I flinch, hold my breath, and brace for impact. The dust stirs as Sugarby slides through the dirt, planting his little hooves—just in the nick of time. He stands up straight on all fours and gives a shake that rattles his whole body. Turnabout is fair play—it's now Sugarboy's turn. Flight didn't work, so fight takes its place. Sugarboy puts his head down, with ears laid back, and unleashes his anger on the dog, as if he is saying, "That's it. Now I'll nip at your heels." Jake sees the fire in his eyes, turns, tucks his tail, and runs for his life as the pony, mouth open and teeth bared, tries his best to land just one bite on the white of his nubbin tail.

This is their routine. They're actually great friends, and often pass the time chasing one another. Neither has ever hurt the other. Both have provided us with reams of laughter and joy. Even their act this morning is not making me feel better.

I walk outside, feel the glorious day, and wonder: Why can't I just be happy? Little did I know that peace and happiness would not re-enter my life for what seemed several lifetimes.

My children, Nathan and Jamie, are rushing around to get ready for a day at the beach. "Hurry and feed the animals," I encourage them. "Get your things together quickly because we're getting a late start." Since they know the beach is waiting, they set out to get the jobs done without the usual resistance. They are eager for life. I am still feeling the sting of my emotions. When I think about last night, I feel ill.

I wonder how I'm going to get through the next ten hours of family togetherness. It's funny, though, because no one seems to notice that I am not happy. My chest is welling up with pain, and my mind is crying. Meantime, my kids need help finding their swimsuits.

Last night was Friday night, and what could have been a nice evening became, instead. Just another embarrassing disappointment. It started out meeting my husband (here I'll call him JJ), his friend, and his friend's companion du jour at a restaurant in Mobile, Alabama,. With good Italian food, Chianti, a few laughs, and congenial conversation, it should have been good.

Who knows what makes a 33 year-old adult act like an imbecile? Looking back, it must have been a set-up to make sure he came out as the all-powerful one in our relationship. What else would make a grown man decide to start throwing ice chips he fished out of his iced-tea glass?

I looked at him with amazement—I don't get a chance to go out much, and manners are very important to me. "Behave" is the Southern admonition that slips out of my mouth like a watermelon seed you spit out. That makes it worse. He now reaches into my glass and tosses an ice chip at my face to further demonstrate his disdain for me as I attempt to keep our dinner within the parameters of acceptable behavior. "OK, I see everyone's looking now. Can we just cut it out?" I try to speak softly. This just brings him strange pleasure as he announces to the audience of attentive bystanders, "If you don't like it, you can leave, but you're not taking the car."

The only way I can deal with this is silence. I look at the stunned faces of our dinner companions. I don't really know them, but I remember thinking how odd they were. She was an attractive petite blonde, he a tall, not so attractive, red-haired man. I felt embarrassed, trapped, degraded, and helpless. JJ was smug, and his contempt for me was so obvious. His friends said nothing. I just sat there, in my usual retreat mode.

The rest of the meal is a blur. The evening is certainly unmemorable, other than the fight. I don't think I ever saw either of his friends again.

As his opponent and wife of 12 years, I had suffered another defeat. I was okay with that—I knew our days were numbered. The decision had already been made—I would leave him as soon as there was an opportunity to escape with my children. It was going to be hard—I had tried and failed several times before. But if I wanted to survive, I knew I had to make a good plan.

The 18-mile ride home that night is silent, and it seems even longer than usual as we head due west along Airport Boulevard. We pass the airport and continue almost to the Mississippi line before taking a left onto Grand Bay-Wilmer Road, headed toward Union Church. We finally make the single turn up to our farm on the hill.

Our driveway is literally cut into the side of an embankment, where some concrete had been randomly poured to keep erosion from washing it away. Nothing pretty about it, just two rough ruts that allow our car tires to roll easily up the grade. As the lights hit the opening, you can see that the sides of the drive are just dirt, and that the hill is sprinkled with oaks, some pines, and a few scrubby looking bushes. We are home.

There won't be an apology coming. There never is. I will just go in and try to stay away from him. The last thing I want is to be next to him. Maybe we can just go to bed and he'll leave me alone. I will get into bed. I will face the wall. My body will remain rigid as I pray he will read my unspoken language. His hands on my skin cause a chill to run up my spine and tears to well up in my eyes.

The phone is ringing and it jolts me back to face the morning. It is my older sister Ann, who is also my only sister. It's unusual for her to call me on a Saturday morning. She's a beautician and usually busy handling a shop full of gossiping ladies. She works hard to style their hair. She is attentive to each one in their proper turn, and for that, they tell her their life stories. She smiles and laughs appropriately. Compliments come from her talkative customers, as does news from the neighborhood. In lieu of a good bartender, your hair dresser is the next best thing.

I sense something is wrong because Ann's tone is different. I can't put my finger on what is different, but I hear something strange in her voice. She asks me what I am doing. I tell her we are getting ready to go to Gulf Shores for the day. Still trying to act like it isn't a big deal, she calmly says, "Can you stop by here on your way? I've got a shop full, but I need to talk to you."

"Sure," I say, "but what's wrong?"

She says, "I can't talk now. I'm busy. Just come by."

I wonder if she and my brother-in-law had a fight.

Only three miles due south, at the crossroads of Old Pascagoula Road and Grand Bay-Wilmer Road, stands the Corner Grocery Store. It's a rundown place. Its old green block building and asphalt parking lot, complete with potholes, is always in need of repair. It is a gas station/ hamburgers-to-go diner/ grocery/beauty shop. Ann and her husband, Otto, own and run the place.

Directly north of the Corner Grocery Store is Phelps Feed Company, and diagonally across the street is Donny's Auto Repair Shop. The opposite corner on the other side is still a vacant lot. Not much else around and the closest real grocery store, Sims Clover Farm, is still a couple miles down the road. This logistical fact accounts for the constant traffic in and out of this homey stop.

To enter the grocery store, you must walk past the two gas pumps out front. Walk in and you will be greeted with a Southern, "Hi, how ya'll doin' today?" The one cash register is on the left and the grill bar on the right. You can order up the best hamburger in town and then shop for other needs. When you leave, the cook will hand you your brown bag of fresh grilled hamburgers and you pay for it right along with your groceries and gas. JJ goes into the front with the kids, and I head around to the back door. The entry on the opposite end of the building is the beauty shop. As I walk around the side, I can't help but notice that the weeds, or the so-called Jap grass, are getting high. It'd almost take a bush hog to knock it down.

When I enter the shop, there must be five or six ladies sitting around at various stages of the beauty process. Ann, spotting me as I enter, lifts a woman up from the shampoo bowl, wraps a towel around her dripping wet head, and tells her she'll be right back. Ann looks at me. *Man, this oughta be good.*

In the small and dingy back room, Ann closes the door behind us and looks me straight in the face. "Paul's wife is dead," she says.

I'm taken aback. I'm not even sure what she's saying. "What are you talking about?" I ask. I'm in a brain fog trying to put the words together.

"Paul's wife, Elizabeth, is dead. It's in the paper, on the front page," she tells me.

"What happened? Did she commit suicide?" I ask her quickly, as if I can't understand what she is telling me.

Ann shakes her head and tells me, no, the newspaper reported that she had been shot and stabbed.

"Oh my God!" I can hear myself say. "I can't believe this." Ann doesn't appear to be sympathetic. She turns and opens the door to walk out, leaving me with a quick shake of her head. "I've gotta get back to work."

I pick up a Sunday paper as we leave the store. I can't wait to get into the car so I can be still enough to read the story. Totally engrossed, I start to read the article out loud to JJ as we drive down the road. It said Paul Leverett, a wealthy businessman in Mobile, found his wife murdered inside their fashionable home in the Airmont subdivision.

JJ stops my reading and asks me, "Isn't that the man you sold insurance to?"

I nod my head yes. The pretty blonde woman in the photo gracing the front page, above the fold, is smiling. It's a beautiful smile. It's the first time I have ever seen Elizabeth Leverett, and she is dead.

A dazzling smile in this file photo from Mobile Press Register.

Chapter 2
Getting There from Here

Lance Corporal Brown and my mom at age 15.
It's the photo Dad carried in his Marine helmet during WWII.

As with most complex stories, I must start at the beginning. My parents married on May 30, 1942. My mother was 16 and Dad had just turned 18. They honeymooned at the Admiral Semmes Hotel in Mobile, Alabama. She recalled the memory of that time with a look of sweet nostalgia. They had been happy early in their marriage.

Dad was soon drafted into the war—he was of age and had to report. He chose the Marines only because he was drafted. Had he not been drafted, he would not have volunteered. It was his duty, as he saw it, and for that reason he, like so many other young men, stepped up to the plate.

My brother was born in June of 1943, in my maternal grandparents' home while Dad was away training at Camp Pendleton in California. Joseph became Grandpa's little man and the apple of his eye. He was pretty and blonde, and he shared the German characteristics of his grandpa. As he grew, he would take the same path as Grandpa and all of Mom's brothers. He would become a skilled master carpenter, a true craftsman, and a blue-collar worker all his life. Our family considers this a good and honorable thing.

Dad was in the 4th Division, the first group of Marines to move across the Marshall Islands, Saipan, and into Iwo Jima. He took a hit of shrapnel from a bomb dropped on Saipan. He said he remembered seeing and hearing the bomb as it barreled through the sky toward him. He remembered hitting the ground, feeling the bomb's impact, getting up, and looking frantically for his helmet and gun (a Marine never loses his gun). His sergeant came up and asked him, "What the hell you looking for Brown?" When Dad told him his gun, the Sergeant, looking into Dad's blood-covered face, told him he wouldn't need his helmet—the medics would be taking care of him. The Sergeant picked up Dad's helmet and handed it to him. Riddled with holes, it had Mom's photo still embedded in the top, split in half and covered with blood. Dad's front line action ended that day—he came home from WWII with a metal plate in his head—and the effects would last a lifetime and affect all of us.

After months in the hospital, Dad slowly recuperated and was finally able to go home. He remembered the surgery on his brain—he was awake, lying face-down in some contraption . . . listening to the saw grinding through his skull . . . feeling the vibration rack his body . . . smelling the burning bone through flared nostrils . . . counting the droplets of blood as it dripped from the tip of his nose. The horror can only be imagined.

Before his release from the hospital, Dad's surgeon gave him a very candid briefing. He had done the best he could, but he was not able to get out all of the shrapnel imbedded in his brain. He said he was afraid he'd do more damage than good if he dug too deeply for the pieces left behind. And he cautioned him that, at any time in the future, some of that shrapnel could try to work its way out. If it did, it could result in serious or even deadly consequences. Dad was instructed to report to his local Veterans Hospital, as soon as possible, if he experienced symptoms that potentially could be attributable to the wound.

My question is: Why in hell didn't the doctor just tell him he had a ticking time bomb in his head that could go off at any moment? It would have had the same result. Corporal Brown was medically retired, sent home with a Purple Heart, his discharge orders (DD-214), saying that his service had been honorable and he suffered from acute brain trauma. He would later receive a Presidential Unit Citation for outstanding performance in combat during the seizure of the Japanese-held islands of Saipan and Tinian in the Marianas from June 15 to August 1, 1944.

*A photo of Mom, Dad, and Joseph, standing
on the porch of their new home.*

And so Dad made his way back to the farm in Alabama, and back to his young, beautiful wife and baby boy. He wasn't the same young man who had left.

Dad was discharged from the military, and received 100% disability compensation, which meant a small monthly pension of about $75.00 a month. Under the VA rules, if he earned even a small pittance on his own, he would lose the disability check. How's that for incentive? Dad spent the rest of his life in fear of shrapnel going off in his head and/or losing that check. He was too honest to lie, and too scared to say, "To hell with them." He would not earn more than what would amount to minimum wage at any job he ever held.

War had made him a man. It had also made him a sick man. He could have been the poster boy for Post Traumatic Stress Disorder (PTSD), though that wasn't a diagnosis used at the time. Maybe some people knew of shell shock or battle fatigue, but not anyone who lived on Route 3 in Samson, Alabama.

What they did know was that he came home with bad memories, night terrors, a hot temper, and a penchant for uncontrollable violence.

The tears shed by Grandpa Carpenter on the day Dad asked for my mother's hand in marriage were soon remembered. Grandpa had told my mother he was concerned about her choice because the Browns were known as a hot-tempered bunch. Mom said she loved him and Grandpa acquiesced to her desires. Now, with such a volatile person, it became difficult to keep the love in their marriage.

Mom told me about one day when they had fought. She cried, left her home with Joseph on her hip, and walked the quarter-mile mile up the hill to her parents' house. Grandma Carpenter was sitting in the porch swing when Mom came up the steps, still crying about Dad's violent tantrum. Grandma sat in silence for a while, stood up from the swing, and said, "I was afraid of that." She then got up and walked over to the stobs that jutted out from the unpainted wood post, took her bonnet, and put it on as she walked down the steps past Mom. She continued quietly across the grassless yard toward her barn. It was the last time Mom went to her parents' home for support.

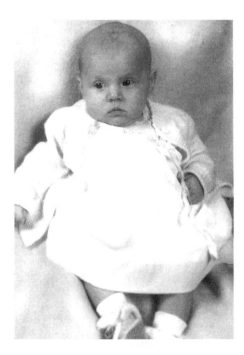

Me at 2 ½ months (photo by Parker Studio, Geneva, Alabama)

Diamond in the Dark

My sister was born in July 1947. She was the first child to be born in the new house built just up the dirt road from my grandparents' home. Grandpa and Dad built it themselves after Dad returned from the war. It was a little white frame house with green shutters and a green shingle roof. It was the first on the road to boast indoor plumbing, which included a bath. Grandpa intended to give my parents the land and the house. I guess he wanted them to live on the farm forever.

They did stay long enough in their new home to produce yet one more child. They named me Phyllis Anita Brown when I arrived in the fall of 1950. I too was born at home, a country doctor at Mom's side. I was a big baby with a tad of blonde fuzz for hair, sweet baby features, and the proper number of fingers and toes. When asked later of that day, Mom says I almost killed her. She was a little woman at 5'2" and, according to her, I weighed 10 lbs. and was 23" long. My birth certificate said 9 lbs. 6 oz. She was probably right—evidently, I felt like 10 lbs. According to my birth certificate, my father was unemployed. Mom said she tried to bottle feed me but I would have nothing to do with it. I was a hungry, crying, and unhappy baby until she gave in to breastfeeding me. So I guess I can't use not being breastfed as an excuse for my problems. I ask myself, in 1950, was it common for a woman to even want to bottle feed instead of breast feed? And, therein may lie part of the problem. I don't think Mom really wanted another baby, so it would be a pretty safe bet I was an accident.

>─┼◆>•○•<┼─<

There wasn't much work in the country, but Dad did finally find some in Fort Walton. It was a long, hard commute. Lunch was packed in a syrup bucket and off he'd go. He walked a mile up the dirt road to catch his ride, and they continued for over an hour, one-way, before reaching their destination. The long commute would eventually become too hard, especially with the prospect of greener pastures beckoning from the city.

I don't know if it was just the work, or the family and the work, but my dad was the reason for our move to Pensacola, Florida. By the time we moved, Dad's temper tantrums were in full swing. "Your dad would fly off the handle over nothing," my mother told me.

I'm sitting happily in front of the house Dad and Grandpa built. You may be able to make out the scar on the left side of my forehead. It was created when I accidently encountered some broken glass.

Chapter 3
The Browns

My paternal grandparents, Ella Victoria and James Mack Brown.

My life growing up in the South in the 1950s plays out in little vignettes in my mind. Some of those memories conjure up warm feelings, especially the times I spent with my grandparents, aunts, uncles, and cousins who lived in the country. Mom's family was from around Samson, Florala, and Geneva, Alabama. Dad's side of the family lived mostly around Defuniak Springs, Darlington, and Gaskin, Florida.

Gaskin, Florida was two miles from the Florida-Alabama line. It was and is a sleepy little crossroad in the middle of nowhere. The Church of Christ is on one corner, a filling station/little grocery store opposite, a Masonic Lodge across the street, and in the last corner sat a (not so picturesque) wood-frame house. My grandparents, Mack and Ella Brown, lived there. It had no porch, and had bare concrete blocks up to the front door. In the spring, a trellis of Morning Glories would bloom big and blue, creating the only beauty that house would ever know. The wood had been white at one time, but was always in need of paint. It was never repainted that I can remember. There were three tiny bedrooms, no bathroom, a living room with an adjoining dining area, and a kitchen with a large storage pantry that connected to one of the bedrooms. When I went into the kitchen pantry, I could crawl through it on my way into the bedroom on the other side. It was the same pantry where Grandma shot a five-foot long Rat Snake resting comfortably on her canned goods. She was a crack shot and only broke two jars to kill it. The house was a great place to play, and Grandma Brown didn't seem to mind children in and out, throughout. The outhouse was in the back yard, complete with Sears and Roebuck catalog for reading and "finishing touches."

Grandma Brown, a twin of English background, was born Ella Victoria Wilkerson. Ella married Mack Brown, and they had five sons and one daughter. My dad was somewhere in the middle, with my favorite, Uncle Burt, the baby. From all I heard, the Brown boys were not only mean as hell, but they had no problem deciding to scrap things out with fists flying.

Ella was tall and handsome, and loved her children above all things. She was a mother whose children could do no wrong in her eyes. She was attentive and giving to everyone, especially her children, but for me, it was special. I was not accustomed to being treated special. When I stayed with her, for a week or two in the summer, she made breakfast just for me. That may not sound like much, but Grandma Brown truly was the only person who did anything only for me. Her pancakes were thin and she piled them high, her egg bread was amazing (it was her version of French toast), but best of all was when she would make fried eggs, circled with crispy edges and golden, runny centers, buttered toast, all finished off with sweet iced tea. At home, we had iced tea only on Sunday—Grandma Brown let me have it for breakfast. I loved her. It is still my drink of choice today.

Ella Brown was a real pip. She loved Sweet Garret Snuff and six-ounce bottles of Coca Cola. At the time, it may have had cocaine in it because she seemed to be addicted. Each morning my job was to go up to the corner store, get a can of Sweet Garret Snuff, a Coca-Cola, and some penny candy for myself. When I returned, she would drink the whole bottle without putting it down. It was amazing to watch and a mystery why it didn't seem to burn her throat, as it did mine when I tried the same thing.

My grandfather, Mack Brown, was a different matter. I didn't really have a chance to get to know him. I don't remember him ever picking me up or hugging me. I guess I was a little afraid of him, and he didn't make any attempt to change that notion. He drove an old pickup truck. In the front seat of his truck, he kept a footed glass tumbler and a box of Kellogg's All-Bran. The glass looked like a great big, heavy wine glass. I thought it peculiar at that time because there was not a single wine glass in our home. I guess Grandpa needed a little help to keep up his daily constitution.

Next to the All-Bran and the wine glass lay the ominous and untouchable double-barrel shotgun. Grandpa worked for the Florida prison system, and his job was to guard the convicts who worked along the roadside on the chain gang. He'd stand at his truck, shotgun in hand, to make sure they worked, or at least didn't escape.

Behind their house were dog pens, filled with long-eared, howling hounds. Grandpa was a hunter, especially a deer hunter, but I'm not sure why he had so many hounds. I certainly didn't make the connection at the time, but I suspect the hounds were for hunting escapees. Hounds will track just about anything if they have a scent.

From everything I have heard, Mack Brown was just plain mean. To keep his five boys in check, he ruled with an iron fist. Dad told me only one story about him and his dad. Dad said he and a cousin had been out in the hot summer heat most of the day. They were hungry, thirsty, and headed home. They stopped at an uncle's watermelon patch and picked one melon growing near the edge of the field. They busted the melon, ate it, and enjoyed the fact it supplied both water and sugar for energy. An aunt saw them and went running to tell Mack Brown that my dad had stolen a melon. Grandpa Brown beat him with a belt, swinging full force, the buckle hitting each time. Dad said, "I lay in bed with welts and sores that ran bloody corruption." He hated that aunt until she died. Strange that he attributed the horrific beating to the aunt, not to his dad.

My visits with Grandma would be in the spring, during garden season, when the empty freezers were calling to her to be filled for the year. If you couldn't can it, you could freeze it. The women of the country tackled their full-time job, each spring, until the harvest was complete.

Being pulled out of bed before the sun came up was not fun. However, riding in the back of the pickup, with baskets and buckets rattling around next to me, bumping along the road to the fields, was. It would awaken us to a glorious new day. We rode several miles up the highway to the turn-off. It was just past The Silver Slipper (a local honky-tonk), where we turned left.

Sometimes that colorful neon sign, in the shape of Cinderella's high-heeled shoe—the only neon for miles and miles—would still be flashing as we passed by. I loved looking at that sign blink against the back-drop of the rising sun.

A couple more turns and we were driving on a dirt road, the dust generating a red cloud behind the truck. We slowed almost to a crawl as the truck bounced and rolled over the slatted cattle gap. The cows mooed their acknowledgement as we passed through their pasture. We turned at the mailbox and drove down a two-trail dirt lane, crossed another cattle gap, and were around the curve before we could see the house belonging to my Uncle Alf and Aunt Belle, who lived on the back of the farm. Alf was another of my Grandma's brothers, my great uncle. This was where a caravan of relatives would form. All of us met for our "good mornings" before going together to enter the fields. We caravanned for our early arrival at the garden, planted with peas and butter beans as far as the eye could see. There were also areas with Speckled Butter beans, Crowder and Purple Hull peas—dew still glistening on the leaves. It got hot quickly, so picking had to be done early.

Everyone set off to work with the usual admonition, "Watch out for snakes." We never walked outside that someone didn't say "Watch out for snakes." Talking and laughing could be heard as each of us moved down our row. I stayed close to Grandma and picked with her. When the baskets and buckets were overflowing, we headed back to Uncle Alf's to shell and "put up" the peas. It was hot, and our hands were gritty with dirt—I hated dirt on my hands. The ride in the back of the pick-up was the coolest place in the summer heat. "Sit down or you'll fall!" I was warned. I obediently complied. While we rode, I was wiping my wind-blown hair from my eyes, so I could watch the dust and smoky exhaust, happy we were on our way back.

Uncle Alf's home was a shotgun shanty with a wood plank porch, a swing on a squeaking chain, straight ladder-back chairs with cowhide seats, and a rocker that awaited any visitor who wanted to set a spell. Above the doorway was a rattlesnake skin that stretched five to six feet long. Maybe they felt the skins would ward off other snakes from settling in too close to the house.

Around the door and tacked to the eaves of the house were hundreds, and I mean hundreds, of rattles cut from snakes that had met their untimely demise. It was fascinating. "Look!" Uncle Alf would say. "This one is the same age as you. He has five buttons and a few rattles." Uncle Alf would laugh and pretend to chase me with the rattle. I'd squeal. He loved it. He was such a good uncle.

After Aunt Belle's breakfast of biscuits, thick-sliced bacon, grits, and fresh-fried yard eggs, we were ready to work. Everyone helped bring up the freshly picked bounty. The enameled dish pans came out and were filled to the brim. I got a pan too, not so big and not so full. The family sat on the porch and shelled peas, bushel after bushel. I shelled a bit, played a bit, and shelled some more. Whenever my pan reached a cupful, everyone would say what a great little pea-sheller I was. Even when I looked at the huge pans of peas the women shelled, I was still proud of my cupful. As the morning gave way to the hot summer heat, I could understand why the harvest had to be done early.

By afternoon, the really hot work began. The big black cauldron was out in the yard, away from the house. The shelled peas were put into clean 10 lb. flour sacks. The flour sacks were tied to the end of a long pole, then carefully lowered into the hot, bubbling bath. My grandma said we had to blanch them. When the peas came out steaming hot, the sacks were immersed into a wash tub filled with fresh, cold pump water. The cooled peas were then ready for bagging and freezing. No other vegetable ever tasted as good as these peas and butter beans grown "up home."

I tried to help when I could. However, I couldn't have done much because I was distracted. I took it as my duty to collect the eggs that were "newly" laid. Sometimes, they were so fresh they were still warm in my hand. I watched the butterflies and mosquito hawks that were everywhere, dancing in flight around the wild flowers. I would do my best to catch them, marveling as the soft velvet of the butterfly wings would rub off in my hand. There were so many and no one seemed to worry about them.

The summer days went by slowly—there weren't a lot of exciting things to do. Sundays were set aside for church. At Grandma Brown's, we always went to the Church of Christ on the Gaskin corner. So many cousins, aunts, and uncles from my mother and father's side attended. It would be the home church for our family for many years, and a visit to the country wasn't complete without attending services on Sunday morning, just to see everyone.

Grandpa Brown died of a stroke in the summer of 1956. I was five years old. At the time, my Uncle Bill had taken my grandma on the first real vacation she ever had. They went to South Florida to see the orange groves, Cypress Gardens, and Silver Springs. Everyone was trying to find my uncle to let him know Grandpa had died. My mom was babysitting for Uncle Bill's children, my first cousins, Kenneth and Rebecca. When Uncle Bill finally called home to check on his children, Mom told him Grandpa Brown was dead and to come home quickly. My Grandma Brown was a little high-strung, to say the least, so my uncle decided not to tell her the truth—he told her one of the children was sick and they needed to go home. Uncle Bill said he drove 80 to 100 miles per hour all the way home. Dad had previously contacted the highway patrol in hopes they would spot my uncle's car and we could get the message to him. No one stopped him—so much for the highway patrol watching out.

As soon as their car came over the hill, Grandma started crying. She knew by all the cars in her yard that tragedy had touched down in her life. She sat in the car for a long time, refusing to come inside. I was in the house watching the adults come and go. After embalming, they always brought the body home for the wake. Grandpa Brown was lying in his casket in the very small living room. It was a pretty emotional scene as they finally led my Grandma through. She had her hand clamped over her eyes, so she would not see him. It was some time later that night when she would come back into the living room to make peace with her loss.

The next day, men were standing all around their trucks in the front yard. My cousin Rebecca and I were both so little. The corner store was just across the road, and one uncle gave us some money. We went to the store and bought candy, gum, Rock'n'Roll cookies (gingerbread cookies), and RC (Royal Crown) Cola. My cousin Kenneth was with us; he was nine years old. We took our treats and went to the backyard, looking for a place to spread out our bounty. We ended up sitting in the shed for Grandpa's hunting dogs while we enjoyed our impromptu picnic. Every time we would laugh about anything, Kenneth would remind us of Grandpa. We would be sad for about two seconds, look at each other, then carry on. It would be safe to say I didn't feel a great loss, only because I didn't feel I even knew him.

I visited my Grandma Brown, on Manning Pond, many times later as I grew up. The times I spent with her are special memories. I never once heard her talk of Grandpa, so I don't know how much she really missed him. Grandma had such a great personality, and I think she did have a demon living in her somewhere, because she loved reading murder magazines. There would be all these gross magazines, like "The Detective," lying around that were about gruesome, horrible crimes, complete with crime scene photos. She would caution me about men, tell me they were only after one thing, and remind me every day not to trust them. We would loll about on our beds, read the magazines, take long naps, fish in the pond, and on special occasions ride down to the cold creek, called Natural Bridge, for a swim. Her home was always busy, filled with warmth and laughter, and always open to our family, especially her boys.

I was 20 years old when she died of a heart attack in 1970. I was pregnant with my second child, Jamie. The Church of Christ was overflowing that day. So many people came. They couldn't all be seated in the church, so the family sat, as her friends filed through to pay their last respects. I don't know how many were there, but we sat a long time as each person would go up, look at her, turn, nod to the family, and walk out. It was said they had never seen so many people show up for a funeral before. I guess the old girl had made a lot of friends in her life. She was a good woman.

At her funeral, I'm as big as a barrel, very pregnant, and I pick my way carefully down the steps leaving the church. I glance up to see an old man standing in front of a long row of bystanders, all there to pay last respects. As I pass, he catches my eye for just a second. The old codger has his eyes on my breasts and, with his mouth open, he flicks his tongue at me! It was such a shock. My eyebrows had to go up, as I looked forward and continued on, shaking my head with the realization that Grandma had been right after all.

Me, Nathan, and Grandma three months before she died.

Chapter 4
Mom's Family

Charlie Hilton and Ibbie Florence (Williams) Carpenter.

A beautiful Ibbie, at 16 years old.

My mother's name is Mary Irma. She hated the name Mary, so she was always called Irma. She was one of six—three girls and three boys (all three boys became carpenters and cabinet builders). Carpenter is not their real name, but it seems to fit. Mother was a beauty. She had natural, platinum blonde hair, and that lovely, easy-to-tan, skin. No matter where she went, someone would talk about how pretty she was. For her entire life, beauty was her claim to fame.

Mom loved her family heritage. Her parents, Charlie and Ibbie, were farmers—Grandpa was also a carpenter. Grandma was part English, and my grandfather was of German descent. In America, our family can be traced back twelve generations to the early 1800's, when the first of them settled here. Grandpa's farm seemed to have everything one would need: The shotgun style farmhouse, the smoke house filled with hams and sausage, a wash house with a canning room, the corn crib, the barn with mule stalls and pig pens in the back, a work shed (where he did his own blacksmithing, and where, if a neighbor died, he would often be asked to make the coffin), his calving and milking barn, and of course, the out-house. Fruit trees were planted around the property, so there were always good things to eat.

Grandma sold her hen's eggs for a little extra money, made quilts entirely by hand, and was always on call, ready with her divining rod, when neighbors were deciding where to drill for their new well. They watched as the willow would shake hard when finding water. She was right every time.

Many of Mom's relatives lived within a five-mile radius of their farm, so the family reunions conjure up memories of lots of children, each with a family story to tell and all sharing a little of the Carpenter blood pumping through their veins.

Many of Mom's family were Primitive Baptist. The churches were so small and poor that one itinerate preacher served many congregations. The once-a-month when they did meet, their service was complete with singing, preaching, communion, and dinner on the grounds, followed by the ritual depicted in Biblical washing of the feet stories. The elders would go back into the church and take turns washing each other's feet, which showed their humility, as was described in the Bible. I liked their much more laid back demeanor of accepting people. They believed if God wanted you, and your name was in the "Lamb's Book of Life," no matter what you did, he'd bring you back to him before you died. It was written ahead of time, and you just played out the scenes while you were here on Earth. Neatly stored in the back of my head became the line: "It is preordained, before the foundation of the Earth, those that will inherit the Kingdom of God."

Grandpa Carpenter was the opposite of my dad's father. I don't remember him in anything but overalls (that's what he worked in), although I know he had a suit because I saw it in pictures. In the evening, he sat in his rocker by the fireplace. He welcomed me onto his lap. He was quiet, and his hands were rough, but his heart was warm and kind. I have no idea how he made such an impression on me, but I still miss him to this day.

The family's farm was about 300 acres of pasture, farmland, and a big pond on the back 40 acres. The Florida-Alabama line was the southern border of the property. Life there had to be tough at times. Grandpa never plowed with anything but mules, Kate and George. I would sit and wait in the ditch until he would finish his plowing. He would leave the field, stop the mules, and I would get to sit on Kate all the way back to the barn. I'd cling to the leather harness as we plodded along. Kate was very tolerant, but not so George. When he was ready for his stall and dinner, he was not up to late afternoon riders. In fact, George was known for both biting and kicking when he got the chance.

During the Great Depression, they came and took my grandpa's mules because a bad crop had left him unable to pay his debt. He walked back into his barn and wept. Thank God a law was later passed that they can no longer take away the tools one uses to earn a living.

My Grandma Carpenter was the stoic, quiet type, but she was a tough little lady and very adept with a peach switch. She certainly tagged me at least once, and I deserved it. At about four or five years old, I was very into being creative and looking for a true "cook's" experience. I used fresh hen eggs I had gathered, straight from the nest, to make my famous mud pie. It seemed like a grand idea at the time. And my culinary confection looked quite pretty on a flat board. It was dark mud, but boasted a sprinkling of white sand for icing and sticks for candles.

Grandma must have known we were up to something, because she walked around the corner of the barn with a peach switch already in hand. She took a look at the empty egg shells lying on the ground near the pie, which were a dead giveaway. My cousin Jerald ran like the wind, leaving me to take the heat. After being afforded the opportunity to do the "switch dance," I didn't break her eggs, without permission, ever again.

It may sound funny, but my mom really did have to milk the cows before starting out on her daily three-mile walk to school. Mom said she took her lunch with her to school each day. She and Dad attended the same school, and one day Dad not only decided to steal her lunch but ate the whole thing. He then invited her to his home for lunch, since his house was in sight of the school. He thought surely she would come, but she declined the invite.

Mom said she liked school and excelled in basketball of all things. I don't know what league they were playing, but this little 5'2" firecracker was named "Best Forward in the State of Alabama" for her contribution to their all-girls basketball team. She had to have been fifteen or barely sixteen when she won the title, because she quit school at sixteen to marry my dad.

My cousin, sister, and I.

Most of the folks up home didn't get away much because there were too many animals to feed, too much work to be done. My Aunt Inez (mom's oldest sister), and my Uncle Phonza, who lived just down the dirt road from my grandparents, finally decided to come and visit our family in Pensacola. Picture in your mind a real "Norman Rockwell family" in an old car riding "full speed" about 35 mph, which was about as fast as Uncle Phonza would allow himself to go.

My mom and dad were working the day our relatives first arrived at our store. I was on the sidewalk in front of the grocery store, just sitting on the electric horse that cost 10 cents to ride. If a paying rider wasn't there, I sat on it, sometimes for hours. My cousin Florence was sent to get me off the horse and bring me back into the store. She picked me up and swung me around. We were so excited to have them. My beloved cousins would be there to play with me all day.

We all went to our home early that day. We had only been home a short while when the phone rang. This was the first house we lived in that, to my memory, had a phone. I still remember the number: it was HEMlock 33911 (433-3911). My mom walked over to answer the call, listened intently, and dropped her head. She backed up, plopped into a nearby chair, her hand went to her face, and she started to cry. There was silence for a moment. My Grandpa Carpenter was dead.

Grandpa had plowed with Kate and George all morning, came in for lunch, laid down on the couch for his usual nap, and made a funny sound. She ran to check on him and knew something was wrong. She went out and rang the farm bell attached to the house. It was usually rung for the field hands to know when it was time to come in. She rang the bell until my uncles, who lived up the road, arrived. Grandpa was dead. Unfortunately, I do not remember his funeral service, nor do I remember their family ever visiting us in Pensacola again. I think my aunt was afraid we were jinxed.

Chapter 5
Burke's Place

Me in my new dress Momma made.
This photo was taken just before leaving Burke's Place.

My earliest years were plagued with illness and problems. The first tale Mom shared was of me, at about six weeks old, suddenly becoming very sick. She said I was a lifeless limp and starting to stiffen up, when I screamed in pain, then finally passed out. They tried everything to get me to open my eyes, but I was unresponsive. Dad raced me as fast as he could to the hospital in Defuniak Springs. Mom said by the time they got me to the hospital, my back was drawn up in a stiff curve. The end of this episode was a country doctor telling them I had spinal meningitis. I'm not sure how he came up with that diagnosis because no spinal tap was done. They soon sent me home. Mom said they couldn't do anything for me. I gradually got better.

Seizures followed the meningitis, and of these episodes, I have no recollection. Mom told me I would start crying, get frantic, and when I could not catch my breath, I would actually go limp and pass out. She would take me to the kitchen sink, turn me over face-first, and run cold water over the back of my head until I'd come to. Dad always believed I was faking it. He thought I was "holding my breath" because I was so spoiled and just wanted my way. He thought a good spanking would get my attention and make me stop. According to Mom, Dad did spank me even while I was still in diapers.

My mom also told me of the day my dad had an "epiphany." They were at the lake with my Uncle Leroy and his wife Thelma. They were going to walk to the other side, and Thelma said she would watch me. As Mom made her way around the lake, I became frightened and wanted my mom, so I started crying and running toward her. My parents saw me running toward them and they started back toward me. They watched helplessly as I fell off the dam into the deep water. By the time they got to me, I was floating face down. Dad pulled me out of the water and laid me on the grass, preparing to try his skills to revive me. About that time, I came to, gasping and crying for my mom. I guess the fact I had not taken in any water impressed my dad. Maybe I hadn't been faking those "pass-out-spells" after all. I continued to be the talk of the family, distinguishing myself as a very difficult child. Only my grandparents and my nanny were brave enough to babysit me for long periods.

I had just begun to walk when I was ten months old. The family folklore is that my sister, who would have been about four at the time, was told to watch me. We were in the backyard while Mom dressed for church. Ann took me to her playhouse, where she had a glass iced-tea pitcher. The pitcher broke and I fell, face first, into it. The blood gushed from my head. Mom said by the time she got to me, I was completely drenched in blood. On a Sunday morning, they rushed me to the hospital in Defuniak Springs. The country doctor they called in was having a party at his home, and supposedly arrived at the hospital drunk. According to Mom, they held me down and put twelve big stitches in my head.

>─┤─◆)─·─O·─◆─┤─<

We moved to a housing project in Pensacola sometime around 1952. Moving from the country to the projects was a culture shock. Mom said

I passed out almost every day when I'd cry to go outside. As soon as they could manage, they moved to a home on the north side of town, somewhere around Ensley.

The house in Ensley was a white wood frame house with a porch spanning the entire width across the front. It was a home rented from landlords named Burke—and the house was always referred to as "Burke's place." Joseph and Ann were already in school. I spent hours alone playing my portable record player, memorizing the tunes of "Tina the Ballerina," "Ballad of Davey Crockett," and "Cinderella." The limited selection of 45 rpm's was played over and over. I fantasized of being a horse-riding cowgirl, and I loved to play with the gun and holster set Mom had bought me. It was a pistol with real popping caps.

Dad went into business with his brother. It was supposed to be a 50-50 deal that would let Mom and Dad run the storefront of a wholesale bait and fishing tackle store. My uncle had a van loaded with wholesale products of fishing tackle, poles, reels, and such that he delivered along the coast from Pensacola to Appalachicola, Florida. Because of the limits on what Dad could earn without losing some of his pension, the brothers got together and agreed that my mom and dad would basically work for peanuts while the business was being built. And so the family business of Brown's Sporting Goods began.

Mom said Dad was so afraid of losing his pension, he would not try anything that could put him over his limit. That fear set in stone the "financial ceiling" of our future. It finished him off by killing his incentive, thus dooming his chances of adequately caring for his family. He always felt the shrapnel left in his head would cause problems eventually. It had to be a terrible time for him as my mom kept pushing him to insist on more money. She didn't trust my uncle, but Dad thought his brother would never do him wrong or cheat him.

Going to work at the store made it possible for Mom to hire a black lady (at that time, we called her a "colored lady") to care for me while she worked. I never knew her name, I called her Nanny. She was short and plump and had huge breasts. She was so good to me, and there was no place better than sitting in Nanny's lap and being rocked to sleep. Mom said Nanny would say I was one little white girl she would like to keep. Nanny is a loving and good memory of my life.

Mom was home with me one day when we walked together to a

neighbor's house just up the dirt road on which we lived. Mom visited with her, sitting in the kitchen and drinking coffee. As we walked back home, I placed my hand in the pocket of my smock dress to play with newly found coins. I had picked up about four pennies and one nickel lying on a table at the lady's house. As we walked back into our home, a penny dropped from my hand, clanging as it rolled across the floor. My mom wanted to know what I had dropped and what was in my hand. I slowly opened my hand to reveal the change in my sweaty little palm. She responded by picking a switch from the bush by our porch. She switched me all the way back up the hill so I could return the money. I screamed, she switched, and she held my hand hard as I did the best "switch dance" ever, trying to evade the biting stings on my bare legs. I had the opportunity to give my apology to the lady, and I endured a repeat of the same process on the way home. My mom was intent on making sure I never again took anything that did not belong to me. She succeeded.

My parents were really into their religion and, for them, Christianity meant you were Baptized into the Church of Christ, where true Christianity could only be practiced. It was a Bible totin', Bible quotin', have-an-answer-for-your-salvation ilk.

My parents were not only strict in making sure we understood the Ten Commandments, but we were to abstain from all "appearances" of evil. To them, that meant that if we were doing something that someone could see and somehow extrapolate a negative image or conclusion from, we weren't allowed to do it—it was a sin. These beliefs were more important than anything else to my parents, and we were held fully accountable to the law of God. When it came to me or my brother, corporal punishment was administered frequently for even minor transgressions. In my entire life, I never remember seeing my sister spanked for anything.

We were all in church one Sunday and I was sitting between Mom and Dad. During the service, Dad leaned over and picked me up in his arms. I panicked that he was planning to carry me out of the church. I looked at Mom, with eyes begging to be rescued. Dad never took me anywhere without Mom—I was terrified. When we got home, I stood in the doorway of the bathroom and watched Dad get something out of the medicine cabinet. He was sick. I overheard him laughing and telling of getting sick during church and just grabbing me up as an excuse to leave in the middle of the service. To him, it was really amusing that I thought I was going to be punished. I don't really think Dad had the ability to think that children actually had feelings, or that his behavior could affect us, other than through punishment, of course. For me, it seemed Dad only had one punishment—spanking. The only question was how hard or long it would be, or how angry he was at the time. If I, ever on high vigilance, scared him, and got his blood pumping, it was a beating for sure.

>—I—◆>—◦—◦<—I—<

I have only a few visual memories of Dad during this time frame at Burke's place. He was a hunter and a fisherman, so guns were always in our home. Children are pretty observant. They are especially attentive to anything that is out of place.

This particular day, my eyes focused on an intriguing object, sitting out in the open, that I was unaccustomed to seeing. My dad was in bed snoring away. I can still hear the rhythmic sound of him sucking in the air, making a loud grating noise, a pause, then a spewing hiss as he exhaled.

I stood at the door listening—watching and accessing the opportunity that had presented itself to me. The four-poster bed stood tall in the center of the room, but my interest lay in the gun propped up on, and leaning steady against, the footboard. The gun's barrel was pointed toward the ceiling, with the polished wood stock resting firmly on the floor.

I listened until I felt confident the snoring rhythm would continue without missing a beat. I crept into the room, squatting so low I would not be visible from the bed. I don't think I was afraid, but I was concentrating intently on not being discovered so I could connect with the gun. I knew I was not supposed to touch it, but curiosity took over. My small hand slowly reached toward the trigger, and I gently placed my index finger on the cold metal. I could not pull the trigger because of the standing position of the gun. My finger pressed down—nothing. I put my other hand on top of my finger and pressed again . . . Boom! The gun went off—I fell back on my butt. Dad jumped up, grabbing frantically for the gun and angrily coming toward me. I looked up and saw a perfect hole in the ceiling. After that, my memory goes blank.

Me, as a toddler. I'm sure whoever took the photo caused me to hold the gun.

Sitting on the Burke house front porch were a few potted plants of differ-ent varieties. The Christmas peppers were so colorful, the leaves were a bright green, and the elongated fruit was plentiful as well as pretty, showing off its bounty in reds, whites, oranges, and varying shades of green. I sat alone on the porch. I picked a pepper from the bush. I knew it was hot, so I did not even try to eat it.

Ah-ha! I had an idea. Dad's hammer was lying on the step where someone had left it after use. I picked up the hammer and started popping the peppers on the step. After a bit, I was discovered by my not-so-attentive caregiver. Then, with pepper juice on my hands, I rubbed my eyes—they burned like fire.

Someone took me from the Burke house to my mom, who was working at the tackle shop. My face was red and swollen, and my eyes still burned. My mom put cold cloths to my face and laid me on a table in the backroom of the store. An oscillating fan was pointed strategically at my face. I fell asleep crying.

Chapter 6
BRENT LANE

*Me wearing my majorette boots and holding Elsie the Cow,
and my big sister with her bride doll.*

I believe a visual image is often worth far more than words. The photo of Ann and me standing in front of our car was taken on Christmas. She was smiling, proudly displaying her wished-for Bride Doll that came with a fancy blue-enameled doll trunk—it had to be expensive. Mom had gotten me an Elsie-the-Cow stuffed animal. It is funny now to see how Borden Milk Company marketed to children. I loved my fuzzy brown cow, with the painted rubber face and sweet expression. Mom had saved milk carton seals and added a few cents to acquire my gift. In the photos, note the majorette boots I have on with my dress. They were my prized possession. I would always have my own idea of what I wanted to wear and what I would not. That became an issue that plagued me and my mom for years to come.

By the time we moved to the house on Brent Lane, I was five years old. The run-down house was made of stucco, but it boasted beautiful hardwood floors. The exterior looked like dirty, whipped meringue on a pie, all swirled and peaked. Even in the 50's, this was an old house, so I'm guessing it had to have been built in the 1920's or earlier. Moving here did get us much closer to the store that my parents co-owned. Convenience had been an issue when selecting this house, plus at $35 a month, my parents could afford the rent. (Obviously, we had not moved into the high rent district.) The biggest problem was I lost Nanny in the move. I missed her and grieved her loss for a long time.

Our furnishings were sparse and simple. Mom and Dad's bedroom held the same lovely four-poster bed, dresser, and chest that they had moved from the Burke house. My favorite things were two boudoir lamps that sat on each side of my mom's dresser. They were of a formally dressed man and woman. He was holding her in the mid-step of a waltz, and her long skirt was swirling gracefully as she turned. The small silk lampshades were white, with a ruffle around the edge. When turned on, the light illuminated the Lalique-looking, smoky glass figures—I found them enchanting. They made me dream of someday waltzing in the soft moonlight.

The dining room held a yellow, marble-colored Formica-top table surrounded with chrome edging—very contemporary at the time. The chairs were chrome with yellow plastic seats. It was at this table where we had to gather each week for Dad to read from the Bible. There would be great emphasis placed on this symbolic tradition of reading God's word. It showed our devotion to our religion. Dad was very sincere, and took this ritual seriously as a solemn duty for our family's edification. I would get so tired of listening. As I would become restless, I would try to leave my seat and sneak over to my mom's lap. Dad would stop reading, and without raising his head, just glare at me over his reading glasses. The look just about killed, so I'd try to move slowly and inconspicuously back onto the cold plastic seat. It was so hard to sit quietly, waiting until the seemingly never-ending reading was over.

It was in this house, in this living room, that my mother received the call of my Grandpa Carpenter's death.

Our residence, 57 Brent Lane, was on a quiet, paved street—quiet except for the fact we were close to the railroad tracks, where all the cheap houses were. We got used to it, and eventually didn't even hear the daily rumble.

My seizures were still a problem. I was anemic and sickly, and I was tired a lot. No one ever had to force me to take a nap. If you couldn't find me, most likely I had fallen asleep somewhere. I should have scored some parental points just for that, because they usually didn't have to make me go to bed. Though my mom said she took me to the doctor, I have no recollection of it.

I do remember the heavy brown bottle filled with bitter, thick yellow tonic. I had to take it every day, no matter the nasty taste.

Unfortunately, I was also a bed wetter. This wasn't popular with the family, so the nickname of "Pee-Pot" was slapped on me and used. There were several other versions of sick nicknames—"Phil-Pot"—or, because my platinum blonde hair was so thin you could see my tanned skin in the part of my hair, "Skin-Head." My dad would laugh at me and tell me I wasn't born but hatched. The other "good one" was that they just didn't know where I came from, and that I must have crawled from under a log like a centipede.

Let me say now that the inflicted pain was not intentional—they were just kidding. I know my parents loved me. The jokes may have been inappropriate, but they were funny to them, and there was no way they knew how the names were affecting me. Neither my brother nor my sister had nicknames, and I do not remember either of them being subjected to ridicule.

The name-calling was not the worst of it. My older siblings were free to express their disdain for me. My poor mom knew if I was hurt, I could have an attack, usually ending in me not being able to breathe, and then "passing out" stone cold. She tried to protect me from my very rough big brother. He was eight years older and resentful that he had to play nice with me. I am sure I was a pest, but I was five and he was thirteen. When he would get angry, I became afraid. My mom would actually leave me and my sister in his care with rights to spank me if he saw fit.

When he would get too rough, I would implore him, "Don't do that or I'll pass out." I was using that threat as my weapon, but the truth was, I really did not want to go through the seizures. My passing-out was like drowning in open air. I would gasp for breath but I couldn't get any air into my lungs. I would frantically gasp until my vision would blur, then I was gone. If no one saw me pass out, I would awake lying in a pool of hot urine, so Mom would have to bathe me and put me to bed. It really wasn't anything I could control.

No matter the evidence, I don't think my brother has ever changed his opinion that my seizures were created to torment him. To this day, not one of my family ever asked me, "What happened?" or "How did it feel when you were in the throes of a seizure?" Everything was based on how it inconvenienced them. That was pretty much the attitude, and I guess I was mighty inconvenient.

I love this photo. I was five.

Over the years, my seizures happened less frequently. My last memory of passing out was while playing in the tree in our yard. The very climbable low-hanging limbs beckoned to me even though Mom didn't like me to climb. I climbed to the first limb, then higher and higher. One limb was long and thin, so I held on tight, and I swung out from the base of the tree, dangling by my arms. There was a board lying on the ground. I had not paid much attention to it beforehand. I dropped easily from the tree. My foot landed on the board. A nail was sticking from the board, which penetrated my thin sneaker sole and went right into the bottom of my foot. I screamed as I managed to get my foot off the nail.

When I saw the blood, which scared me, I became hysterical. As I started to run to my mom, who was inside the house, I felt it. I recognized what was coming, because my throat would not let any air in, no matter how much I gasped. I could feel it surrounding me like a bubble of fog closing in around my head. As I ran up the steps and onto the porch, my vision was blurring, my hand reaching out to the screen door.

When I awoke, my sister was standing at the foot of the bed. She was saying, "Please, wake up. Please, wake up." My mom was bathing my face with a cool rag. She let me go back to sleep.

I don't remember ever waking to my mom crying or holding me saying, "please wake up." Usually, I just woke up in a bed somewhere. Maybe it happened so often when I was very young, she became hardened to the drill. My mom said I eventually just grew out of the seizures after some doctor treated me with vitamins and penicillin. There was never a conclusive diagnosis.

Some of my days would be spent in the hardware store with my mom while she worked. I remember spending a lot of time playing in and around that building. There was a man there who must have worked with my dad. I don't really know what he did, but he may have been a driver of our distribution van. I really could not describe his face if my life depended on it.

Behind the store was a parking lot with a garage. I was playing behind the store one day and the man was sitting there on something low. I think he was smoking. To me, he looked like a cross-legged Buddha. He had on jeans and a t-shirt. He called me over to him. I was not accustomed to not doing what I was told. He pulled me over to sit on his lap. I didn't want to sit on his lap, and I tried to get up and push away. I was now facing him. He pulled me back down and now had unzipped his pants. He pulled his penis from his pants and told me to touch it. When I resisted, he held me tighter and made me touch his erect penis. When again I tried to pull away, he laughed at me. With mean-looking eyes, he warned me, "If you tell anyone, you will be the one to get a spanking." I believed him, so I didn't tell.

There was another time that I can see so clearly, but it had to have been in a different indoor location, maybe in the back of the store. I try to remember the face and the details, but I can't. I just remember lying on the side of a bed. My legs are dangling and my panties are down. I see that from a bird's eye view, not as if I'm lying there. A man is standing by the bed, my legs are being pulled apart, and I am crying. I see the belt. It is doubled, and it is lying next to me within reach.

"Lie still," is all I hear. My legs are so little. He is looking at my vagina. I think he stops because I am crying, or maybe someone is coming. Anyway, at this point, my memory goes blank. I guess I can say I was fondled at belt-point. I try, but I can't recreate the face in my mind, and I am not sure where we were, but it really happened. Again, I didn't tell anyone. I was too afraid, and I didn't want to get into trouble.

Diamond in the Dark

My sister had a girlfriend, Tricia, whose house was across from ours when we lived on Brent Lane. I would sometimes go with my sister to visit and play at her house. Tricia's mother was something else. She was the first woman I ever saw smoke cigarettes and drink beer. She was nice to me and Ann, often taking us all for ice cream at the drugstore counter. Banana splits were the specialty and cost thirty-five cents. A split banana, filled with scoops of vanilla, strawberry, and chocolate ice cream. Toppings of chocolate syrup, pineapple, and strawberry. Flavors I had never known, all topped with whipped cream, nuts, and a cherry. It was so extravagant and delicious. I was in awe of such wonderful things, and I soaked up the feeling of sitting in that booth, my bare legs sticking to the plastic bench, feeling the newness of the experience—and loving every second of it.

One evening, I got to go to a real restaurant with them. Tricia's mom ordered a Busch Bavaria beer, in a can, as she smoked a Lucky Strike cigarette. I watched her closely as she raised the tin can to her lips. The blue can featured a snowy mountain scene and blue waters—my mom neither drank beer nor smoked. It was an Italian restaurant, and it was there I saw my first pizza. I didn't have a clue what it was when the waiter set it down on the table next to ours. It was about 16 inches, very thin, with little more than red sauce and Parmesan cheese. I watched in fascination as the skinny woman with long black hair and red finger nails picked up the limp, red triangles. Her languid manner made me feel as if she was savoring each bite. I watched as she ate the pieces, on-by-one, until all the slices disappeared. It was a curious thing for me to see the lady eat that whole pizza. For me, spaghetti and meatballs were exotic enough, and I ate them with joy and happiness on my face.

The fly in this ointment was Tricia's stepfather. His name was Reggie. He was tall and thin, had reddish blonde hair, and he too smoked and drank. A can of Busch Bavaria was never far from his grasp. What I hated about him was his mouth. His top lip was strange. When he smiled, his top lip seemed to curl up and you could see the lining, or pink, inside.

I was in their home one day when he grabbed my arm. He said, "Hold on, you pretty little thing. Come give me a li'l shu-gah." He leaned down and gave me a big, mouth-open, wet kiss, sticking his tongue in my mouth. I was pushing at him, trying to get away. I was learning to push back. He was so disgusting I wanted to throw up. There must have been others nearby, so he quickly let me go. I was afraid to tell on this man. It was better not to risk telling things that I didn't understand.

My first year of school was traumatic. With no kindergarten to prepare me, I was marched off to Brentwood Elementary School at the ripe old age of five. School started in September, and I wouldn't be six for a while. I wanted my mom. I cried each day, and they would bring in my sister to console me. I actually ended up doing well, but I had a tough start. I seemed always to be one of the youngest in my class.

For every bad thing that happened to me, it seemed a good thing would happen, too. My teacher chose me and a little boy named Rusty (yes, he did have red hair) to represent our class in the annual parade for Pensacola's Fiesta of Five Flags. Mom made my beautiful costume, a Grecian girl, full-length, toga-type dress of sheer pink organza, worn off one shoulder, with a wide gold braid on the scarf draping from the opposite shoulder. There was also gold braid at the hem, gold sandals, and a wreath of flowers for my hair. I remember everyone telling me how pretty I was in my pink toga—everyone but my sister, who was a little jealous of me having such a beautiful costume to wear. She was the one who always loved the girly things, not me, so it was very unusual to see me so feminine in pink.

Me on Pensacola Beach at Fort Pickens.

Diamond in the Dark

The good times had by our family always seemed to be centered around my dad's love for water sports and fishing. Pensacola Beach was the sugar white sand heaven my parents and all of us children enjoyed. At the beach, our family would meet Uncles Bill and Bert, with their wives Betty and Derlie respectively, along with my cousins Kenneth and Rebecca. Those were the ones who lived in Pensacola, but we had more relatives who visited during the long summer season. My mom's family would also come—Uncle Dewey and Aunt Ina with my cousins Michael and Randy. We enjoyed the surf of the emerald-green Gulf of Mexico, but most family days were spent on the calm waters Bay side. In the 50's, there was an abundance of sea life for all to enjoy.

At that time, the Bay was thick with sea grass, crabs, scallops, oysters, and fish of all kinds. There were so many crabs that even a small child could carry a crab net and just scoop them up. The trick to this was chicken scraps. Dad would get chicken necks and tie them up with string, put a weight on them, and throw them out about ten feet from the shore. We would put ten or so of the bait bundles out along an area of a quarter-mile or so. All we had to do was start walking down the beach. The clear water made it easy to see the bait and the crabs that would come up to feed. As the crabs would latch on to those tasty, rotten chicken necks, it was easy enough to scoop them up. It was a fair chase, because the crabs would often see us in time to make their getaway. The splashing, running, giggling chase would be on, sometimes successful for us, sometimes not.

Scalloping was a little different. I was just learning to swim, so I would dog paddle like crazy trying not to let my feet touch down on the grassy, creepy, scary Bay bottom. Crabs could clamp down on your toes with their big pinchers. Stingrays could whip their tails around and tag your leg. Schools of minnows could swim along and nibble at your toes or any bare skin. The scallops hid, in their clam-like shells, in the living grasses below. We wore our tennis shoes and my brother would drag his feet on the bottom to keep from stepping on a stingray.

My brother had a system for scalloping and picking up oysters. He took a big tin wash-tub and placed it into the center of a black inner-tube, then tied a string end to the handle and one end to his waist. He would happily snorkel along in the shallow water picking up the scallops or oysters, and tossing them into the floating tub. I would cling to the inner-tube, which was black and rubber, and joyfully dog paddle along, watching the tub grow full and heavy from the crustaceans.

If you were not squeamish, you felt alive and part of the living spirit of the Earth we shared. It was beach life in Florida. Little did I know that, in my lifetime, I would see that paradise maimed and ruined, first by Mother Nature with her raging hurricanes, then finished off by "big oil." Big oil, the epitome of greed, would try to put a final round into the head of a struggling victim. I am so thankful that I experienced the exquisite white sugar sand of Pensacola Beach while it was still in such pristine condition.

At the end of the day, our family and friends would often gather together at the picnic tables on Wayside Park. We kids would play. The adults would cook up the bounty—fish so fresh they were almost flipping as they were dropped into the hot grease. The scallops were fried along with the hushpuppies. The ladies brought baked beans and cole-slaw. And sometimes our meal finished off with a big churn of homemade vanilla ice cream. Rebecca and I would sit on the churn to hold it down, and the boys would crank as the cream hardened. It was family time I will always cherish.

Though my parents were members of the Church of Christ, I am sure all of my parents' friends were not church-goers. One couple would come over to play cards—a big guy named Dullath, a fishing buddy of my dad's, with his thin, red-haired wife. She was nice, and they all seemed to like each other.

These friends suffered a terrible blow to their marriage. The thin red-haired woman was diagnosed with tuberculosis. T.B. was a word only whispered about because it was too bad to say aloud. I didn't know what it was, but it was the first time I heard of a sanitarium. This lady was taken from her family and sent away to this place to die because there didn't seem to be a cure. I know my parents tried to offer their support and friendship. I never saw her again.

The story that my little ears overheard, in bits and pieces, was that my parents had gone to a party or get-together where drinking was involved. My dad left the room for some reason and came in to find Dullath with lipstick on him. That lipstick may have been in my mom's shade.

That night, the three of us kids were home alone watching television, while our parents were out for the evening. I don't know what time it was, but Dad came home alone, and he was so drunk he could hardly walk. He staggered through the living room and went straight into the back of the house. No one had to tell us there was a problem. He obviously was on a mission, and obviously, his children all looking at him in fear was not a concern of his at the time. I could hear him in the bathroom.

Then he noisily continued on into the master bedroom. We were all afraid, but there really didn't seem to be anything we could do, so we had to wait until he came back out. He emerged from the bathroom with his pistol in his right hand. The gun wasn't in a cover or anything. He was disheveled. His shoes were untied, the laces long and flopping. He was stumbling about so much I did not know what to do. I had just learned to tie my shoes. *I need to tie his shoes*. I timidly moved from the shadow of the room. I looked up at him and asked, "Daddy, can I tie your shoes?"

He turned and looked at me as though he was surprised I would speak to him. He pushed me away and made an indiscernible remark as he walked out the door. I can't remember what my brother and sister did next, but I watched him through the window as he staggered down the front steps of our home, across the yard, and then down the street, his shoes flopping, laces untied, and his gun in hand. I still vividly see his staggering silhouette as a car's bright headlights shined in his face. I knew something terrible was going to happen. I was afraid for him.

There were numerous fights while we lived on Brent Lane. Mom said it was because they found out that the paperwork on the business Dad had with my uncle was not as they thought it would be. Mom pressed Dad to have an attorney look at the papers and he finally agreed. Mom had been right. They did not own what they thought was half of the business. Dad was so upset by the thought that his beloved brother had not given him the deal he thought he was getting. Dad would have died for his big brother. He felt betrayed and depressed. Instead of facing up to the problem and confronting his brother, he just gave in. He backed out with nothing to show for all their work. According to Mom, Dad said, "If he wants it that bad, let him have it." If there was a turning point when things got worse for us, this was it.

Now it seemed that if Mom and Dad had a disagreement of any kind, the fight escalated quickly. We wouldn't even know what was going on before we were in the midst of totally fearful chaos. One evening, a fight started in their bedroom, with things crashing and breaking—there really was no way for me to know how it started. I do know it ended with everything in Mom's room destroyed. The screams were Mom's, the crashing of glass was from the beautiful boudoir lamps with the ballroom dancers hitting the wall and falling in shattered pieces to the floor. I loved those lamps so much, but I knew they were gone.

The police were called by someone. Dad was crying. I could hear the sobs coming from the bedroom as the policeman walked through the house. One of the cops stayed in the room. He was nice, and he was telling Dad, "Mr. Brown, you are going to have to try and get yourself together if you want to work on the police force with us." That cop had to have known Dad couldn't work as a policeman if he had these kinds of problems with his wife. I guess they would say anything to defuse a situation. Before that night, I did not know Dad wanted to be a policeman, or that he had applied for the job. Needless to say, Dad's dream was shattered just like those lamps.

All of our family loved our trips back to the country and family home. My brother, sister, and I spent most of that time with my mom's sister, Aunt Inez and Uncle Phonza. From our perspective, they had a Norman Rockwell-like life. Their whole family, including the five children, lived in a three-room shack with no plumbing or a fireplace but an overflowing abundance of love. No one fought there, and the parenting style was much kinder. Eventually, they were able to build a nice cinder-block home and left the little shack behind. It was good for them, but I liked the shack better.

On one of our visits, we were all playing in the front yard of their new house. I was about seven years old, my sister about eleven, and my cousin thirteen or so. Jake (an older cousin) drove past in his dad's car, which produced giggles and laughter. Jake, about seventeen years old, was so handsome. The conversation turned to Jake's sexual exploits, and my cousin told of one girl who had her pants pulled down. I listened closely as the older girls discussed things in whispers and laughter.

It was the first time I was privy to a discussion like this, and I thought it would be an opening to get some help. I mustered up my courage and told them that a man had pulled *my* panties down too. They both turned and looked at me with wide, judgmental eyes. Immediately, I wished I could take it all back, but I feared his words would come true. He had warned me I would get into trouble if I told.

Within seconds, the girls began giggling and chanting as they pointed at me, then turned to shun me. They huddled together, turned their backs on me, and ran away. I felt empty, alone, and physically ill,

Wow! That didn't work. When my panties were pulled down, I must have done a terrible thing. I felt so ashamed and humiliated in front of the two older girls. Their reaction to me was confusing and painful. I'm not sure what I thought they could do to help me, but they obviously weren't prepared to deal with that kind of disclosure. I decided not to ever talk about the incident again. When it comes to pulling down panties, there is shame, even if you are five years old and an adult is the one who hurts you. The girls never mentioned the incident to me again.

Chapter 7
NORWOOD

Our family photo just before my brother left for the service.
I thought my mom was the most beautiful mom ever.

During the summer of 1958, my mom and dad were able to purchase their first home in a lovely little neighborhood of modest, cinder-block houses, most of them with flat roofs and colorfully painted exteriors. Mom chose a pink block house. Even at eight years old, I had developed some sense of aesthetics and found the pink house with white trim interesting, though not in a good way. It was extraordinarily feminine. I was always somewhat embarrassed when I'd have to give directions to the pink house.

When Grandpa Carpenter died, he left my mom fifty acres and the house they had built on his property. My dad, always afraid of debt, told my mom that if she wanted to buy a different house, she'd have to sell her inheritance. She sold the fifty acres and the house to her brother for about $3,000, and that was the down payment for our $8,500 pink house.

Diamond in the Dark

The Norwood subdivision was a horseshoe-shaped, drive-lined neighborhood with a canopy of Live Oak trees. Looking down into my new neighborhood, I sensed a cool, tranquil invitation to a new life. The huge trees wrapped over the top of the drive, creating a welcome respite of cooling shade for our intense summers. The biggest problem was that they had added gray jagged rock to the concrete to build all the streets within the very small subdivision. Trying to walk barefoot on the pavement was like dancing on a sizzling skillet. Our feet toughened over time, but it was always a challenge to walk barefoot in our neighborhood. The Pensacola cinder-blocks, as they were called, were very basic but sturdy concrete-block homes, built to withstand the frequent hurricanes that came up the coast.

Our cinder-block home—address: 5826 St. Benedict Avenue—had three bedrooms and one bathroom. It was right in the curve of the horseshoe lane. As you rounded the curve, you drove straight into our driveway and covered carport. There was no landscaping, no paved driveway, no heat or air-conditioning, and just one bank of cabinets in the kitchen. The best feature of the home were the hard pine floors that glistened with a thick coat of shellac.

Huge Live Oak trees filled our small yard and created much needed shade for the long, hot summers. That was a good thing. However, I had no idea how much mess could be created by oak trees. They are in a perpetual state of growing leaves; blossoming with little bloomy things that fall off, completely covering the ground and filling the air with pollen; or becoming heavily laden with acorns that fall by the thousands. You have to rake and rake and rake, which we did. Take my word for it: Oaks are better to admire in someone else's yard than to have in your own.

We were all so thrilled to get a new home of our very own. We wouldn't have to rent any longer, and the pride of ownership hit my mom with full force. She was a worker, and she sure didn't mind putting us to work either. There were things she wanted to accomplish immediately and things that would follow in time.

First, the yard needed grass, so we were all on hands and knees poking little holes in the ground, sticking a grass plug in, and covering it with our hands. We couldn't even think of affording sod squares, so sprigs had to be planted and nurtured into a lawn. Kids proved to be really good at sprigging.

My mom loved flowers, and flower beds were soon designated for the yard. She bought rectangular concrete blocks, and with them we lined the front of the house and around the two oak trees. We set each block in dirt at an angle, with each resting on the back of the next. They looked like a ric-rac of white ribbon around the two oak trees in our front yard. My job was to paint each block white to match the trim of the house. Mom filled the beds with azaleas and other flowers.

The winter was coming, so they added a floor furnace in the most central location of the house, which was the middle of the hall, leaving about 10-12 inches of flooring on each side of the grate. It made sense to put it in the center so the heat could reach both ends of the house. Of course, we didn't know at the time that, before we left that home, just about every person in the family would suffer "checker board" burns seared into their skin from stepping or falling on the blazing hot grate. No matter how hard we tried, all the kids in our family got burned at one time or another. We all became adept at the side-step over the furnace—step to the side with your right foot onto the small rim of wood floor, then step over the furnace with your left. We could almost do it in our sleep.

My mom once told me that her goal was to be able to pay for groceries *before* we ate them. She knew we all needed more, but she had quit school at sixteen to marry Dad and she was ill-equipped to work most jobs. And, as she plotted her future, she had to take into account that she would not get any additional help from Dad. Her sister was a successful beautician who owned her own beauty salon business set up in her home. Mom decided she could do the same, so she set out to take her GED and prepare for beauty school.

She passed her GED with little problem and went on to prepare for beauty school. It was fun to help her study. I could tell it was all so new to her. Mom would sit me down and name all the muscles on my head, neck, and shoulders. She would give me facial massages. I was so impressed with how hard she studied.

Mom also practiced her manicures on me, and she practiced cutting hair on me. From fourth grade on, my hair was always kept short. As soon as it started getting any length, she would go into a frenzy of cutting it back. Easier to wash and keep would be my guess, plus I had a little natural curl that she thought looked best with the shorter length. I swore if I ever got old enough to make it stick, I'd grow my hair long.

The beauty of beauty school is it doesn't take long before you can hang out your own shingle, which is exactly what she intended to do. "Irma's Beauty Salon? What do you think?" she would ask. I heartily approved, and I was proud of my mom.

Mom did her year as an apprentice at Ensley Beauty Shop. She worked hard and long hours. She was often so tired when she got home that she depended on her girls to help with dinner. I loved cookies, cakes, and sweet things, so it was during this time that I learned to make things for myself. I first mastered the oatmeal cookie recipe on the back of the Quaker Oats box. I liked to cook. This was the beginning of my love affair with the kitchen. The kitchen would become my retreat and my refuge as times got hard.

Dad would not agree to borrow money to help Mom open her own shop. Mom wanted to do as her sister had done and enclose our carport to make her salon. With figures in hand, she loaded up me and my sister for our drive to the country. My Great-Uncle Alf was home (the one in the shack with snake skins all around the door) and seemed to be waiting for us as we drove up his long, dirt driveway. After the normal welcome of hugs, Mom sat next to the fireplace. Uncle Alf was rocking back in his big handmade rocker as he listened intently. Mom told him of her desire to open her own shop.

Mom looked nervous as she shared with him her crude drawings of what she wanted to build onto our house: a shop that would hold two head wash basins, four hair driers, a small supply closet room, and a half-bathroom. Looking back, I am proud of her—she went for two chairs instead of just one. She wanted to make more money and planned to hire an extra worker. I sat quietly, wanting to hear every word.

She finished by telling Uncle Alf that she would repay him so much a month with six percent interest on his money. He didn't think about it long before he called out loud to his wife, "Belle, bring me my checkbook." The rest is history, and I thank that wonderful man for giving my mom a chance. With his generosity and love, he truly changed our lives.

My 4th grade school picture.

Mom built her shop and paid the money back without ever missing, or even being late on, a payment. That shop was her life, other than church, and it was also her only social outlet. Her clients became her friends, and she and her friends visited every week for the length of time it would take to do a $3.00 shampoo and set. With the regular appointments each week, the ladies would have a shampoo, have them set in hair rollers, sit under the drier for thirty minutes to an hour, and have their hair styled by back combing, or as we called it, "ratting." Mom would "rat" the hell out of it, smooth it over, and spray it stiff. The customers were good until next week—same time, same place.

My brother was 16 and in high school when we moved to Norwood. He was in the tenth grade and madly in love with a girl named Margaret. I walked with him to visit her, which was pretty often. They were in love. I giggled when I caught them kissing.

Joseph did well in some areas. He had a beautiful voice and was the first sophomore ever to be chosen as one of the 13 "Voices" at Pensacola High School. It was quite an honor. I would sing along as he walked around the house singing about such Biblical ne'er-do-wells as Shadrach, Meeshach, and Abednego, who were banished to the fiery furnace. The chorus was great—it told of the poor man dying and then he "lived" so well, and of the rich man who died and went straight to Hell: "Dip your finger in the water, cool my tongue, because I'm tormented in the flame." Religious messages permeated my life from every direction.

Joseph had grown up and changed from a pudgy little fellow with freckles into a slim and handsome young man. He was active in the church, sometimes even leading the song services. He kept himself busy mostly by working with Dad and on other little projects. He spent days putting a lawn mower engine onto a makeshift go-cart. Always busy, Joseph loved to hunt and fish with Dad—that common interest would last throughout their lives.

Reading was not easy for Joseph, so he found it difficult to keep up with high school. He would call me in and I would sit at the foot of his bed while I read to him from his social studies, science, or geography books. He would lie on the bed and look at the ceiling. I felt special that I could read his books and help him pass his tests. He was smart, logical, and a hard worker. So why couldn't he read well? When he was in the military many years later, we found out why—he was dyslexic.

Dad was hard on Joseph. We had finished all the landscaping to be done in the front of the house, and it was time to start on the backyard. And good news! We now had a tool to make the sprigging easier. It was a long, horizontal bar with prongs like a fork and a handle. You stepped on it like a shovel, thereby creating about ten holes at once for the sprigs.

"Joseph, you need to get these holes done in the backyard so we can sprig it this afternoon," Dad said as he left for work. I guess Joseph thought he had plenty of time, but he didn't do what Dad had said to do. I saw Dad drive up, and I followed him to the backyard to survey the job—it wasn't finished. My dad's face was red. He turned on one heel and stormed off into the house yelling for Joseph.

I was afraid to go in, and though I stayed outside, I still could hear the crack of the belt. Joseph was in front of him, and Dad beat him from inside the house out the door. My brother cried, and tried to block the shots, but he did not fight back. I was crying. Dad yelled at me, "Go in the house." I ran in and watched out the window as Joseph cried and wiped his face. With each press of his foot on the shovel, his tears ran, and his nose ran, and everything dripped until he wiped it away on his t-shirted arm. It was after dark before he was finished and allowed back in the house.

I could never look at the backyard grass again without envisioning the tears I saw on my brother's face. The lesson I took away from this: Screw the damned oak trees and the grass.

Mom allowed me to do things even if I really didn't know how to do them. She thought I was smart and could learn by doing. I was very good at drawing, and I loved to paint. I had painted "Edward Brown, 5826 St. Benedict Avenue" neatly in block letters on our mail box—pretty good for a kid.

She brought home a board, about five feet long. Most likely it was just a 1' by 6' board cut to the length of the front window of her shop. She handed me a couple of brushes, some white paint, and some black paint. First, after it dried, I painted the board white. I carefully traced out the block letters for "Irma's Beauty Salon." It was all done in free hand, aided by a yard stick and ruler.

I painted carefully. I dribbled. I cleaned it up and painted again, until it was perfect. I am sure it wouldn't have been what I would use today, but my mom loved it, and she hung it over the big window of her shop. Together, we walked out to the driveway and gazed proudly at her new sign. Her business was now official. For weeks, all the regular ladies came in and I got big smiles and compliments for my sign. I bet they were really laughing at us to themselves, but I didn't know, and I not only was proud of my handiwork but inspired to do more. Mom gave me that precious gift.

All the walls in the house were white. I wanted to paint my room. Mom, of course, wanted me to paint it pink. Mom took some money out of her gray steel cash box that sat on the shelf next to her station, and we bought a can of pink paint. I got to work with excitement.

The room's grand finishing touch were two sets of pink and white striped café curtains with matching bed spreads. The twin beds were new and made of hard maple. There was a dresser and a night stand, and I got a new desk. The windows were high. If I walked up to the windows, I could barely see out over the window sill. They were the roll-out, Jalousie-type windows used at the time. The point was, the café curtains had a space of about 12 inches between the bottom tier and the top valance. It was so high that no one could see in the room, but light or darkness could be seen across the middle.

As I would lie in my bed at night, I would often sleep with the windows rolled open. I loved to feel the breeze come in during the summer, and I loved to cuddle under deep quilts in the coolness of winter. I learned to be comforted by the whistle of the train I could hear in the distance.

Dad and my uncle must have come to some accommodation because Dad was soon working at the new warehouse for Brown's Sporting Goods. Dad was handling the inventory: fishing poles, tackle, live and artificial bait, crab traps, and most anything having to do with catching a fish.

If not real busy, my dad and my brother would sit at the work chair with a long cane pole in front of them. The pole would turn and they would thread colorful string around the pole, putting on the metal loop eyes for fishing line to run through. It was fascinating to watch as each new row of the string fit snugly next to the last row. It was then tucked neatly under and burned at the tip to seal the nylon thread. When finished, the string was coated with shellac and sealed to the pole. A cane pole was now ready for fishing; you could run your fishing line through the threaded eyelets. The profit was much greater since it was ready to use.

My uncle had found really cheap labor in my dad and my brother. Dad was as honest as anyone could be. I am sure my uncle could have paid Dad under the table and he would have made more money, but then Dad would have to lie. My uncle benefited from his honest, faithful employee who worked for about $50 a week. This money was deemed to be Dad's spending money for huntin', fishin', and drinkin'. Mom got his disability check to run the house, which meant that he was through with his obligation to household expenses. Mom worked and paid for anything extra from her beauty shop earnings. She worked long hours, Tuesday through Saturday every week.

Mom and Dad were still having problems in their marriage, and money was not the greatest of them. Dad would work during the week, and on Friday leave to go up to the country to his mom's house for the weekend. He used that as a time to go on a little "toot," as Mom called it. Dad was a binge drinker. When he drank, he was mean. It was always better if he left home to do his "tooting."

The fights progressively got worse and worse. Dad's temper was so quick to flare. As soon as he walked in the door, you could tell he was drunk, and my mom just couldn't stand it. She would say something about the drinking, and a fight would ensue, or she wouldn't say anything, give him the silent treatment, and a fight would ensue. If he drank, we knew the violence would start. We walked on eggshells, but nothing helped.

If I knew Dad was drunk, I tried to stay out of his way. I was in the bathroom one day when I heard screaming from the living room. I jumped up from the toilet and was washing my hands when the bathroom door burst open. I stood motionless, shocked, with nowhere to run. Dad grabbed me by my arm and slung me out the door into the hall. I hit the wall on the opposite side so hard I almost fell onto that dang floor furnace. I was rattled, but okay—this time.

At least it was better than what my mom ended up with. Many days she would go to her shop nursing a black eye, prints on her throat, or bruised arms. She talked about their problems to her customers, and the ladies sympathized with her. She became the martyr and played the victim, with no way out. Maybe it helped her to have people to talk to, but it also made our family's dirty business common knowledge to all.

The police would often show up during the brawls, but they would just talk to Dad and he would go to bed and sleep it off. When the cops had been at our house most of the night, I hated to go to school the next day.

When he saw what he had done to Mom, Dad would be very penitent. He said he didn't remember beating her—after all, he had been drunk—and he was so sorry. Then on Sunday, we'd all put on our nice clothes and go to church, where Dad would hear the preacher's admonition to love your wife as you love the church. He'd wipe the tears from his eyes, and at times he would respond to the preacher's call to come forward and ask for forgiveness. He'd walk to the front of the church, and sit on the pew with his head down as the preacher would come and quietly sit next to him. Their backs were to us as they exchanged whispers, and sobs could be heard as the preacher would stand to face the congregation. The preacher would sadly and solemnly give a vague description of Dad's misdeeds and we would all be asked to bow our heads in prayer as the preacher would pray to Almighty God for his forgiveness.

For Dad, it was cathartic and soul cleansing. He was determined in his religious belief to start life anew. Family Bible readings would resume. We would have weeks of reprieve, sometimes months, before the next binge, and the same cycle.

By the time I was ten years old and in the sixth grade, the battles had become more frequent and rougher. The bedroom I loved became the place where I would lie in fear and dread. Those café curtains with the open space between the lower panels and the valance became my beacon—the warning light for the terror that was ahead.

Whenever Dad was late coming home, we knew it was because he was getting drunk somewhere—otherwise, he was on time every day. If he wasn't home by 9 or 10 at night, we knew there would be hell to pay no matter what we did. And I could always tell that time was near as the cars made the turn around our horseshoe street, and the car lights would beam in to the bedroom wall on one side. I would be at attention that someone was coming. I would lie still and watch the lights pan from one side to the back wall, and then the other wall and out. It wasn't him. If the lights came straight in and stopped, he was in the drive. I would lie quietly and pray.

One of those evenings, the three of us children were in the back bedrooms. We soon heard screams, with Momma pleading, "Edward, stop! Edward, please!"

Ann and I ran into Joseph's room. He was angry and frantic. He did as

Dad usually did. He went to his closet and pulled out his shotgun. Crying with fear and dread, he pulled back on the gun to put something into the chamber. He felt he had to do something. Dad was killing Mom, we were so afraid, and terror gripped our bodies. What could we do? We didn't want Mom hurt, but we didn't want Joseph to kill Dad.

I don't remember if Ann pulled me or if I pulled Ann. We were holding hands. We were running, the floor furnace rattled and banged as we ran across it, we entered the living room, and there we saw Dad sitting on Mom's chest. She was on the couch, her hands pinned down, her face red and wet with tears.

Ann and I fell to our knees together. Somehow, we were in sync as we put our hands together in prayer. "Daddy, please get off Momma," we begged. "Please don't hurt her. Daddy, please, please, let her go."

He didn't let her go, but he turned and looked at us, as if we woke him from an intense dream. Gazing into our crying faces, he calmly declared, "I'm not hurting her. I'm just holding her down." He sat there—a minute or seconds, I can't remember. He then stood up and walked—maybe "staggered" is a better word—out the front door and drove away in his car. I don't remember what happened after that, but I have never talked of these things to my siblings. As always, we pretended that if you didn't talk about it, it didn't happen. Our greatest bond was our ability to go on in silence, with no real hope of change.

Margaret's mom was very unhappy that my brother Joseph and her daughter were engaged in a very serious puppy love. Margaret soon found herself being "deported" to New Jersey to live with an aunt. Her departure was yet another reason my brother used when he decided to quit school and leave Pensacola. Mom signed so he could join the Air Force at seventeen years old. I was nine and my sister almost thirteen when he left home. Good for him. He had managed to escape.

Chapter 8
BIRMINGHAM 1961–1962

The three escapees and co-conspirators.

When I started the sixth grade, violent episodes in our home became so common that they somehow ran together in my mind. School had always been my best outlet for positive reinforcement. Almost every time there was something special happening at school, I would be chosen to be involved. It began with me playing a Greek princess in Pensacola's Fiesta, followed by the school's folk dancing exhibition, the big fourth grade school play, where I was chosen to sing a duet with Cynthia (I do not know why because I can't sing), and in the fifth grade, I was Mammy Yokum with a corn-cob-pipe, when our school presented *a L'il Abner*-themed float in the Fiesta of Five Flags Parade. My self-esteem would have been in the toilet if not for the loving teachers at Brentwood Elementary School.

My parents never seemed to worry about my school work, so they never gave me any assistance with homework. And I would not have even considered going to school without having done my homework. As long as my grades were good, all was fine.

Mom worked every day and didn't have any desire to be a part of my school life, nor was she community-minded. She never made cookies or cupcakes for school, was never at class parties, and never was a room mother. I wished she could have come to class because I thought she was so much prettier than the other moms.

Though they had no interest in supporting school activities, my parents did participate in other things. They did have friends that they would bowl with or play cards with. They seemed to enjoy their Canasta buddies (Canasta is similar to Bridge). We went with them to a friend's home one night while they played cards. The evening went late and they were drinking. I don't know what happened, but Dad was visibly angry when we left.

Riding home that night, Mom must have said something, or maybe it was that she didn't say something—it could have been either one. Dad immediately generated fear throughout the car when he raised his hands and started to beat the steering wheel in a rage that seemed uncontrollable. I was in the back seat, totally helpless and along for the ride. In 1961, seat belts were not used, so I was pushing back in the seat as far as possible, trying to steady myself in it.

All of a sudden, Dad slammed on the brakes, and with brakes squealing, I was thrust forward, hitting face-first the seat in front of me. It hurt. I was trying to hold on. Mom was screaming, "Edward, stop! You are going to kill us!" It didn't help.

Dad had his left foot on the brake and his right foot on the gas. He would speed up, then slam on the brakes. I fell onto the floor board of the back seat, tossed back while the yelling continued in the front. I don't know how many times he sped up, then braked—it seemed as if the sequence would never stop.

When it did stop, everything was silent. I was still wide-eyed with terror, but I knew better than to call attention to myself. The silence continued. We didn't talk of the episode—ever.

One day, I came home from school, as usual, but Mom and my sister were in the house frantically packing. Mom had decided to leave Dad. She met me at the door and told me to get my things together..

"Momma, where are we going?" I asked her.

"To Uncle Hub's house in Birmingham," she said.

We grabbed pretty much all our clothes and the few things we couldn't bear to leave behind. I grabbed a small plastic horse figurine and a couple of stuffed animals. I didn't realize just how little we had—and it was piled from seat to ceiling in the car. I turned around and couldn't see out the back window.

We had to get out before Dad discovered we were gone, because we knew if he drove up, he'd hurt Mom. He'd never let us leave without a fight, and none of us was up for a fight.

But what about school? I wondered. *What about my friends?*

The three of us were co-conspirators, linked by blood and fear. I scrunched myself into the middle of the front seat. Mom said not to worry, because her brother would give us a place to stay. He would protect us.

Uncle Hubert, or Hub as we called him, was newly married. He had worked with a partner in the cabinet building business. The partner died. Uncle Hub ended up leaving his wife and son to marry the dead partner's wife. I liked the first wife much better, and I missed my first cousin Carlton.

The new wife had a son just my age. He liked me, and we immediately became fast friends. His cat had kittens and he gave me one. I named him Skeeter. The typical antics of a kitten took my attention away from our tough situation and gave me something to love.

After that, Mom dragged us through a series of really cheap apartments and houses as she tried to find a job and a home. Her options were pretty bleak. And so was Birmingham. It was dirty from coal mining.

Dad found us pretty fast. The negotiations started by phone, then all of a sudden, panic set in because he was coming to Birmingham to get us. At first, Mom didn't want to go home. Then again, maybe a new venue for our family would do the trick, she thought, so a deal was worked out and Dad would come up and help Uncle Hub in his shop, Mom would find work, and we'd stay in Birmingham. A new start, a new place, and things would be better in Birmingham, right?

We made the trip back home to retrieve our furniture and complete the move. Before we finished, my birthday arrived, so Mom let me invite a few kids to our home, in Pensacola, for a party as my going-away present. We had cake and punch. We played pin the tail on the donkey. It was really a sad little affair.

They rented out the Pensacola house, and we packed up everything in a big truck driven by a nice black man. The problem was we were taking the "thing" with us that we had run from before—Dad. He had cried. He was sorry. We always had to forgive him.

About halfway through our six-hour drive, we stopped in some small town to order hamburgers at a walk-up restaurant window. We ordered our food through the little opening and went back to our car. We were in the heart of the South—the "Bible Belt." The people in the window would not take the black man's order. I couldn't believe it—they wouldn't let him buy food. Dad went up and ordered his food, and when it was ready, I took the bag to him. I cannot describe the look in his eyes. Even a child can recognize such an ignorant injustice. I could not understand. "Do unto others as you would have them do unto you." What the heck did those words mean? It hurt my heart.

Dad went to work with Uncle Hub. In the military, Dad had been a demolitions expert and a sharp-shooter. He had worked as a diesel mechanic for a while, and he worked in the sporting goods business, but none of those skills translated into the fine art of cabinet making. Plus, Uncle Hub wasn't thrilled to work with the man who had been beating up his sister.

We rented a small two-bedroom frame house just a few blocks from Uncle Hub. My sister and I had to share a room. We both made friends quickly and liked our new schools. I was enrolled at Hillview Elementary. It was nice to have a new cousin going to the same school.

The funniest darn thing was, at our recess time, we would all play tag and touch football. I liked to play with the guys. A pudgy boy in my class liked me so much he would come up to me from behind, lock his arms around my shoulders, and not let go. I don't know where it came from, but I just grabbed his hands and arms, which were on my chest, bent over, and flipped that kid over my back. He hit the ground hard. Needless to say, he didn't bother me again. And my popularity rose considerably since I was now recognized as the girl who flipped Roger over her shoulders.

Several of the kids from school met at the skating rink every Friday night. Vicki invited me to a sleep-over at her home, giving me a chance to get to know her family. A nice home, good food, lots of fun. I visited often. Their mom wanted me join the Thetro Girls with Vicki. *Why not?* She took us to their secret society meetings held in ornate, drafty old buildings and led by a bunch of old ladies from downtown Birmingham. They were the Daughters of the American Revolution and really did have a secret inner-sanctum, passwords, and a strange hierarchy. They were kind, and more than a little strange.

When we new members were presented to the court, we wore long evening gowns and were marched into the auditorium with much pomp and circumstance. I wore a strapless pink gown of Chantilly lace and organza borrowed from Vicki. The dress made me feel like a princess. I was being introduced into a world I had never known. My mom wasn't there to see me—in fact, none of my family was there. It was okay. I was already comfortable seeking a life of my own, separate from my family and its chaos.

Vicki lived across the road from an uncle who had horses. He liked the fact that I was so in love with the animals and I liked to ride. All of his children were afraid of them. One day, I was ecstatic with joy as he put me up on Beauty, his beautiful black-gaited horse. I rode him up the lane and around the farm. I trotted him, then pushed him on into his smooth racking gait. I was in heaven. Her uncle turned to some of those family members watching me and said, "She just sits on him and rides." After that, every time we went over to her uncle's, he would bring out Beauty and I had the time of my life. Vicki was my new best friend.

We celebrated Christmas that year in Birmingham. My big gift was a jewelry box of black lacquer with a Japanese scene painted on top. We always got one present and some clothes, or socks, or such. I'd never gotten a lot, so I didn't expect much. A horse was out of the question. It was always my wish, and the answer was always the same.

In my eyes, there were three things that made a person or family rich. The first—to have a horse—was the ultimate possession of the luckiest people on Earth. The second was a two-story house. There was something about climbing a grand staircase and being able to look down that made me feel big and above the fray. The third was a swimming pool. I didn't know anyone who had all three.

I can't leave the subject of Birmingham without thinking of the five inches of snow that fell one day while we were in class. The windows almost completely covered one side of the classroom. The teacher walked to the window and said, "Class, come see the snow." The big white snowflakes were falling so fast, the ground was being covered, and the landscape was quickly changing to all-white. It was my first time seeing snow stick to the ground. Our teacher let us stand at the window and watch. As a smart teacher would, she talked to us about the snow and the uniqueness of each flake. I found it to be so beautiful, and we couldn't wait to play in it. My cousin, who was accustomed to the snow, knew all the cool things we could do.

Three snow-days followed. It was a winter wonderland of snowmen, iced-over ponds to slide on, snow angels, and snow ice cream. We ate until we had a serious brain freeze. It was exhilarating, and I felt so alive in the cold air.

Mom and Dad were starting the same crap again. *Why? Why can't we live in peace?* Dad wasn't happy cleaning at my uncle's cabinet shop, so of course he started drinking again, and the fights soon erupted. We were right back at the same place. Dad was messing everything up. Why couldn't he just leave? I hated him.

One night, he came in while Mom was away. I was in the kitchen alone when he stumbled in the back door—drunk of course. He wanted me to get him some food. I went to the stove and put some of Mom's homemade soup in a bowl and set it down on the table in front of him.

He sat down and started to slurp the soup. He was such a slob! Every time he put the spoon to his lips, I would cringe as he loudly sucked the broth. I couldn't take it. I looked at him from across the table. I knew I was taking my life in my hands, but I didn't care. I said to him, "You eat just like a pig."

The noise stopped. His elbows on the table, his head over the soup, he looked up at me with a glare that made my blood run cold. His eyes were evil. I know he wanted to kill me. Then, in the most deadly voice possible, he said, "Don't you *e v e r* say anything to me about my eating again."

We were coming to the end of our short six-month stay in Birmingham. We needed to go home. Nothing had changed. Dad's problems had resurfaced, even though we were in a different place. The welcome Uncle Hub had extended us was worn out, but even going back home to Pensacola was rife with problems. Mom had to call the folks who had rented our home and tell them to get out. They weren't at all happy about having to leave so quickly.

A few days before we left, Dad did not come home at the usual time. He was probably worried about the move, so we prepared for the worst. It was after dark when he drove up in his truck. We waited, but he didn't come in. We waited . . . and waited some more. Mom finally went out to the truck to see what was wrong.

She came back in and said he was sitting in the truck, drunk, with his shot gun pointed at his head. "He said he is going to kill himself!" she cried. She was going to try to stop him from shooting himself by getting him to calm down, and just come inside, so he could go to bed. We begged her not to go back out. I was so afraid for her. *How much easier it would be for all of us if he'd just do it*, I thought. At that moment, I didn't care. He always won, either by intimidation, threatening Mom, actually hurting her, us, or now himself. I was willing to give him up. It would be the solution to our problem. After several hours, he finally stumbled into the house, the back door banging as he fumbled his way to the bathroom. When he came out, he found his way into the bedroom, slamming the door behind him.

It was over for the night. We went to bed. I wished him dead.

The day we were to return to Pensacola, the moving truck pulled up in the drive to load our things. Skeeter was afraid and ran for the woods. I looked for him all day. I called and called. I was frantic, knowing that if I didn't catch him, he would have to survive on his own. I didn't want to lose him. I called until I was hoarse. We couldn't leave him. He never reappeared and our truck drove away with me in tears over Skeeter.

When we arrived at our home in Pensacola, we found it had been vandalized by the renters. We had to make necessary repairs. We were so busy that Birmingham now seemed more like a long vacation than a home.

When I returned to Brentwood Elementary at the end of March, my friends welcomed me back. My teacher was kind. No one asked me any questions. I settled back in quickly.

There were four classes of sixth graders, and each class voted their favorite for the Annual May Day Court. I was chosen to represent my class. I had only been home two weeks when the whole school made their choice for May Day Queen. All the girls were told to dress nicely. We all complied the next day, but I said something silly like, "I didn't really try to dress up. I think if they like you, it won't matter if you are dressed up or not." The four of us were marched into each classroom with a big number hanging around our neck. We entered all first through sixth grade classes. We were lined up in front of the blackboards, like cattle at an auction. After we introduced ourselves, we would leave the room and the votes would be taken by raised hands.

I was very uncomfortable with the whole thing. I was embarrassed. JoAnn handled it well. She was very pretty with long dark hair. She looked at ease and her dress was so becoming.

JoAnn was selected May Day Queen. I was Maid of Honor, and Ramona and Alice took the title of Maid. I did not like people looking at me, or judging me on my appearance against someone else's. I decided I would never compete in such contests again, and I never have. That was the closest I ever came to entering a beauty contest.

The Annual May Day Play and Court Presentation was something else. They built a platform about four steps up in our school auditorium. The court was presented to the standing-room-only audience of parents, there to see their children in the big production. We entered the ribbon-lined walkway to "Pomp and Circumstance." The Maids went first, and then me, the Maid of Honor, all three of us in long, exquisite turquoise dresses. The last to enter, Queen JoAnn, was presented in white, as lovely as a young bride.

Me and David as part of "May Day's Royal Court."

We climbed the four steps to our platform, the Maids one by one, then me. I, of course, had to step on the hem of my skirt while trying to go up the stairs. No one told me to hold up my dress as I stepped up. I quickly recovered, making it to my seat a little embarrassed for stepping on my dress. Queen JoAnn came up without missing a beat. She was a much better queen than I would have been. The Royal Court sat on our high platform as we watched the school play, "Tom Sawyer."

I asked myself, "How can it be that I am part of this Royal Court?" I looked at the crowd stuffed into the school's auditorium. It was filled with moms, dads, grandparents, and children, all there to enjoy the play (my mom was the only one to attend from my family). I sat on the lofty perch, looking out at the crowd. We were the little diamonds of our school, all dressed up and sparkling. I thought of Dad, of Skeeter, of all my friends I had left behind in Birmingham. I couldn't help but think to myself, *No one here would ever suspect what has happened to me this year.*

Chapter 9
SUMMER OF 1962

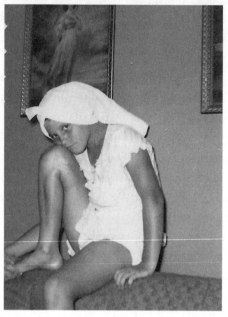

Me getting ready for bed. I see someone old beyond her eleven years.

O h, the pre-pubescent summer of 1962! Of all my summers, it generates some of the best memories. The memorable adventures of the four of us traveling across America, for the first time, is one that still brings a smile to my face.

My brother, Joseph, wasn't with us. During his first year of being in the military, he was transferred to Tacoma, Washington, and he was working at the Air Force base. He met a local girl, and I guess things happen quickly in Washington. I acquired a new sister-in-law and a new niece pretty fast.

My mom and dad were grandparents. Mom was the ripe old age of 36, Dad was 37. The child was named Sheryl Marie.

Sheryl? Sheryl? That name sounded familiar. Oh yeah! That was the name of Joseph's first little girlfriend to whose house he had walked two miles to give her a box of candy. He was about fourteen years old and in puppy love. I hope his new wife didn't know that he named their baby after his first girlfriend.

My parents' answer to the news of their first grandchild was, of course, to load everyone up in the car and head to the great Northwest. Dad loved the idea of a family adventure, and committed himself to the impending 3,000 mile road trip. The travel budget could be easily summed up with the phrase "on a shoe string." We'd "pee in a can, and drive on through." It was great! We didn't know any better.

I learned so much during that summer. Mom and Dad had done some homework. We left Pensacola armed with the AAA Trip Tic. (For those not familiar with a Trip Tic, the AAA, pre-Map Quest, would give you maps in a spiral notepad. These maps would provide a street by street, turn by turn, route for every city along your chosen route.) This was pre-interstate days. We were routed through every main street of every Podunk town, and we wove our way through the center of every major city along the way. My eyes were opened to the size of this great country.

No one loved the U.S. more than Daddy. He pointed out each new site, each colorful vista, each rushing stream, all the prairie landscapes, all the tall buildings, big trees, wild animals, and even barnyard animals. Everything was beautiful. Pulling off the road, he would get out of the car and call our attention to the newest attraction. He was like one of the models on "The Price is Right," standing proudly as the curtain opened to reveal yet another surprise. He was so proud to be able to show us America

Mind you, he wanted to make the trip in five days, so we were confined to the back seat of the car for about 600 miles a day. Dad was happy as a clam just driving and looking. He probably missed his calling as a long distance truck driver.

Mom sat with an ice chest almost between her legs on the front floor board. Drinks were stored in the chest, and snacks did not come from every 7-11, but from Mom, dispensing them from her never empty snack bag. She was big on peanut butter crackers and Pay-Day candy bars.

As the days would slowly come to an end, we would scout for the motel sign that had the bright AAA marking. As Dad said, the AAA's had been inspected. They were clean and basic, not fancy, and the air-conditioners worked well in the summer heat. We would make a stop at a local grocery, so Mom could run in and pick up food for the next day, and then we'd settle in to a room. My sister and I always had one and the same request, "Please, the motel must have a pool. Please, please, please, get us a swimming pool." On arrival, Dad would be so tired that he'd be ready to flop onto a bed. Ann and I would head to the pool, and we would swim until they ran us out.

Mom's chief request of a motel was that it have a kitchenette. We would wake to Mom frying chicken or making sandwiches for our day on the road. She planned ahead, and each day we would lunch somewhere in a park or along a road under a shady tree. We'd pull over and enjoy whatever she had lovingly prepared for our day. She was the best mom she knew how to be, and that meant taking care of the food for the family.

I don't remember Ann being interested, but I loved the maps. Before we got to Washington, I had figured out the map thing, and as we went through the small towns, I could spell Mom from her navigational duties. Five days riding and learning to navigate finally brought us to the door of my brother, his wife, and our precious new family princess.

Mom and Dad exploded with love and pride. Sheryl was special. She was the new and the innocent of our lives. This beautiful little girl, twelve years my junior, would grow to be more like my little sister than my niece.

My brother, raised on the Gulf of Mexico and accustomed to life on our beautiful gulf shores, had been busy finding all the waterfront activities he could. Because of him, our experiences on the West coast included clamming for Razor clams along the shores of the Pacific Ocean. The water was so cold it cramped my feet. We delighted in the size of the huge Dungeness crabs (they dwarfed our Gulf Coast Blue Crabs), and the oysters were the size of a tennis shoe. Each one was three bites. Our oysters were small one-bite size. We marveled at all nature had to offer. We were in awe of this "big" bold West Coast that my brother now called home.

We visited the mountain forests and took the drive up to Mount Rainier. As we drove to the tourist area at the mountain's base, we circled a huge valley with meandering little streams running through the valley floor. There were clumps of snow still standing white. Ann and I decided to make our way down to the valley to pick up some snow and touch the cold clear waters of the mountain stream. We carried our big snow balls back up the steep valley wall. As we made it to the top, Dad was taking pictures and just standing there waiting. He told us to turn around and take a look at where we had just been. When we turned, there was a mother bear and her two cubs walking along the stream's edge, at the same spot where we had gathered the snow. It was a close call. Our vacation could have turned out really bad, really quick. But, we were safe and a little more respectful of the mountain wildlife.

My brother's wife took us up into the mountain area where her father lived. She wanted us to meet him and to see his mink farm. His place was not much more than a tiny house, but his sheds were another matter. They were long—about 100 feet, with cages above the ground. I walked along the side of the cages, looking at each mink running within its very small enclosure, which looked pretty much like rabbit cages to me. The minks were pretty, weasel-like creatures. They were grouped according to the color of their pelts—black, brown, and honey-colored. I, of course, wanted to pet them all. I was told they were wild and untamable, and would bite my hand off.

We stayed for a while, and her father fed the minks by throwing a big glop of mushy ground meat and cereal on the top of each cage. They needed to eat well and fatten up before the winter, he said.

"Why?" I asked.

The answer left me pale—they would all be killed and skinned for their fur. Hundreds and hundreds killed and skinned. It made me ill. I never wanted to go back to that place again.

In 1962, the Seattle World's Fair opened, and it was a sight to see. We walked the grounds and went into all the exhibits. They were free once you paid the initial admission. Dad was enthralled with all the educational displays and really tried to get our attention focused on them. We were more interested in the rides. We were finally able to get on a couple—everything was so expensive. We watched as people lined up for the glass elevator ride to the top of the Space Needle. They said there was a revolving restaurant at the top so you could see the city 360 degrees as you sat and ate your lunch. We did not go up. I don't think we even expected to be able to do all those very pricey things. But we were there! We saw it all. Thank you, Dad.

Most days in Washington were rainy or drizzly. Joseph lived about three short blocks from a mall that featured a pool in the center. This pool possessed a treasure—a gray-black-speckled baby seal. I was comfortable venturing to the mall alone, and I spent every second I could gazing at the antics of this precious puppy that swam. Before the end of the week, the feeding crew knew me. They allowed me to pet the seal as they force-fed him the fish fillets that would keep him alive. They told me he wouldn't eat in captivity, so I watched as they stuffed the fish down his throat. I sure hated to leave that pup.

My brother had made a number of new friends. They would stop by to meet his visiting family. One friend was tall, had dark hair, and is easiest to describe as the cool "Fonz" character from "Happy Days." He was nineteen. I was seven years younger. We talked and laughed. He tickled me and I giggled. He visited us several times during the week. I developed a big crush on this guy and it was mutual.

He took me and my sister to the movie one afternoon. Electricity would run up my arm if he touched me, and I thought I blushed easily when he kidded me. He most likely was a bit surprised that he found me to be so cute. He kept a respectable distance, but kept on telling Joseph he couldn't wait for me to turn sixteen and return for a visit. I was wishing I *was* sixteen already.

The time flew by. We all cried, hugged, kissed, and said good bye. The baby was cradled gently in my mom's arms. She relished her last kisses with Sheryl. We promised we would come back.

We returned home via a desert route—Dad's idea for our further enjoyment and edification. By day three, we were all more than on edge. Looking out the side window, watching the scenery go by, can make you sick. I would lie down and try to rest, but Dad would wake us up every few minutes to make sure we didn't miss a single view. He wasn't going to let any experience go to waste.

Needless to say, my sister and I participated in the usual kid crap. "How much farther?" asked every hour, along with lots of "Are we almost there?"

And of course, the usual back and forth of "she's on my side," "she's kicking me," and "she's pinching me." Ann always resorted to pinching me when no one was looking. We were somewhere in the middle of New Mexico or maybe Texas. A huge green fly had gotten into the car. It kept buzzing and flying by our heads. We would swat at it, and it would quickly maneuver away. Finally, the offending insect landed on the window next to my head. I slowly raised my hand and hit him dead on. He was still buzzing under my hand. I smashed and then rubbed him across the window. You could hear him pop. His guts left a trail across the glass. *Yay!! I killed him!*

Ann took one look at the smeared guts and seemed ready to throw up. She cried to Mom that I was making her sick by smashing the fly. Mom must have been at her wit's end by then, because she came over that seat like a pit bull coming over a fence. Her hands and arms were raised. I was in recoil trying to avoid, or at least minimize, the blows I knew were coming. She landed a few on my head and shoulders. She slapped me with her open hand over and over. She looked toward Ann to see if that would be sufficient to shut her up. I remained in the fetal position for a few moments to assess the damage.

I was hurt, but my feelings were hurt as much as the physical pain. *Didn't you want the fly dead?* I asked myself. I really thought I had done a good thing. Even Dad may have been shocked at Mom's response to this one, but he'd back her up if she had killed me. Ann had been avenged. We now rode quietly. My attempt at being the hero had been a miscalculation on my part, and I had the bruises to prove it.

>−+◂▸•○•◂▸+≺

Our family was trying to heal, yet again. We were strong in our faith and our church—during one of those "on the wagon" periods. Maybe that's the reason my sister decided to profess her belief in Jesus Christ and her desire to be baptized.

Dad was very solemn when he told me that we were going to church because Ann had decided to be baptized. I announced clearly to him that I, too, was ready to profess my faith and be baptized. I felt I was just as big and I wanted to go forward with my sister.

When the invitation was extended to those sinners who wanted to come forward, profess their faith, and be baptized into the body of Christ (that is, the church) and to come now while the congregation sang "Just As I Am" from our hymnal, my sister and I, holding hands, walked down the aisle together.

We had been persuaded by our years of church, Sunday school, Vacation Bible School, and from the ever-ready pulpit of Dad. We were right in our hearts and our minds. Together, we stood in front of the church while the song was sung into the second verse. The singing would stop and the preacher would ask again for anyone who wanted to come forward. I felt my heart enlarging to the point of bursting.

The preacher held our hands in his, Ann's first and then mine. We answered in front of our parents, and the congregation, but mostly before God. We both sincerely professed our faith and belief in Jesus Christ as the Son of God. We were baptized by full immersion, in the name of the Father, the Son, and the Holy Ghost. We believed we rose from the waters, sinless and forgiven after being washed in the Blood of the Lamb. We were "white as snow," and like children, we would now walk in the newness of life as part of the body of Christ our Lord and Savior.

Me and my dog, Dutchess.

Chapter 10
BRENTWOOD

I tried out for cheerleader the summer before the seventh grade. We all waited for a week after the tryout to see if our names were among the eleven chosen. They would be posted on the gym door, like a proclamation of the chosen ones from God. The squealing, jumping up and down girls, ecstatic with joy, did not include me. I didn't make it. Many of my friends did. I didn't make it, probably because I didn't have a clue about cheerleading. I could jump like a gazelle, but the cheering thing needed work.

The year still proved to be fun for me. I was named Valentine Sweetheart of the seventh grade class, and had lots of little boys paying attention to me. I was invited to parties at the homes of my classmates—that was the big thing then. To have a party, just provide some music, food, and punch and you were good to go. The kissing and making-out that we did at that age makes me blush even now. At twelve years old, we were in full-blown romances (without the sex)—puppy love at its best.

Diamond in the Dark

As puberty arrived, I started attracting older boys. The boys of my age and grade were silly, small, and mostly uninteresting. They really weren't prepared to deal with a girl like me. I liked the attention of the guys if they were a few years older. Many of the boys in the ninth grade were fifteen. There were even a couple of really fine guys who were sixteen and could drive. (They may have been the ones that were dumb as dirt and had failed a year.)

My sister and I attended the same school that year, I in the seventh and she in the ninth grade. However, we did not run in the same circles.

Both Ann and I had to deal with our parents' strictness. Dad was always overbearing when it came to rules on what we could and could not do. Mom was backed up by Dad. Whatever she said, he made it stick. However, if Dad wasn't around, Mom could be manipulated a bit.

Dad held us to a dress code that was conservative beyond belief. Most of my clothes were home made. Mom was a fair seamstress, but most of the things she made weren't at all stylish. And because we lacked money for clothes, I felt highly motivated to learn to sew in Home Economics. I had a talent for sewing, I liked it, and I became a very good little seamstress. I started making my shorts, skirts, and tops. That allowed me to hem them as short as I wanted.

Dad didn't believe in sun bathing or swimming with boys, and under no circumstances could someone get a glimpse of an uncovered belly. That pretty much put a two-piece swimsuit out of the question. So that was exactly what I wanted—a two-piece Bobbie Brooks swimsuit, which I figured was worth its weight in gold. While making do, I actually took a one-piece suit and cut it in half. The make-shift job was less than perfect, but no matter. I hid it in my purse when I headed toward the beach. I'd change there. I was much happier when I had my pretty smooth belly out there for the world to see.

And I finally saved enough money baby-sitting to buy that $18 Bobbie Brook s suit of blue and white checks with white edging. Though the bottom had little shorts, and they came all the way to my waist, it was in style. The top was high and very modest. I didn't have any cleavage to show anyway. The suit was deemed spectacular, by me and my friends.

From the Bible, I knew I was supposed to obey my father, but I decided to make up my own mind about what was right and wrong. I began to covertly rebel. There was no way to express my disdain for all the stupid rules. If you even looked as if you wanted to disagree, you could be in for far more than you bargained. I found a way around every unbending rule. For example, skirts could be rolled up as you walked to school, making them a full three or four inches shorter. I had pretty legs, and I fully intended to show them, just like the rest of the girls.

Thank goodness I had a lot of girlfriends. They allowed me the chance to spend many weekends away from home. Mom always said yes to my invitations to go away for the night. It was probably easier for her not to have to deal with me. While away, I learned many things. At each visit, I watched the family interactions and fully appreciated the dynamics each family had to offer.

The father of one of my friends, Cindy, with whom I often spent the night, would come into the bathroom whenever we were in the tub or shower. His excuse was there was only one bath in the house. He'd come in and take a whiz while we stood behind the shower curtain scared to death he'd pull it back. *He didn't, but what was that about?*

My friends and I became wise beyond our years. We learned to field (and rebuff) the advances of the wayward husband driving us home after a long babysitting gig. Or, better yet, we would make-out with our friends' big brothers if they were good looking. I remember reading a book dealing with ancient methods of keeping girls virgins. The pictures of women in crude chastity belts caught my attention, but the caption was even better. It went something like this: "Putting a girl in a chastity belt is like trying to keep fleas in a croker sack."

My grandpa had used croker sacks of rough, loose woven material, to keep whole corn in, but the weevils crawled in and out with ease. I guess my dad didn't understand, or wasn't willing to accept the reality of young people growing up. His philosophy was, "Don't go near the water until you know how to swim."

During the eighth grade, my brother was sent to Korea, so his wife and Sheryl came to live with us. Our small three-bedroom, one-bath house, just got even smaller. My bedroom was the only one with twin beds, and it was actually the largest bedroom in the house, so I ended up sharing it with them. That year, my sister-in-law sat up till midnight writing letters to my brother. Sheryl was asleep in her baby bed, and each night, I begged for the light to be turned off so I could go to sleep. I had to get up early for school. My sister-in-law was able to enjoy the luxury of sleeping in late with the baby.

Sheryl was worth it. She was a joy, except we could hardly get her to eat. I'd sit for an hour trying to get her to eat half a peanut butter sandwich. She learned to just hold the food in her mouth, so she couldn't possibly take another bite. Sheryl enriched our lives in a way that is hard to explain. I very much enjoyed that precious little girl. I'd dress her up and take her with me for walks to the school for games and such. She became my new little sister, and that feeling for her has never changed.

There was a big party, being held on a Saturday night, at the home of one of the school's football players. He was a star player and I really wanted to go. Mom said no.

Later, two of my friends, Dale and Diane, who were twins and lived just up the street, asked me to spend the night with them. I begged and begged until Mom finally agreed to let me go to spend the night with the twins. Everything was going well. For the party, I dressed in one of the twins' outfits, and their mom dropped us off at the party—three little thirteen-year-old girls just as cute as can be.

The party consisted of a record player under the carport of a very modest home. There were chips and snacks with a bowl of punch. His mom was on site, watching out for us throughout the evening. One of the twins and I were bored, so we went inside and sat down at the dining table, talking with the host's mom. She was a hoot and so sweet. And she was enjoying our company as much as we were hers.

The other twin walked out front and got into a car with some guys who had driven up. This twin was known to drink a little beer if someone had it. Neither I, nor the other twin, would touch the stuff. The story is that she had turned a bottle up, to take a swig, just as my mom drove up behind the car. Mom was livid at seeing this, and rightly so, I guess. But it wasn't me. I wasn't drinking beer—I never drank beer. I was inside, innocently talking with an adult.

Mom had decided to go somewhere that evening with my sister-in-law, and without the baby. Mom went to the twins' house to get me to take care of Sheryl. The twins' mom told her where I was and how to get there. I guess Mom probably seethed her entire drive over, because I had lied to her in order to go to the party.

Mom came to the back door and knocked. Needless to say, I was speechless. She said, "You're coming home with me now." I followed her to the car. At that point, other than to hug and kiss a guy, I had never done anything. I was not sexually active. I was a little girl.

I got into the car and as my mother drove away, she was yelling at me, calling me a little whore. "Who do you think you are? You act like that whore!" She likened me to a girl who was a friend of my sister—a beautiful girl four years older than me who had a terrible reputation.

I kept telling her, "I am not a whore. I was just talking with his mom and having a nice time." As she drove down the road, she hit me over and over with her right hand. By the time we got home, I felt I had been run over. Her words were spinning in my head. *A whore?* I was thirteen and my mom was calling me a whore.

When we walked into the house, my sister-in-law was in the living room. She was staring at me, disbelief on her face. Mom left the room and disappeared into the back of the house. I could hear her angry steps as she banged across that damned floor furnace. I just stood there, not knowing what to do.

Mom quickly returned to the living room, this time with a belt doubled in her hand. I couldn't believe it. She grabbed me by the arm and ordered me to her shop. We walked outside and then into her beauty shop, which served the same purpose as the old-fashioned wood shed. She turned toward me and said she was going to teach me a lesson about what happens to whores. I returned her anger with words I will never forget. They were true then, and I would make them true forever. "I am not a whore."

She grabbed my arm again and told me to bend over the chair. It was one of the hair driers she used each day in her shop. I bent over, and the cold vinyl of the chair's seat gave under the weight of my hands. She pulled the belt back as far as possible, and hit as hard as she could, over and over. My will was strong. I was indignant at the injustice of this, and my body tightened to the core. I would not cry. If she killed me, I would not cry.

I don't know how many times she hit me. Maybe it was five, maybe seven. It didn't matter. The damage was not to my butt and legs, as much as it was to my head, heart, and soul. I was outraged at the names she called me. In her haste to find something to spank me with, she had chosen a heavy plastic type belt and not leather. There had to be some reason I was able to withstand the full blows without a single tear.

When she was spent, she finally stopped. I stood up and turned to face her. My body was rigid and straight and my head held high. I asked her in the most condescending way I could muster, "Are you finished?"

She started to say something like, "If I you think you can behave." Before she finished her words, I turned my back on her, and with the most upright and indignant posture I could gather. I walked out of the room. That was the last time my mother beat me.

My ninth grade year was a year to remember and cherish. Our school was seven to ninth grades, so we were basically seniors and they treated us as such. We enjoyed all the same things they did in high school. We had a football team that played intra-mural games against all the other city schools. We played on Saturdays at 4:00 p.m., and the high school games started at 6:30. We thought and behaved like seniors.

I made cheerleader for the ninth grade and my team chose me as captain. We had a new gym teacher, and she wanted to give some different girls a chance to be on the team. She was not tempted to have the same "cliquish" girls who got the gig in the seventh grade keep it for three years, though she kept a few from the years before. We had to be the worst cheerleading team ever. We didn't know what we were doing, and she didn't know how to teach us anything. But we loved being on the squad, and all of us looked peppy in our outfits. We did our best.

The selection of Who's Who was a tradition at Brentwood. The votes came in for who was the Most Studious, Most Likely to Succeed, Biggest Flirt, Most Popular, Most Beautiful, and the coveted title of Best All Round. Jimmy Hobgood and I won Best All Round in what amounted to the King and Queen of "Who's Who." Those who were voted "in" were introduced to the crowded auditorium of our fellow students, teachers, and parents who came to see the presentation. It felt good to be on the arm of the best looking guy in school. Yay! *Siss, boom, bah!* If there was a clique, I was in it.

Dad had long since returned to his binges. However, we were still expected to be in church every time the doors opened. The conflicts in my life were vast. It was as though I had a life completely removed from my parents. I made good grades. I lived at home. While at home, I was respectful and obeyed the rules. Every chance I could get away from home, and there were many, I took them. I ran my life within my own moral parameters. I knew good behavior from bad, and I feared my father, as we all did.

None of my friends cared that the police might have been at our home the night before. If they did, they didn't say much. It was just accepted that you didn't want to come to my house or mess around with Dad. I had guests over very seldom, and when I did, they were girlfriends who knew we had to be "good."

Mom's beauty shop was thriving. She and another lady worked five days a week, "from can, to can't," as she would often say. The telephone line that came into the shop was vital to my mom's business, and was getting way too much action from her two teenaged daughters. The answer to the problem of teen-aged gabbers was a Godsend—for Ann and me, they installed a wall phone on the narrow wall that separated our bedrooms. The phone had a fifteen-foot cord, so we could take the phone into our room and close the door. What a luxury! We had our own phone line.

Some of Dad's binges were worse than others. One night while asleep, I was awakened to the ringing of the phone. I got out of bed and answered it sleepily. It was Mom. "Mom, where are you?" I asked.

I got an almost whispered voice, like she was afraid Dad would hear her. "Phyllis, wake up. Your dad is asleep in the den. Get his gun and come next door."

"What? What time is it?" I was very confused. I was scared. It was about 2 a.m. "Just do as I say," she ordered. "We are at the Paynes' house."

I hung up the phone and slipped on my pants and shoes. I walked quietly to the den. It was dark and I was afraid to turn on a light. There was a small lamp still on in the den and I could see my father sprawled across the sofa-bed, at the foot of which was his gun. He wasn't moving, but he was snoring sporadically. The gun was in a leather holster, and I was afraid if I picked it up, it would wake him. I held my breath and slowly lifted it from the bed. He did not wake up. *Why do I have to get his gun? Why can't I just run?*

My steps were as quiet as I could make them. The fear in my heart was almost unbearable. My stomach was cramping, and my arms felt like hot water was running through my veins. I reached our front door and ran into the night air. It was dark, except for the street light, which gave me enough light to run across the yard to the house next door. The door opened without me knocking. They were waiting there, looking out the window, to see if I could get out of the house without incident. They closed the door behind me and Mom took the gun.

Dad and Mom had been arguing, so to get his way, he got out his gun.

Mom said that he had shoved her to the floor and pinned her head against the wall in the corner of the room. He said he was going to kill her. She started coughing, but managed to tell him, "Edward, I am so thirsty, I need a drink of water." He actually got up to get her a drink of water, and that is when she ran from the house. She ran for her life, and the neighbors took her in. I was asleep through the whole thing. It's funny, but that's what my parents usually said when the cops came, but this time I really was asleep.

We spent the night at the Paynes. The next morning, we were anxious, but we went home. Dad was still sleeping it off. Life returned to normal. The only time anyone talked about it was when Mom would tell each and every customer about what he had done. She would work with the bruises on her face, neck, and arms. She was a victim of domestic violence, and it became her claim to fame. The only way she could fight the abuse was to tell about it, so tell about it she did. The mere fact that she could tell her story over and over each day, and garner the sympathy of her clients, somehow seemed to validate her misery, her victimhood. Her friends made her feel better when they sided with her on how bad he was, but she stayed.

Every Sunday, when we drove to church, we would pass a family home with a pasture alongside. It held two horses that I loved looking at. Sometimes I'd take a carrot to stick through the fence. The sweetest of the horses was a fabulous Dominoe Appaloosa.

Some of our church members owned horses, and occasionally I'd be invited to ride at their place. I was already a good rider, for a child without real training. The stable owners felt comfortable giving me one of the better, more challenging horses.

On one of the Sundays, a sign appeared on the fence, "Horses for Sale." I became excited at the thought of buying a horse. Dad said we would go out and take a look at them later and "see" about it. I was walking on a cloud. Just the thought of a horse of my own made my heart race with anticipation. Dad said next weekend would be a good time to go.

Every day that week, I dreamt of going out to see the horses. I came in from school and started my usual chore, cooking dinner. As I was standing at the stove frying something, Dad came in the door. It was early, about 5:00, and unusual for Dad to come in drunk at that hour, but he was. Not hard drunk, just tipsy. He seemed to be happy, but I knew it was going to be a problem when Mom came in. I had the radio playing as I cooked, so the music was blaring.

Dad, who never danced, couldn't dance, and hated dancing, decided now was the time he is going to try. He wanted to dance with me in the kitchen as I was cooking. He grabbed my hand and pulled me to him to sway with the music. He was out of time and off step. I found him totally disgusting. I tried pulling away as he slovenly attempted to be Fred Astaire. When I pulled away, his eyes flickered with anger. He held my arm hard and shoved me back and into the cabinet. "Who do you think you are?" he asked. "You can't even dance with your daddy? I wouldn't buy you anything if you were the last kid on Earth."

In our home, any attempt at independence or thinking for yourself was unacceptable. I didn't go along, so that was that—no second chance. The horses were not mentioned again. My heart bled with pain and grief at the loss of something I had only dreamed of. He had the power to take dreams away in mere seconds, and he used it.

Our routines at home didn't vary too much. One week I would cook, and the next week my sister would cook. On my week, it was my responsibility to wash the dishes and clean the kitchen. One ordinary evening, the phone was ringing, so I left my post to talk with my boyfriend *du jour*, who was just calling to chat. I was stretched out over my bed, fully enjoying our silly talk. I heard Dad calling to me to finish cleaning the kitchen.

I told my boyfriend that I had to get off the phone, my dad was calling me. He thought it was funny and he kept talking. I didn't want to just hang up on him, but that was what I needed to do. *Why couldn't I just hang up instead of continuing the conversation?*

Suddenly, the bedroom door burst open, banging so hard my body jumped like I was shot. He came at me as an attacker, his eyes blazing with anger. He tore the phone from my hand and threw it—it banged with a loud crack as it hit the floor. With fury, he turned on me, pinning both of my arms to the bed as he flipped me over onto my stomach. I screamed, "Daddy, Daddy, don't, please. I'm sorry. Please don't hit me."

He put one knee up on the bed and held both my wrists together with his left hand. Then his open hand started hitting me on my butt and legs. He was so strong and he was furious with me. The blows came, one, two, three, four, five—*oh God, would they ever stop?* When they finally did, and the screaming turned into soft sobbing, Dad moved to the phone cord and snatched it out of the wall. "When I tell you to do something," he said, "don't ever make me tell you twice."

My boyfriend heard my screams. He knew what had happened. I can't imagine what he was thinking as he listened to my pleas. I sobbed from being hurt, and I sobbed from the shame I felt. There is no way to describe the broken soul that lived in my body that day.

I could not call my boyfriend back—the phone was dead. I didn't see him until school the next day. He came up to me, quiet and concerned, and asked me, "Are you okay? I heard you. Why did your dad do that to you?" I didn't have an answer. My friend really did care about me. It was nice to feel his concern, but it wasn't enough to overcome the shame. I would try to do that by walking proudly, pretending it didn't happen, and never speaking of it again.

I write this as an admonishment to parents. If you are strict and your children respond appropriately, just maybe you have it right. If they are not responding to your style of discipline, you may want to take a different tact. Just as some children learn in different styles, some also respond to punishment in different ways. Adopting the old world maxim of "do as I say, and not as I do" inspires conflict within. I was committed to finding my own path, around him, because there was no way to work with him.

I didn't have the internet, or any of today's distractions. All I had was a life in the midst of other weak humans. I began to see the "no's" of my life as just another obstacle. I did fear my father. He did instill a strong sense of respect for God, country, and a higher authority. That respect for authority helped me in the long run.

I began to recognize that my parents didn't want anything but the best for me, yet they operated from a totally different perspective. For me, their perspective overshadowed all their good intentions. They just had no clue on how to parent, other than to instill their religious beliefs and their very skewed concept that fear of personal pain would cause a person to make better choices. It just didn't work for me.

＞━┝━◆＞━◯━◇＞┝━◄

Managing money came naturally to me. In junior high, a $2.00 allowance had to cover my 30 cents-a-day lunches at school. We never got a free lunch, because Dad would not furnish the required written information on his income. Thank God anorexia was unheard of by my peers. I always looked forward to and ate my lunch. From elementary through junior high, it was usually the best meal of my day.

I babysat. I could probably fill a book on bad experiences during babysitting gigs. The ones who had no food in the fridge or cupboards to feed the children; the parents who did have food, but were mad because I fed the children too much; the ones who left for a movie and never came home until the next morning. It was amazing what people were able to get away with in the 60's. I babysat for the money, so no matter the conditions, I would go back if they needed me.

I learned to help the kids. If I could find a bag of cornmeal in the cabinet, I'd make cornmeal mush (basically it was just fine, gruel-like grits), or if there was a bag of flour, I'd make a big pancake that could be covered with margarine, or jam, or eaten plain, if you had to. We always had food to eat at our home. It didn't have to be fancy, but kids needed to eat. The kids loved me.

Making excuses for my grades during my ninth grade year would be just that—excuses. Belonging to every club, being head cheerleader, my head in the Beatles craze, plus chaos at home was more the norm than not. Couple all that with an attitude and, as you can expect, the result was less than desirable. I wish I could just blame it on someone other than myself. I took pre-algebra and did not do well. I didn't ask for help, though I didn't "get it"; I figured I just needed to study and study hard. I didn't.

I made a 59 on my third quarter report, missing a "D" by one point. I brought it up to a "C" by fourth quarter, but it was too late. It knocked me out of the running for cheerleader in high school. The interesting thing was that I didn't get in trouble for my grades. A two-piece swimsuit would rain hell on my head, but an "F" in algebra was no problem. *The irony?* It was the only "F" I ever made in my life. But no matter what Dad said or did, it was the first of hundreds of two-piece swimsuits I'd wear.

>─┤◂▸•─O─•◂▸┤─◄

Starting in 1965, Pensacola opened its first all air-conditioned high school. It was touted as cutting edge. I was horrified. Our neighborhood was one street into the new district. Pensacola High School, the best public school in our town, would not be where I'd go. I was devastated. I now had two choices, either the new school, Woodham, or Tech High, a vocational school in town.

My sister had long since decided to be a beautician when she grew up—something I definitely had no intention of emulating. I knew I did not want to stand and work like my mom did each day. However, I did ask what Pensacola Technical High School had to offer, which was where my sister attended. She went half-day to classes, half-day to beauty school. They offered other technical jobs, and they had both football and basketball teams. My sister was a cheerleader for them, and pretty much "Little Miss Everything." She really thought she was "it" and acted accordingly.

Ann had a couple of her cheerleading friends come to our house to spend the night after one of their games. On that Saturday morning, I was awakened by Ann and her girl friends, standing in force around my bed. "Wake up, wake up," they said. I looked at them, slowly sitting up in the bed. They were bigger than me, and older than me, and they were all standing around my bed and glaring at me. My sister said, "We just want you to know, we don't want your kind at our school." One of the others said, "Yeah, do you understand? You're not welcome at Tech." They walked out single file, with smug, arrogant looks plastered on their pudgy, mediocre faces. They had completed their mission.

Well, that certainly simplified things for me. I guess I would be going to Woodham after all.

Chapter 11
SUMMER OF '64

I was fourteen and ready for the tenth grade at the new high school.

I had a special girl friend with whom I shared so many childhood memories from fourth grade through high school. Sheila, an only child of an only child, had everything I would have given anything to have. She had a big bedroom with a satin comforter, instead of a hand-made quilt. She had her own TV in her room, her own bathroom, an Australian Shepherd dog (his name was Rex), and really quiet, sweet, Christian parents. Most important of all, Sheila had a horse.

Sheila's mom was a diabetic, and I was fascinated to watch the insulin shot she gave herself every morning. Her skin was so tough from the daily shots that it was sometimes hard to get the needle to penetrate. Those times, she would have to hit her skin two or three times before the needle successfully penetrated her leather-like hide. She drank dark bitter tea with saccharin. She was kind and plain, never wore any makeup, and was a person without pretense. She laughed easily at the antics of Sheila and I. Her giggle was sweet, and her indulgent nature made it easy for me and Shelia to have fun with her.

Diamond in the Dark

John, Sheila's dad, was such a good man. Mr. John was a welder by trade. Each day, he dutifully grabbed his lunchbox of freshly-packed sandwiches, stood at the roadside waiting for his ride, and returned every day, almost to the minute, at 4:30 p.m. At about 4:15, Rex would take his position on the front porch, waiting patiently. Just like clockwork, Mr. John's ride dropped him off at the gate. Rex would bark and take off, running to meet him. He'd enter the gate as the excited Rex would jump and wag his tail with joy. Mr. John always stopped, opened his lunch box, and gave Rex the brown bread crusts he had saved for him. Rex would have been devastated if he forgot, but I don't think he ever did.

And did I mention Sheila's horse? Oh, my God, what a horse! Actually, he was a pony of Hackney breeding. He was about 13.2 hands tall (that is about 4'5" to the top of his withers/shoulders). "Silver" was snow white with clear, baby blue eyes. He was round and plump and the most beautiful horse I'd ever seen. Sheila's dad loved him too. Occasionally, he would even get up on him and let him do his little pacing gait around the yard.

Silver's favorite trick was to pace along just as sweet as can be. The second you weren't paying attention, though, he would stop short and make a quick, lateral move of about three feet that would make Joe Namath proud. If he didn't put you on the ground, it was a miracle.

Sheila somehow had a sense of when Silver was going to make this sideways bolt. I, on the other hand, stayed on guard at all times. He did unseat me a couple of times, but I managed to stay on by pulling myself back into position.

Shelia and I took turns riding Silver. He'd be decked out in his little black saddle with shiny silver conchos (round decorative medallions attached to the saddle) and buckles. Sometimes her dad would hook him up to a two-person sulky, and Shelia and I would fly around their yard. By the way, their yard was a manicured and fenced-in area of probably three acres or so.

One time, Shelia was acting like a spoiled only child and took off on the sulky faster than normal. I don't know if she was showing off for me, or just "showing" her dad what she could do. Silver's feet were flying and his head was bobbing in a rapid up-and-down motion. Shelia bounced the reins, which slapped down hard on Silver's back. She shouted to Silver, encouraging more speed. I was hanging on tight as we rounded the turn by the back porch. I realized Sheila had cut the turn too close. The wheels groaned, the sulky made a tearing sound, and all of a sudden, we were sitting in a sulky with no wheels. Silver was pulling us along the ground, the broken cart digging into the earth as the horse dragged it around the house.

I could hear her dad yelling in the background, "Whoa!! Silver," then astonishingly enough, the frightened horse did stop. He then craned his head around and looked at us with those blue eyes, as if asking, "What the heck happened?" We were all okay, except for the sulky.

I think that episode took a couple of years off her dad's life, but Shelia didn't get into any trouble. My dad most likely would have spanked my butt for showing off like that, but her dad didn't. He was calm, concerned, and restrained in dealing with us.

I spent so much time with them or in their home—many weekends and long summer days playing in the pasture at her grandparents' home, going to their church, and accompanying them on day trips to the country. I think they grew very fond of me. Shelia rarely came to my home, because I really didn't have much to offer. Besides, it was much more fun at her house. If her parents knew of our family problems, they never showed it. Even if they knew, I don't think they ever would have ever said anything—they were so nice.

Shelia and I shared many events we could laugh about. As we lay sleeping late on a Saturday morning, Red entered the bedroom. Red was a neighbor boy born with Down's Syndrome. He came in flashing his badge and showing us his new gun and holster set with bullets stuck all around the belt. He had on a cowboy hat and boots. He talked loudly, telling us about his new outfit and that he was Matt Dillon (the "Gunsmoke" marshal). His garbled language was something Shelia translated for me. Red was about twenty years old and a regular at their home. It took a while, but I soon learned to understand his speech and accepted him as a playmate.

Red taught us a lot about what it was like to be forever frozen in a childlike world. One day, he would be King Kong, the next Roy Rogers, and the next day someone else. He lived in a fantasy world of happiness and make-believe, and though usually very docile, some genius gave him a play bullwhip. He came over while we were in the yard, and it wasn't long before we had scaled the oak tree to get away from him as he tried to crack the whip. We laughed, and he laughed, but someone had to come get him before we could come down.

Across the street from Shelia's home was an elderly couple that loved children. In fact, he was a Scout Master for a local Boy Scout troop. On a visit to their home one day, Shelia and I were asking the man some questions. Somehow he was telling us (we were then ten) that he loved his scouting camp trips because he usually ended up with a scout's mother in his tent for the night. I was shocked. His subsequent tales about bedding his wife every day both fascinated and repelled us.

On our last trip over to his house, we found him sitting in his recliner, wearing nothing but boxer shorts and a robe. He kept moving around in his chair until he was exposing himself and pretending not to realize he was doing so. It was truly disgusting, but we never told on him. I felt sorry for his wife.

I missed Sheila when I was away in Birmingham, and when I came home, my friendship with her resumed as if I had never been gone. By then, Shelia's dad had brought in a second horse, so both of us could ride at the same time. He was keeping the horse for a family until they could take her back. Her name was Misty and she was bigger than Silver—more like 14.1 hands high. Misty was a sorrel or reddish-colored horse with a white blaze down her face. I thought she was just beautiful. Her dad said Sheila needed to have another horse, so she could have company when she rode.

That company was almost always me. It opened a whole new world to us, as we rode all over our side of town—through fields, woods, and over to Sherwood Farms, where we met more kids to ride with us, filling our days with happiness. It just couldn't have been any better, unless of course, Misty had been mine.

Sheila and I had finished the ninth grade and we were spending a lot of time riding together. We rode through the vacant land between Old Palafox and Pace Blvd. In 1964, it was just open fields and trails. (Now it is Car City of Pensacola.) We crossed the highway, entered the Sherwood Farms riding stable, added a few more riders, and continued to head west through the woods. The path we took led us into a new middle class neighborhood called Crescent Lake.

We must have been a sight to see—nine horses, with riders walking through the streets like a parade. The kids were running to see the horses, and moms were standing next to the street, holding their children closer to them as they pointed at us. It probably was pretty unusual to see so many horses walking through their neighborhood.

We rode past the houses and down to the lake. Crescent Lake had a pretty big dam, and there were a lot of swimmers jumping from the dam into the lake. The dam was at least eight feet above the lake. No lifeguard, no gate, no fences—just kids having summer fun. I'm really dating myself here, because the liability issues now would have closed the place down.

Some of the teenaged boys started to walk over to us. They all wanted to pet the horses. My eyes immediately ran to one boy. He was really cute. He had white-blond hair—bleached, in fact. You could see the dark roots coming in, and you knew this was the latest surfer boy craze.

He approached me first. He wasn't real tall, but he had a great body. He was brown as gingerbread, had a chest full of hair, and his Levis jean shorts were still dripping wet. He petted Misty, talked about how pretty she was, and made a little idle chit-chat.

When we left, I asked Sheila, "Did you see that guy?"

"Wow, he is tough." "Tough" was our term for "hot," which, of course, we could never have gotten away with saying in front of our parents

I was smitten with this guy from the start. His name was JJ. I now rue the day I met him, but that's life, and that was the start of a long, hard row I'd have to hoe, as my old grandpa would say.

Chapter 12
Woodham

My sixteenth birthday photo taken in front of the pink house.

Entering the doors of Pensacola's brand new high school, I was a fresh-faced sophomore at the ripe old age of fourteen. This was not going to be easy. These kids were from all over the county and included many who hadn't attended my elementary and junior high schools. They were bused in each day, some from as far away as West Pensacola's Belview, and Ferry Pass, and from upper middle class areas across the bay. These so-called Gulf Breeze kids were showing up en masse at Woodham. We "Brentwood kids" were in the minority.

My eyes were wide as I watched kids driving to school from Gulf Breeze in their new cars. Girls wearing beautiful, name-brand clothes and real jewelry walked past me, tossing their long, straight hair. They wore makeup, and many were very pretty.

We had only been going to school for a few days when I ran into the same gorgeous guy I had seen at Crescent Lake during my horse-back ride with Sheila. He was just as "*tough*" as I had remembered, maybe more so. He had on khaki pants and a Banlon shirt (Banlon was a brand of polo-type pullovers in a light sweater knit). The hair on his chest was exposed by the V-neck of his sweater. He was a man. He was eighteen, I was fourteen, and therein was the problem.

We hit it off. It wasn't long before he asked me out on a real date, but I wasn't allowed to date. *Ummmm.* It was time for a creative logistical move on my part. I had one wild girlfriend whose mother was known to be really cool. She let her daughter do pretty much anything, as long as she showed up for church on Sunday to sing and play the piano. JJ had a good friend who ran with him, and he possessed the same name. It was JJ and JJ. Soon, we had the plan—I would spend the night with my friend, and we would double-date. How hard was that?

The beginning of the date was not very memorable. In fact, I don't even remember what we did. It was getting late, and the guys asked us if we would like to see their land. "Land? What land?" we asked. We all laughed as they pretended to have some special piece of land they owned. It was fun, and not surprising, when we drove up to the hillside of Bayview Park to see the view. They thought it was hilarious, and obviously it had worked on a lot of other girls before us.

It wasn't long before JJ had pulled me close for a first kiss. We made out. I loved his kisses. The couple sitting in the back seat was not as enthralled with each other, but JJ and I just couldn't seem to get enough. The kisses were gentle and sweet.

The voices from the back seat kept saying, "We are ready to go." My JJ balled his fist up in a playful manner and shook it at them in a gesture aimed at buying more time. We wanted to get lost in our kissing. For me, it was a sensory overload. I had never experienced anything like it before.

I fell in love that night. I fell in love with a young man four years my senior. I didn't know I was falling hard for a person who had never known anything from his parents but abandonment, lies, and betrayal. His scars were hidden, but they were carved deep into his soul.

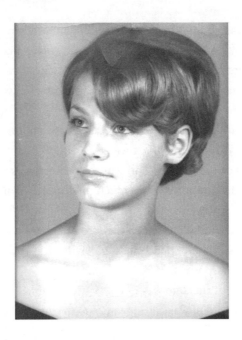

Mom never let me have long hair like all the other girls. I was sixteen years old.

There were loads of good times I shared with JJ. He was working for his parents, so he not only had a new car but money to spend on our dates. We went to drive-in movies (usually not seeing most of the movie), we went to dances at Fireman's Hall, The Armory, The Casino on the beach, and The Place. We went for burgers, soft-serve ice cream, and even to a couple of good restaurants.

On Saturday or Sunday afternoon, many of the guys would bring friends to the park. We'd hang out and watch them play football without pads. They could get rough, and it was not unusual for someone to leave for stitches, or to end up in a cast. JJ split open his eyebrow on a big play, which sent him to the emergency room for a dozen stitches or so. They were a tough bunch of boys.

That year was JJ's senior year and I was a sophomore. As we dated, JJ got more and more possessive, with him controlling who I could talk to, what I should wear, or how I should wear my hair. He would walk me to most of my classes and seemed to catch me whenever I even spoke to a guy. If he saw me talking to a good looking guy, he would tell the guy to leave me alone—he could intimidate most young men. He had to love me a lot to be so jealous. It was cool to be his girl, and everyone knew I was off limits.

We began telling each other how much we were in love. It escalated, and by Junior /Senior Prom, we were ready to commit to our love. I wore a dress of a soft "whipped-cream" fabric. At least that's the name Mom gave it when she handed me the neatly folded, soft, lime-green material, along with a Simplicity pattern, for a straight-skirted long formal dress. Mom said if I wanted a dress, I could make it. I was careful to take my time and do the best job I could. It was simple but nice enough. I wore it that night as we danced to the music of our prom band. JJ was supposed to wear a tuxedo, but he refused and wore his suit instead—they let him in anyway.

We didn't care about anything anyone was saying. We had each other. I guess I meant that literally, for that night we left, and for the first time, we "had" each other. Mom and Dad were out of town, so we went to our house. He and I got into my sister's bed and, for the first time, made love to one another. I, frankly, was not impressed with the whole thing, most likely because I expected something wonderful, even magical. It wasn't. In fact, I was scared, and it didn't feel good. I made him keep the light off while we showered. It was the first time I had let any guy see me naked. When all was over, he turned to me and said, "I thought you were a virgin." Hell, I thought I was, too. He was the first man I had had sex with, and I gave him the best thing I had. Now, he had made that seem trite and dirty, treating me as if I had given him a second-hand pair of jock shorts.

As time passed, JJ seemed to forget about that initial disappointment. We went out every weekend together, with most dates ending in us making love somewhere. Thank goodness, the first night was not indicative of things to come. We grew together, and I believed—or should I say "convinced myself"— that we truly loved each other.

Some time during the winter, JJ's parents' house burned down, and they moved to a home on a dead end street off Hillcrest. It was a flat-roofed ram-bler overlooking two fishing ponds divided by a dam. The cinder blocks were painted gray, making the house look drab and ugly. His parents had been out of town when their house on Lenox Avenue caught on fire—they lost every-thing. This was a house they bought to live in, while they prepared eventually to rebuild their home.

I started visiting them on a pretty regular basis. His mom liked me and his dad flirted with me—I thought he was a true sleaze-ball. JJ's dad played golf, while his mom stayed home and drank vodka and orange juice. The fact was they both pretty much drank like fish. I still had fun at their house, because they didn't seem to have any rules for JJ—he came and went as he pleased. We went to his house, not mine, because my dad hated him on first sight. That whole year we dated, he avoided my dad by picking me up at strategic times.

Despite the relationship, I was making good grades. I am not sure how he made it, but JJ did graduate from high school that year.

The summer after his graduation was wonderful. The pond behind JJ's house was good for swimming. We had a huge tractor-sized inner-tube tire, and I could curl myself into a ball inside it. He would roll me around the pond and over the dam. I'd be so dizzy, I'd almost drown when he rolled me fast into the water. As friends and lovers, we had a great time swimming—we were like two mating dolphins.

He taught me to drive that summer. How I managed not to kill both of us, I'll never know. We spent loads of time at the beach, riding in his old Hillman that he used as a beach buggy. The car had no floorboard in the back seat, so, if you rode in the back, you had to keep your feet up or you'd be running along like the Flintstones. He came over to my house, driving the Hillman, to pick me up for a trip to the beach. He walked up to me as I was coming out the door. The Hillman, which was still running, somehow jumped into reverse. It went backwards, in circles, across the road and into the vacant lot across the street, while JJ was chasing it down. Finally, he managed to get the door open and jumped in. We laughed until we almost passed out.

As a regular in his home, I started noticing family photos around his house. They still had all their framed family photos, and some prized knick-knacks I had seen in the other house. His mother somehow hadn't lost any of her jewelry in the fire, nor did she lose her nice winter coat. Why would you go on vacation, in the summer, and take your photos, knick-knacks, and your winter coat with you? A normal person wouldn't do that, unless they thought their house might burn down. Even funnier, the same thing happened again to them a couple of years later. They were out of town and the ugly gray house just happened to burn down. They rebuilt back on Lenox, the old family photos still intact and on display.

JJ and I dated throughout 1966. We acted like a couple in everything we did. He threw a fit when my dad announced we were taking another driving vacation to Washington state. Dad and Mom were ready to see my brother and his family again, especially Sheryl. Our trip went well, and this time, the guy I had thought was so cute years before was of no interest. True to my Scorpio sign, I was in love, and I was faithful to JJ.

We came back by way of California, with us staying at Laguna Beach with relatives. One of my old boyfriends, Thom, was living there. I knew how to contact him, but I didn't bother. Again, faithful to a fault. *Did I mention stupid, too?* Disneyland was fabulous, as was the trip to the Grand Canyon. Our foray into Mexico, at San Juarez, became a shopping extravaganza. Another lovely and quite educational vacation, thanks to my mom and dad.

By the time I was sixteen, JJ wanted to leave Pensacola and get married. I didn't. I wanted to finish school and enjoy my high school years. However, he bought me a beautiful ½ carat diamond engagement ring for my sixteenth birthday. I didn't show it to Mom or Dad, because I knew they'd throw a fit. I kept it in my purse, wore it to school, and took it off each day before returning home. I wasn't comfortable with being engaged. I wasn't ready. My feelings for him were changing, and his demands had started to wear thin.

Thom had been a boyfriend, on and off, during my junior high school years. He was the handsomest of all the guys I had ever liked. He was also the older brother of one of my classmates. Think Paul Newman with clear, sparkling blue eyes, but with black hair, and he was just as sweet as he could be. He loved being the young surfer, spending all his free time on our beautiful beaches, focused only on catching the next wave. During the times I spent with him, we did fun things, like surfing, dancing to the bands at the old aqua-colored Casino (it was a landmark of Pensacola Beach), going to Fort Pickens at the end of Santa Rosa Island, and always finding a place for a kiss or two along the way. With the old forts at Pickens as our playground, we passed the time and visited the old cell where Geronimo was once held captive. I really liked Thom, maybe loved him, but I think the problem was he was just too nice. His real name was Thomas. That he shortened his name to Thom and not just plain old Tom says quite a lot about him.

The Air Force evidently got Thom's attention. As I was entering the eleventh grade, he joined up and was stationed in Texas. I received two of his military photos. He was so good looking, all decked out in his working, deep-blue uniform. Both black and white photos came in a letter that said he'd be coming home for Christmas.

Maybe he's grown up some and isn't just a surfer boy anymore. My day dreams got the best of me. I decided to break up with JJ, so I would be able to see Thom when he came home on military leave.

The break-up with JJ was not pleasant. In fact, JJ threw a fit. I gave him back his diamond ring. He started calling me horrible names. He made terrible disparaging remarks about my character. The hardest thing was to hear him calling me a whore. I was the same girl he had been dating, and loving, for over a year. I had been totally loyal and faithful to him, and now I had to listen to completely outrageous remarks, like: "I'll start dating another girl, and I know *she's* a real lady, not a slut like you."

His words twisted the intimate feelings we had shared. He turned our feelings into vulgar words used only to degrade me. He left me in fear of the gossip and slander he could create—gossip that would tear my world apart. These were not "Sex and the City" days. A bad reputation was a devastating blow then, and I could not stop him from saying terrible things to others about me. JJ just wasn't going to buy in to the "It's not you, it's me" deal or "I just need some space." He was angry, and he was going for my jugular.

I fully intended to see Thom and enjoy his company while he was home. I refused to be blackmailed. As soon as Thom got home, he picked me up and we had a really nice evening: a drive-in movie, a few kisses, and a chance to find out how we were doing at this point in our lives. He was a gentleman and never—and I mean never—tried to go any further than to kiss me. My curfew was always the same time—11:00 p.m. No matter the occasion, Dad's curfew was set in stone. Promptly at 11:00, we drove into my driveway and parked directly in front of Mom's beauty shop. We sat there, just for a moment, saying our goodbyes and making some plans for the following day.

All of a sudden, lights from behind were beaming into our car. JJ had staked out my house, and he pulled in behind us, jumped out of his car, and came around to the passenger side. He climbed into the car and was sitting next to me on my right. It all happened so quickly. I was sandwiched in between the two guys. JJ's comment was something like: "You need to make a decision right now. Do you love him or me?"

The night air had been cool that evening, but now you could feel the heat emanating from the tense bodies. I could smell the whiskey on JJ's breath. Fear gripped me as I sat trying to figure out what to say and do. I heard the words come out of my mouth, "Right now, I don't like either one of you." JJ immediately slapped me in the face—so hard my head flew back against the seat. I had never before been slapped in the face so hard. Somehow, I didn't feel any pain—just shock. At that moment, Thom swung his fist over my head and landed a blow somewhere in JJ's head area. They were both now fighting, with me under them trying to cover my head. I was screaming for them to stop.

Mom and my sister-in-law must have heard the commotion, and were soon at the driver's side of the car. Mom opened the door and yelled, "Stop before you kill her!" Mom pulled me out of the car. Blood was coming from a mark on Thom's forehead—JJ always wore a big ring on his right hand.

Once out of the car, I walked away and toward our front door. Thom got out of the car. When JJ got out, it was very obvious to everyone that he was drunk. Mom went over to talk to him. She asked him if he had been drinking. *Duh!* He could hardly stand up.

JJ was now focusing on Mom and what she was saying to him. From nowhere, Thom pulled back his right hand, his fist clenched tight. He took two steps, then threw his full weight behind a punch that landed squarely on JJ's face. The sound clapped as JJ, already too drunk to walk, fell backward like a dead tree, straight onto the concrete driveway. He was out, down for the count, and was still as a dead man. We all ran to look at him. I couldn't believe what I saw. "Is he dead?" I bent down to see him up close. A few seconds later—and they seemed like an eternity—he woke up, looked up at me, and sat up. Mom pulled me away, her words stabbing me, "Go in the house now! YOU have caused enough trouble."

I had never known Thom to fight, nor even talk of fighting. He had a good father and a reasonable upbringing. This had been a totally unexpected attack on both of us.

Yet Mom blamed all this on me—not the person who had stalked me, nor the person who cursed, called me names, and slapped me. She blamed me! The guys soon left, and Mom came in, only to tell me again I was the one who had caused the whole thing. "If you hadn't been acting like a little whore," she said, "it wouldn't have happened."

My head was spinning at the injustice of it. I was trying to get away from a guy who was abusive. I was not running around on him; I had broken up with him because I wanted to see Thom when he was home. I had been honest.

Thom and I had enjoyed a nice, age-appropriate evening, and we were home at my curfew. Still Mom put me "on restriction."

I had a good Christmas that year, even with all the craziness in my life. Ann came home from college for the holidays. There were several fun-filled parties to attend. They were not at our house, and thank goodness. Friends with functional families were holding them. One of those special families was the Ramseys. Ann was dating one of the two Ramsey brothers, but they must have had at least five more cousins, all about the same age. Their dad, a beer drinker, surely loved those kids. Their mom was so sweet and tolerant of us all. They were a good Catholic family, but we could still dance and party in their small home, which was overflowing with love and acceptance. Even a priest would attend the parties, conspicuously having a drink or two too many. This was just the weirdest thing on earth to me. I had never seen a man of the cloth drink. I knew that one of the Ramsey brothers thought my sister was something, and I guess they were falling in love. He was a Catholic. JJ was also Catholic. My dad would throw a fit if either of us ever married out of our faith, much less a Catholic. Both my sister and I knew our parents would not approve. In the big scheme of things, we weren't so bad, but in our parents' view, we were walking on the wild side.

Going back to school after Christmas break was hard. I returned as a "single" woman because JJ and I had broken up. I wasn't sure what I was going to do. With Thom gone, I was left to deal with JJ alone. I told my mom I wanted to leave Pensacola, and asked her if I could go live with my brother in Montgomery. She dismissed the idea as absurd, so there was no use pursuing that option. I wanted to run, but I had no place to go. JJ's words had not only been hurtful when I broke up with him, but they had struck fear in my heart. His reaction was vicious, his words vulgar, and his behavior unpredictable. He had no problem turning our teenaged intimacies, which had been filled with "I love you"s, into weapons of degradation. I knew he would share that opinion with all who would listen. I was terrified.

JJ continued to call me, and before I knew what was happening, I was back talking with him. That seemed to be easier than dealing with what I perceived to be the repercussions of a permanent break-up. I just couldn't bear the shame of him saying to others those horrible things about me. I was damaged goods. Who else would want me? So I caved.

I figured that going back with JJ would quiet the beast. I could live with that better than becoming one of the girls the guys talked about at school. The term, at the time, was "pig." A girl who was promiscuous, or one who had given in to sex, regardless of the circumstances, moved into the zone of no return. She was labeled a "pig," and most of the kids who I ran with were not reluctant to use the term every time a girl's name came up.

How nice it would have been if I had had just one person to confide in, who would tell me this would not be the end of the world. I needed to know I wouldn't be ruined forever. None of my friends *ever—and I mean ever—*admitted to having sex. We all tried so hard to make everyone think we stopped short of the *dirty deed*.

Some time toward the end of January, JJ invited me over to his house on a Saturday afternoon. His parents weren't home, and with much prodding, though we now considered ourselves back together, we ended up having sex in his bedroom. It was the dumbest decision I've ever made, and I've made some really dumb decisions.

In the eleventh grade, I was voted Treasurer of the Student Council. I enjoyed reasonable popularity in school, especially since I had managed to pull my reputation out of the fire just before being burned. JJ, who was having problems with his dad, was ready to leave Pensacola and go back to Grand Bay, Alabama, where the grandmother and uncle who helped raise him lived. We would go on a date, and he would try to convince me to just leave with him. The last thing I wanted was to get married, or leave with him. I didn't want to leave school. Yet we did share one strong common bond: We both were products of dysfunctional families, both hoping one day to get away from them and make a better life. As bad as mine was, though, his was far worse.

JJ's dad had recently purchased a little bar that had a couple of pool tables and a juke box. It was basically a local dive that drew only low-class losers— people who just wanted a bar stool to sit on while pouring cheap alcohol down their gullets. JJ's dad owned it, and used his wife as free labor to take care of customers. JJ told his dad if he ever went in there and found his mom serving beer, there would be hell to pay. Well, of course, that is exactly what happened.

After finding his mom with swollen ankles and serving beer, JJ went home, got his 12-gauge Browning shotgun, loaded it, returned to the bar, and put a couple of rounds in the ceiling. He and his dad squared off. His mom cried, trying to stop the fight between father and son. Somehow, JJ could engage in this sort of behavior without anyone calling the police. And JJ prevailed—his mom got off early that night.

The phone in the hall, outside our bedroom, was still the best thing my parents had done for me. It was my outlet and my one connection to my friends, especially JJ. We talked for hours—so long, in fact, that we were once accused of listening to each other breathe. I didn't have a television in my room—there was only one in the house. That television was dominated by my dad, and he had no problem telling you that the TV was his. He would tell us, whenever we had a program selection that differed from his, "When you get a house and a television of your own, you can decide what you want to watch." Any dissent with Dad and you risked life and limb.

My brother and his wife were visiting us and the family was in the den, I assumed watching television. I was lying across my bed talking to JJ on the phone. Dad had been drinking, and I guess Joseph had had a drink or two with him. It was family time, and we loved having Joseph and his family visit.

Suddenly, I heard yelling and screaming that sent chills up my spine. I told JJ, "Something is happening. They are all screaming." The house carried the sounds and vibrations of the altercation taking place at the other end. I was afraid to go into the kitchen, but JJ told me to go see what was happening, and he would hang on to the phone. I ventured the short distance down the hall and into the dining room/kitchen area. As soon as I rounded the corner to the dining room, I heard my sister-in-law screeching like an owl caught by a bobcat. I could see the back of my father—he had my brother pinned to the floor.

I don't know how it all started, but Joseph's wife grabbed the broom from its resting place in the kitchen and was holding it as a weapon. She was like a mamma grizzly defending her cub. She held the broom by the straw end, one hand on the base of the straw and the other just above. God bless this feisty woman who chose to fight for her husband. My mom was standing in the kitchen, watching as the scene played out. She did nothing. She never had the courage to physically fight for herself. How could she fight for anyone else?

The broom handle was raised and blows came down as hard as a broom stick could drop. Each swing made contact with the back of my father's head and shoulders. She was screaming, "Get off him! Stop and get off him!" My brother and sister-in-law were fighting for their lives. Dad finally stopped and got up, but as he was releasing my brother, I ran back to the phone. JJ was waiting; he had heard everything. He was cool as could be, and he said he was on his way to get me.

I stayed in my room. Within ten minutes or so, JJ was in the drive and I ran to join him. I left home crying to the one person who understood how bad it was, and how much it hurt to have so much violence in my home. He consoled me. We affirmed to one another that the one thing we wanted was a life that did not include the drama we had seen in our parents' lives. I hated the way Dad's violence was destroying our family. At this point, I did not recognize that JJ was part of my problem, not a cure.

My brother said that Dad drank so much that he started to hallucinate, got out his shotgun, and was going to shoot the ducks that were "flying on the ceiling" of our dining room. Dad was watching those ducks as if they were real and getting ready to open fire. Joseph tried to stop him and the fight ensued. Just what our battered family needed: a crazy, drunk, hallucinating war-veteran, opening fire on the "flying ducks" in our dining room.

Chapter 13
The Weddings

Me and JJ on "Seniors Rule Day." I was being shown how to wash his car for a spoof photo in our class newspaper.

Come back with me briefly to the end of February 1967. I was sitting in French class, which happened to be my favorite. Miss Pavlic, a Natalie Wood lookalike, was one of the prettiest teachers in our school. She was young, and I really wanted to emulate her ability to speak French. I was sitting at my desk, repeating the phrases she gave us.

All of a sudden, I felt sick. I thought I was going to throw up on my desk. Trying hard to choke back the vomit I felt rising in my throat, I stood and walked quickly out of the classroom. I couldn't ask permission—I'd barf. My face was flushed, and I could see how red it was when I entered the girl's restroom at the end of the hall. I threw up, then wiped my face with wet hand towels. I thanked all the lucky stars that no one else was in the restroom. I looked at myself in the mirror. I asked myself: *Are you pregnant?* Panic gripped me. The fear of being pregnant was worse than anything I had ever known.

I started counting backwards, and realized I had been late starting my period. I kept hoping and praying I was wrong. At home, I lay in bed and tried to think of what I could do if I was pregnant. *Oh, God, please, please, please, don't let me be pregnant.* I fell to my knees beside my bed and begged God to forgive me of my sins and not to punish me by bringing a child into the world when I had no way to care for it. I had nothing to offer. What would I do?

JJ took the news much better than I thought he would. He was ready to leave Pensacola at any time, and he said we could get married in Georgia. But I didn't want to be married. And I didn't want to have a baby. I was sixteen, and I was not prepared to even think of being a wife, much less a mother with a child.

Every day, I went home and I would run, jump, do hand springs, double round-off flips, and back flips. I'd bounce and kick with all my might. I thought maybe—just maybe—if I was late starting my period, all the bouncing and jumping would make me start. It didn't work.

Though I continued to go to school, I felt sicker each day. I told no one but JJ. I had no one in which to share a secret so dire, no one to trust with a predicament I knew would change my life forever.

Again and again, JJ offered to marry me. He reminded me of the beautiful diamond he had given me. He finally said to me, "If you wait until you're showing, I'm not going to marry you." That thought sent waves of nausea through my body.

It was now March. After school each day, I returned home sicker at heart than the day before. One day when I walked into the house, Mom was standing at the breakfast bar. There was a phone on the wall, and she had obviously been making calls, or she had been on the phone with someone. She walked to the end of the bar, stopped, and faced me with a contorted, strange look on her face. I walked up to her and asked her what was wrong. She moved closer, her body language confrontational, and she said something in such a tone that the words went through me like an ice-pick: "Your sister is going to get married, and when was the last time YOU had a period?"

It sounded so mean and accusatory that I didn't know what to say. I mumbled something about having just gotten finished. I certainly couldn't or admit anything to a woman without love or kindness in her voice. Confiding in her would only allow her to make me feel dirty and rotten. I just couldn't share anything so private, so intimate, with this angry person who seemed to revel in catching me in the wrong. She would never listen to me, or make me feel loved or protected. I knew there would be no kindness. She was my adversary.

I decided to keep it to myself, my secret—my decision.

Figure the odds of me getting that one right.

Preparations for my sister's wedding, the bridal shower, selecting her attendants, picking out bridesmaids' dresses—all began immediately. It would be a Sunday afternoon wedding at the church where we attended. Ann chose a short white lace dress for herself. Her old friend from Pensacola and I would be bridesmaids, and a new friend she had met in college would be her maid of honor.

There was so much to do in so short a time frame, but somehow it was all pulled together. Ann's shower was a huge success, and the den was filled to overflowing with gifts. She was set with linens, dishes, pots, toasters (two of them), electric mixers (I think she had three), plus all manner of miscellaneous household goods. It was quite a haul, and something to see in our very modest home. In fact, I had never seen so many gifts in one place before.

My mom had been playing with a technique of fabric painting called Tri-chem. It was a type of liquid embroidery, done with tubes of wash-proof paints. That was right up my alley, since I loved art and painting. I had chosen to embroider a set of pillow cases with a design that had a hillbilly couple standing in front of an old outhouse, complete with a half-moon on the door. I appreciated the humor: The Daisy May-Li'l Abner-type couple stood with their backs to each other on one pillow case. With their arms crossed and noses in the air, the caption read "Some Don't." The matching case had the same couple kissing, with cute puckered lips together, with a caption reading "Some Do." The design seemed more appropriate for my situation. I did a great job, and I prized my art work. I wanted to keep the pillowcases, but my mother said I was selfish, and she made me wrap them as my gift to my sister.

Mom and everyone got a little crazy in those weeks leading up to the wedding day. The usual consequence of stress in our home was that Dad went on a binge, which he did. It was the Thursday before the Sunday wedding. I went to school. I was at wit's end, still not knowing what I was going to do. I came in the front door and laid my books in the usual place. Mom was busy in her shop, talking non-stop about the wedding. She called me to come out to the shop, and while she combed a lady's hair, she told me to go inside and cook the frozen vegetables that lay thawing on the kitchen counter. Nothing was unusual about this, so I went in and started dinner.

I prepared everything Mom had on the counter. We had black-eyed peas with snaps, creamed corn, fried okra, a pan corn bread, and sliced fresh tomatoes. It was a vegetable dinner, and it was hot and ready when Dad came through the door. He was drunk. I knew it when he walked in like a John Wayne sidewinder. He sat down at the table and started to eat. I sat at the other side, eating quietly. The last thing I wanted was to sit across the table from him, but the food was good to me. He ate with the bad manners of a drunk, and each forkful triggered less tolerance in me. Finished with his meal, he got up from the table and said in a surly tone, "From now on, I want meat with my dinner."

I just looked at him. In as matter-of-fact a tone as I could manage, I told him, "We didn't have any meat to cook."

If looks could kill, I'd have fallen over then and there. He turned on his heels and grabbed for the back door, almost collapsing as he went down the stairs and out to the storage room. I didn't know what he was up to, and just continued cleaning up the kitchen. All of a sudden, the back door burst open and in he walked in with a frozen ball of something wrapped in white butcher paper. It was taped up and frozen, hard as a rock. He slammed the frozen bundle onto the kitchen counter and snarled at me not to ever say there wasn't meat in the house.

I guess I could have blamed Mom. I could have said, "Dad, I just cooked what Mom laid out for me." Or maybe, "Gee, Dad, I'm sorry. I didn't know it was there." But no, I said in a very sarcastic tone, "You got enough to eat, didn't you?" I knew full well that anything other than a subservient tone would be dangerous, and when he was drunk, I was putting myself into a very precarious position.

There was no turning back now. With glazed eyes, he stared through me, as if I was the enemy. I backed up against the cabinet and watched him lunge straight at me, grabbing at my arms. His right hand clinched around my wrist as he pulled me into our den, which was right next to the kitchen, where he slung me at least ten feet. I hit so hard I bit my tongue. I then bounced almost completely off the couch.

He ran over and grabbed me, lifted me up by my shirt, and pushed me back down against the couch, leaving me in almost a sitting position. His left knee came up on the couch, and his right hand was pulled back in a fist, hard and tight. His face was within twelve inches of mine and he looked like a vicious dog. His eyes were dilated, like two black holes in his head.

Dad was missing his two bottom teeth—no one ever noticed the empty space until he was mad. I could see the empty space, and his back teeth were grinding. He had his left hand holding a fist full of my shirt, leaning painfully hard against my chest. I then realized he was going to hit me with his fist, full force, right in my face. I braced for impact, accepting that I was doomed. It was as if he was fighting another man or the enemy.

Something must have gone through his mind as he looked at the fear in my eyes, because he stopped. He shook me, shoved me back, and then stood up, slowly releasing his coiled fist. "Don't ever speak to me like that again or I'll kill you," he said. He stormed out of the room. I ran to my bedroom and cried. I cried in fear, I cried in hatred, I cried because I didn't know what to think about what had just happened to me. He came so close to smashing me in the face with his hard fist. I sat down on the edge of my bed, and my mind slowly processed the incident. I fully recognized that I had "smarted" off at him. I knew that I shouldn't have done it. I guess I just didn't fully calculate the "off-the-scale" response I would receive.

My final assessment of the situation was jelling in my head. I turned and saw myself in the mirror. Hunched over, I looked teary and pathetic. I stood up straight and walked slowly closer, then closer, until I was face-to-face with that young woman in the mirror over my dresser. My eyes met the reflection of my soul. I studied her for a moment. Then I asked myself, out loud, in a clear resolute voice, "Why am I afraid? Nothing can be any worse than this." It gave me the strength I needed to do what I felt I had to do. I then began to mentally prepare for my departure from that house.

Still, I knew I had made a terrible mistake, and now I was forced to marry it!

First things first, I had to get through my sister's wedding. My handmade, sage-green satin dress fit my slim curves beautifully. The small pill box hat, with the sheer veil, rested softly on my head. It looked as though it had been chosen just for me. Unlike many bridesmaids, I wasn't unhappy with my dress—in fact, I loved it. I felt beautiful.

JJ and many of my friends came to the wedding. Dad kept telling JJ, over and over to the point of embarrassment, "JJ, when you decide to take her, I'll give you fifty dollars and a ladder to get her out of the house." His joke was at my expense. "Yep, I'll gladly give you fifty bucks if you'll just take her off my hands," Dad said yet again.

Fifty dollars was all I was worth?

It was okay, because we didn't even plan to take that from him.

Many years earlier, I had sat in church while a beautiful teen-aged girl from our congregation walked down the aisle, her very pregnant body making clear she would be having her baby out of wedlock. I will never forget her bravery, her willingness to humble herself before the congregation. There literally wasn't a dry eye in the house. I could not envision me choosing to be in such a position. At least the father of my child said he loved me, and he wanted to marry me. Marriage was my only viable option.

I made a plan and, the hope was, I'd make a clean getaway undetected. Mom usually knew everything going on in our small house, so it would be a challenge to leave without her discovering me. Maybe her preoccupation with my older sister's wedding would work in my favor.

Mom had given me a dark green, three-piece set of hard-side luggage for my sixteenth birthday—a large suitcase, a medium-sized one, and a small cosmetic-overnight bag. I packed my clothing while Mom worked in her shop—I tightly packed as much as I could cram into that big case. On top, I laid a simple baby-pink wool dress. It was a church dress that Mom had made for me, an A-line dress that looked like something Jackie Kennedy would wear. Round at the neck, with long sleeves, it would be my wedding dress.

There would be no choosing a beautiful white dress for me. There would be no bridesmaids, no fanfare, and no rice-throwing at my departure. I knew I didn't deserve to have a wedding like that, nor could I imagine pulling one off myself. I couldn't bear to face either of my parents. I had no reason to believe they would deal with my situation with anything but anger and condescending rage. They had never been there to offer me anything but tough judgment and harsh discipline. Neither would help my situation now.

On Wednesday night, after everyone was in bed asleep, I counted the money from my hiding place. Having saved for months, I had accumulated $68.00. That was not much of a dowry, but at least more than the fifty bucks

Dad had promised. Like a thief in the night, I carried my suitcases out the back door and down the stairs, and hid them behind some boxes in the storage room. I stole my way back into the house, not sure what excuse I would use if discovered. Mom hadn't moved, so it was easy to crawl back into bed. This was my last night in my parents' home. I just lay in bed in silence, listening to my heart beating, staring at the ceiling, and praying that somehow God would protect me, even though my mission was somewhat misguided. God knew my heart. He knew I was sorry, and he knew I was willing to try to make things right.

Lights—I saw lights. A car was coming around the block. I watched the lights pan around my bedroom wall—left wall, back wall, right wall, around and out—as the car completed the turn. I tried to find solace in knowing I would never again have to lie in terror as I waited to see if the lights stopped on my back wall, indicating Dad had turned onto the drive. As I relived the memories in that room, the next morning arrived at a snail's pace.

Mom had not been in the habit of getting up to get me off to school in years. I always set my own clock, got up, got dressed, made my breakfast, and left in time to meet the bus. Everything went as usual that morning. I left out the back door, pulled my suitcases from the storage room, and handed them to JJ. He did not seem to be nervous. He threw them into the car and we were off. He was twenty years old and I was sixteen. I had absolutely no idea where we were going, or how to get there. I really didn't know how he knew, but I guess he spoke to someone about where you could take a sixteen-year-old girl to marry without parental consent. I was anxious—he was full-throttle and ready to go. I asked him, "Where are we going?"

"Georgia. Bainbridge, Georgia," he answered. "They will marry us there. You don't have to worry."

I gave up the reins of control and prayed he knew what he was doing. I snuggled close to his side in the front seat next to him. It was just me and him now. His closeness brought me some comfort, but I wondered if I was jumping from the frying pan directly into a blazing fire.

JJ and I headed east toward Tallahassee. He turned north on Highway 27, which wound its way toward the little town of Bainbridge. I didn't know if I had ever been to Georgia before. On the outskirts of Bainbridge, we stopped at a sign that read, "Marriage Blood Test Here." We pulled up to a white one-story building that looked like a commercial building you'd see in any city. We walked in and paid our money. They drew our blood, and we were certified good to go in no time. I honestly do not know how they could have tested for anything in such a short period of time. But we received our paperwork and headed into Bainbridge to get our marriage license.

We entered the state building, where we were directed to go. I did have a Florida Driver's License, but it had my birthday indicating I was sixteen. When we reached the window, they asked our names and ages—JJ said twenty (which he was) and I said eighteen (which I was not). My knees were shaking like I was robbing Fort Knox. The man looked at me, looked at JJ, and completed the license with no further identification. It was a pretty surreal moment. How could this be so easy? With license in one hand and directions to the local Justice of the Peace in the other, we left the courthouse.

We stopped at a local gas station to fill the tank. I opened my case and pulled out the neatly wrapped pink dress that had silently waited there for me to put on. No one would be there to help me zip it—I would do it alone. JJ took his bag, and he went into the men's restroom. We changed and came out together—he in his only suit, me in my homemade dress. There were no cameras to record the ceremony. Actually, I wish there had been. It would be interesting to see that couple through my eyes today.

When we arrived at our destination, we stopped out front and took a deep breath. It was a white wooden, two-story house, with a wide front porch, on a lovely street. The scene at the home of the Justice of the Peace could have been taken directly from a William Faulkner novel. We held hands and walked to the front door. It was as if we were resigned to the fact that marriage was something we had to do.

JJ knocked. I don't really remember who answered the door, but we were invited into the foyer. We tentatively walked in, and we were asked to sign the register on the side table to the right. We leaned over to sign in, and heard a man enter the room from the other side. We were somewhat surprised to see a man dressed casually, and I watched as he pushed his way into the foyer in his wheel chair. I was not prepared for that scene. I don't know what I was thinking, I wasn't expecting romance, but I wasn't expecting to be married by a person in a wheel chair. A nice man with kind eyes, he looked at me for a few seconds and asked, "How old are you?"

He had to have known I wasn't eighteen. I looked him in the face and said clearly, "I'm eighteen years old." He took the license, studied it for a moment, and then asked if we were ready. He rolled his wheel chair in place, and we stood before him, both of us trembling.

The ceremony was short. I guess it included all the necessary parts to be legal, but I really don't remember "Plighting my Troth" or anything too fancy. It was, "Do You?" and "Do You?" and "therefore I pronounce you husband and wife." I wasn't expecting bells and whistles, but this was so sad, so naked, that I was ashamed to even speak of it. It was done. Dear God in Heaven, the deed was done.

When we left Bainbridge, Georgia, we drove west toward Mobile. It was getting late by the time we drove back through Pensacola. I knew my mom would be worried about me, so I asked JJ to stop at a pay phone so I could call and let her know I was okay. My sister-in-law, who answered, said they were worried about me, and they knew something had to be wrong. I assured her I was okay, and told her that JJ and I had gotten married. She turned and relayed this to my mom. I could hear the murmuring through the phone. The first thing that came out of my mother's mouth was, "Ask her if she's pregnant."

Not "let me talk with her." Not "where is she?" Not "please come home," but a hateful, "I knew it," and then an insulting, "Ask her if she's pregnant?"

In response, I said I didn't know. It was true. I had not seen a doctor. There were no "over the counter" tests available. I guess I could have said "yes" because I wouldn't have gotten married otherwise. But somehow saying that would have made me feel so awful. Admitting anything to her was like admitting I was dirt. I knew that now she would have the satisfaction of knowing I was dirt all along. And by her standards, maybe I was.

My sister-in-law told me not to come home. She said Dad had his shotgun out and was threatening to kill JJ. "Whatever you do, don't come home. Dad will kill him," she warned. Then she said, "Hold on." Mom was talking to her. When she came back to the phone, she told me they planned to take Dad out somewhere, to give me a chance to come by the house and grab a few more of my things.

When we drove up to our back door, I was so nervous. My sister met me as she opened the door to let me in. She gave me a condescending look, almost rolling her eyes. We didn't touch. She was almost four years older and she knew I had screwed up. Wordlessly, I grabbed my few things and carried them to the car. I left for Alabama without any words of comfort from my older sibling. It hurt me, but maybe she just didn't know what to say.

We headed on toward Alabama. JJ had been a regular on Dauphin Island during his teen years, and that is where he wanted to take me on our wedding night. It was so late by the time we made it to the island, we were both exhausted. We pulled into the Holiday Inn, which I found out later was the only decent motel on the island. Of course, we had no reservation, and the motel was full. We went a little farther down the street and found a small motel that had a room. It was cheap. We were just so tired we decided to take it.

My experience, up to this time, had been in the AAA motels my mom and dad would choose along our vacation routes. They were simple, inexpensive, but clean. Nothing could have prepared me for this squalid little room, with its sandy floors and questionable bedding. Our first night as husband and wife was awful, to say the least.

1967, our first Christmas as a family.

Chapter 14
Potter Track Road

Our family photo 1969 (Photo by Olan Mills Studio)

Twenty-four hours later, our disastrous wedding night behind us, we headed for our first home together. JJ assured me we could live with his uncle and grandmother until he could find work. Since I didn't really have any other options, it certainly seemed like a good plan. After all, we were in love, married, and felt ready for this adventure. We talked of what we would do differently with our family. We both wanted to work hard and make a life for ourselves free of the dysfunction we both experienced growing up.

Driving up to our new home was something I could never have imagined. I certainly came from humble beginnings, but it did not prepare me for this.

JJ's uncle was a wonderful man who had been injured in a kerosene explosion that almost burned his leg off. The accident happened sometime around 1947. After years in the hospital, he had managed to keep his leg—it took a will that I could not comprehend. His uncle, now a confirmed bachelor, carried the scars of his injury on his body and in his heart. I later learned his fiancé, and the love of his life, dropped him like a hot potato during his lengthy hospital stay. He was a big, good-looking man who reminded me of Rock Hudson with gray hair. He visited his doctor three times a week for new bandages and continuing care.

The trailer home was one he could afford. He was a proud man—he wouldn't go on welfare or disability—who worked as a paper carrier for the Mobile Press Register. He was afraid to go into debt because he could not predict how long he could work. So he lived within his very limited means. I had the pleasure of getting to know this man and I cannot say anything about him that isn't good. He truly was a special person who deserved, and received, our respect.

We arrived that afternoon, March 24, 1967. My new home was a trailer smaller than what some people pull around as a camper. It was about 42 feet long and 8 feet wide. It was a very old eyesore, painted a rust-red color (pure Rustoleum), that was parked under the shade of a big oak tree. The nicest part was the very private lot, about three-fourths of an acre, on which it sat up on a hill. The lot backed up to farmland, so there were no homes behind or on one side of us. The closest house was another mobile home about 100 yards down the hill. On the backside of the lot stood a dilapidated chicken house with chicken-wire fencing all around the perimeter. The "girls" in the pen kept the family with a never-ending supply of organic eggs. This was before we knew to call them organic.

JJ's grandmother was a small, completely gray-haired lady, a one of a kind treasure. Granny wore a cotton house dress with an apron. The apron had pockets where she kept things you would normally keep in a purse, and she never went outside the door without her bonnet. This little old lady lived off nothing but an old age pension of $77.00 a month, and the support of her beloved son, JJ's Uncle Buddy. She must have been in her early 70's when we arrived at their door with the surprise announcement of our marriage. They took us in with no questions. In fact, his uncle moved to Pascagoula with a friend so JJ and I could have his bedroom.

Me and Uncle Buddy, years later.

JJ's granny raised him after he was left in her arms at six-weeks-old. According to Granny, JJ was too much trouble for his mom and dad to care for, so she took him in and cared for him as her own. He lived with her until he was about sixteen. That was when JJ's parents lured him to Pensacola to work in the family business and finish school. The prodigal son had now returned, and his granny and his uncle welcomed him with open arms. If they had had a fatted calf, they would have killed it for his homecoming.

That afternoon, the three of us—Buddy, JJ, and I—crowded around their camper booth table and we shared the story of our elopement. The mottled plastic bench fit tightly with the three of us. There was nothing but a galley aisle separating the table from the stove and sink, where Granny worked her magic as we sipped sweet iced tea. How she could cook full dinners on this gas apartment-style stove amazed me. I soon learned that every meal was complete with one of her incredible "hoe-cakes" of either flour or cornmeal.

Granny would fill the hot sizzling frying pan with a big flour biscuit dough ball, or she would pour in a cornmeal batter, let it sizzle until it was brown and crusty, flip it with the skill of a chef, and remove it to a plate. It was cooked to tender perfection, and rimmed with crispy little edges. No one went away from the table hungry when there was a hot hoe-cake to round out the meal. In the coming years, she would teach me many things. She would become my first adult friend. Never judgmental toward me, she was always ready to listen and mentor. Her wisdom came from the hard life experiences she had endured.

In the first few weeks of our marriage, we were happy and excited about starting a life together. JJ began looking for a job, and I made an appointment to see the doctor that JJ's uncle had been seeing for years. He was a general practitioner, and at that time, obstetrics was part of his practice. With no insurance, we knew we would have to pay, out of pocket, for all medical services. We probably had $150.00 between the two of us.

The good thing was JJ was hired and within the first month went to work at Ingall's Shipbuilding in Pascagoula, Mississippi. He was hired as an employee in the civil service system (a GS-07)—we were all delighted. He would be working in submarine overhaul, a blue collar worker who would pack and take his lunch each day. I would rise early along with him. I'd make the sandwiches, take care in wrapping the cookies, put chips in a little bag, and always include a napkin. This was the way it should be, right? *I will be a wonderful wife*, I thought. I was anxious to make a good home for me and my husband.

Having never endured a pelvic exam, my first visit to my new doctor was traumatic. I cringed at the thought of anyone looking at my bottom, even if it was a doctor. But he provided me the first medical confirmation that my suspicions were right—I was indeed pregnant, though I surely didn't want to be. The doctor explained to me the importance of good nutrition, while my mind was off somewhere wondering what I was going to do with a real baby. I felt like Prissy in *Gone with the Wind*, thinking to myself, *I don't know nothin' bout birthin' no babies.*

I got my vitamins filled and went home in a daze, just trying to digest the whole thing. I hated to give my husband the news on how much we would owe for the birth of our baby. It seemed like more money than there was in the world. JJ took the news much better than I expected. He said he would start working as much overtime as he could get, and that is exactly what he did.

From the start, we lived on a tight budget but, with a concerted effort, we made the numbers work. From the start, keeping the family checkbook became my job. JJ brought his check home each week, it was deposited, and we paid our bills first. If anything was left over, we saved every penny we could.

JJ's Uncle James came over the following weekend. He was an old scoundrel, but a lovable one. He was married to an Air Traffic Controller, who was twice as big as he was. She was smart, funny, and an absolute delight. We hit if off really well. She liked to eat sweets, and I loved to make them for her. Soon after their arrival that weekend, JJ told his uncle we would be having a baby. "There's no way you can know she's having a baby this soon," he blurted out. Then, the wheels turning in his head, you could see the "light" come on! "Unless she was already . . ." The situation was obvious, so no one mentioned it again, which was fine with me.

I spent my days with Granny. I watched soap operas with her, and helped her do chores around the house. I listened to Granny as she would tell me the family stories. She had raised JJ in poverty. As a baby, he was fed Carnation milk mixed half with water. She had made his shirts out of flower sacks, and they had eaten whatever they could—usually dried beans and cornbread or whatever food she could provide. And, she told me, they moved many times in his first few years of school. He had to be held back in school, a couple of times, because he was never in one place long enough to get a decent start. What she lacked in material things, she made up by giving him everything she could—she was totally selfless.

My pregnancy was going well and I started to gain weight. With the high carbohydrate-fat diet, my waistline seemed to grow exponentially. I didn't really show in my belly, though I gained two sizes in the first few months. My new husband began immediately to call me nicknames like "Queen Lead Bottom," and "Miss Round Pound." I would try to stay busy and active, but there was little I could do, since I had no car and we lived too far out to walk to anything. I really wanted to help out financially, and explored the possibilities of finding a job.

Across the street from our home was a potato shed. I had no idea what that was, but found out that one of Granny's friends owned the big barn where they processed potatoes. It was a family-owned farm, where they grew and harvested the potatoes, bringing them in to the barn, by truck, to be graded according to size. The potatoes were then bagged and sold to Lays Potato Chip

Company. After a cold call job request, they agreed to let me come to work.

Working at a potato shed was hot, hard work. The field hands would bring in large trucks filled with freshly dug potatoes. The trucks backed up to a conveyor belt, and the potatoes were sent rolling through the barn, on wide, bouncing, rolling racks, producing mind-numbing noise. I was now an official potato grader. The grading was pretty simple. I'd pick out all the rocks, dirt clods, rotten potatoes, or foreign objects as they rolled in front of me and several other graders. This was a monotonous, dirty, stinky job, under any circumstances, but during the first months of pregnancy, it was horrible.

As those rotten potatoes would roll by, I'd get a whiff and my stomach would contract. As we would finish up grading a truckload, I would get up and walk behind the shed to puke. I was only paid for the time the conveyor belt was actually moving, so I'd wash my hands and face, then return to my position by the time the next truck was dumping its load. The little bit of money I earned was spent on things for my new baby that would be arriving in October.

Six months pregnant and my new single wide!
Mom and Dad with Nathan during one of their many visits.
Me and Nathan celebrating his second birthday.

My parents were able to put their feelings about my elopement aside and started calling me to see how I was doing. Sometime around my fifth month of pregnancy, they made their way to Granny's house to visit. Dad and Mom came in their camper, and that was where they spent their nights. Mom was appalled at the condition of the place. They visited for a couple of days, and then drove along the coast, en route to the VA clinic in Biloxi. That same route brought them back through Pascagoula, where they stopped at a mobile home lot. They came back with exciting news that they had found a beautiful new mobile home for me and JJ. We were shocked.

They now seemed to want, so badly, to do something for us. Mom said to me, "I am so sorry I never did anything for you. I always thought I'd have time for you after Ann was gone." Those words validated my feelings and I believed her. I could see she was genuinely sorry. Now she really wanted to help me rise above the conditions we were living in, so we rode to Pascagoula and looked at the home. It was 55 feet long and 10 feet wide, two bedrooms, and one bath. The living room had deep green carpet and dark wood paneling. There was a white wooden rail, with two steps up into the kitchen, and new appliances in avocado green. The ceilings were white, with dark wooden beams running from side to side, giving it an English Tudor feel. The bathroom even had a washing machine, also in green. In comparison to where we were staying, it was a palace.

JJ was reluctant to accept the help, but he finally agreed. We purchased our first home, with Mom and Dad borrowing the 10% required, or $678.00, to make our down payment. Note: I said they borrowed the down payment money. My parents didn't even have $678.00. But they did have good credit and they co-signed for that loan. Our payments were $78.00 a month.

That gift of love spoke volumes to me. They wanted to be back in my life. My parents did love me, even though there had been many mistakes made along the way. Dad ended up going over the $50 contribution to my elopement he had promised, but he never said he was sorry for making the statement. I never told my mother that Dad had attacked me. It was a family tradition to just "let it go." I forgave them, I believe they forgave me, and I appreciated my parents' gift and involvement. Soon, the trailer was placed on JJ's uncle's property. Our first home was beautiful and I kept it spotless.

JJ's parents also gave us a wedding gift of sorts. They turned over JJ's car payment to us, since he was no longer in Pensacola to work for them. His parents did come over to see our new home. I will never forget meeting them at the door, and showing them through our home, which entailed the grand entry of our living room, our lovely kitchen (it took 1.2 seconds to take it in), a short walk down the hall to see a tiny bedroom on the right, the bathroom, and the master bedroom with its built-in vanity, and one double closet with sliding doors.

That SOB turned to me and asked, "Is that it?" His face was close to mine and his gaze was fixed. I looked straight into his face, stepped back, and for the first time, I noticed he only had half of an ear on one side. Half his ear had been bitten off in a fight when he was a young man. I thought I'd bite off the other half.

Maybe all the pressure of actually starting our family was hard on JJ. Maybe he just couldn't cope with all of the responsibility. Many times he wouldn't come home, though I always waited for him. I felt alone, empty, and frightened. He worked the second shift to make more money, so I would be alone at night to hear every creak and pop of that trailer. I couldn't sleep because fear would grip my heart. He would get in at midnight, which felt like dinner time to him. He would eat and I'd eat with him. I just kept getting fatter, or more pregnant, so he just kept distancing himself from me. The biggest problems came when he would not make it home at all. I'd wait, walk the floor, and watch for the lights to come up the drive.

More and more he would not make it home. The time from midnight until dawn seemed twenty hours long. I would turn off all the lights so I could peek out the windows to see if I could see anything or anyone. I was miserable and many times afraid.

After one of his no-shows, I finally heard him at the door about 3 a.m.. My body was bulging with child. I was angry and I was fussing. I knew he was up to something, and I was not going to be quiet about him making me suffer through another night of fear. I yelled at him and he pushed me. The argument escalated. He pushed me hard, and I fell down on the bed with a bounce.

The day before, we had worked on putting a baby bed together, so at the foot of the bed were his tools. As I watched him grab a pair of plyers, I tried to push him off me. He was sitting on top of my baby and he had my hands pinned down.

"Where have you been?" was all I could say. He sat on me and held the plyers to my lips. "I'll shut you up," he said. I was terrified. He was about to grip my lips in his plyers.

When I started crying, he told me that if I didn't keep my mouth closed, he'd close it for me. "You always start shit and you can't finish it," he mocked. My tears gave him what he wanted. He stopped. But he had set the stage for the rest of our marriage: "I'll do what I please, and if you say anything about it, I'll hurt you . . . bad."

>→•→•—○—•←•←

I continued to prepare for our baby, and I kept myself busy most of the time.

I collected a lot of baby clothes, and I spent time preparing the nursery for our new addition. His parents actually bought us a real baby bed. We had no idea what sex the child would be, but JJ would not even entertain the thought of a girl. He wanted a boy—a football player. What would we name him/her? JJ would not agree to any reasonable suggestion. Jeremy, Jason, James, Mason, all good, solid boy names were tossed around. The name he finally settled on, "tongue in cheek," was Poindexter—actually Poindexter Grunk. The father of my child thought this was funny. I was dealing with a person incapable of dealing with anything in a mature way.

As the time approached, I carefully packed my green cosmetic bag with all the things I'd need to bring my baby home from the hospital; a lovely soft blanket, and a sweet outfit for both boy and girl. Mom had crocheted a precious little sweater, cap, and bootie set for her grand baby.

My delivery was difficult and long. Labor started on my birthday, as I turned seventeen years old, and it progressed through the night and into the next day, with terrible pain in my back. My mother came as soon as she could, and she and JJ waited for hours. It was about 7 p.m., before James Nathan arrived to meet his young parents. He looked pretty pitiful with his bruised, flat forehead, and forceps mark from being turned and dragged into this world. But he made it, and I passed out, exhausted. At that time, hospitals kept women for three days, so JJ visited each day for a short period and then was gone.

For my departure, JJ was supposed to bring me my green suitcase, which had been packed for a month. I had left the case sitting in plain sight, on the vanity of our bedroom. The morning we were to bring Nathan home, I waited for JJ to arrive with all my precious things, so I could dress my baby to take him home. I waited. And I waited longer. He finally showed up, hours late. I asked him about the suitcase and he said, "I couldn't find it."

My baby had nothing. I asked, "How on Earth could you not find it? It was right there on the vanity." Our master bedroom was all of 10' X 12'. "What do you mean, you couldn't find it?" I asked him over and over.

One of the gifts I received while in the hospital was a little blue and white suit from Granny. It was too big for my little Nathan, but I had no choice but to use it. The nurses came in to say goodbye and I could tell they felt sorry for me—I read it on their faces. My mom took off her white sweater and I wrapped Nathan in it. It had been so important to me to be able to bring my baby home in sweet clothing befitting the welcome of a precious child. This made my heart ache with pain and disappointment, and with equal anger at JJ for not caring.

When I arrived home, I walked to the master bedroom. On the vanity in open sight sat my green suitcase, with all my baby's things packed neatly inside. JJ had not been home. While I was in the hospital, recovering from bearing his 8 lb. 9 oz. child, he had been out screwing someone else.

James Nathan was a delight. With his clear skin, big bald head, dimpled smile, and strong limbs, he was beautiful. The first thing JJ did was sit him on a football. Football seemed to be the only hope he had for his son, and that was really the only true direction that I saw JJ try to give him. I wanted him to grow to be a confident, well-educated young man. I didn't give a rip about the sports thing.

JJ did not ever seem to be interested in caring for his son. Except for one time, he never changed a diaper. Nathan was about 14 months old, and JJ stayed with him while I went to the grocery store. I was usually timed for such outings, so I was always in a rush to get back home. Nathan needed a diaper change while I was out. JJ attempted to pin one on, so when I came in, he told me he had changed his diaper. As Nathan stood up, the front of the diaper dipped below his genitals, fully exposing himself. Actually, it was pretty hilarious—even Nathan thought so.

Nathan was certainly the center of my life and I did everything for him I thought a mom should do. I enjoyed being a mom, and at that time did not miss my old school life, or Pensacola. For a while, I honestly felt my life was better. I guess I was pretty much desensitized to violence at home, so it didn't even ring a bell for me just how wrong the whole relationship was. I had no place to go, so I really didn't consider leaving, even when things were at their worst.

Over the next couple of years, I became accustomed to JJ's fits of anger.

No matter what the disagreement, in his eyes it was "might makes right!" He would get especially difficult when he was drinking whiskey. Beer was bad. Whiskey was lethal, at least on his mood.

One evening, he started in on me, and ended up flipping our coffee table upside-down by throwing it into the air. The entire table flew up, almost to the ceiling, then landed with a wham against the wall. I ran out the door and over to Granny's. His uncle was there and he came into the room and told JJ in a calm but strong voice, "JJ, leave the girl alone." Thank goodness he did leave me alone then. I had taken to heart one of my mom's lessons to me: "When all else fails, run like hell."

After I went back home, I walked around the coffee table. For two days, it was balanced against the wall, standing on one end, before he finally set it back up straight.

Nathan

We often packed the car and journeyed back to Pensacola, only 90 minutes away. We spent the holidays dividing our time between my parents and his. It was never really comfortable. I didn't like his parents, and he didn't like mine. JJ often used the trip as an opportunity to dump me and the baby so he could visit friends and try to relive the unmarried good old days. One weekend, he met up with the old friend who had been on our first double date to "the land."

The two of them got drunk, ending the evening in a bar fight. JJ managed to get himself arrested and taken to jail. His friend said it took four officers to get him into the police car. Nowadays, that's called resisting arrest. Now, they would taze you in a heartbeat, but JJ always got away with totally outrageous behavior. I can't remember the actual charge, but it was minor. Mom and I went to the jail to bail him out with a property bond on her home. I didn't have a clue about jail bonds. We went into a room to talk with JJ, and he just stared at the wall, refusing to speak to either me or my mom, and Mom was there to get him out. Mom got him out and we headed back to Grand Bay the next day.

On the way home, we stopped at one of his cousins somewhere in Baldwin County. He managed to get in a few slugs of whiskey, and I was none too happy about him or his drunken demeanor. He finally threw the keys at me and told me to drive. He wouldn't have done so if he hadn't just gotten out of jail.

In an era of no seat belts, we had let Nathan sleep on the back seat of the car. As we headed west over Mobile Bay by way of a dangerous causeway—the causeway was a four-lane road that was built at sea-level across the bay—I became aggravated at the way he had treated my mom, the mess he was in with the law, and the way he was treating me.

In the blink of an eye, JJ's mood changed to crazy anger. He moved from the passenger side of the car to the center, threw his left leg over my right leg, and pushed his foot on top of mine. I could not take my foot off the gas pedal. While I started screaming for him to stop, he was laughing like an insane person. The car was building speed rapidly and there were other cars on the road. I was so terrified, but I could do nothing but try to keep our car from hitting other cars. I was weaving and dodging cars at a horrific speed. I knew we were going to die, but I could do nothing—nothing but cry, hang onto the steering wheel, yell for him not to kill his child, and beg him to stop. After what seemed like an eternity, he pulled his foot off mine and said to me, "Keep your God damned mouth shut."

I did.

My life was wrapped up in my baby. JJ's was wrapped up in whoever was available at the time—if he wasn't out screwing around, he was missing a chance to because he was busy doing something else. I felt alone much of the time and pretty disconnected from the outside world. It was a depressing time—the Vietnam War was in full swing and heavy body counts were reported every day.

Gaining twenty-nine pounds during my pregnancy left me unhappy with my body. I started dieting and I lost twenty pounds in four months. I started looking pretty and swore to myself that I would not put on that weight again. I mistakenly thought that by losing weight, my husband would no longer feel the need to seek other female companionship.

I am not really sure how I did it, but Nathan seemed to thrive even with a seventeen-year-old mom who was learning as she went along. I loved him so much. I played and talked with him. His great-grandmother and his uncle were a big part of his life, and I am so thankful they were there for both of us.

There was an ad in the local paper for a palomino colt. They wanted $150.00 for him, said the nice man who answered my telephone inquiry. I hadn't really planned on buying a horse, as much as I had always wanted to, but the ad was intriguing. The guy who owned him lived a mile or so away from us, so I quickly made arrangements to go see the horse. He was beautiful—two-years old and gentle as could be. His golden coat was shiny and his mane and tail were almost completely white. He looked at me with soft horse eyes and I was his. I wanted that horse so badly I could taste it.

I went home and told JJ and Uncle Buddy. They agreed to help me by putting up a fence in the back where I could keep him. Then it was up to me to figure out how to buy him. I didn't have $150. I was seventeen, had no job (the potato shed work was over), and no prospects. Though I didn't have a set of male *cajoñes*, I did possess a great set of eggs.

I borrowed my uncle's car and went into Pascagoula, where we had our checking account. Dressed nicely, I walked confidently into the loan department, where I was directed to the desk of a nice young man in a suit. He asked how he could help me and I said, "I'd like to borrow $150."

The guy looked at me a little puzzled and asked me the purpose of the loan. When I told him I wanted to buy a horse, he chuckled a little, then looked back at me and decided I wasn't kidding. He told me to just wait a minute while he talked with the senior loan officer. He left the desk, walked across the floor, and spoke to a man who was obviously the boss. They both looked at me and whispered a bit, and the young man came over to me and said they would approve a signature loan for me in the amount of $150. They had a good laugh, I am sure, but to everyone's surprise, I came home with $150. I turned the check over to the guy selling the horse, and he handed me the lead rope, allowing me to take possession of my first horse.

I named him Star Dancer. "I have a horse!" I could have shouted. I was dizzy with happiness. The horse somehow survived, though I didn't know a thing about horse care, like how much to feed him. We didn't have pasture land, and we didn't have the money for a lot that that horse needed, but he seemed to be fat and happy. I took my time and won his confidence as I broke him myself—he never bucked. I'd ride my Star Dancer through the woods and around the dirt road behind our home. Happiness was riding my horse, and the only thing better would have been to have two horses to ride. The money was paid back to the bank, always on time.

We were having repair issues with the car JJ owned when we got married. The Comet Caliente was a repair nightmare—he had it all suped up with a four-speed Hurst shifter and other accoutrements that made it a serious gas hog. We badly needed to trade it in for a more economical and dependable vehicle. Of course, JJ wanted a Corvette, which was a very practical car for a married man with a baby and car seat. He was running wild and he really resented the fact he had to trade his car in for a Ford Falcon, but it was one of the few models that fit within our severely limited budget.

I don't think we had the Falcon long before he failed to come home at the regular time. I waited for him. I suddenly heard something that sounded like a car skidding on the pavement right in front of our house. Immediately after that came the sound of someone flooring the car's gas pedal, causing the wheels to spin. I was keenly alert to the sounds. I opened our windows to better hear the commotion.

In seconds, I heard another skid and the thump of a wreck. *Oh my God, someone has crashed almost in front of our home.* Within a few minutes, some-one was banging on the door—I looked at the clock and it was 2:00 a.m. Then I heard JJ yelling, "Open the door and let me in." I opened the door—he was drunk as he could be. He pushed past me. I was afraid to say too much with the plyer episode still fresh in my mind. "What happened? Where is our car?" I asked him. He wouldn't tell me, and instead, just walked down the hall, took a whiz, and climbed into bed.

The next morning, there was a knock at the door by a local sheriff. When

I answered the door, the officer wanted to know if JJ was home.

"Yes, he's here. Is something wrong?" I asked in a concerned voice.

"Will you have him come to the door?" the officer asked coldly.

I hurried back to the bedroom to get JJ. I whispered as I was shaking him, "JJ, JJ, you have to get up. There's a sheriff at the door." My fear did not appear to faze him one bit. I stood there, staring at him. I could not understand his nonchalant attitude. JJ slowly got up, went into the bathroom, and closed the door behind him. He stayed long enough to take two shits. When he came out, he totally ignored me, calmly walked to the door, then stepped outside to talk to the officer.

After the officer left, I found out it was our car upside down, in a ditch, at the bottom of the hill. JJ had just left it there, walked home, and gone to bed. He was neither arrested nor charged. We just paid to have it pulled out and repaired. When it came to police encounters, he was always smug, as if he had some secret knowledge that he could do as he pleased and would never be held accountable.

One of the few photos I have of me and Star Dancer.

Chapter 15
Saxon Manor

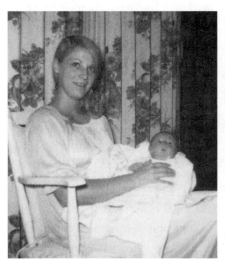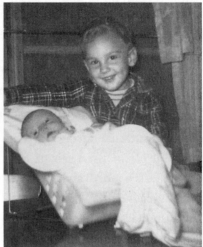

Nathan and I welcomed the new baby, Jamie Lynn.

J's uncle's job was delivering newspapers, so I looked forward to going through our paper page by page every day. I would read and share the local news with Granny. We would sit and talk about the strange things happening in our world. I listened to her—she had a very interesting perspective. I avoided telling her much about the Vietnam War because I felt sick thinking of it and so helpless to make any difference.

On a Sunday in the fall of 1969, an advertisement appeared in the classified section of the paper. I read it. I read it again. It said something about government assistance to first-time home buyers. Qualified buyers could get a three-bedroom home with only $200 down. According to your income, the government would subsidize your payment so your actual payment would be much lower than otherwise. The ad gave the real estate company's name and phone number to find out more.

I read the ad over and over. I had just turned eighteen years old, and I was pretty naïve about business, but I did get my horse loan and paid that off. This was just too good to be true. I waited impatiently for Monday morning to come so I could call the number. I was on the phone as soon as it hit 9 a.m. The voice on the other end assured me that if I was a first time-buyer, my husband had a job, and we had a dependent, then we would qualify. I just needed to come into the office to see the available floor plans. I was so excited I could hardly contain myself. When I told them, JJ and Uncle Buddy were skeptical of the whole thing and laughed at me.

I borrowed my uncle's car and started out for Mobile, Alabama. I had never driven into Mobile alone before. I carefully took down the directions and started out knowing that Nathan would be just fine with Granny until I returned.

The meeting went well. They took our information and did a preliminary analysis, which indicated we were well within the income range to qualify. For a three bedroom, 1 and ½ bath, 1,700 square foot house, we would have to pay only $109.00 a month and the government would subsidize the difference. The realtor explained the whole process. His name was Hilton Robinson. He told me that each year, they would reassess our income and the payment could go up if we made more money. I couldn't believe it—I drove home riding on a cloud.

It was difficult to get JJ to agree to go with me into Mobile. He thought I was pretty much full of crap and there had to be some kind of catch to it. I pushed and pushed until I got him to go with me to see the model home. He had no intention of moving to Mobile, so they agreed to not only let us choose a lot anywhere in Mobile County, but pay a maximum of $2,500 for the lot and then build us a house. All we had to do was give them $200 to start the ball rolling. We scraped the money together and launched the project.

Directly across the street from our uncle's home, a developer had constructed a paved dead end road, but it was only about one-quarter mile long. Nearby the entrance to Saxon Manor were two nice brick subdivision markers. Each lot was about 100 x 200 and for sale at $2000. We started our paperwork. It was November 1970 and I was nineteen years old when they finally approved us for this special loan. I was ecstatic.

They had purchased the lot in Saxon Manor and the building process started in the beginning of 1970. It seemed to take forever but it was finally happening. The thought of a new home was so exciting. We were also trying to have our second child. We wanted children three years apart, and Nathan was now over two years, so no birth control after January 1970. By March, I was pregnant. My sister and I laughed at our genes—we both were as fertile as cow manure.

I walked over to the new house each day. I enjoyed the walk, only about one-fourth a mile away, and it was such a thrill to see each step of the process. The guys framing the house were paying too much attention to me, because the first time JJ walked with me to the house, he became angry about the way the construction guys talked to me. I thought they were just being nice to talk about our home and the construction process, and I honestly did not think I had been flirting. I just wanted to see our home being built. JJ threw such a fit that he said he would kick everyone's ass, and tear the damned house down, if I went again without him. He started with the name-calling and berated me every time he saw someone look my way.

By the end of the summer, our new house was almost finished. We had to go through the loan-qualifying process again to make sure nothing had changed since we had been deemed eligible the previous November. We really didn't understand that the mortgage was totally dependent on meeting the income levels again. JJ had received a cost of living raise at the first of the year, and in May he had received his annual merit raise or step increase. The raises had put us over the income limit. It was crazy. We had qualified, and had been approved. Now we didn't qualify.

After my long struggle, the committee in my head was yelling, "You've got to be kidding!" JJ now made in excess of the allowed amount for a couple with one child. "But I'm pregnant," I told them. "My baby will be here in October."

The house would be completed soon, so the same realtor, Hilton Robinson, came to Grand Bay to see how it was coming along. He then came to our house to bring additional papers for us to complete which would let us count our second child to qualify. When Robinson came in and sat down in the living room, Nathan was playing on the floor and I walked into the kitchen to get something. I could feel Robinson's eyes on me. He said, "When are you going to start looking pregnant?" The way he said it was making me very uneasy.

I said something back like, "Believe me, I'm pregnant," then ignored the remark. We finished our business and I was glad when he left. I told JJ about it and we both laughed at the guy for being such a jerk.

After they recalculated our loan application, we still made about $50 a month too much, even with two children. JJ actually went in and asked for a pay decrease so we could qualify for the house. After the government gave him the cut in pay, we waited for his leave and earnings statement to reflect the decrease, resubmitted the application, and the income ratio finally worked.

The realtors came back again. Now they said they couldn't hold the home until after our child was born in October. "It's August," I argued. "Even if you put the house on the market, a buyer most likely could not close before October or November. So why can't you wait for our baby to be born?" I was using every argument I knew of to keep the contract from collapsing. JJ was sick of it—all of it.

The Robinson creep told us if we paid $200, he could hold the house. It's funny, but we didn't even have $200. We signed a note and paid him $50 a month to pay off the $200 note. In retrospect, it was most likely illegal for him to do that, but we didn't know any better and we were willing to pay it. Our baby was born on October 31, 1970. We closed on our home in November and moved in soon after that. I felt victorious.

Our new brick house was larger and nicer than any home either of our parents had ever owned. It was truly the nicest place either JJ or I had ever lived. I had left home at sixteen, married, had two children by age 20, established my credit, and now we had a beautiful new home. Most of the time, these accomplishments were satisfying to me, and I credit them with sustaining our marriage. At times, things were bad, but I was not about to strike out on my own, and I sure wouldn't go back to live in the house under my dad's rule again. It probably helped that I was no longer in touch with my friends at school. That left me not much to compare myself to.

Nathan and Buckshot

My days back then were spent caring for my children, sewing—I made drapes for the entire house—painting, refinishing furniture, and caring for our horses. We fenced in a small plot behind our house that backed into the woods. If you went into the woods, the land rolled down gently to the creek. No one was ever back there, so no one cared, or seemed to care, that we were using a small piece of their land.

I had sold Star Dancer, and after we settled in at the new house, I bought Brandy, a huge black quarter horse. I rode her often and hard, until one day when I was trying to do a fast figure eight in our back yard. She tripped, completely fell, and rolled over on the ground. Thank goodness I had gone in the opposite direction so she didn't roll on me. The old girl was a good horse, but not as agile and athletic as I needed, so I sold her pretty soon after that.

We purchased an adorable pony for Nathan when he was four. We named him Buckshot. I wanted so much for Nathan to enjoy this pony, the one I never had as a kid. From the start, he did. I saddled Buckshot each day and let Nathan ride. On his own, he finally was able to ride to the end of our little street, turn around, and return up the hill toward home. "I can ride by myself, I'm a big boy," he'd say. I let him ride to the bottom of the hill as I stood keeping a watchful eye. One time, after Buckshot made his turn toward home, he took off like a blue streak up the hill. Nathan was doing a great job of staying on and, though I tried to catch him, Buckshot dodged me like a fullback and ran around the far side of the house on a path headed right under a television antennae wire. That wire caught Nathan and flipped him backwards off the pony. Nathan hit the ground with a thud. He cried—can't say as I blame him.

Watching this episode had scared me to death. Nathan was both scared and hurt a little. He walked over to Buckshot, now standing by the paddock fence, grabbed his reins, and led the pony over to me. He was all red-faced and teary as he blurted out, "You take him. I want something that runs off gas." And he stuck to it. Nathan never again had much use for horses.

Buckshot then became Jamie's pony. At eighteen months and in a diaper, she would try to climb up his leg to get on. Her love affair with horses had just begun. I couldn't have been happier.

Our family photo (Olan Mills Photography).
Me on my black and white Paint, Lucky's Squaw.

As before, JJ was having a hard time finding his way home. He had developed some expensive hobbies, which took both a lot of money and a lot of time away from us. He went scuba diving with a friend who had a wife and six kids. We enjoyed their company fairly often. He also decided to join the Pascagoula Country Club so he could learn to play golf. That gave him an excuse, almost every day, not to come home until late, and it was a constant drain on our budget.

Outside our home and family, church was my only outlet. I attended regularly and taught Sunday school to the four-and five-year-olds. It was very important to raise my children in the church, but that always proved difficult with no help from their dad. It didn't matter. I had always gone to church and I wanted my children to have the same religion as I did. At that time, I felt it was the best thing my parents had done for me.

By the time Jamie was three years old, both JJ and I had horses—an Appaloosa for JJ and a gorgeous black and white Paint for me. I bought "Lucky" when she was a two year old so I could break and train her myself. She was gentle broke, never bucking once. This was a young, athletic horse that allowed me to ride like the wind. I left my troubles behind me while we flew through the woods at breakneck speeds.

But the horses became another way for JJ to inflict pain on me. If he was angry at me for anything, or if he got angry because the horse was afraid of him, he would go into the pen and meanly "shoo" the horses away. They were terrified and ran for their lives. It was fight or flight, and for them it was flight at top speed in a very small pen. He would yell and chase them until I begged him to stop. He was going to kill or hurt them really bad by running them into a fence. This didn't even take into consideration what he was doing mentally to the horses. His Appaloosa would be absolutely "wall-eyed" in fear. I was so angry that I ran to the fence and challenged him, "You bully, you hateful bully! Stop before you hurt them!"

He came away from the fence, walking toward me until he stood just in front of me. I can't remember what I said, but he grabbed the front of my shirt in his right hand, and his big hand twisted the fabric as his fingers dug into my chest under my shirt. Then with one hand, he lifted me off the ground, which amounted to strangling me. The pain was streaking through my chest and neck as he shook me. I couldn't breathe. "Keep your damned mouth shut. Do you hear me?" he warned. He pushed me back as he let me go. I was barely able to keep my feet.

I heeded the warning and kept my mouth shut.

I soon recognized that I was reliving my mother's life. She knew it, too. Mom pointed out to me that I had "one just like your dad." Clearly, she was referring to JJ. Worse, I now was putting up with the same things she had endured all her married life. I wanted to be a better person. I wanted better for my family.

I prayed harder.

I had quit school early because of my pregnancy. In the 60's, the thinking was that young, unmarried pregnant girls should not stay in school with other "children," because your pregnancy would somehow scar them. At sixteen, I had only two choices. The first was to have a baby out of wedlock and become a disgrace to my family. I just couldn't see myself walking down the aisle to beg the forgiveness of the church. The second was to marry the father of my child and try to make the best of it. There were no other options for me, so I chose to marry my mistake. Making that choice left me without a high school diploma.

Mobile had an adult high school that was part of Murphy High School. I was able to go for just two weeks to prepare to take the GED test. I took the test and passed all five segments with flying colors. I was so happy that my best score, a 98, was in mechanical logic. I was now twenty-two years old, I had two children, the adult high school was 32 miles away, and it offered classes only at night. I did the best I could under the circumstances. I didn't know how I would do it, but I always knew I would continue to further my education beyond the high school equivalency.

The most significant of the many violent events that took place in our Saxon Manor home started about 2:00 a.m. JJ entered the kitchen and turned to quietly close the door, as if I wouldn't know he was slipping in. I stood across the room, in the den, and I yelled at him with all the intensity I could muster, "I hate you! I hate your guts!" It could have been a scene from a Lifetime made-for-television movie. I had summoned all the bravery I had to confront him because I knew I would end up paying.

I wouldn't speak to him and went straight to bed. The argument started again as soon as he was out of bed the next morning. He actually wanted me to screw his sorry ass after his outing the previous night. I had no idea where he had been, or with whom, and I wanted no part of him. I told him, "Every time you stay out and do this to me, you kill a little more of my love for you. Do you understand what you are doing?" He tried to pull me in for a kiss. The children were in the den and he was starting this shit again. I pushed him. I was hurt and upset, and I didn't want his hands anywhere near me.

JJ didn't just one-up the ante, but he raised it even higher. He reached into our closet, where he kept his .22-Colt revolver, hanging in a western-type holster. I stared at him as he grabbed the pistol, which was always loaded. So now what was he going to do? I tried to turn, but he grabbed me with his left hand, clamping down hard on my arm. I tried to get him to let me go while trying to keep my voice down, so the kids wouldn't hear. I couldn't believe that he had cocked the loaded .22. Holding the gun with his right hand, he buried the barrel into my stomach.

Feeling that barrel sink into my belly, I figured he was really going to shoot me. My tears spilled involuntarily. I was paralyzed by fear, and my body folded as my knees gave way. I thought, *He is really going to kill me. Oh my God! My children are in the other room.* My brain protected me as it took me into this dreamlike, surreal place. I accepted the reality that I was going to die. There was no more fight in me.

When he felt my body completely succumb to his threat, he let me go. Then, turning toward the closet, he fired that revolver either five or six times (I don't know if one was in the chamber when he grabbed the six-shooter). He emptied the gun through my clothing and through the wall. He turned to me with a threatening grimace. "You keep your mouth shut or I'm going to kill you," he said. I believed him.

As soon as he walked away, he went out the door and out of the house. I ran toward Nathan, who was coming down the hall after hearing the noise. I consoled him. Somehow, Jamie was still asleep on the floor pallet the kids had in front of television. The Saturday morning cartoons were blaring. I turned the sound down and walked back into Jamie's bedroom.

Our master bedroom and Jamie's room backed up to each other at the end of the hall. The closets both shared the center wall. I can't remember if the bullet holes went through the doors on the other side, or if the closet doors were open. However, my treasured suede coat, with the luxurious mink collar, now had bullet holes running through it. I loved that coat, and now it was not worth wearing. I turned from the closet to look at the full bed in Jamie's room. The bullet holes had gone into the bed at about a child's height. Bullets were now embedded deep in the mattress. Jamie's baby bed was on the other wall, and she and Nathan often played in that room. I suddenly realized for the first time that he could have killed our children.

It was my fault, according to him. I had made him do it. And he never apologized. To make up, his usual mode of operation was to pester me until I let him have sex. However, after this episode, he now had a new line. Whenever he wouldn't come home, he would always mock me by saying, "Well, I guess I killed a little more of that love tonight, didn't I?" He'd throw his head back and laugh like hell. At that moment, I truly believed the devil lived inside him.

Chapter 16
Union Church

Jamie (by Olan Mills Photography) and a photo I took of Nathan, Jamie, and Sugarboy, shortly after we moved to Union Church.

My sister's husband was now out of the Air Force, and they were back in Pensacola, working, she as a beautician, he for the railroad. Mistakes made on the railroad are not too forgiving. Otto had a close call, and was soon looking for another line of work. JJ helped him get a job, and he began schooling to become a radiation control monitor. He and my sister were soon living in Grand Bay. I helped them move and get settled in. It was good to have them close.

With JJ, Ann, and Otto all working full time, I kept Ann's two children for her. From Tuesday through Friday, her children (my niece and nephew) were like mine. I had four children in my care, all under five years old. Needless to say, I was busy.

JJ and I had bought a five-acre piece of property in Grand Bay, Alabama, with plans to build a home on it one day. Ann and Otto had purchased a beautiful 2.5 acre lot in Cantonment, Florida. They were hoping to someday return to Florida. They were telling us of their property, so while on a visit to Pensacola, we took the short drive out to Cantonment to take a look. We ended up buying a lot next to theirs. We thought that someday we might all return to the Pensacola area. The prices were cheap and the payments were low.

We sold our government-subsidized home in Saxon Manor and made a $2,000 profit. The payments had gone up to the max because our income had more than doubled over the previous few years. JJ was moving up fairly rapidly in the government system. We rented a lovely little white frame house right in the middle of Grand Bay. It was across the street from the local high school and next door to the Church of Christ, where I was an active member and Sunday school teacher. We were lucky to find such a nice house, in town, with more than an acre of property. The back was all chain-link fenced, and within that fence was a horse paddock and shed. Perfect for Lucky (my paint horse) and Smokey (Jamie's new, very large Shetland pony).

One problem: Smokey was getting mean and unmanageable for a young child. Since he was a large pony, I was afraid he was going to end up hurting Jamie, so I put him in the huge pasture behind my sister's new house until I could find a buyer for him.

On a Saturday afternoon, I took Jamie and Nathan to a horse show at a local arena. We were having a great time, watching the barrel racing event, and laughed out loud when a little girl came riding out on one of the smallest ponies I had ever seen. He was a dappled gray, and the little girl had long since outgrown him. She was running the little fellow wide open as they rounded their first barrel. She was giving him extra encouragement, with a riding crop, when the pony decided he did not want to be encouraged. Instead of going faster, he started jumping around, a buck here, a buck there, which was eating up her time. She finally rounded the second barrel to the laughter of everyone in the crowd. Her finish time put her outside the running for a win, so she got off as soon as she was out of the arena and scolded her obstinate pony.

I walked around to talk to her and let Jamie meet her. We told her she did a great job, but maybe she was just a little too big for her tiny mount. Jamie petted the precious little fellow, with the girl introducing herself as Diane. The pony's name was Sugarboy. I loved that little guy from the moment I saw him. His legs were the size of broom sticks. His coat was slick and shiny. He looked like a perfect little horse, not like a blocky pony. Diane let Jamie sit on Sugarboy. *Voila!* A match made in heaven.

Diane's dad came up and the conversation turned to a little old-fashioned bartering. I told them that I had a pony that was too big for Jamie, and since Sugarboy was too little for Diane, let's trade. Diane said, "Oh no, I can't." She grabbed the reins, and Sugarboy sat back once again, simply being obstinate.

I told her she could come by and ride Smokey any time she wanted, and see if the much larger pony would work better for her. We had Smokey in a pasture about one mile up the road. "Why don't you come by on your way home and meet him?" That is what they did. Sugarboy was in their trailer as they pulled in to meet Smokey. I met Diane and handed her a halter. I pointed to the big gray pony grazing quietly in the field. Diane walked into the field and petted his head. The pony offered no resistance as she slipped the halter over his head. It was love at first sight, and the perfect size for her. Diane was a great rider, so Smokey wouldn't get away with the antics he had pulled with Jamie. Sugarboy would be much happier with a little girl who wasn't using a crop to ride the barrels. Sugarboy came out of the trailer and Smokey went in. Jamie now had the beautiful, lovable, little Sugarboy to call her own. Sugarboy became her friend, playmate, and a beloved family pet.

⊳⊶⊙⊷⊲

Our home at Union Church.

It was a good thing I was so busy with the children. It kept me from worrying too much about my philandering husband. Even though I was taking birth control pills, JJ initiated the process to have a vasectomy. It was a fairly new procedure and he actually wanted it, arranged for it, and had it. It wasn't my wish, so I was pretty sure he was tired of worrying about spreading his seed and being held accountable.

I kept looking at property when I had a chance, and I found a great buy on a house just north of Union Church. It was a very small, brick, three-bedroom, one and a half bath, on five beautiful, hilltop acres. We sold both the two and a half acres in Cantonment and the five acres in Grand Bay to come up with the needed down payment. We were still short of what we needed, so my dad came up with difference. We soon moved into our new home at Union Church. We assumed a $22,000 Farmers Administration loan with payments of only $77 a month. We also paid my dad for his loan. Now we finally had a proper place for horses and our children to play. Jamie was four and Nathan was seven when we moved into our house on the hill.

It was here that my children would get to enjoy the country life. Our family got to sit on our front porch and watch our cat have her kittens. The kids had tree swings and tree houses, ponies, and mini-bikes. Nathan learned to drive the tractor, and he and Jamie both helped in the garden. And at Christmas, we would all go into the woods together to find, cut, and drag home that special cedar tree growing along the creek behind our house. I wanted so much to enjoy my children and watch them grow up knowing and understanding a little more about nature.

It would be in this house that JJ and I would journey through the last leg of our marriage. The time passed. We had good times and terrible times. We stayed together because we just did. Over the years, I left him a couple of times. Once, he found me and the kids at a cousin's in Pensacola, and he came to get us as soon as he found where we were. I went back because I had no way to sustain the separation. I had no money, no education that gave me a real marketable skill, and I didn't want to burden friends or family. Besides, JJ loved me, and he always wanted me back. And when I came back, things were good—for a while.

Our hilltop farm was everything I wanted or needed as a place to live. I was trying to live the dream of farm life. I bought a beautiful, registered quarter horse from a big ranch in West Mobile. She was an incredible King-bred, unbroken, and two and a half years old. The ranch owner financed her for me, since she cost a whopping $750. I paid him $75 a month, which I paid off early. Her name was King's Bay Annette, a regal name for a bay with cutting horse blood, but she was truly spectacular. JJ and I broke and trained her. She was my love. At one time, we had a horse, a pony, a goat, a cow, hunting dogs, a cat, and Flip, my bulldog—a real menagerie.

King's Bay Annette

In Mobile County, you could be a substitute teacher with only a high school degree. I became a substitute teacher at both the elementary school and the high school. It was great part-time work. I could get up, get JJ off to work, get myself and the kids ready for school, and be home in time to clean the house and have dinner on the table by 5:30. I spent all the money I earned fixing up our home, on the children, or on our horses.

When I tired of the teaching gig, for extra money I started selling home interiors, which specialized in home accessories. The lovely merchandise was marketed and sold through home parties. I had a blast going to parties and working in my little business. At that time, I took orders, the products were delivered to my home, and then I had to distribute them and collect the money. Soon, my house had home interior wall art, shelves, and what-nots, etc., in every room. That was nice, but our newly built addition to our home (a big den with a fireplace) had become a warehouse, because I had become too successful. I lacked the space to sort and distribute. We were not going to build a warehouse for Home Interiors, so that too soon ended.

Mom and Dad found a house in Grand Bay on a visit to see all the children and grandchildren. They sold their home in Pensacola, moved into a lovely brick home, located, almost dead center, between my family and my sister's family. It was great to have them close by.

Nothing much changed with JJ. He was still running around. He had given up golf and scuba diving for hunting (deer, dove, quail, and raccoons), and fishing (anything that would bite), and then he bought a shrimp boat, so he and my dad could shrimp together. He said he played on a softball team in Pascagoula, so he often did not come home at night. I never saw him play.

My husband's routine was to leave work early on Friday, then head to a hunting camp farther north in Alabama. I would not see or talk to him again until Sunday. No phones there, except a pay phone at a café near the camp. Thus, we had no communication. He would promise he'd be home for dinner on Sunday, so I rushed home from church to make dinner for him. He might or might not show up for dinner. I'd usually wait around until Sunday evening before he'd drive up.

There was always some reason he couldn't come home at the agreed-upon time: He couldn't find his favorite hunting dog; they were looking for a deer that was wounded; or the Jeep was stuck in the mud, and they waited to get it winched out. When he'd come in, he'd throw his hunting gear and dirty clothes on the floor in the living room. After all, I had all week to get them washed and ready for his next weekend. And during deer season, it *was* every weekend. I asked him one time during the season to stay home with me and the kids. He said, "Unless I'm dead, I'm going." When deer season ended, 'coon huntin' began. It was always something.

My love of my horse, cooking, art, and sewing somehow kept me on that hill for days—just me and the children. I always kept busy, and often amused myself over long weekends with paint and pallet. I sold a few still-life pieces, and I once traded a desert painting for an Irish Setter puppy of very good breeding. Many of my paintings of landscapes, portraits, horses—any subject that caught my attention—were given to my relatives as gifts. I painted the worst picture of the little white house where I was born in Samson. I based it on an old photo. Mom cried with joy when she saw it. As I write this, it is still hanging in her home. It was so bad, I have to laugh every time I look at it, but she has always cherished it.

I also did a painting of an open Bible that had a red book marker, a hurricane lantern, and reading glasses lying on the oak antique dining table I had refinished. The pressed back chair sits turned slightly as though someone had walked away just for a moment. This is yet another bad painting, but in Mom's eyes, it was a true treasure. She always saw it as a symbol of my fight to save my marriage. They kept preaching to me that a man can be converted by just witnessing a long-suffering wife and her good works. I was still trying.

No, I wasn't a great artist. However, my work was appreciated by many who did not have a true discerning eye for "real" art. It was good enough for me, and it gave me something to look forward to each day. I would get up, clean the house before 9 a.m., and then paint or sew. I could become so involved and wrapped up in my work that, before I knew it, the day had passed. I was very good at being alone.

Between tiny-mite football, little league baseball, cheerleading practice, and baton lessons, the kids were involved with so many out-of-school activities. Weekdays were always full, and on most Sunday mornings, they and I would be sitting in church. It was more difficult for me in the evenings, because JJ didn't like me going out at night. His heart was hard, most likely in perfect concert with his penis. He was the only one who went out at night.

At the beginning of 1975, I was 24 years old. I was enjoying my children, who were getting to the point where they didn't need supervision every second of every day. It gave me more time for myself, and I was always looking for something productive to do.

By sheer fluke, I caught a piece of a conversation on veteran's benefits, and learned there was money for kids to go to college if they had a parent who had received a 100 percent VA disability. Could this be true? I called Dad. He said, no, you don't get the benefit if your child was married. He really believed that. It upset me so much that I went to the Veteran's Administration office in Mobile.

The end of the story? I did qualify. I could have gone to college on my dad's benefits and I never knew it. Dad thought I had lost the benefit when I married. Then I found out that the benefit had nothing to do with marriage, but the funding ended when I reached age twenty-six. The government would not only cover my education costs, but also pay for child care. I felt like I had hit the lottery. After coming down off this high, I set out for Mobile yet again.

The VA benefit guy was so nice. I took a test that helped to determine my aptitude, and then I took the college placement exams. The VA guy said, "Your scores are high enough that you can do anything you want to do." He continued with the fact that my math and science scores were good enough to get me into pre-med, which he highly encouraged. That thought was so far out of the realm of my comprehension, I didn't even know how to wrap my head around pulling that one off. The problem was that I needed funding for four years, and I was less than two years away from being twenty-six. *Damn!*

I explored every option I could find. A four-year program was out, I thought, because there would be no way to finance college for four years. I didn't want to go for a year and then have no way to continue. I researched and called everywhere, trying to make a good decision. I took a test, at the Old Providence Hospital on Springhill Avenue, for x-ray technician training. The test took the better part of the day.

Two weeks later, I was called in for a post-test interview. The nice man politely told me he was extremely impressed with my test results. I was so happy to hear him say my score had been the highest in the class. He did have concerns, though, because I had two children, and he had not had good luck with women finishing the program if they had children. He was not going to be able to offer me the program for that reason, *but,* because my math scores were high, the head of nursing said she would be happy to have me in her nursing program. I was devastated. I didn't want to be a nurse. That kind of blatant discrimination today would allow me to own part of Providence Hospital, but in those days it was just fine.

I ended up selecting an eighteen-month program at 20th Century Business College. I took accounting, bookkeeping, and income tax preparation. That probably was not the best choice I could have made, but at that time, it was the one program I thought I had a chance to finish. I did well in school, made a great friend who started as my babysitter, and on completion in 1976, I went to work for a tax season with Marian Curley, an attorney in Mobile, who did income tax preparation. It was, all around, a good educational experience for me, and I am glad I went. I have often used those skills since—business and tax accounting are needed for just about any endeavor. It would have been better if I had gone on to college, but without a crystal ball, it was the best I knew to do at that time.

Chapter 17
It Will Never Be the Same

One of the first Colonel Dixie stores.

Holding down a great job at Ingalls Shipbuilding, JJ was a government employee with wonderful benefits and good pay. Yet, he started on a rant about how he hated the work, and how much he wanted to leave. He came home one day and told me of how he could "get rich" by buying a dump truck and hauling dirt and asphalt for a living. That way, he would be his own boss and not have to worry about the demands of his bosses at Ingalls. There had been a few tales of altercations between JJ and some other employees, but I never got the straight scoop on this. I just knew he badly wanted to leave the shipbuilder.

He found a truck, which we bought for around $16,000, and he went to work hauling dirt and asphalt. He made big paychecks, but the truck needed continuous repairs, which took ever bigger portions of the paychecks to repair.

We had no idea how we would be able to keep everything afloat. His big pipe dream ended with us in terrible financial straits. For a young family that had previously done so well, this dump truck scheme was taking us under.

Somewhere toward the end of 1976, a gentleman met me during a business transaction with my mom. I remember Mom introducing me to him and his wife. He was a member of the Church of Christ, which is how he knew my family. After speaking with me for a while, he told me they were recruiting agents for his insurance company, and asked me to call and make an appointment for an interview. I did just that.

I showed up for the interview in a polyester gray pinstripe suit that I had made. The suit fit perfectly. I had on a clingy white blouse. To top the outfit off, I put on a tie—of white pearls. My size 6 frame was slender, and I looked polished as I entered the interview. The old guy's tongue was hanging out, so I was hired for the job that very day. I was to attend classes, study for the State of Alabama Insurance License exam, and start out making $600 a month plus commissions. It was the best offer I'd had lately. I accepted the job, but would not be able to start until after the first of the year. I had a lot to do to get ready to go to work full-time. Making arrangements for the children was at the top of the list.

The great swine flu epidemic hit in 1976. I had never taken flu shots, nor did I ever see a reason to do so. In the fall of 1976, there was non-stop news about a terrible flu hitting the entire South. Mobile and Pascagoula were reporting a record number of cases. The hospitals were full, and there were so many people in the Singing River Hospital that some were actually housed in the halls because they had no rooms for them.

It started with a cold and a scratchy throat. I got sicker every day, and by December 23, I was so sick I could not get out of bed. My fever shot to 104 degrees. JJ was home for the holidays, so he was with the children. I was lying in my bed, crying. As the tears rolled down my face, they felt like hot water running from the corners and down the side of my head. I ached so badly, I felt like an old person who could hardly move her limbs without crying. I had started my menstrual cycle the day before, but it stopped when my fever stayed so high. JJ said I was delirious for a couple of days. I have no idea why he did not take me to the hospital, but he didn't.

JJ did help me get to and from the bathroom, because I couldn't walk alone. Never before, or since, have I been so sick. I even missed sharing Christmas with our family. On December 27, two days after Christmas, I was finally able to eat some soup that JJ brought me in bed. It tasted so good, since I had not had food in days. I started feeling a little better and was finally able to get up. It had been a nightmare.

The next day, JJ got me up and said he needed to take me to my mom's. He was going crazy having to stay in the house, taking care of me and the kids. We drove to Mom's house and within a short time, a guy with a Corvette drove into her driveway. JJ said he was going away with his friend for a while—he needed to get out, he said. He left me and the kids in the dust. I could almost hear him using Martin Luther King's line, "Free at last. Free at last."

I was still unable to care for the children. Thank goodness Mom did that for me. But things went from bad to worse. My cycle, which had stopped, now restarted. The high fever must have been the cause, but now I was dying from cramps. I alternated between thinking I was having another child, to feeling as if I was hemorrhaging. I hurt so badly, I actually thought I would die. My mom was very worried about me, but I made her promise me that if I died, she would not do anything to try to find JJ. I didn't want him anywhere near my dead body.

No need to worry about that. He did not come back for two days. He didn't even call to check on me. I was sure he was far too busy.

How you treat someone when she is sick is a good indicator of how much you care about her. The one thing that had been proven, over and over during my relationship with JJ, was if I ever really needed him, he would not be there. Put another way, there was only one thing I could depend on with my husband, and that was, I *couldn't* depend on him.

It took a while to get over the flu, and then to get started on my new job. In an office of about 22 agents, there were only two females—I and a very nice, somewhat cherubic, African-American woman who would work in a Mobile area considered at that time to be a black neighborhood. I was destined to become the office darling. I was young, enthusiastic, and polite, and I really did want to do a good job.

I was working for National Life and Accident Company as a debit agent and in direct sales. My area was northwest Pensacola, all the area north of

Airport Blvd., Spring Hill, and out toward the airport. Springhill is "Old Mobile," aka the hotsy-totsy area, where many of the doctors and lawyers lived. The route extended all the way westward to Young's Neck Road, where rednecks lived in country homes. It did not present a problem, because I could get along just fine with people from both ends of the economic spectrum.

It was so difficult to keep it all together. I was learning a new job, JJ was working hard, and on the weekends I had to help him. There were times I was under the dump truck with a grease gun, shooting grease into whatever joint he identified. I knew he was now in a bad position, but so was I. We were still losing ground financially. We thought we would end up losing everything on his dump truck gamble.

He finally got a truck job, north of Mobile, somewhere near the camp where he had been hunting for years. He would go there, work all week, and come home on the weekend. I would take care of everything else—the home, the kids, the animals, the new job—and give him almost all my paycheck each week, so he had gas and money to live on. After I gave him my pay, I was usually left with $20 to $30 for the week. It was okay. He had to run the truck and I could survive.

I was selling insurance like crazy. The ladies in the office admin department complimented me on the quality of insurance I was selling, and I also grew in favor with the guys. They fought over who would help me with my book, and were delighted with the fact that my debit book always balanced easily—I never borrowed, or "farkeled" (fooled around) with the money. Evidently, some of the guys "borrowed" until pay day. The year was passing, my insurance business base was growing, and eventually I received heavy bookends for being on pace to hit the million dollar level. I didn't give a rip. I gave the bookends to the manager, who thought they were gold. I guess I wasn't truly invested in this company. I was just doing what I had to do.

I reported to the office each day, opened my debit book, and recorded all the premiums that came in the mail. After about 9:00 a.m., I went to homes and knocked on the doors of those who paid in person. Most paid promptly. I also asked for leads. My people liked me, and I was able to get into people's homes to sell "love." If you love your family, you protect them. Family coverage and whole life policies—that was the name of the game. The commissions were good, and whole life was an easy sell in the 70's.

March 23, 1977 was our 10th wedding anniversary. We planned to go out on the town, sharing a nice dinner and maybe even taking in a movie. My mom was going to keep the children and allow them to spend the night, so we could have the whole evening without having to hurry home.

I made sure my schedule was clear and my timeline for getting ready was all set in my head. My plan was to get home around three in the afternoon, pick up the children from the regular sitter, and take them to my mom's house. Then I'd go home and take some time for myself, so I could look really nice for the evening.

The plan was working pretty well even though I was running a little late. It was about 4:00 p.m., and I was driving toward the sitter's house. I passed JJ just about the time I got to where the interstate crosses Grand Bay Road. I waved as we passed but I couldn't help but notice the scowl on his face. Also, he didn't wave.

I saw him in my rearview mirror after he passed me. He was driving very fast, and then he slammed on his brakes. He spun a donut in the road, and burned the tires as he began chasing me. I pulled over onto the side of the road. He was so furious—he wanted to know what the hell was wrong with me, being so late. "I'm not late. I thought I'd still have plenty of time to go home and get dressed so we could go about 6:00," I told him.

I apologized and asked him what he wanted to do. I didn't think we would be leaving so early. He said he wanted to get back to Pascagoula and go to a special place where he liked to go. I asked him what he wanted me to do. The arrangements were made for me to go get the kids, take them to Mom's, and meet me there. That was what I did. I left my car at my Mom's house. I didn't have a chance to change, to prepare for the evening—nothing. I would go out for my tenth anniversary celebration in the same clothes I had worked in all day.

I was heartsick.

We drove to Pascagoula and went to some little bar where I'd never been before. When we arrived, the bartender said that the girl who was there to sing, during happy hour, was already gone. JJ was furious. His thoughts were not at all about us. He really wanted to get there to see that girl. This would all make a lot more sense to me years later, when a friend of JJ's told me JJ was seeing some girl there who was a singer. At the time, I didn't put it all together.

The next stop was a cheap Mexican restaurant. I told JJ I really didn't want to eat there. I expected something a little nicer for an anniversary dinner. He stomped on the gas and drove like a crazy man, all the way to Mobile. We had a terrible dinner and then headed to the movie.

The only movie we could agree on was a documentary on whether there were space aliens. It was actually interesting, but as we sat in the movie, JJ, with his arms crossed in front of him, slept. I looked at him with sheer disgust. I hated him. I actually hated him.

It was at that moment that I decided our marriage was over. In my heart, it was over. In my brain, it was over. But I knew the break would not be easy. Nothing with JJ ever was.

The following day, I had a chance to tell him how I felt. With my tears flowing, I described how he had ruined our anniversary. I told him with all the feeling I could muster that I did not love him anymore. I told him, "I no longer care what you do or who you do it with. I don't care where you go, when you come back, or if you come back. Dinner will be ready each day at 5:00, whether you're here or you're not. It makes no difference to me." He did hear me loud and clear. He just didn't believe me.

This was my stand, I thought. After ten years of trying, the bonds of our marriage were forever broken. I never said, "I love you" to him again.

The only thing JJ cared about was having sex. He wouldn't take no for an answer. I didn't want him to touch me ever again. He held me hostage, in our bedroom, until I had sex with him. When he would penetrate me, my fists were clenched on my chest and tears were running down my face. He did not care, and in fact, he did not appear to notice. I took an oath to myself: From this day forward, I will work toward the goal of getting away from this man. I would have to find a way to leave him. However, that way just wasn't apparent to me.

Going to work each day made life easier. I got up, started my daily schedule, and the days passed. My premium collections were finished for the time being. This meant I had time to kill, since the debit book was completely up-to-date. I was down to scouting for prospects, and worst of all, making "cold calls."

As I drove up Airport Blvd., I passed all of the familiar shops, apartment complexes, houses, and then the strip mall. Scott's apartment complex was nice, and the entry street was lined with shade trees. It was inviting, but I resisted the urge to drive in. I hadn't heard from him, so there was no reason I should try and find him this afternoon. Okay, I shouldn't. I knew I shouldn't, but I couldn't resist calling him.

After meeting Scott a few weeks earlier, in a beauty shop where I had to collect a payment, I had thought of little else. He was there in some type of sales capacity, so we had a chance to exchange our hellos. The guy was magnificent looking. He was tall and handsome, and had rusty blonde hair, a little too long, and combed neatly back. He had the charm and look of Kevin Costner—a smooth, gentle, sexy personality that could pull in women like a magnet. He had spotted me the same second I saw him. The eyes have it. Stop! Stop! Too late! The connection was made.

For me, it was truly the first time since marrying in 1967 that I had acted on an attraction to anyone. It was so strong, it caught me off guard. Scott was the first man who appealed to me, since I had clearly verbalized my mental and emotional separation from JJ. My marriage was over. I didn't know that it would be this man who would be the first to break my "armor," penetrate my soul, and guide me gently into a new place.

We chatted politely. I gave him my business card. It wasn't long before he called me at work. He was amazing! He actually made my heart beat faster and my face flush.

Scott asked me to come by his apartment for lunch. I knew I shouldn't, but I did. Scott and I met several times at the apartment. We would have fabulous lunches, like a tuna sandwich or a bowl of soup. Okay, maybe it wasn't the lunch, but more the company. I soon found out the apartment belonged to a friend and not to Scott. No matter whose apartment it was, I found him interesting, funny, non-threatening, and gorgeous, to say the least.

He was in some kind of life transition. He told me a story of getting kicked out of med school. He said it was because he had actually performed an abortion on a female friend. He said at the time he thought he was helping her, because she was so distraught she was threatening to hurt herself. The story was so far out there, I just didn't really think of all its implications, so I just didn't process it fully. I was thinking of other things. My feet were planted firmly in the sky.

I needed to pay attention as I drove. The strip mall was coming up and it was the easiest place to kill time. The sign said Colonel Dixie—a local fast food chain and a hometown equivalent of McDonalds/KFC combination. With a pay phone in the dining room, it was the perfect place to stop, rest, and grab some of the best fried chicken in town. The chance of getting Scott on the phone was slim. He worked, too, but the possibility seemed to be more compelling than the smell of Southern fried chicken.

As I pulled around the building and into the parking lot, I noticed a big station wagon parked against the loading area, behind the restaurant. It was a green and brown Pontiac Safari, like an old woody, that reminded me of my surfer friends in Pensacola.

My silver Chevy Vega with black racing stripes got attention as I whipped around for my choice of parking spots. The place was pretty much empty, so I knew I could have some privacy when I made my call. I hoped Scott was home. I needed to hear his voice.

Some outfits you never forget, because they just make you look and feel great. My hair was down, long and blonde. My sage green polyester shirt was soft, draping my breasts. My shirt was tucked neatly around a 24-inch waist, and belted into tight, smooth-fitting pants. The pants were matching green and cuffed at the bottom. Brown leather huarché shoes were comfortable with solid wood stack heels. The shoes were special to me—they had cost $38.00, an extravagance given my $160.00 a week paycheck. As I have gotten older, I have come to think that when a woman wears an outfit that hugs her body so closely, it's because she longs for the hugs that aren't in her life. (Okay, maybe it's just me.)

The Colonel Dixie crew inside was friendly and took my order of a Diet Coke with a chicken snack—fried chicken, fries, and a soft white roll. I smiled to myself when I saw the white shirt and silly white paper-hat the guy behind the counter was wearing. The tiny logo on his hat had an uncanny resemblance to something you would see at the Kentucky Fried Chicken place down the street. The thought now of eating from a red and white paper tray filled with extra crispy fried chicken brings back memories of food that could fill an empty soul. Heaven only knows just how empty that soul of mine was that day.

Waiting on my food would give me a chance to call Scott. A quarter would get a dial tone on the black, wall phone. I put my money in and dialed the number without having to look it up. I knew it. The ring was echoing in my ear when he came on the line. With my back to the dining room, I leaned closer into the phone frame as I propped my elbows on the shelf. His voice was so mellow and so welcoming that I asked myself, *Why have you been so anxious about making this call?*

There was a gentle tap on my shoulder and I turned around quickly. A guy had walked up quietly behind me and was handing me a note on a little piece of folded white paper. As I began looking down at the note, the man walked away. I was trying to talk to Scott, but I had to quietly laugh, amused and disbelieving. I told Scott, "Some guy just tapped on my shoulder and handed me a note." I read the note. I said, "The guy wants to talk with me when I get off the phone." I didn't know who he was, but I thought it was really weird.

My conversation continued, but I could see the guy walk out the side door as he passed in front of the big glass window. He was not real tall, maybe 5'9" or 5'10," a little plump around the middle, with dark hair combed straight back from a receding hairline, and his clothes—green plaid shirt, khaki pants, a leather belt with a silver western style buckle, and nice brown boots—struck me as "country gentleman casual." Some dark hair was peeking out of the top of his shirt—a very masculine man. He was peculiar. He was intriguing.

I heard Scott on the phone. He was asking me to come over to the apartment. It was what I had hoped to hear. I made plans to be there in about thirty minutes or so. As I hung up, I thought about how good it was going to be to see him. I looked out the window, and the guy was striding confidently back toward the door. Now I would find out what he wanted.

He said, "Do you mind walking outside with me for a moment? I want to ask your opinion on something." My forehead probably wrinkled, but before I could protest, he said, "Don't worry, I'm Paul Leverett. I own this place, and this is a business question. I just need your opinion . . . if you can spare a moment." His eyes were questioning.

Curiosity kills the cat, and curious I was. I followed him to the parking lot and continued to watch this strange man. He walked out ahead of me, about 40 feet into the parking lot. He stood in the lot with his arms out, making a wide gesture. He said, "They want to put a drive-up photo booth right here," pointing to the ground. "Do you think you would use a photo booth if Kodak put one here? You know, a kiosk where you can drive up, drop off your film, then pick it up later," he said. I had a little trouble envisioning a photo booth, but I told him I might use it.

As though it was an after-thought, his brow furrowed and he asked me, "Who are you? I don't think I've seen you in here before." I told him my name and that I was working as an insurance agent for National Life and Accident Insurance Company. I added that I stopped there often in the afternoon, for a late lunch, and to use the phone. I didn't have much else to say, so I told him my lunch was probably ready by now so I needed to go in and pick it up.

He walked in with me. Then he said, handing me his business card, "I have a daughter that I do not have any insurance on, and I have insurance on all my other children. Do you want to give me a quote for insurance for her? She's eleven years old. Give me a call when you get a quote for me. I need about a $10,000 policy."

Still a little puzzled by this bizarre meeting and the strange but engaging man, I sat and ate my lunch alone. *What a day!* My focus now was on going to see Scott. Mr. "Colonel Dixie" wasn't even a blip on my radar.

I didn't know how to describe what was going on within me. The husband whom I despised was away, doing whatever he did while he was away. I was home taking care of my children, working each day—holding the fort down. I was twenty-six years old. I wanted to be touched, held, and caressed by someone who could elicit something from me other than disdain. I "needed" to feel consensual love.

I arrived at the apartment where Scott was staying. He was so handsome he made me weak. He was humble. I had no idea where he was in his life. I did not know that he was the one who would allow me to leave my self-imposed fidelity to a dead marriage. He greeted me with warmth, openness, and a gentle, welcoming hug. We talked. I can't remember what we talked about, but we talked and laughed, and the afternoon passed much too fast.

We sat on the sofa. My heart was big, my mind was open and, most of all, my body was receptive to this man. As we closed the gap, with our bodies sitting close, we held hands. He opened my hand and looked down into my palm, as he held it softly in his. He asked me to close my eyes. It was the most sensual feeling I had ever experienced. As I closed my eyes, he ran his fingers gently over my palm. He traced the outline of my fingers with the touch of a butterfly. Then he asked, "Can you feel this?" He was tracing the outline of my hand, but not making contact with my skin. I felt the static of his being. I felt him breathe. It was an "Avatar Moment."

Our kisses started simple but got longer and deeper. They were gentle connectors of two souls who needed each other. He was not pressuring me. Most men, at that place, would be in a full court press by now. He was giving me time and quietly letting me work through things. He knew he had nothing to lose, and I was caught in a dilemma that was obviously tearing at everything I had held strong to, until now. Suddenly, I just couldn't do it. I said, "I have to stop."

He let me go. "It's okay," he said. He was sincere.

Leaving was hard, but I had to go. I made myself drive away knowing there was so much hanging in the balance. I felt I was losing my sanity. I knew this was an incredible place to be, because my body was throbbing. I felt every inch a woman, and I couldn't remember the last time it had felt good to be touched. Mindlessly, I drove down Airport Blvd. I asked myself, "What will you do?" I then listened, because my body had spoken, and I heard it loud and clear. I also heard my own admonishment, "If you do this, you will *never* be the same."

At that point, the devil was on one shoulder, and the voice of caution and goodness on the other. It was a pivotal moment in my adult life, and one that would haunt me to the end of my days. It might sound small and trivial, but this was where my life changed dramatically. I thought I was ready.

I went home to my children, my pets, and my life. My children were so sweet, and I loved them so much. Their dad was away and the kids trusted me to take care of everything while he was gone. I tucked them in, as usual, and kissed them good night.

Our home, high on the hill, was a simple dwelling, with no other houses in sight. Our master bedroom window looked out over the barn and the pastures beyond. I stood at the open window, my arms resting on the sill. Looking out, through the screen, I could see the stars and moon shining so brightly—they lit up the dark sky. The night breeze touched my face. It seemed perfect. Here, I felt so close to God.

I prayed for strength. I prayed for forgiveness.

It wasn't long before I returned to his apartment. Scott was patiently waiting. I went fully understanding my transgression. I needed him. He met me with such gentleness. He led me to his bedroom and asked me if I was sure. I was sure that no one needed anything more than I needed him at that moment. He made love to me. That sounds so trite, but he actually made *love to me*. It really didn't seem to be about him, because all the focus was on how he made me feel. He took off my clothes, slowly, and laid me on the bed. As he entered me, I felt like a flower blossoming in the rays of the sun. He was more than I expected, and he was everything I desperately needed.

My life was all new now. I had changed course in the storm. I couldn't wait to hear from Scott the next day. I was excited at the thought of seeing him again.

Work always came before pleasure. I did everything I was supposed to do at home, and set out with my new heading, directly into the storm. The first thing was to get a quote for the Leverett guy on his daughter. This was a first to have someone just say, "I want a $10,000 policy. Just give me a quote." I ran the numbers and gave Mr. Leverett a call at his office. I was surprised to get him on the phone so easily.

I gave him the quote, and he said he definitely wanted the policy. I told him I needed to get an application filled out and signed. He didn't seem to mind at all, but wanted to know if I would mind coming back out to the same store to get the information. We set a time, and I met him there. It was really straight-forward. He was friendly but not at all flirty. I talked with him about my business, and he kept asking me questions. We ended up having a hot dog while we sat in the dining room of his restaurant. It was nice to have someone buy me lunch, even if it was a hot dog. In his restaurant, they called it a Dixie Dog. It was covered with chili and cheese, loaded with calories, and melt-in-your-mouth delicious.

I completed the paperwork as he gave me his check for the entire annual premium. That was also unusual for my clients. Even if they could, most people paid by the month, and a few still paid by the week. I asked about his other insurance. He was very receptive to listening to my sales pitch on our insurance products. The whole thing ended with him telling me he would be willing to allow us to work with him on his estate planning. I told him I would take care of turning in the small policy he had purchased, and I'd get back with him on the additional information I would need. It was all very professional, I thought.

Returning to my office, with a check in hand for his daughter's insurance policy, I felt really good about making the sale. I told the others in the office about this very good lead. Before I knew it, they flew a guy in from the Tennessee headquarters to go with me to meet with Leverett. This was a big fish and they didn't want me to let him get away. Leverett ended up giving us his financial statement and everything we needed to do a full estate-planning proposal. The office was abuzz with the talk of me working with such a wealthy man. "Phyllis is landing a big fish," so all the guys were excited and happy for me.

Insurance was going well, but I didn't get a call back from Scott. I was crazy with worry. My heart was also broken. It was weeks before he called me again. I was in my office when the call came and I heard his voice. I said, "Well, the prodigal son returns." He laughed. I tried to keep my heart from beating out of my chest.

He said he was sorry for not calling. He had had an emergency, and he had to go to Texas for an interview. He was only back in Pensacola for a few days to get his things, because he had taken the Texas job. He asked me, "Will you come see me before I have to leave?"

Knowing full well that I was being stupid, I nonetheless agreed. He was no longer at the apartment in Mobile. Now he was staying at a family home in Bayou La Batre. I was very familiar with where that was—just south of Grand Bay, Alabama. I had lived there many years. The locals call it Ba-la-ba-tree, as though it's one gushing word. He wanted me to come there, to see him and spend the afternoon. I juggled all my appointments and followed his directions to the canal home on the bayou. I drove through the countryside until arriving at this seaport community.

Going through town, I could smell the salty, fishy air. I went slowly over the small town's bridge, glancing toward the horizon with all manner of shrimp boats in view, their green nets draped gracefully, always ready for the next drag. The port is the home of Forest Gump's Shrimp Boat Business, Bubba Gumps. I was right in the heart of Bayou La Batre, and the music on the radio was blaring out Linda Ronstadt's newest hit "Blue Bayou."

My destination turned out to be a quaint little gray house just across the street from the canal. I couldn't help but notice the pretty white birds resting along the water's edge. I pulled into the driveway, got out of my car and, with only a few steps, was knocking softly at the door. When I saw him, my heart almost stopped. He opened the screened door, took my hand, and pulled me in.

He made us a glass of iced tea while he told me more about himself, his family, and the memories he had of that bayou home. He was dealing with some demons, and still feeling guilty about a terrible gun accident. A group of teens had been standing in the driveway of that home, excited and ready for hunting season, when a gun fired. All were surprised by the piercing sound as the ammo hit the concrete driveway. It ricocheted up and into the heart of Scott's twelve-year-old cousin. Scott held the gun, and his cousin lay dead. The pain was still apparent.

To redirect our conversation, he stood and led me out back to see the garden he had planted—some tomato plants, peppers, and squash seed. We soon came back inside and made small talk, until the small talk just wasn't working anymore. He stopped, pulled me close, and we made love that afternoon. It was bitter-sweet. I knew he was leaving and would not be back. I kissed him goodbye and drove home, knowing I would never forget him.

The #3 hit "Blue Bayou" was playing again on the radio. This time I turned it up loud. It was as though Roy Orbison and Joe Melson had written the song just for me. Linda Ronstadt's voice will forever play in my mind as I remember that day—that beautiful, incredible, late summer day in 1977. I drove away in my silver Vega, my heart aching, and softly singing along with Linda.

> *I feel so bad I've got a worried mind,*
> *I'm so lonesome all the time,*
> *since I left my baby behind on Blue Bayou*

The sweet interlude with Scott ended just the way it should have—quickly, because it was the result of pure sexual magnetism. Of course, there's nothing wrong with pure sexual magnetism. If I had gone off to find him again, I'm sure I would have ended up like Diane Lane in *Under the Tuscan Sun.* I'd be standing there, heartbroken, while he came out with someone a lot better looking and younger than me.

I didn't grieve for long the loss of our intense but fleeting relationship. However, I did learn something. It was just another stepping stone toward ending my marriage, and I really wanted, and needed, to legally end my marriage.

Returning my attention to the insurance business kept me busy most days, and even some evenings, when I had to schedule appointments for people after their work day. I had a great baby sitter and friend I could depend on to care for my children. She could pick them up after school, along with her children, and keep them until I got home.

Jean (I will call her) had started babysitting for me while I lived in Saxon Manor. While there, I had started taking golf lessons at the country club, so I hired her as a babysitter. She took on the job, and we gradually became great friends and confidantes. She was the one person I could talk to, woman to woman. On days I had off, she would come to my house and we would talk for hours, play Scrabble, or just watch television together. She was smart. Some discounted her because she wasn't beautiful, but that really didn't matter at all to me. She was a good friend. Before long, I was going to need a good friend.

The headquarters guy, from Tennessee, came down for the big estate planning appointment with Mr. Leverett. We met in Leverett's office, where he had a huge Polar Bear skin stretched out on the back of a wall. He took great pride in telling us his trophy was for the third largest polar bear ever killed. At thirteen feet tall standing fully upright , the bear had actually been attacking their party when he killed it. This all took place when he was stationed on

Saint Lawrence Island while serving in the Air Force. He also had walrus tusk, deer, elk, and duck trophies mounted. Obviously, he was an avid hunter and sportsman.

Robust and confident, he answered all the questions about his business and family with what, to me, seemed like complete candor. He was nice. He had a big, contagious smile, and such a positive outlook. When we finished, he wanted to show us around the office and warehouse. It was an enjoyable afternoon for both me and "Mr. Headquarters."

"Mr. Headquarters" and I drove back to my office to share our big potential sale information. I might make one of the biggest commissions in quite a while, if we could just land this account. I felt the entire thing was a fluke, but was ready and willing to make the commission. It would be a tidy sum to stash away for my getaway.

Chapter 18
The "Master" 1977

This photo was taken within a month or so of meeting Paul.

My children returned to school the end of that summer. Jamie was starting the first grade and Nathan the third grade. They were eager to begin as students at Grand Bay Elementary School. The bus stop was right in front of our house, so it would sure make things easier for me.

The business friendship I had developed with Paul Leverett continued to be interesting. He was always happy to meet with me and help me with anything I asked him about. It was the first time in my life I had a person who responded to my requests for help. I approached him for donations to ball teams, the Fall Festival at the children's school, and other activities. He was always good for ice, red-and-white Colonel Dixie cups, plates, and napkins—anything except food. He said he had a policy not to give away food. "You can't make money if you give away the food," he'd say.

By this time, I had moved away from calling him Mr. Leverett to just calling him Paul. He treated me with respect and always kept a cautious distance.

I never once caught him ogling me, nor did he say anything to me that would even suggest the fact he found me attractive. I actually thought his reaction to me was just the opposite. The whole situation was peculiar, but I just couldn't put my finger on why.

My babysitter girlfriend had been looking for a full-time job. I told Paul about her and he said, "Just have her call me and I'll see what I can do for her." That ended with him giving her a job which consisted of sitting at a corner somewhere on a highway and counting cars. That's right, counting the cars that went by, in order to document traffic counts. High traffic counts could be enough to justify creating a new store at a certain location. He paid her well and she was happy. She thought he was such a great guy, and I was starting to think so too.

I truly cannot remember why I was supposed to meet him out at the Airport Blvd. Colonel Dixie. I drove in, parked, and went inside to the dining room. He met me and asked me if I was up to going out for a picnic lunch in one of the fields he was getting ready for dove season. He was telling me how pretty it was and he wanted me to see it. I wasn't busy, so I agreed to follow him "not far down the road," as he put it.

We drove out past the airport and it wasn't far before he turned off to the left into a pecan orchard. His green safari station wagon was in front of me, with its bumper bouncing as it passed over the deep ruts in the road. There was an opening but no actual gate. He made the turn and I followed. I was thinking to myself, *I don't really know this man. He could be an axe murderer.* I clearly remembered wondering, *Why on Earth would you follow into the woods a man you don't really know?* With everything telling me it was a dumb thing to do, I kept following.

It was a beautiful day. There was a little coolness in the air and the sky was so blue. The pecan orchard was pretty, with new green sprouts bursting out everywhere. When we finally came to a stop in the middle of a field, he got out and met me at my car door. He talked easily, as though he was giving me a lesson on nature, hunting, and caring for the land. He was president of the hunting club, which gave him the job of managing the lease and the club's many hunting fields.

He opened the back of his station wagon and dropped the tailgate for us to sit on. His ice chest was right inside, so he popped open the top, pulling out little Coca-Cola bottles. I told him, "I'm sorry, but I only drink diet drinks." I watched him dig until he found one, wiping the moisture away, opening the bottle, and handing it to me. We sipped our soft drinks and talked of the beautiful field that stretched for acres all around us. It was obvious we both appreciated the beauty.

Paul was a hoot. By that, I mean he was such a character. Seeing him talk with his hands was like watching an animated cartoon. He laughed easily, and seemed curious about everything. "And now for lunch!" he announced, as if he was presenting Act Two of a play. He brought out a red and white paper bag filled with the newest addition to the menu—a Dixie Chili Cheeseburger and french fries. Staring out from the tailgate seat, we enjoyed a simple lunch, laughing at his hunting stories.

Afterward, he explained how it was legal to plant natural fields of corn or millet in order to attract wild game. I had heard of people who would illegally "salt" an area in order to attract deer, but I had never heard of baiting fields by planting legal crops that attracted the animals you were hunting. I had never even heard of millet. He then shuffled things in the back of his car, pulled out a bucket, and showed me these tiny seeds that looked like sesame seeds.

He stood up and waved his hand, indicating I should follow him as he continued his lesson on dove hunting and feeding. As sincere as a college professor, he tried to teach me the fine art of dove enticement. You plant millet, watch it grow, and the birds will come.

Walking out in front of me, he turned and asked me, "Do you know how to determine how recently a dove has been feeding in the field?" He was motioning me to come closer. He was looking intently toward the ground. This guy was so damned funny, I was almost mesmerized. Stumped by the question, I answered "no."

"Here," he said emphatically. He pointed his finger at the ground and I walked closer.

"You must come down here," he said as he squatted down, pulling the grass apart with his hands. "See this?" He looked up at me, then down to something on the ground. "Come here," he said. "You can't see from there."

I got down close enough to see the small blob of bird poop he was point-ing to. He said, "This is a dove dropping. See how it's brown, swirled, and white on the top?"

I was looking at this little pile of bird droppings, almost like a cone-top of a soft ice cream. The bottom was dark and swirled up. The top finished off in a white peak. I was amazed, not at the fact that it was dark and white (chicken shit is the same way), but at the fact that he thought this shit was amazing.

I laughed to myself: *This guy may be a little nuts. But in for a penny, in for a pound.* I looked closer. He then, very sincerely, asked me, "Do you know how to tell if it is fresh?"

I was down, my face within a foot of dove shit. "No, how do I tell if the dropping is fresh?" I answered.

He looked straight into my eyes and said, "You stick your tongue on the white part to see if it's still warm."

I looked at him, he looked at me, I laughed, he laughed, and we enjoyed the joke. Okay, he got me on that one. We stood up and walked back toward the car. I was thinking this guy is both cute and bonkers. However, if anyone ever needed a laugh, it was me.

He continued on, telling me how many buckets of seed he put out each year, which was such a huge number I found it hard to believe. He used five-gallon plastic buckets, with re-sealable tops, to store the seed, and then distributed the seed by hand.

He told me of his baiting techniques that had proved to be successful for years. That was why the guys of Mobile paid those fat dues to belong to his hunting club. Paul knew how to naturally and legally bait the fields. The hotshots didn't mind paying the big money to shoot the birds that came to eat in Paul's baited fields. He smirked as he told me, "In this hunting club, I'm known as the 'Master Baiter.'" I laughed.

My heart was cheerful and I enjoyed every minute with this unique and humorous man. We walked back to the cars. I sat on his tailgate to rest after the walk around the field. He took one of the seed buckets out of the car and turned it upside down on the ground right in front of where I was sitting. He sat down on the bucket, and looked up at me from this lower position. He gently took my hands and rested them gently in his. He looked up at me and asked, "Do you mind if I hold your hands?" I looked down into his sweet brown eyes. He was sincere. Then he said something like, "You're beautiful and I want very much to kiss you."

This was not expected. He hadn't made his intentions known before now. He had never even paid me a compliment. Yet, intuitively, I always felt there had to be an ulterior motive to his kindnesses, and now I saw it. He stood, pulled me up to stand, and kissed me. This strange guy was so sweet, so willing to pay attention to me, I let him kiss me. I was actually surprised when the kiss turned out to be really nice. He pulled me closer—I balked.

I turned and walked over to my car. I was getting into my car when he stopped me. He kissed me again. It was nice, but I was confused. I wasn't ready to consider this man a potential suitor. He was too old, a little too heavy, and a lot too married. I was just not interested in that kind of involvement.

I told him I had to go. He apologized for upsetting me. I said it was okay, that I needed time to think. I wasn't mad. I wasn't anything. I just needed to leave.

I drove away. I watched him from my rear view mirror, gathering his things, his seed bucket, and packing them neatly away. I just kept driving. My mind was already reliving the events of my first close encounter with the "Master Baiter."

Chapter 19
Getting to Know Paul

Captain Paul Leverett, USAF, stationed on St. Lawrence Island, Alaska.

It didn't take long to find out that Paul wasn't one to be offended easily. He called me often. I accepted some of his invitations to lunch, some I had to turn down, or I'd relent and take a ride out to Eight Mile to check on a store or go with him to a friend's house while he delivered some of his homemade wine. He didn't really seem to care if anyone saw me in his car—we were just friends.

One weekday afternoon, I agreed to share a lunch with him. He seemed a little nervous and upset and asked me if I would be willing to go to a private place to talk. I said okay and then followed him to an apartment he said belonged to a friend. We sat in the living room for only a couple of minutes before he told me that his wife, Elizabeth, had tried to kill him. I was taken aback, but he continued with the story.

He said Elizabeth had come into his office and fired a pistol at him. He told me the caliber, but I am not sure I remember correctly—I think he said a .38. He said he ran into the warehouse and was throwing shelves over while trying to dodge more bullets. According to him, she fired most, if not all, of the shots before he could jump out to grab her arm and take the gun away from her. He said the sales or price tag was still hanging on the trigger. She had bought the gun at a pawn shop that day, went to his business, and almost succeeded in killing him.

"Did you call the police?" I asked him. He said they were called by some of the staff. I asked him about pressing charges and, if so, would she go to jail? I told him that I thought, at a minimum, she should be charged with attempted murder. She was firing in a place of business with other people who could have been injured or killed. I really couldn't believe she could try to murder him and walk away as if nothing had happened.

He said he was not going to press charges. He said he did not want to see his children's mother put in jail, and all he wanted was to make sure it never happened again. He ended by saying his wife had to write a letter of apology to the Colonel Dixie staff for scaring everyone.

I had a difficult time understanding his decision, but then I had dealt over and over with a violent partner, so I had no room to find fault with him. The only difference was that JJ had always done the dirtiest part of his work when there was no one to see but me. It's interesting how a mind works, because I was rationalizing that, *at least*, JJ had never actually fired *at* me with his mind set on to killing me. Elizabeth was trying her best to kill him, according to what Paul was saying, and they were in a public place where innocent bystanders could have been hurt or killed.

I then asked him, "Why would your wife want to kill you?"

This is the story he told me. Because this story began on that day, and continued thereafter, I will start at this point. I saw Paul over the course of some time, before more details of his relationship oozed out. I listened intently to the strange home-life stories he divulged with such sincerity. There were so many symptoms of a marriage that had fallen apart, but the beginning was infidelity—his infidelity, of friggin' course.

I had no way to contradict anything he said. I kept thinking, if a woman goes into a business office to kill her husband, with the tag still hanging on the pistol, he was dealing with someone he had pushed over the edge. There had to be more to the story, and there was.

Paul completed college at Southern Methodist University in Dallas, Texas, joining the Air Force on completion. He had been dating a woman who he said he was very much in love with at the time. She seemed to love him, too, and marriage plans were tentatively made for when he finished his stint in the military. The relationship went on throughout the beginning of his service. Paul received his first permanent orders, to St. Lawrence Island, Alaska. He was to live for a year at this isolated Air Force detachment. He said his good-byes, promised to be faithful, and then left for Alaska.

After he arrived on St. Lawrence Island, he crossed someone in charge, which resulted in his being relegated to a duty no one else wanted. He was ordered to go out into the cold weather, scour the coast of Alaska, and pick up anything that could have washed ashore from the Russians. At that time, we were spying on the Russians, making sure they didn't get too close to our shores.

That bad duty turned out to be a hunter's paradise for Paul. He went out with the Eskimos and Inuits, the natives of Alaska, to roam the coast. He actually liked the assignment. He was out in the open land, enjoying the company of people who knew how to survive, and they were hunters. It was during this time that he killed his giant polar bear, numerous walruses, and seals, plus he returned with a full collection of hand-carved walrus ivory, and scrimshaw, and many pieces autographed by the natives who carved the elegant ivory pieces. He also returned with several "osiks" of different sizes. Osiks vary in size from about 12" to 18" long, and are the bones of the walrus penis. He talked of Alaska as a truly great adventure.

Now back to the girl story. This part of the story came to me much later in our relationship. While in Alaska, he had not been with a woman in a long time. He was having intense pain in his groin. He finally had to go to the doctor about his "problem." On examination, Dr. Baggett pushed into the area around his lower groin, which caused a blast of semen. Paul said, "Old Doc Baggett said I needed to go find a girlfriend or I could just come back to see him anytime." The doctor laughed at him, Paul found it amusing, and I found it exceedingly disgusting.

At long last, his tour in Alaska came to an end. He anxiously returned to meet the love of his life, Norma Summers (not her real name). She had been waiting for him to return. He knew Norma loved him. She would be so happy to see him, right? He arrived at her front door full of anticipation, only to find she was now engaged to another military man. She explained to him that she really didn't want to hurt him by sending a "Dear Paul" letter while he was in Alaska. Being replaced by another military guy did not sit well with Paul. He consoled himself with numerous ladies who were readily available to young handsome military men. He ended up living in Mobile, checking into Brookley Field, which was where he met his wife-to-be. He said she was beautiful, slender beauty pageant winner. She had coal black hair and a perfect smile. He said he fell in love or lust with her almost immediately. The fact that she already had a little girl, by a first marriage, was not an issue for him. He said he loved Elizabeth, and he grew to love the little girl as well.

Paul and Elizabeth—sometimes he called her Liz—soon married, and they had two boys and a girl together. He said by the time Liz had her second child, she had already gained a lot of weight. According to Paul, she mushroomed before his eyes. She would never be able to gain control of that problem again.

He worked for years for Scotsman Ice Machines, selling their products on the road to hotels, stores, etc. He drove over the entire Southeast territory, and evidently did very well. His wife was often jealous. She lamented his frequent absences, she hated that he was "always" gone, and her obsession with her weight grew to overshadow everything else. He said it was her weight that had made her so jealous of everyone or anyone who didn't have a weight problem. She put him through hell, he said. Of course, he told me he had never been unfaithful to her, and he actually sounded very convincing. He said he kept his nose to the grindstone, drove hours and hours each day, and returned home to his family at the end of his route.

The following he told me was his favorite sales story, and I really have no doubt it was true. Paul said while he worked at Scotsman, he drove through the countryside, ending up in the middle of nowhere. He came to a crossroad and looked out across the open field. A man in overalls was standing in the middle of a vacant lot, a shovel in hand, his foot starting to dig the first scoop of dirt. Paul passed the farmer, drove a short distance, stopped, turned around, and went back. He said he parked and walked out to where the old guy had started to dig. "Hello there. What are you doing?" he asked the man. The old guy took his time but finally replied, "I'm about to build myself a store." Paul said he asked him, "Well if you're about to build a store, don't you think you'll need some ice machines?" The guy acknowledged he would need them, so Paul sat on the hood of his car and took the farmer's huge order. Paul loved that story. I loved hearing him tell it.

He left Scotsman when they cut his territory. He said it was the penalty for doing so well. He said a salesman builds an area, it becomes very profitable, then the company divides it up among the new guys. Basically, they penalized him for doing so well. He quit, or so he told me. He then went into business with a partner, and together they opened a fast-food restaurant chain called Colonel Dixie. The fast-food restaurants sold great fried chicken, red beans and rice plates, with big squares of cornbread, a selection of hamburgers, and their namesake, the Dixie Dog.

The stores did well, he made more money, and he eventually moved his family from Foul River to his present home, off in Airmont, at 663 Montcliff Drive, which was a roomy 6,000 square feet. They had "moved up-town" so to speak, and they all felt like they were millionaires. The whole family bought into living the extravagant lifestyle befitting a successful restaurateur.

I listened to his tales; I really couldn't tell which came first, the chicken or the egg. His wife was jealous and going crazy, because she believed him to be cheating. Or he was cheating, so she became jealous and crazy with rage. Either way, it wasn't pretty.

He said she would do totally irrational things, like taking the kids into the car and saying she was leaving him. He asked her how they would live. Liz said they'd eat the ten-pound bag of onions she had in the car. Crazy shit, for sure, was going on in that relationship. I was sympathetic to him. After all, I understood dealing with crazy shit.

During his many years of marriage, and constantly being accused of cheating, who happened to call him? You guessed it! Norma Summers, the woman who had jilted him when he returned from Alaska. She looked him up and gave him a call. Norma was having trouble with her marriage to the colonel, and now she was thinking of getting back to her first love—Paul. Of course, Paul, the dumb fuck, went to meet her.

He told me he had to do it. It was like a matter of principle to him; his competitive spirit had kicked in. He wanted to enjoy screwing the colonel's wife because, after all, he had taken her from him so many years ago. Paul and Liz were not doing well, and Paul's testosterone level was still high.

Paul met Norma often. According to him, they engaged in a wild and blazing affair that took them to other cities. One such place he told me he met her was Callaway Gardens in Georgia. There they "honeymooned" for several days. He indicated they were madly in lust—I mean love—and both considered how they would leave their respective mates and marry.

The whole affair ended when Norma's husband, the colonel, found out and called Paul's wife, after which all hell broke loose. Paul and Liz's marriage then took a different turn. I thought, *No shit!* The marriage was irretrievably broken. There was no trust left. They separated. Paul moved out. Some papers were filed for separate maintenance, and a deal for divorce settlement was discussed.

They ended up back together, with Paul anteing up with an almost four-carat diamond ring as a show of good faith. She took the diamond, but it didn't erase the pain he had dealt her. I could not blame his wife for hating him/loving him/hating him. I understood the pain that spousal betrayal can inflict on a woman's heart. However, I thought trying to kill him might have been a bit over the top. According to Paul, there was never a peaceful moment in their home again. A war of anger, revenge, and punishment had begun.

He revealed other past incidents over time. One time, he told me his wife fired a shot into his car windshield and busted it out. Another time, she took a bat and beat the headlights out and put other dents in his car. There was a day he called and said she had just tried to run him off the road. He was driving on Azalea Road, coming into the neighborhood, and she tried to crash into him with her car. Paul said their youngest son was also in the car with his mother when she made that attempt to collide.

I asked him if he was still sleeping with his wife during these tumultuous times. His answer was "sometimes." He said he had tried to make love to her one afternoon when they were in the house alone. "She was so sweet to me and we crawled into bed," he said, "but just as I was on top and ready to start, she grabbed me by the balls and about tore my nuts off." I laughed. After that, he was always leery of what she might do, and so relaxing in the home became difficult.

He told me he had tried to get her to give him a divorce. He wanted a divorce, but she wanted everything he owned. In his words, she wanted to ruin him. She would not believe that his best offer of settlement was all he could give her. She thought he had hidden accounts, Swiss accounts, money growing out of his ears. He said he kept telling her, "If you kill the cow, no one gets the milk."

His stories of his home-life were as bad as mine, and maybe worse. He said she often visited his stepdaughter in Texas. En route to one such visit, airport personnel asked her, "Did you pack your own bags?" Elizabeth answered, "Yes, but my husband might have put a bomb in it for all I know." Security at the airport did not find this amusing, and it became a full-blown bomb scare investigation. The accusation had been totally baseless and, according to him, it was finally dropped as a bad joke on Liz's part, but it had been a very trying time for him.

In another incident he related to me, he was in the shower, naked and wet, when she came into the bathroom and attacked him. He ended up fighting with her, pushing her out of the bathroom, and then out of the bedroom so he could lock the door. After that, he said he put a keyed deadbolt on his door and always locked himself in to take a shower.

He would tell me that constant health complaints suggested his wife was also a hypochondriac. He said she had seizures, took very strong medications, and would tell people she had a brain tumor. All the people at her beauty shop were concerned for her well-being. She often went to the shop with her Bible, to sit and read while under the dryer. According to him, she had a seizure while at the Las Damas Beauty Shop. The seizure hadn't lasted long, but it had scared everyone there, so the shop owner called him to come get her. When he arrived, she was sitting under the hair dryer, Bible in hand, looking as though she was reading. She looked up and saw him coming toward her. The first words out of her mouth, as she closed her very expensive monogrammed Bible, were: "*You God-damned mother-fucking son of a bitch.*"

Paul said she would sit and write in a diary, or journal, as they were riding down the road together or while she was at home. He said he really didn't care what she wrote because he knew it was probably crazy, twisted crap. He said by that time, nothing he did was ever right.

She said she hated him, then she loved him, then she hated him. He told me he had offered her $250,000 up front as a divorce settlement. In the late 1970's, that was a lot of money. Then he agreed to give her $60,000 as income every year, plus she would get a new car every two years. The kids would be kept in their expensive private schools. She could continue to belong to the country club or whatever she wanted. He agreed to give her the moon for his freedom, but she wanted more. According to him, he would never let her do without, but all she wanted was to stay where she was, retain her social status, stay married, and most of all continue to make him pay for his indiscretions.

One of the hardest things for him, he said, was that the kids had been taught to lie and to deceive him for gain. He said he found his daughter in his bedroom one day as he opened the door and came out of the bathroom. He said she was just about ten years old, and it was obvious her pants were stuffed with something. He held her arm, called for her mom, and made her mom look in her pants to get the item out. He wanted to see what she had, but knew he couldn't strip-search her, so he made her mom look. The child had his billfold in her pants. After much fighting and yelling, said Paul, the truth came out. His wife had put her up to going in to take the wallet, so they could get money for shopping. He said he was furious at the thought of her mom teaching the child it was okay to steal from him.

That seemed to be the pattern. She was not going to leave, she had it too good where they were, and she fully intended to punish him for his transgressions by attacking his pocketbook. After all, they thought he was a millionaire, and his partner in the business seemed to live far better than they did. They all "knew" he was holding out on them and socking money away somewhere. Paul said he kept telling them that he was not hiding money and he gave them the best and most he could without bringing down the whole business.

I was a good listener. I felt sorry for him. I had no reason to question his truthfulness. After all, he had told me the Norma story, and he certainly didn't come out looking good on that one. He didn't need to lie to me. He told me about things guys don't usually share, even with other guys.

Chapter 20
The Lake

Photo taken by Palmer Studio, Mobile, Alabama.

We worked with Paul on his estate planning. Everyone at the office had really pushed for this sale, but it just never happened. By the time the sale was "past its prime," Paul and I were more than just friends. We were inching our way toward becoming romantically involved.

Yet I was able to spend little time with him. I was busy, and he was busy, so maybe every couple to three weeks we would make an appointment to meet. He would call me at work and ask me to meet him for a picnic to try out some new food concoction they were working on at Dixie. They might have a great new sandwich, or be working on a new breakfast meal. He loved taking the dove he shot and turning it into a spicy, deep-fried, crispy delicacy. He would start with a cleaned dove (it looked like a tiny chicken), stuff a small, round cherry pepper into the bird's cavity, fill it with ground sausage, dip it in breading, and deep fry it like the chicken they sold in their stores. Whatever the excuse, we would try to find time just to get together and talk. Lunch was just the most expedient conduit for the connection.

Hunting season was never far away. He talked of hunting and said he would go to work each day and hunt every afternoon. I found it interesting that someone would get up, go to work, hunt in the afternoon, and then be back at home every day by dinner. From everything he told me, he kept to his routine regardless of his relationship with Liz. His wife no longer had to endure him working out of town, nor being absent just because he decided not to come home.

One day, he called me and asked if I could meet him for lunch, which I did. I parked my car at the Sun Ray Food Store on Schillinger Road and I slipped gently into the passenger seat next to him. It was like finally getting to go on vacation—a great relief. I now had someone on my team who was there for me. I had on a denim one-piece jumpsuit that fit like a glove, my leather huaraché sandals, and my hair was blown in the Farrah Fawcett style. I felt young and pretty. He didn't appear to notice.

As we were driving down the road, he said something about me looking beautiful that day. It was the first time he had ever complimented me, and it really surprised me. His eyes left the road for a second, and he met my eyes with a questioning expression. He asked, "Could you ever like an older, fat guy?" I looked at him. He was serious. I told him if he would ditch the chocolate chip cookies he kept in his front seat console and move from Coca Cola to Diet Coke, he might not have to deal with being overweight. At the time, I honestly didn't know if the culprit was the Chili Cheese Burgers or the food he was eating at home. I leaned back against my door and just looked at him. Riding with him felt good and comfortable.

It was a beautiful day for a drive. We left the highway and turned onto a dirt road. We rode to a couple of fields where he wanted to make sure everything was okay. He said he had a guy working for him named Bill McEvoy. Bill was supposed to put out the millet seed in the pecan orchards before the hunts. Along a two-trail lane that had knee-high grass on both sides and between, we rode out to a picturesque little lake. I sat up straight, watching intently as he plowed through the weeds like they weren't even there. It was a nice car and he drove it like it was a four-wheel-drive hunting vehicle. That in itself was strange to me.

It was mid-afternoon, my stomach was growling, and I was ready for the picnic. He drove to the opposite side of the lake and parked on the dam. We got out and walked around to the rear of the car, and he opened the back of his green Safari. The ice chest was there and our lunch was still warm in the red and white boxes. He lifted the storage lid and pulled a blue blanket from the spare tire area. He brought the blanket over and spread it out next to the car, overlooking the lake. We sat between the shade tree and the car. The shade was lovely and the breeze calming.

After lunch, we walked the perimeter of the lake, tossing some leftover crumbs so the fish would surface, swish, and nibble while making bubbles; the crumbs disappeared quickly. It seemed as if we were the only two people in the world. He looked so nice in his khaki pants and safari shirt, with the dark hair from his chest poking its way out to be seen. He also wore warm, soft leather boots that boasted no frills or embellishments of any kind. He looked every bit the epitome of a country gentleman.

He walked over and took my hand. He told me of the guy that leased him the land, while continuing to make small talk about his love of the country, hunting, and how wonderful Mobile County was to offer such a combination: work he loved, and the sport he loved. It was perfect, he said. He could never have had the same situation in Texas.

We sat down on the blanket and had a cola. Soon, he made his move, and we ended up kissing, lying under the open canopy of blue sky. I was thinking how crazy it was to be here like that. I was nervous. He didn't seem to mind at all. He kissed me while his hands started to wander. They touched my breast and came down to my waist and my hips. I couldn't believe I was here, in the open, making out with this much older man.

He talked to me, gently unzipping my suit. As he continued to undress me, I balked. I really didn't know how to process being out in the open, on the dam. We held and caressed each other, kissed some more, and eventually my jumpsuit was completely unzipped. I was about to slip one arm out when I heard something.

Holy shit! I just about jumped out of my skin. I was off that blanket, up on my feet with my suit zipped, in just about .23 of a second. My heart was pounding as I listened intently. I then recognized the sound of a tractor, or combine, moving down the road and getting quieter as it moved slowly into the distance. We laughed. We sat back down, and it took a while before we were able to relax again. I was suffering such conflict in my head: *Do I or do I not?* I really wanted to be with him, but I wasn't at all sure about sex. I had never had sex with anyone but my first husband, and then Scott. They were both young and handsome.

This was just so foreign to me, but I intuitively knew it was coming. I had enjoyed the courting, waiting to see his true intentions. He had played his cards well, because I would have rebuffed any approach by him earlier in the relationship. This intriguing man had manipulated me with patience, attentiveness, and understanding. I couldn't just leave—I would be a tease—and I wanted to keep this one comforting connection. I needed this connection.

My mind returned over and over to Scott. I said to Paul, "I can't do this. I could get pregnant." He looked at me and said he had a condom. He got up, went to his car, and came back with it. I tried to relax. I wasn't truly happy about where I was right then. I had enjoyed the long prelude so much. A younger man would have never waited so long, and I almost felt I owed him. I really don't think I would have let it happen if Scott had not already paved the way. With Scott, I was so sexually attracted. He was young, and gorgeous, and passion had prevailed. This man was older, but his touch was nice—so I let him make love to me. I was surprised at how sweet he was. I was even more surprised at how he felt, and how we melded together. Never would I have thought this older man would have the ability to make me feel warm and loved from head to toe.

As I left that day, I was confused. I thought to myself that maybe, just maybe, I shouldn't think about the guy that "flips my switch," then leaves as soon as he has what he wants. Maybe an older man would treat me better. At this point, he couldn't do any worse than his predecessors.

As summer was winding down, my silver Chevy Vega started giving me problems. It would overheat. Occasionally, it would jump out of gear, and someone would have to go under the car and do whatever repairmen do to get it to change gears again. My car was so important to my work, and it was in terrible mechanical condition. Several times during that summer, I found myself stranded, my husband out of town, no one to help me, and totally at wit's end. The only person I could call and ask for help was Paul. More than once, he sent someone to get me back on the road from a breakdown somewhere.

JJ was gone most weeks working with his truck. When he was home, he often came up with some excuse to head toward Pascagoula. He did not want to take our Ford Bronco, with its big monster mudder tires, so he took my Vega. This would be yet another time when he left and did not make it home that night. It wasn't until the next day that I got a call to come pick him up because he had burned up the engine in my car. He said he was so drunk, he pulled over on the side of Highway 90 and fell asleep with the car running.

The A/C was on and it must have overheated. He woke up with a sheriff tapping on the window. I don't know which was worse: the lie he was telling, or the fact he had destroyed my car. I often wondered if he did it on purpose to sabotage my job, but most likely not. Where do you go until the wee hours of the morning, drunk, for a legitimate purpose?

During the repair process, I learned the Vega had an aluminum engine block. After overheating, the block warped. Numerous attempts were made to repair it, but it was just totally screwed. JJ would take his dump truck and head off somewhere to work. I was left at home with his hunting truck (his red Ford Bronco with monster mudder tires). This was pretty hilarious. I drove it to work. I drove it to church. I had no choice. After church, I had to wait until no one was looking so I could raise my leg high enough to pull myself up and into the truck. The tires were three to four times the size of regular tires, so the truck was at least 36" off the ground.

One afternoon, I met Paul and he asked me to follow him to a field off Airport Blvd. somewhere. I remember following him off the road and down a two-trail dirt road, bouncing along the path behind him. When I got out of the truck, he was laughing at me, talking about how cute I was, a petite blonde maneuvering this big truck down the bumpy path. He came toward me with a big smile and a yellow rose stuck in one of the small Coca Cola bottles offered as his gift. He said something about the "Yellow Rose of Texas" as he placed the bottle in my hand. I looked at it. I looked up at him. The pride of presentation was all over his face; it reminded me of my son, when he would pick the wild flowers in the back field and bring them to me. He said he had been watching me through his rear view mirror as we drove back into the field. He had gotten a kick out of the somewhat incongruent image—big truck, little woman. I wasn't offended. It *was* ridiculous. The whole situation was ridiculous.

At that time in my life, the only thing that helped me through was this interesting relationship. After listening to his tales of paying the price for infidelity, I ended up allowing this man, seventeen years my senior, to help me, love me, and be there, just for me.

He made it clear that he had been the one to first commit adultery, but he was so convincing when he said he had tried to go back to his wife and make things right. That Liz could not overcome the pain of his infidelity seemed plausible to me. Liz took him back to make him pay big-time. The stories of the shooting, of her running him down with cars, or smashing his car windshield with a bat, always came to mind. I felt sorry for her, but if you can't forgive someone, it would be better to take the money and build another life for yourself and your family. At that time, I was hoping that JJ would offer me something similar. I would have taken it in a heartbeat.

I sat under the tree on the blue blanket. I leaned back against the tree and watched as he walked around the field, scattering the seeds that would eventually bring in flocks of hungry doves. To me, he was a handsome man— handsome in a clean-cut, pressed, ironed, and affluent sort of way. He would soon come back to our blanket, hot and sweaty. We sat together and shared a cold drink. But we shared more than just that—we were now friends. Friends who cared about each other . . . really.

I did not want to be in an adulterous affair. I had continued in church, and its principles were what I knew. I believed in what I was taught there, and my life was going against everything I knew was right. My conscience was relentless and always tugging at my mind.

JJ and I got a lucky break. The truck that was killing us financially finally sold. I think a friend of his in the truck repair business finally assumed our loan, because he saw what it was doing to our family. I never knew who the guy was, but wherever he is now, in my book, you are a saint.

Another good thing: JJ was hired back to work at his government job. With this stability, we knew we could get our financial affairs in order quickly. In March of 1978, for our eleventh anniversary, JJ bought me a new Grand Prix. It was my dream car, a yellow cream with a half-vinyl top. It looked just like a Cadillac. I decided to quit my job, go back home, and try again to be the person I knew I should be. I turned in my resignation to the insurance company. I truly believed I could get control of my life by taking this drastic action. Looking back, I know I sabotaged the first real success I had ever tasted.

Though Jamie had completed the first grade, she was not progressing as well as I thought she should. I wanted to send her to Mobile to a Christian school—one connected to the Church of Christ. I knew she would just continue to fall behind where she was. But I went into sticker shock at the price of private school. I talked with JJ, and he was adamant: No way he would consider paying the extra expense for private school.

Quite a few children from our church in Grand Bay were riding the bus to Mobile Christian School. The preacher's wife had been the driver, but now was unable to continue. Everyone was very concerned that there would be no bus service to take the children the 32 miles to school each day. They approached me, the only one not working a job, with a plea to drive the bus. "What? Me drive the bus?" Instead of a salary, they offered me free tuition and books for my children. As farfetched as it was, I ended up agreeing to drive, so I could help everyone else, and help my own children, at the same time.

Jamie started the second grade and Nathan the fifth at Mobile Christian School in 1978. Each morning I would drive from our house, south to my sister's store, where the big yellow bus was parked. We got in and headed out on our route east to Theodore, Tillman's Corner, and then on to school. I'd park the bus in the school lot, then get into the school-owned, 1965 Plymouth, which sounded like a rattle trap as I puttered home. I was due back at bus time, late afternoon, to drive the kids home. I guess it was worth it, but it was embarrassing for me. I made the commitment to drive for the year, because I knew if I quit, everyone would be left with no transportation for their children.

I was so involved with my children and my everyday life in Mobile, and JJ was so involved with his life in Pascagoula. We simply went through the motions of being a family.

Since I was in Mobile, at the kids' school each day, I became active in all the school activities. My daily trips into Mobile also gave me plenty of opportunities to see Paul.

In one of our long conversations, he told me he had given the Independent Methodist Church, off Hall's Mill Road, five acres on which to build a new school and church. I was impressed. He then brought up something about his wife voting against him on a critical church issue. Paul was a deacon. Members stood up to be counted on all such votes. According to him, they said, "All stand who are in agreement," which he did. They sat back down and then they said, "Will all stand who disagree." Liz stood. He felt as if she stood against him. It didn't seem like a big deal to me, but he obviously felt the sting of embarrassment.

Paul had his battles to fight and I had mine. However, it was nice to have a friend who listened and cared without offering advice.

There were days I would drive in, leave the school in the old rattle trap Plymouth, and drive straight to a townhouse subdivision just west of the school. I'd drive to the back, park, and jump into Paul's waiting car.

We never lacked for things to talk about. My favorite story was of his childhood. He was born Paul Fawcett Leverett, Jr., in Dallas, Texas. His mom and dad divorced when he was very young, and his mother and aunt raised him. His dad owned a chicken processing plant, which he said he visited, but not often. Paul had pigeon cages in his backyard, and at twelve years old, he would dress out the squab (a baby pigeon right off the nest) and take them by bus to the Waldorf Astoria Hotel, in downtown Dallas, where he sold the chef his squab. The chef, who obviously liked this precocious little boy, would pull up a stool so Paul could sit and watch him cook. The chef would make a special dish for him, and Paul would sit in the kitchen, eating his gourmet meal, feeling special and accomplished. I would say he was both for having a business of his own so young. I was simply amazed by that story.

Paul, often with a laugh, would refer to himself as the "greasy Mexican" or "the Mexican Jew." I was not sure why, other than he was olive-skinned, with dark brownish black hair. His mother's maiden name was Laudner. His references to her certainly sounded like she may have been of Jewish heritage. I was not sure about his dad, but he was an entrepreneur who passed on those traits to his son.

Paul was very athletic, very competitive, loved baseball, and attended Southern Methodist University on a full baseball scholarship. While in his first year at college, he was in a car wreck with a bunch of kids and broke his arm and elbow severely enough to put him out of commission for baseball. In order to keep his scholarship, he became what amounted to an assistant to the coach. He said he did a little of everything for the team, including washing the jock straps. Paul loved the game and idolized Babe Ruth. He just wanted to stay with the team.

I could tell by his stories that he had such a tenacious spirit, he would do whatever he needed to succeed, and because of his mom and aunt, he had a great respect for the abilities of women. He never made light of what I was doing to get my kids into a good school, but we both had to laugh at the school's stupid ass car, banging and clanging down the road.

At that time, there were about eleven or twelve Colonel Dixie stores around the city. Every couple of weeks, I would take some time and just ride around with him. I think all, or almost all, of his store managers were women.

That fact impressed me, and I asked him why he had so many women working for him. His answer went something like this: "Women who have families to care for have few options in Mobile, unless they are professionals of some kind. The women who work for me are usually middle-aged women who started in the stores at the front and worked their way up. They're making a good salary now, with benefits, and they've proven themselves to be loyal and dedicated to the job. Plus, I've experienced less theft when dealing with women managers."

Not only were Paul's store managers women, but his accountant was a woman, his marketing person was a woman, and his real estate agent was a woman. All were older women respected in their fields, and none of them was young or particularly attractive. It was evident to me that he just preferred dealing with women. I felt it was a good sign—that he had a healthy respect for females—because I had certainly seen some bad men with no respect for us at all.

Paul always traveled with an ice chest in the back of his station wagon. We would ride out to different farms and often stop if some of his friends were working in the fields. He would get out and take them a Coke or leave a bottle of his homemade wine at their door. Every month, he would go by and see an old lady named Daisy. She lived alone in a little house on a dirt road. She did have land, and I guess Paul leased one of her fields for hunting. He would go to her home, take out a bottle of wine for her, and come back to the car with a handmade quilt. The quilt was pieced, but the fabrics she used were mixed textures—some of cotton, but most of double-knit polyester.

I asked Paul why he would need the quilts, especially since they were not very attractive. In fact, in comparison to my Grandma Zorn's quilts, they were awful. Nor did I think they would be especially comfortable. He said Daisy was living on a pension, and he had told her he would buy every quilt she made for $100. Daisy knew a good thing when she saw it and cranked out a quilt a month. Paul said it was a fair trade. I didn't think so, but it made me feel good about him.

It was during this year that my friendship with Paul grew, as did our love for each other. I was fascinated by this man and his eccentric ways. I was not proud of it, for I knew it was a sin every time I saw him. I wished so many times that it wasn't so, but it was. We met when we could because we enjoyed each other's company. He never said he was getting a divorce. In fact, all his statements were of the impossibility of such. He seemed resigned to dealing with his plight. We didn't talk of our relationship being contingent upon his divorce.

I never envisioned being his wife. That was so remote an idea that I couldn't entertain it. My marriage might have been over for me emotionally, but it was far from reality that I could leave JJ and live to tell the tale. Paul and I were just there to enjoy each other in the precious moments we could steal.

Chapter 21
TEXAS 1979

*A hot Texas summer, so my Jamie found shady
respite at the edge of a dry river bed.*

In 1979, JJ got an opportunity to go to work on a new nuclear power plant being built in Glenrose, Texas. If he took the job, he could get a promotion, and they were working a lot of overtime on the plant, so he would make much more money. The decision was two-fold: Better job with more money, and it was going to be a last-ditch attempt to resuscitate a marriage that was down for the count. I was hoping that, if we could just change our environment, get away from family and other distractions, if we could go back to depending only on each other, maybe a miracle could save us.

And the move would also give me a chance to put some distance between me and my conflicting relationship with Paul. It had not helped me be a good wife, nor helped me be the Christian I wanted to be. I prayed a lot. I was weak. I was willing to try harder to make things work. It was soon settled, so we made plans for a move to Cleburne, Texas, population 24,000.

Before the move, I had been plagued with a lot of female problems. My gynecologist had told me that I should have a partial hysterectomy. I had planned to do it, but canceled two weeks before surgery date. I didn't have to have it, and it would be so hard to make a move while recuperating from the procedure.

There was one additional issue—my dog Flip, believe it or not. Flip was my best buddy and friend. He was a pit bull, white with a brown spot over his eye just like the RCA dog. If I was standing outside in our yard, he would sit on my foot. If I was sun bathing on a blanket, he would position himself so at least a paw was touching me somewhere, even if it was against my big toe. If I sat in a chair, he would come up and lean against my leg. If I did nothing, he'd put a paw up. If there was no reaction, he'd slowly raise his body and have both front legs on me. This would continue until he had his entire big body up in my lap so he could be loved like a lap puppy.

Flip was a faithful friend who guarded our house all day, every day. Flip, being male, did have a down side—he was a night wanderer. When the lights went out for us to go to bed, he would be in his guard position on the front porch. However, many mornings when we woke up, he would have a surprise waiting for us. He'd bring us dead opossums, raccoons, and rabbits. Once, he brought us a dead skunk. He smelled so bad that he was banned from the porch for a couple of weeks. Flip would present his catch with great pride and butt wagging—his tail had been cropped at birth, so he just wagged his entire back half. His night missions involved either hunting or fighting. Sometimes, in the morning, he would look like someone had used a nail gun on his head. Teeth puncture wounds suggested a fight over a female dog. I loved him so much.

The problem: He had heartworms. He was an outside dog and this was pre-heart-worm medication days. We nursed him in and out of the swelling and jaundice several times, but now he was weak, and his liver was failing him. The cure for heartworms is basically a poison, which the vet said he didn't think Flip would live through. If he did survive the meds, he would most likely not survive the trip, since we would be moving this free-roaming country dog to the city. He would just be too stressed. The vet recommended we put him down.

When I told my husband, he said, "It's your dog. You can put him to sleep." It was the only choice I thought I could make under the circumstances.

I called Paul. I needed someone to care about the pain that went with the decision to put my Flip to sleep. Paul's answer was for me to bring him to Mobile and he would meet me at his vet's office. I met him and we went in together and stayed with Flip until he was asleep. He wouldn't let me pay, and he arranged for Flip's body to be buried. It meant so much not to have to go through that alone.

We packed up our things and moved just as soon as the children finished school. Cleburne, Texas was a small, friendly town. We found a lovely house to rent in a very nice middle-class neighborhood. It was much nicer than our home in Alabama. When showing us the house, the realtor said it was in the right location—an excellent school district. She looked straight at me and said, "It is where the more affluent children go to school." I just stared at her for a moment. That was a new concept for me, to consider children to be "affluent." To me, parents might be affluent, but kids were just kids.

Welcome to Texas, where the more money you have, the better the school district. In Alabama, if you wanted your kids to have a good education, and you could afford it, you anteed up and sent them to private school. Our new home town was clean, the people were friendly, and the public parks and community facilities were so much nicer than those in Alabama. Texans have oil money.

I joined the Church of Christ in Cleburne, so I immediately went on the visitation list. The ladies at church welcomed me to their Bible study. I tried hard to get my mind and my heart right with God.

The neighborhood had loads of kids who played with my children all that summer. We hiked in Dinosaur Valley, swam at Lake Granbury, and were regulars at the perfectly preserved Old West town of Glenrose. Glenrose featured a dinosaur museum and the best of Texas cooking, at a boarding-house-style restaurant on the corner. Those Texas women sure knew how to cook. We loved exploring the area, so our family spent quality time together each weekend beginning the first month after our arrival.

During the day, it was so hot. I pretty much stayed home with the children, did arts and crafts with them, read a lot, and cooked special new Texas recipes. The kid's favorite was Doo-Doo Cookies (chocolate no-bake drop cookies)—a recipe given to me by a new neighbor friend, Lawanda. She had a Texas drawl that made my Alabama accent sound fast. At first, I thought she was kidding, but no, she was *a gen-u-wine Texan*, possessing a true Texas drawl and a butterfly tattoo on her butt just above her bikini line—my first friend with a tattoo.

JJ made a new friend at the plant. He was an older man (probably 45 or so) and he was, as we call it, a geographical bachelor—meaning his wife was somewhere else and he came there alone to work. He had loads of free time, so he sought the friendship of my husband. JJ seemed to latch on quickly to this new buddy, spending more and more time with him. JJ was working a lot of overtime along with this guy, so they often left work to have a beer or two before he made it home.

I have to say the new friend seemed nice, he was interesting, and he was an avid pilot who owned a small one-engine, Piper Cub plane. We met him at the air strip and received a thrilling birds-eye-view of their worksite (the Glenrose Nuclear Power Plant) as well as some other beautiful local sights he pointed out. It was exciting, and a little scary, and it gave me the sensation of being inside a mosquito, buzzing for all you're worth, while looking for a place to alight. After that ride, as enjoyable as it was, I decided I wasn't really interested in flying in tiny planes again—I'd checked off the "little plane" column.

About six weeks after arriving in Texas, I received a phone call from Paul Leverett. I was shocked to hear his voice. I thought we had agreed to stop all aspects of our relationship, and I asked him how on Earth he found me. He said, "It really doesn't matter how far you go, I will always be able to find you." Well, that was a little heady, thinking someone would track me down. He went on to say he was very concerned about me and was just checking to see how we were adapting to Texas.

Since he *was* by birth and, *by the grace of God*, as they say in Texas, a true Texan, he wanted to stay in touch with me to see how I liked his home state. He said he missed me. As much as I knew this would undermine the whole reason for us moving to Texas, I was weak when it came to someone showing concern for me. It felt good to talk to him. I got to tell him all about the things we had done and seen. I was sick a lot, still struggling with my female problems. JJ really couldn't have cared less about them. He was just pissed if he couldn't get laid.

The workdays were very long. JJ left early and came home late. Within three weeks, we were arguing again over his not coming home on time. I was so tired of making dinner and watching it get cold. I could see he was falling right back into the same old habits. I really had no way of knowing where he was going or what he was doing. We continued to stay in Texas and pretended to make it work.

He was making good money, so we started looking for a home to buy. We put our house at Union Church up for sale, but felt we should find a place of our own in Texas instead of renting. It was also fun to spend time getting out and looking at what this place called Texas had to offer. We looked at homes next to beautiful lakes. We saw prairie hillside farms with vistas as far as you could see—it was big country, with hot open fields, "tanks" (we called them ponds), and heavenly breezes that made the heat bearable.

We looked at a place called Pecan Plantation (a subdivision with an air strip), which was located just outside of Granbury. The neighborhood had homes built into cliffs or perched on hilltops, with a backdrop like those for a western movie. Most of the houses had hangars underneath, for people who flew into Dallas to work each day.

We ended up liking a waterfront home best. It was about an acre and a half overlooking a lovely lake. I fell in love with the two-story brick that had been finished out by an interior decorator. This spacious, upscale home had foyer wallpaper that was flecked with a velvet design, a winding staircase, chandeliers, and bathrooms with bright, shiny metallic wallpaper. I'd never seen anything quite like it. The children loved it, and best of all, we could afford it.

We had just about survived the long hot summer. One weekend, we were looking for a new home for our family, the next week JJ came home on a Friday evening announcing that he and his friend would be going to a big party the next day on a turkey ranch somewhere unspecified. It was "just a guy thing." The group from work would be there for the all-day event. Wives were not invited. "Nope, no women are going to be there, just men," he said.

He went. Into the night, he still hadn't come home, and I was livid. I would have bet my right tit he was somewhere screwing his brains out with another woman. I knew he hadn't gone to a turkey ranch with just guys. P-l-e-a-s-e, give me a break. His normal pattern had resumed, but my patience had long since disappeared. Pretending to be a happy family sucks. My mind whirred with anger and frustration as I faced the same old problems. *I cannot, I will not, go into debt for a home in Texas when this is all I have to look forward to,* I thought. At this point, I knew it was the pot calling the kettle black, but I had put up with his crap for ten years before I said it was over. Now I was trying to do the right thing, trying to resist temptation, and he was right back to the same thing. It was hopeless.

When he finally returned that night, we argued. He didn't come in wanting sex, so I figured that one out. By morning, my mind had been working overtime. I told him that I wanted a divorce, and that I was going home and taking the kids. We argued, and he got angry. He would not let me leave me alone. He pushed me, then tried to kiss me. He barred my exit and kept me in the bedroom. We talked and talked and talked. He would not let me leave the room or leave me alone—he held me captive all day until I submitted to having sex with him, which I did just to get him to leave me the hell alone. For him, make-up sex fixed everything. He got him some, and I could have spit in his face. Oh, God, how I loathed him!

But I knew I had to bide my time. Trying to fight him head-on was going to be futile.

As I laid stone-still in bed that next night, I decided I would play like everything was just fine. I would call Mom and let her know I was leaving JJ and would be coming home. I would stay with her and Dad until I could get some furniture back into our house there. We had all our things in Texas, and I knew I couldn't pack and move with him barring the way.

I thought about it a lot and tried to plan my escape. I decided to write him a letter. I spent hours with pen to paper saying everything I couldn't say to his face. There were no minced words. As the song put it, "I don't want you, I don't need you, I don't love you anymore, and I'll walk out the door." I also said I planned to be long gone by the time he read this letter (again like the lyrics of the song). I went into a lot of detail on what he had done to me, how he had killed my love, how much I despised him, and what he had done to our family. A sabbatical in Texas couldn't repair the damage. "We have no marriage," I wrote. I sure didn't want to be around when he read my letter.

Paul called me on a Monday morning following what was, for me, another weekend of hell. I told him of my decision to leave. I just could not stay in Texas and go into debt for that expensive house. It wouldn't be fair, and I knew I'd really be stuck then. I was ready to come home and put my kids back in school there.

He asked me if I had any money. I told him I had some, but not a lot. I just needed to get to Mom's house and I'd be fine. He said he didn't want me to be on the road with no money, so he said he would wire me money. *Wire money? Western Union?* I had never used that service—I had never had a need for it. He called me back a little later and told me to go to a store in town and I could pick up the money to help me get home without worrying. Needless to say, I was shocked beyond belief when I picked up the money. He had sent me $1,200. That was more money than I had ever put into my hands for a trip.

I had a hard time believing he sent me that much. I had not asked him for anything. When I spoke to him and told him it was too much, he acted as if the money was nothing. He said, "You know I will help you any way I can. The money is not important to me." He said he wanted to make sure I could get back safely. I couldn't believe someone would help me like that. I truly appreciated what he did for me and my children.

The kids had already started to school in Texas. They had only been going a short time, but I couldn't help it. JJ left for work. I packed my suitcase, then woke up the kids. I told them we were going home and leaving their dad. Jamie was fine, Nathan was extremely upset—exactly opposite to how I thought they would react. Nathan knew more about how JJ treated me, but he was still upset to leave him.

I left the letter on the dining room table and we headed east toward Mobile. I drove fast and didn't stop anywhere for long. I was afraid to stop. I feared JJ would find out and catch up with me, even though I knew this wasn't a logical fear.

For me, there was no turning back. The letter I wrote had ended it for me. Surely he would have to honor his contract, stay at his work in Texas, and not follow me home. I kept thinking of his possible reactions. He had obligations. He had to stay—right?

Please, dear God in heaven, tell me I'm right.

Chapter 22
Hurricane

Posted by Bill Murray, abc 30/40 Weather Blog at AlabamaWx.com

The drive back to Grand Bay was long and traumatic. I was running for my life, and for my children's lives. Not that I thought I was going to be killed, but I was running from a life that had been killing me inside for such a long time. In truth, I felt I was running *to* a life, though not sure what kind of life would lie ahead.

I craned my neck to look into the rear view mirror. I looked older. My summer in Texas had been so hot and dry, and my skin felt parched to the touch. I'd never felt heat like they had in Texas. No matter how much lotion I used, I looked like I was trying to turn into a raisin. The air-conditioning was on full force even in September. I was looking forward to a little humidity in the air so my skin could return to normal. Why I focused on my skin I have no idea.

During the drive, Jamie started to sing. The radio was in a static zone so we resorted to self-entertainment. The one thing missing in both mine and Jamie's chromosomes was the ability to carry a tune. She sang the songs she made up as we drove along. Nathan was holding his hands over his ears and begging for mercy, "Mamma, please, make her stop." I was conflicted, not wanting to stifle Jamie's creativity. I did let her sing for a while, but finally stopped her before Nathan bailed from the car. I was sorry I deprived her of a musical gene, but I didn't have one to pass along.

When we arrived in Hattiesburg, Mississippi, I started to "feel" home. The highway to Mobile turned into a narrow two-lane road, with trees and foliage hugging both sides. All those tall pines, reaching for the sky, were shading parts of the road as we kept our heading. I could smell the trees and the lush greenery—the pine scent filled my nostrils and I breathed in deeply. The inviting aroma of my "Sweet Home Alabama" translated into a feeling of welcome—the forest opening its arms, allowing me to return to where I should have been.

We arrived at Mom and Dad's home to hugs and warmth. There was concern for me and my children. We were all tired from the day in the car. I warned my parents that this might not be easy.

As soon as I was able to slip away to Mom's bedroom, where I could access her phone and have a moment of privacy, I called Paul. A call to Mobile from Grand Bay incurred a long distance charge, so I could not speak long. I told him we had arrived safely and thanked him yet again for helping me leave without worrying about money. I appreciated what he had done for me. He said he was happy I had made it home safely, and told me I should help my parents prepare for the coming storm. He had loads of work to do in preparing his business and employees for Hurricane Frederic's impending wrath.

I knew that as soon as he got home and found the letter, JJ would call. I was right—it wasn't long.

Mom tried to screen the call, but I finally took it just to keep her from being caught up in my problem. "No, I'm not coming back," I told him. "Didn't you read my letter? I meant every word of it, JJ. I do not want to be your wife." I began to sound like a repetitive recording. "Why won't you listen? Why won't you hear what I say?" I pleaded over and over, "Don't come here. It will do no good. Our marriage is over." I spat out the words before hanging up the phone.

My worst fear was now reality; he said he was coming as soon as he could. I let my parents know, despite their total preoccupation with news reports of a hurricane in the Gulf of Mexico. It looked like it might be headed right for us. We became glued to the television, watching and waiting for the latest weather report.

JJ continued to use every trick in his arsenal to make me come back on my own. He badgered me, saying how much he loved me, needed me, and couldn't live without me. Neither the badgering nor the bullshit worked—and then the threats started. He threatened that if he had to come get me and drag me back, he would. Then he started on the scare tactic of the terrible hurricane coming our way. I had to leave for the safety of the children, he said. I told him I'd rather die in the storm than return to the misery I had with him. I meant it.

I dug my heels in and stuck to my position. Doing so became even harder when Nathan said he wanted to go back—that he wanted his family together again. He couldn't understand why I no longer loved his dad, and I had no intention of telling Nathan of the transgressions committed. He was way too young to understand. I looked at his precious face and saw the repercussions of trying to shield children from the pain of ending a marriage. I felt it was abuse to include the kids in situations they didn't understand. I hugged him, but I'm not sure it helped. Jamie seemed to handle everything just fine. As long as her mom was with her, she was okay.

The hurricane news kept getting scarier. I remembered the fierce hurricane that had hit the Mississippi coast in 1969. Hurricane Camille was one you wouldn't forget. We had fled from Grand Bay back to Pensacola and stayed with my mom. It was just a bad storm in Pensacola, but we came back to devastation all along the coastal areas. Almost 300 people lost their lives in that high-water hurricane.

We began getting our supplies together and preparing, as they say here in the South, to "hunker down." Once it gets really close, you lose the option to evacuate. Even though Mom and Dad's home didn't feel like waterfront property, we actually were on pretty low ground because it was only a couple miles from the water. Their home was on Old Pascagoula Road, due North of Dauphin Island, and about one mile east of the Alabama-Mississippi state line.

By early morning on September 12, 1979, the news was reporting Hurricane Frederic to be a Category 4 hurricane, with gale-force winds reaching 130 mph. The projected route was right at us. JJ called that morning and said, "If you don't leave now to come back, I am coming there."

I did all I could do to dissuade him from coming. What was he going to do—stand in front of the house and hold his hands up to stop the winds?

As the day wore on, we worried incessantly over the impending storm. The newscasters were preaching doom and destruction, and we were all feeling the air change. As the barometric pressure dropped, we could feel the difference.

Diamond in the Dark

The storm was heading right for us and we prepared for the worst.

By late afternoon-early evening, we started to see the first signs of Frederic. About dusk, we saw the few trees in my mom's yard turn over, revealing muddy roots and leaving huge holes in the earth as they were uprooted. We were lucky that none of the trees fell on our roof.

We talked of JJ attempting to come down the road from Hattiesburg and we knew he'd never make it through that pine forest. *Good*, I thought. *He'll have to turn back, or better yet, he'll keep going but won't make it.* I thought to myself that I shouldn't think that way, but I really didn't want him to make it, and I didn't care what kept him away.

I asked Dad if he thought the house could withstand the high winds. Dad was unsure, and I could tell that even he was afraid. Concern was written all over his face, as Mom and I tried to keep the kids away from the windows. We made a pallet in the hall and sent them to sit there, much to their chagrin. They wanted to watch, too, but every warning was to stay away from windows. I walked back through the house and made sure there was a one-inch crack in at least one window in each room. That would relieve the pressure in the house as the hurricane moved inland.

My parents' home was a nice three-bedroom, two-bath, ranch-style home with a brick veneer and a large bay window that faced the backyard. It was opened wide, and allowed the sun to come into the house, lighting the whole dining area. What had been a lovely feature of Mom's house yesterday had turned into our most vulnerable point. We stood at the window, about four feet back, and watched the wind whip and hurl objects though the yard. I was amazed how the storm drew me in. I could not help myself, so I stood and watched. I was mesmerized and seemed to internalize the power I had only heard of before.

Dad's aluminum shed, which he built with the utmost care and attention, was anchored into its cement foundation. The sliding doors were the first to go. They flew off, bounced, rolled, then disappeared into the rapidly darkening eve. I just kept watching as everything inside the shed started to fly out of the opening. The rain was pelting the window and the wind pushed its way again into the shed. The sides of the building began to expand, as if it were taking a big breath and holding it for a second. As the wind slowed, the breath was exhaled. The shed was "breathing" bigger and bigger breaths, until it started to lift and leave its foundation. One side pulled up, maybe a foot or so away from the cement. Then it settled peacefully back into place.

I couldn't make myself leave. I wanted to see that shed give way to Frederic. It was terrible—and yet so damned cool. The next gust took the shed up another foot or so, then allowed it to settle, this time not so straight, back onto its home. The shed was reluctant to go, but in the end, the last remaining attached side was ripped away. The next gust had the shed standing straight in the air, then, like a snap, it was loose. All the pieces flew in unison into the air, reminiscent of the *Wizard of Oz* house lifted by the tornado. It was gone.

Darkness was now settling in and visibility was almost non-existent. We could hear, but we couldn't see. There was a banging at the front door. It was JJ, standing there in the storm's fury. The son-of-a-bitch had made it. He always seemed to defy the odds. He came in, the kids were glad to see him, and I was sick.

I asked him how he had gotten through the road from Hattiesburg. He said the state troopers had a road block and they were stopping everyone and turning them around. He said he went around the block and sped past them. Blue lights flashed, rain and wind whipped, debris blew into the road, and then the blue lights stopped. The state trooper, he said, probably just gave up and said to hell with the guy who was willing to risk his life.

JJ told us of trees falling like fiddlesticks into the road and the ditches around him. He said at times he had to drive around trees falling behind him, narrowly missing his car. He was, as the saying goes, "hell-bent" on his destination. I believe the devil protected him—the devil always did. He loved the guy. God protects fools, drunks, and children. The devil protects his angels, and he surely did his job that night.

My heart was heavy, but my children needed me more than ever. The rain and wind were so loud it felt as if we were inside a drum banging on the outside. The water was now coming into the house by way of the laundry room door. It was funny how, as the storm moved in, the wind was pulling from the north side of the house toward the eye of the storm directly south of us. The water was flooding in as Mom, Dad, and JJ scurried to mop it up or block it with whatever they could find.

I walked through to check on the kids. Surprisingly, they were okay. We had done a good job of not conveying the fear that lay heavily in our hearts. I walked back to my mom's bathroom. It faced the back of the house; in fact, the window looked straight out over the place where the shed once stood. I walked in, thinking I'd pee and then go back to the others. The bathroom was hissing, and I identified the sound as coming from the window. The crack I had made earlier was almost gone, and the wind was trying to get through, even after the wind had almost jiggled it closed.

My thought was to reach out with my left hand and raise the window higher, making it easier to allow the breeze to flow in to relieve the pressure. I reached out. My fingers touched the little lip of the window, the tip of my ring finger on the pane. At once, the room filled with air. The shower curtain flew up and everything was whirling. I thought the whole window had blown out. I felt the gust of wind from every direction around my body. It was so strong and powerful.

The sting of pain in my hand made me look down. Blood was everywhere. I looked back at the window and could see that only one little pane had blown out. Just one pane had allowed all this—it was crazy. I looked at my hand. The blood was running freely from my hand and now up my arm. My first thought was how I would warn everyone. I thought the house was about to blow up in the wind. I also had to get from the bathroom to the kitchen without my children seeing me hurt. I knew they would be hysterical if they saw blood all over me.

I wrapped my hand in a towel and closed the door to the bathroom. It was our only defense against the wind. I was afraid for all of us as I walked down the hall toward the kitchen. I passed my children, huddled in the hall bathroom, asking them, "Are you guys okay?" They said something, but I just kept walking.

I walked down the hall and into the den. My step went swish, as I felt the wet carpet give under my foot. Everyone was mopping frantically. I was looking at them and then at the big window just beyond. I could only envision the window breaking, with wind and glass coming through the room. I told them, "We all need to go to the hall. The bathroom window exploded and we need to get away from windows."

They heard me but continued to mop and throw towels to try and stem the tide of water running into the house from under the back door. I yelled at them, "We have to get into the hall! The windows are going to blow out!" This time they heard me and turned to look at me. I opened the towel to show them my hand. When they saw the blood, they dropped everything and came toward me. I was so lucky. Every time I think of it, I know that glass could have landed in my face or eyes, and there would have been no way to get medical help. We would have had to wait until the next day. My ring fingertip was blown open like a firecracker. The glass had gone through and exited through my fingernail on the other side. It hurt, but I knew it would hurt more the next day.

As the disaster preparation people tell you to do, we gathered in the hall. It was the center of the house and other than the very small hall bathroom, it was the only room without a window. I was so concerned about what was happening, I ushered my children from the hall into the bathroom. I had them get into the tub and lie down on blankets I had thrown in. In survival mode, JJ and I pulled a twin mattress from the back bedroom and laid it over the tub to protect the children. We then sat down on the floor next to them. I reached up and put the palm of my hand against the wall. I could feel the entire house trembling from the pressure. I was so afraid the house would blow apart, and it would not have surprised me had the roof flown off and the walls fallen in.

Mom and Dad were in the hall, and we all were praying we could ride out the night. Mom started singing hymns of comfort. We offered silent prayers. She sang "Amazing Grace," "Sweet Hour of Prayer," and "Rock of Ages." It was haunting as her voice trembled with her melody. The songs made us accept our dire situation. We were all quiet, thinking and waiting for the next thump against the roof, or the whistle of the wind finding another space to creep through.

JJ whispered to me that the second half, or backside, of a storm was usually worse than the first half. I knew in my heart that the house would not stand up to much more. It seemed a welcome miracle when the noise stopped—it was eerie to hear the silence. We looked at each other and we knew we were inside the eye of the storm. *How long would it last?* We were afraid to leave the inner hall because we had no idea how long we had before the back half of the storm would arrive. We went into the living room and, other than water on the floor, everything was holding up. The back bathroom was in shambles, even though only one small window pane was broken.

It was another thirty minutes or so before the winds began again. I was so ready to cry. Nathan and Jamie were asleep. I prayed they would stay asleep in the little tub nest we had made for them. JJ and I sat, snuggled against that tub, for the next two hours. We kept waiting for the winds to get worse, but thank God they did not. The storm's second part did not seem as bad as the first. Sometime around midnight, things had calmed down to the point where we no longer felt ourselves in abject danger.

We were all okay. We were all completely exhausted and oh so thankful.

>━┤◄►━○━◄►┤━<

On the morning of September 13, we awoke to meet the new day and to face the aftermath of Hurricane Frederic. We opened the front door to clear skies. The calm after the storm had a golden glow that seemed to cover everything like an iridescent blanket. The hue was so very unusual. It was like walking into a strange new world. We all found it so odd that it could be so clear and calm, when just a few hours before, the turbulence had brought us to our knees in fear for our lives. We looked around at all the trees that were broken or torn from the ground. The few pitiful, spindly trees left standing bespoke the horror they had endured. Not a single leaf remained on a single tree.

The ground was saturated, and we squished across the soggy lawn. Where the shed stood, there now was a concrete foundation and nothing more. Even Mom's kiln, where she had made her ceramic pieces, had disappeared into the night. Using camping equipment, Dad now readied the morning coffee. Coffee never smelled so good. We had a full breakfast in no time thanks to Dad.

To that point, Hurricane Frederic was the most financially devastating storm ever to hit our region. Luckily, loss of life was not so great. The coastal recovery would take years. It was ironic that my marriage was in about the same shape, but with less chance of rebuilding.

JJ stayed for a couple of days, and tried to get me to go back to Texas with him. I refused and stood my ground.

Each day we realized, more and more, just how bad it was all over the county—no power, no gas, not much of anything. I was outside cleaning up debris and looked up in time to see Paul's car drive by. He was going very slowly. I waved. He waved. He was gone. I knew he was just driving by to see if I was okay. It made me feel better just to see him for that one brief moment.

There were only three bedrooms in the house and Mom and Dad had not shared a room in years. The kids were in the third bedroom. There wasn't much I could do to keep away from JJ. He wouldn't leave. I wouldn't fight him, because that would involve everyone in the house. He agreed to leave and go back to Texas, but only if I'd have sex with him. I was so disgusted with him that I almost threw up while he screwed me. Nothing could deter him, no matter how much I hated him. He left the next day to go back to Texas.

I tried to talk with my parents the following day about me and JJ, about our marital problems, and the fact that he had been running around on me for years. I didn't tell Dad that I, too, had been unfaithful. I couldn't face his judgment of me. He sat in his chair and almost cried. He said he couldn't bear the thought of his baby daughter burning in hell. He recited the "party line" from the church—that there is no basis for divorce unless it is for adultery, and even though I thought JJ had committed adultery, I could not prove it. He said I would be living in sin and that I would never be free to marry again. According to Dad's interpretation, there would be no forgiveness for an adulteress.

JJ went back to Texas and made some kind of arrangements with his employer, Brown and Root. I could not believe he got out of that contract so easily. We had only been in Texas for three months of a two-year contract. I cried when he said he had pulled it off.

Our home—the one we had left in Alabama—was only a few miles up the road from my parents. It was empty and JJ made arrangements for moving all our things back there. I never went back to Texas. On his return, he came to see my parents, badgering them to persuade me to leave. I would not. My mom told him to leave me alone. JJ turned on my mom like a badger. He told her to stay out of our problems or he'd kill her too. Mom looked like she had been slapped—I could see the recognition of his power cross her face.

He had no qualms about threatening anyone, but I never thought he would stoop to threatening my mother's life. I knew I could not stay there and put my parents through that kind of trouble. They had had so many problems for so long, and now their lives seemed to be better. I wouldn't intentionally drag Mom through anything that could put her, or Dad, in jeopardy.

In the end, as much as I did not want to, I went back home once our things were there. We had no electrical power or running water for over six weeks. The hurricane, or a bolt of lightning, had taken out the power station only about a quarter-mile from our home. The station had to be completely rebuilt and new lines had to be run again. We had to wait our turn, so it was mid-November before our power was reconnected.

I maintained the position that I wanted a divorce. My children knew I wanted a divorce. I told them I was not going back to their dad, even though at the time, I did not have a place to go. It was a horrendous situation.

JJ got mad at me one evening while I was cleaning up from dinner. I wanted nothing to do with him. I was going for the wall phone in the kitchen. I turned just in time to see him throw a knife at me. There was no time to react. The knife stuck into the wall about a foot from my head, embedded in the maple paneling.

I saw the fear on my son's face. I ran to him, and together we ran from the room.

November brought more bad news. My brother called and said he had been diagnosed with cancer. He had a growth, and they would have to take off his entire upper lip. He was devastated. I was horrified at the thought of my handsome brother being in such a position. He needed me.

I was very upset the day I called Paul. I told him of JJ throwing the knife at me and of my brother's illness. He listened to my anguish. He was always there for me, and he never made any demands on me in any way.

The next day, he called me at home. That was really unusual for him, taking a chance and calling my home, but he did. He said he needed to talk to me in person, and wanted me to meet him at one of his dove fields not too far from where I lived. I met him that afternoon. I was anxious to see him and I welcomed his warmth and love.

He met me with a long hug and told me he had something for me. He reached into the pocket of his jacket and pulled out an envelope. He handed it to me as he said, "It's a ticket to go visit your brother." I just looked at him in disbelief. He had purchased a ticket that would allow me to be with my brother during his surgery. I hugged him and thanked him profusely for doing such a wonderful thing, but in the back of my mind, I really didn't know how I was going to pull it off. *How could I leave my children?*

I went home and announced I'd be leaving for Washington to stay with my brother. I told JJ my mom had bought me a ticket, and I would be leaving in two days. During our entire marriage, my dear husband had never once taken solo care of our children. I had never once been anywhere without them. He was the one always leaving for his hunting trips or work, and I was always there to hold the fort down, so to speak. "It's your turn to stay home and take care of the kids," I told him. I didn't ask. I was going no matter what.

My trip to be with my brother was good for me. It was the farthest I'd ever traveled alone. It helped me grow up and it was exhilarating to be free of JJ, even for two short weeks. I knew I needed the divorce—I was determined not to spend my life with a man I had grown to despise.

JJ just couldn't, or wouldn't, connect the dots—that his treatment of me had a direct correlation with my response to him. The words he said to me kept rolling over in my head, "If you really loved me, nothing I could do to you would change it." He believed this to be true, but he was someone whose own mother had her teeth beaten out of her head, after which she continued to stay with his father. His grandmother didn't have it much better. She had given birth to five children (one, whom she had called Buddy-Doo, who died before he could walk, she grieved for all her life). JJ's grandfather had left her for his second family across town. She had then worked in the fields, and washed clothes, to try to feed them. She didn't speak ill of him and she never remarried.

My brother and sister-in-law were very pleased I'd been able to come up to be with them during this really tough time. It was difficult to see my brother go through such an ordeal. However, the surgeon did an incredible job. We had all been so afraid he would be terribly disfigured, but the surgical result far exceeded our expectations. We were very pleased to see that a mustache would soon be able to cover the vast majority of the scarring.

I kept the phone conversations home to a minimum, but I had to call to talk to my children. I continued to tell JJ, emphatically, that under no circumstances would I come back home to resume our marriage.

When I arrived back in Mobile, JJ was to pick me up at the airport. As I got off the plane, I could not believe my eyes. JJ was standing there with Nathan and Jamie, all holding bouquets of red roses for me. The children ran up to me and were so glad I was coming back to their daddy. I looked at JJ in disbelief. What a low, self-serving trick. He had told my children we were making up, and I would be coming home to "them" as a "family" again. The children were so happy. I thought I would throw up.

JJ had talked to church elders and they wanted to come visit our family to help guide us back on track. I felt trapped and miserable. There was nothing he would not do to get his way. JJ, the man who never had anything to do with church, actually went before the church and was baptized, though not for any of the right reasons. In my opinion, it was just a final ploy to head off my resistance. I watched as he was baptized. Normally, this act would have brought me to tears. I had prayed for him to become a Christian. But for me, it was just too late.

However, my dad did forgive him. My dad told me about how we can't get forgiveness if we don't forgive. He stressed again that there could be no divorce in the church except for adultery and I had no proof. JJ denied it and now he had been baptized. It was as if my trip to Washington had been "check," and his so-called baptism amounted to "check-mate."

I cried every day. I was so depressed, I wanted to die.

Several days passed before I was able to meet Paul at one of the dove fields. We parked our car under a tree and talked. He was anxious to hear about my trip. I thanked him for helping me be with my brother. It had meant so much to me, and he was the one who had made it possible.

I told Paul of JJ's baptism. But I then told him of my decision not to see him or continue our relationship. It was just too hard, and I didn't have the strength to fight it any longer.

Paul reached over and grabbed my arm, turning me around to face him. I saw anger in his eyes, though it was for one fleeting second. That one second was enough to know that he did have it in him to get angry—really angry.

In writing my story, I have tried to maintain the perspective I had at the time when these events were happening, and to describe what I felt at the time each incident took place. It is, however, important to note that after that one incident, I did not see another glimmer of anger directed at me for the remainder of our relationship. I can't explain what could have been going through his mind that day, but years later, I would hear of things that might have been happening during that time which could have put him on edge.

His attitude immediately changed to one of care and kindness. He asked me if I thought it would help to go and talk to a psychiatrist about my dilemma. Paul said he knew a good person, whom I could talk to objectively and seek the help I needed to make clear and better decisions, for my life and my children's lives. It sounded really strange—that Paul was recommending a shrink for me—but I took him up on the offer. I told him I would love to be able to talk to an objective person who could help me.

Paul actually arranged an appointment for me with a Mobile shrink. The shrink was very interested in me and my problems, or so it seemed at the time. He was around forty-five or so, and a nice-looking man. We talked and I told him of my married life and gave him some highlights of the abuse I'd suffered. I told him I had had an affair, and the guilt was overwhelming. There was a real spark of interest in his eyes. "Who is he?" I actually told him the name and watched him as he thought a second, looked up, and said, "I guess I don't know him." To me, he seemed more interested in a gossip tidbit to drop at his afternoon golf game than in my dilemma. I guess shrinks need gossip food too.

He gave me the ink blot test and a couple of other tests, which kept me there for about two and one-half hours. Actually, it turned out to be a marathon first visit. I sat around for a short bit until he came back in to talk with me. His analysis was this: You are okay, you are processing appropriately, and I do not feel you need to come in for additional treatment, unless you just want to come in and talk with me (*wink, wink*). When that didn't elicit a response from me, he put back on his doctor demeanor and said, "The only reason I would want to continue talking to you would be to determine why you continue to stay in such an abusive relationship." Then he said, "Your husband needs to be in therapy. If you can get him in here, I'd love to be able to work with the person who really needs treatment."

That was pretty definitive and validating. I made a call and, within minutes, Paul was at the office to pick me up and drive me back to my car. He didn't probe as to the outcome. It was as if he knew I was okay. Paul knew I was dealing with real problems, and others that were self-imposed by my belief system. What the appointment did was give me one more support block to continue moving forward to freedom.

Our last Christmas together as a family.

Christmas 1979 was on us quickly. The family tradition would be honored that year even though my heart was not in it. The main thing I remember about that holiday was that I received a beautiful green velour jogging suit from Paul. When he brought it to me, it was in a lovely box. He chuckled a bit when he told me the suit had been delivered to his home instead of his office. When he had arrived home, it was on his bed, and both his wife and his daughter had been disappointed. It did not fit either of them. I don't know if he ended up buying another one to fit his wife or not. It was soft and absolutely scrumptious in both its color and feel. I loved it and I wore it all Christmas Day. JJ asked me where it came from and I said I had bought it on sale.

I made a Christmas gift for Paul. He had been such a good friend and I wanted to give him something. I could not afford to buy him anything he would want or need, but I knew that he had a favorite poem that he had lived his life by. He had lots of little proverbs and sayings he would spout, like: "The harder you work, the luckier you get." Paul was an optimist, and a hard worker, and he believed in his ability to persevere. He loved baseball and Babe Ruth, often rattling off Babe's batting stats, including the hundreds of times he struck out, but still the Babe was known for his home runs. He loved an inspirational poem by Calvin Coolidge, called "Persistence." It was that poem that I chose to put on a plaque for him. He recognized my effort and he seemed genuinely pleased with my gift.

> *Nothing in the world can take the place of persistence.*
> *Talent will not; nothing is more common than*
> *unsuccessful men with talent.*
> *Genius . . . will not; unrewarded genius is almost a proverb.*
> *Education will not; the world is full of educated derelicts.*
> *Persistence and dedication alone are omnipotent.*

This poem spoke volumes to me. Though I wasn't lucky enough to possess great talent, genius, or formal education, I, too, hoped I could succeed if I didn't give up.

Chapter 23
New Year 1980

Dad and me at Christmas.

My New Year's resolution was to leave the relationship and survive long enough to get a divorce. I had been told often that I could not leave a man who was not only physically abusive, but who had taken a certain sick joy in mocking me every time I told him he was killing my love for him. His response was usually, "Don't even try to think. You're too stupid." He had succeeded in slowly torturing our relationship to death, and then he refused to accept the consequences of his actions.

We no longer had any animals on our farm except Sugarboy. I would have sold him, but Jamie threw a fit. She was already too big for him, but he was a pet we all loved. I couldn't figure out a plausible reason for finding him a new home. Any act like that would raise a flag that I might be preparing to leave. I thought that if we did have to leave him, JJ would either sell him or find him a home. There were certainly plenty of people who would take a free pony. I let Jamie have her way and figured I'd deal with the pony later.

I had taken a part-time job working at Mobile County Co-Op selling feed, seed, and fertilizers. I was concentrating on taking care of my children, and trying to stay sane. I was also trying to save a little money. My girlfriend in Mobile told me she would let me share her town home if I needed a place to stay. I knew going back to my parents' home would not work—I'd never put Mom and Dad in jeopardy again. My mom had not taken the threat against her life lightly, and even my old Marine dad was afraid of JJ. It was either that, or the knowledge that to stop JJ, he'd have to kill him, and Dad didn't want any part of that. I couldn't blame him.

My mom decided she wanted to have a private detective follow JJ and catch him in the act of adultery. She really wanted to expose him for what he was—get back at him for his threats, and shut Dad up about the "can't get a divorce unless it is adultery" religious view he kept spouting. At that point, I didn't care about any of that, because I accepted my own acts of infidelity, so the proof of JJ's infidelity, at this juncture, was a moot point to me.

To me, it didn't really matter that I had spent ten years being faithful and honestly trying to be a good wife. I had given up, and now I was just as guilty as he was. In order to make things right, I'd have to go before the church, repent, and accept my position as a long-suffering wife who could bring her husband to goodness and repentance through prayer and good works. But I knew that wasn't going to happen.

Mom's desire to hire a detective was of concern to me because, number one, I felt it was a waste of money. Number two, I was afraid someone would rip my mom off, and she didn't have that kind of money to blow. I told her that, if procuring a detective's services was going to make her happy, call Paul and ask him if he knew of a detective who was reputable and reasonable. She called Paul, and that took off with a life of its own. I had nothing else to do with it, and really didn't care about the outcome.

I hadn't seen a doctor since before leaving for Texas. So much stress since then could only have worsened my female problems, so I knew it was long past time to be seen. I talked to Paul on the phone one day, and just in passing, I mentioned to him I had finally scheduled an appointment with a doctor in Pascagoula, Mississippi.

I was prepared for the doctor to chastise me for canceling my surgery, scheduled for just before I had left for Texas. My turn was up and the nurse escorted me to the examining room.

The doctor came in, did the usual chat, and came back for the pelvic exam. He said in a surprised tone, "What is this?" as his gloved fingers jabbed hard into my vagina. I almost jumped off the table. He moved closer and pressed on my stomach from the top while pushing hard with his fingers from inside. "You have something here that is huge!" he said. His pushing and probing hurt, and he was really scaring me.

The doctor didn't try to sugarcoat his diagnosis. He had found a tumor, maybe a large fibroid cyst, but he really didn't know what it was. My mind was racing. *Could it be malignant?* The upshot of that "gut-wrenching" exam was that he wanted to schedule me for immediate surgery. It was as if he had found a bomb inside me and didn't even want me to go home—just head straight to the hospital.

To say I was terrified would be an understatement. The doctor described what he thought should be done—a hip-to-hip incision, so he could open me up and explore the situation.

"*Explore?* Excuse me. Did you just say explore?" I needed some clarification. I had walked into that office an hour and a half earlier, thinking I might need a "tack-up," as was told to me before I went to Texas, but the idea of exploratory surgery, as suddenly sprung on me, was just not working for me.

Vanity was rearing its head now as I envisioned my flat, tanned belly becoming a scar zone. I couldn't think straight. The growth had been there for a long time, and I was in a lot of pain from all the vigorous probing. At this point, I felt too stupid to think.

I told the doctor I was going home. I wanted to think about this and get a second opinion. He looked like I had slapped him. I didn't like him. He had shown no restraint in scaring the shit out of me, and had hurt me badly with his exam. He might not be someone I'd want to take a surgical knife to me.

It was March and it was cold. While trying to dress in the silent examination room, I had chills. By the time I left the office, I could feel it was dark outside. *My goodness*, I thought. *How long had I been in there?* I had in my hand the doctor's recommendation for immediate, exploratory surgery, to remove the apple-sized object growing somewhere in my uterus, or in that general vicinity. Too bad sonograms weren't being used by his office. In those dark ages, women were just supposed to listen to their doctor and believe whatever diagnosis he came up with. With this one, though, I balked. As I left, I looked around and determined I was the last patient in the building.

All the other offices had already closed, locked up, and turned out the lights. I was alone, and somehow that cold, empty, open lobby seemed fitting. I walked toward the grand, winding staircase that spiraled down through the plant-filled atrium. The marble under my feet tapped with each step I made as I slowly descended into the dark hallway, leading to the parking lot doorway. As I stepped down from the last step, I looked up to see a man step from the shadows. I could not believe my eyes—it was Paul. He had shown up, unannounced, and had waited to make sure I was okay. It was so like him. I walked straight to him, and he held me while I cried.

Paul reassured me that I would be okay. He said he knew a great doctor, in Mobile, and he did not think I should consider surgery in Pascagoula. He would make some calls and the next day would let me know what could be done. It was so good not to be alone, to have someone who cared about me.

As I headed home, Paul followed me to the last turn and waved bye. I drove home to tell JJ of my problem. "Concerned" was not a word I would use to describe his reaction.

Within two days, I had an appointment with Dr. Sewell, one of Paul's hunting buddies. His exam was gentle, his comments soothing. Because I was not interested in having more children, the easiest thing was to have a partial hysterectomy. He was also pretty sure he could do the operation vaginally, so there would be no scar. He was the one I would entrust my surgery to, and it was scheduled for mid-March 1980. When I told my mom, she immediately seized on the opportunity to have JJ followed while I was going to be "out of commission," so to speak. JJ had certainly proven he was not into delayed gratification. Mom was betting he'd use every moment of that opportunity for personal pursuits.

My surgery was a success, with no problems encountered. The evening after my procedure, JJ left early, so he "could check on the children." *Right!* Within about ten minutes, Paul was standing at my bedside. He looked down at me and told me I looked great for just having had surgery. He said he was just checking to make sure I was okay. He patted my hand and then left, all within five minutes of arriving. I didn't see him again during my hospital stay, which was several days, and went to my mom's house afterward so she could help me during recovery.

I stayed with my mom for about two weeks. I wasn't supposed to drive, and I didn't. My doctor recommended not driving for six weeks. So I spent the time at home, my girlfriends visiting me for company. One girlfriend took me back for my checkups, as I continued to get my strength back.

Mom received a report from her detective on JJ's activities. I was still ambivalent about the whole thing. When Mom gave me the report, I had to laugh.

The report read something like this: Agent had suspect in view as he was leaving his place of work, on such and such a day at such and such a time. Suspect approached his Toyota pickup. He opened his truck, stood on the running board, and looked all around the parking lot, as if to make sure that no one was trying to observe him.

Suspect got into his truck, and proceeded down Xxxx Road, at such and such rate of speed. He was constantly adjusting his rear view mirror. Suspect sped up, made a U-turn, and headed in the opposite direction. Suspect had his window rolled down, his arm and hand extended from the window, and he was giving the oncoming traffic the finger. He was laughing as he drove up the street, turned, and disappeared.

I laughed so hard. JJ never said one word to me about it and I never asked him. He was devious, wicked, and always leery of everything. If there isn't anything to hide, who would go to a workplace parking lot, stand up on the side rail, and survey the lot just before leaving?

There was one additional report, where an agent viewed him from a distance, unable to get photos, of course. He was in the parking lot of the Singing River Hospital talking to a girl in a nurse's outfit. The girl had long brown hair. Perhaps he was just arranging for a medical exam later in the evening, or maybe getting ready to play "Doctor."

I told Mom not to worry about it, but she was so disappointed. The hiring of the detective wasn't for me. It was all about Dad and his theatrical rendition of doomsday for his daughter's meeting with St. Peter. Report or no report, my plans had not changed. As soon as I could find a way to make it stick, my marriage would be history.

Chapter 24
Exodus

Dad and me on a happy day.

From March through the beginning of May, I focused on recovering from my surgery and on basic survival. I used doctor's orders as an excuse to maintain personal space and welcomed the sanctioned reprieve from sexual encounters with my husband. However, when the six-week check-up was over, the pressure resumed.

It was naïve of me to think that my own feelings would overcome his need for sex with me. He just did not care, did not receive the vibe of hostility and revulsion, or just refused to let it deter him from his "God-given right as your husband."

Weekends proved to be the most difficult. I can't remember how the fight started, but I remember being in the master bedroom. He had pulled me in and shut the door as the children watched TV in the living room. I sat on the bed. I watched him walk across the room, bare except for his underwear. I looked at him, studied him a moment—he was, I thought, handsome, tanned, muscular, and possessing an enviable "six-pack" for a thirty-three-year-old guy. His arms were that of a weight-lifter, and his waist and hips were narrow. I knew he had to be attractive to many women.

My thoughts then turned to how to get through this next encounter with him. I looked at him as he approached. He had something in his hand. I looked down and saw him with some sort of condom that looked like a damned squid. It actually had tentacles. I went berserk, kicking him and pushing him away. He must have lost his mind thinking he could use such a thing on me. He hadn't asked me, because he knew I'd think he had lost his damned mind. He became angry, and I was crying. I retreated to the very small half-bath that adjoined our room. I was at the sink wiping my face with a cold, wet cloth. In his anger, he stood behind me saying he was sick of me constantly being "out of commission."

I tried to leave the confines of the small space and he pushed me back in. There was no place to go, so I fell back and down onto the toilet seat. It was really the only place to fall, because the tiny half-bath was full, with only the sink and toilet, side by side. He stood in front of me and exposed himself, demanding, "Suck my dick." His crudeness disgusted me beyond belief. I told him, "No way. You'll have to get your girlfriend to do that for you." The thought made me sick.

He grabbed me by my hair, his fist wrapped tight, and shook my head. I pushed at him, turning my head. He let go, and I fell hard to the floor. My head and neck hit in between the toilet and the wall. The pain shot down my neck. As he pinned me down, I felt helpless in the face of such power and anger.

At that moment, I could hear my sweet Nathan knocking at the bedroom door. He was calling for me, "Momma, Momma." I called back to him in the calmest voice I could muster, "Go watch television. I'll be there in a minute." The thought of yelling "Call 911," never, never, entered my brain. I believed it would have done no good.

Intuitively, Nathan knew something was wrong. He had no idea what, but he knew his mom was in trouble; otherwise, I would have been there imme-diately for him. Nathan didn't leave; he just kept knocking at the door. I could "feel" Nathan listening to his mom's struggle. Again, he called, "Momma."

I was looking up at JJ from my position on the floor. I asked him to please let me go, so I could take care of Nathan and Jamie. Now both Jamie and Nathan were standing at the door listening . . . and waiting for their mom. I was finally released, but I could feel his wrath bursting from every pore.

I know he must have been very frustrated, finally having realized that no matter what he did or tried, nothing would work. I was "dead" to his advances, and there was nothing he could do to make me interested in him. Confused and angry, he decided I was frigid. I don't think he could entertain the idea that his wife truly hated him, but I did.

What was even more amazing was how, each day, we moved from one violent skirmish to another. The majority of the time, we functioned on auto pilot. The deal killer was that I was no longer able to abide the intimacy a marriage required. My heart was somewhere else and, no matter the cost, I could not even feign affection for my husband.

Mayhem

On May 31, 1980, Elizabeth Leverett's death became front-page news. Her death was a shock to everyone. How could such a thing happen to one of Mobile's prominent families—in their home, in the middle of the day. I had never known anyone to go through such a horrendous event before. Because of knowing Paul, the impact of the tragedy seemed so much greater, so much more personal.

We listened intently to the news each day. It was always the lead story of every local broadcast. Everyone, everywhere you went, was talking of the terrible murder. The initial reports on television were horrible, even to the point of showing a stretcher being wheeled out of the big Airmont house. The Mobile Press Register coverage always started with the same words and phrases: Wealthy businessman's wife murdered in the exclusive Airmont sub-division. Then it recounted how she was shot and stabbed.

Her photo, on the front page, showed a very pretty, middle-aged woman flashing a radiant smile. Her hair was actually white as cotton, and some news accounts reported that the dark brunette had recently dyed her hair blonde. I found this interesting, because growing up with a mom beautician, I knew there was no such thing as "dying" your hair from black to blonde. You had to bleach the hell out of it to get that white color. She was also referred to as a mother of four, and a wealthy socialite.

According to all the news accounts, a robber had entered their home that Friday afternoon, and on Mrs. Leverett's return, she interrupted a burglary in progress. Consistent with that, her car had been taken, then found just blocks from her home. Eventually, the reports revealed that a very large diamond ring of hers was missing. Everyone had an idea or a theory. People were spending hours speculating on what could have happened. Sympathy for the family was huge. That Friday evening, the family was supposed to be celebrating the graduation of their son. It was a time when joy and pride should have reigned supreme. Instead, they had the job of mourning, then burying a wife and mother.

Whatever they did to bury her was quick and quiet. I don't remember reading much about her funeral in the paper. I didn't see anything in the news about a huge showing of community support or sadness. I was sure it was there, I just did not see it reported. All I could think was that, no matter how bad her relationship was with Paul, no one deserved to meet such a horrific and tragic end.

It wasn't long before the innuendoes started rearing their ugly little heads. The brutality of the crime was staggering. People grappled with why someone caught in the act of a common burglary would choose to shoot a woman, and then just about decapitate her. The scene depicted was a throat slit almost all the way through. Trying to determine a motive, many wondered aloud if she had been raped. I don't recall if that was reported, one way or the other.

As in any crime or murder, the police looked at the family members first. Where were they, what were they doing, and what were the dynamics of the family relationships? It appeared from the outset that Paul (her husband), Lee (her youngest daughter), Mark (her graduating son), and Mark's guest that day could not have been involved. They were all out having lunch, making the graduation purchase of Mark's new Grand Prix and touring the Colonel Dixie business so Mark's girlfriend could see the restaurant chain's office spaces and kitchen. There was certainly nothing unusual about Paul showing off the thirteen-foot polar bear skin gracing his office wall.

I read each article with great interest. It relieved my mind to hear that Paul could not have been a part of anything that had happened to her. I thought of the stories Paul had told me of her trying to shoot him on two different occasions, trying to run him off the road with her car, and of her beating his car lights out with a bat. Out of revenge, and a sense of love betrayed, she had tried to punish him physically, by openly trying to kill him, and mentally, by constantly beating him over the head with his transgressions.

Even after their breakup, after she had chosen to take him back, Paul said that she would just sit and write in her journal, as if to let him know she was documenting all their personal struggles. And to me, Paul's worst story was of her sexually stimulating him, then trying to tear his genitals from his body. Her rage was strong and unpredictable.

All these tales told by Paul related the tumultuous years they had stayed together, basically tormenting each other. The animosity over Paul's infidelity with Norma, years earlier, would not allow her to let it go—it had consumed her. There was also a lot of anger on his side, over her not being willing to give up her social standing, or her exclusive Airmont home, no matter how big the financial offer of settlement. That was the history between them, as told me by Paul. Because of these stories, which I had heard first-hand from Paul, I was relieved to read the circumstances that seemed to clear Paul of any connection to her death.

The last thing I wanted to do was to be part of a tragedy that had started so many years earlier. I felt sorry for all of them, on both sides of that family. They had been at full-bore war when I first met him. I absolutely refused to take any ownership of any of their marital problems.

In June, on a Sunday afternoon, my family sat together around the dining table. The table seated only six, unless you added the leaf that stood in the kitchen closet. The antique table was of walnut, and I had refinished it in my spare time. I loved it from first sight, and spent hours restoring it to perfection. I was so proud of my work, and the results added visual warmth to our home. The chairs were assembled to match as closely as possible. They were antiques, with stamped patterns in the upper backs. I was proud of how the satin varnish accentuated the beauty of the early colonial pattern.

It was a late, after-church lunch. The meal was over, the children had moved on into the living room to watch television, and I continued to sit quietly, looking beyond the glass doors, lost in my thoughts. All the food and plates sat silently, as if waiting patiently for me to start the clean-up. I was looking straight past JJ, who always sat at the opposite end. The glass doors behind him allowed the light to shine around his silhouette, and rays streamed in brightly across the cluttered table. JJ got up, walked around toward me, and placed his hand on my shoulder. He leaned down to kiss me on the nape of my neck. I felt as if every hair on my neck and head stood straight up. A chill sent an instant shudder through my body. Spontaneous and unanticipated, tears spilled from my eyes and a gasp stuck in my throat. I couldn't do it. I couldn't take it. I put my head down, soft tears pouring forth uncontrollably.

For so many situations in life, someone has been there before and written a song about how it feels. Loretta Lynn made popular a song written by Lola

Jean Dillon, "When the Tingle Becomes a Chill." Sounds stupid, but it was dead on for me:

Sometimes at night when you're fast asleep,
I lie there alone in the darkness and weep.
So sorry and sad but that's part of the deal
When the tingle becomes a chill.
I'll swear by the breath in my body that's true
Ah. but a woman can't help the way that she feels
When the tingle becomes a chill . . .

Suddenly angry, JJ stepped back and, from the corner of my eye, I saw him start the swing of his open-faced right hand, which landed hard and solidly across my left shoulder and back, in what felt to be a full-force blow. My head snapped back and then forward. I fell over, my face almost planting itself into my plate. I tried to get up and get out. To my surprise, he let me by, and then grabbed the back of the chair where I had been sitting.

Nathan and Jamie had heard the hit and were now in the hall. I joined them to turn and watch their father destroy our dining room. He raised my chair over his head, blasting it into the center of the table. The beautiful wood split apart and the chair scattered everywhere, in what seemed like a million brown splinters. We cowered as we watched in disbelief. He picked up a second chair and beat it to pieces across the then-sagging table. Then the third chair. Anger spent now, he quit, throwing the last piece of a chair leg against the wall and storming out.

There was no way to describe the fear I could see in the liquid eyes of my children's faces. Maybe it was the perfect metaphor to our story. He used all the strength he had to shatter the table he knew I loved. He had done the same with our marriage. He had used every emotional tool possible to destroy the very thing he now insisted he wanted to keep.

That was it! I decided I had to leave. Emotionally, I had no other choice. I called my friend in Mobile, and told her I was taking her up on her offer of refuge for me and my children.

On Monday, I left everything behind but the clothes we had on and what I could pack in a couple of suitcases. It was hard, but I had no time to move any household items. Taking Jamie's pony was not an option. I thought he would be better off to stay in his big pasture. JJ would feed him and take care of him.

We arrived at the townhome with our small quantity of clothes and a huge amount of anxiety in our hearts.

After our arrival, I stayed inside most of the time. I was so afraid of him finding me. The children enjoyed the townhome complex's pool—it was a luxury for them—but I was forever vigilant that JJ would pop up from out of nowhere. My long-time friend Jean was there to support me, and my friend Sarah (with the apartment) were prepared, as much as I could prepare them, for what could happen when he found me. I hired an attorney and I filed for divorce.

I couldn't turn back now.

June brought another interesting dimension to my life. Sheryl, my beloved and pretty niece, came to visit for the summer, having just graduated from high school. We had all pitched in to send her a plane ticket for a summer visit to the family's Southern contingent. Though Sheryl was spending most of her time at my mom and dad's house, it came as no surprise that a local boy found her within a week. Her new boyfriend, Roy, was the eldest son of a very wealthy local businessman who owned Hill and Brooks Coffee Company.

She and I enjoyed meeting the Hill family. Their farm was hundreds of acres in Grand Bay, Alabama. I escaped one day and met Sheryl to ride a couple of the Hills' ranch horses. We rode for what seemed like miles across their property. It was Southern summer hot in Alabama. The golden mare I was riding was so beautiful. We were walking along the dirt road, with all of us having a great time, when, in an instant, my mare decided she wanted to roll in the thick sand of the dirt road. When she dropped to her knees, I jumped off and stood aside to look at that stupid horse, upside down on her saddle. She rolled back and forth on her back, then finally turned over, stood, and shook off like a wet dog. We all laughed. I tightened the saddle, got back on, and we continued the ride.

We talked a lot while riding. Later, both Roy Hill and Sheryl came to the apartment to see me. They were fascinated, and wanted to hear the horror stories of my marriage and impending divorce.

I called JJ that evening and told him I had filed for divorce. He went ballistic. He said he would kill me before he'd let me divorce him. He swore to me that I would not live to see the courtroom. I believed him.

He called everyone I knew, looking to find me and again threatening my mom, because he thought she would know where I was. For that reason, I did not even tell my own mother where I was staying.

Somehow—and I didn't know how—JJ found out my location. When he showed up, unannounced, I was upstairs sorting and arranging the children's room. My heart was almost pounding out of my chest, as I stood stone-still to listen. My roommate answered the door and JJ shoved his way in. He said, "I'm here to see that whore you've got living here." I called from upstairs for him to leave her alone. Sarah had to be terrified, but she started for the phone. He told her, "If you call the police, I'll cut her throat."

JJ bounded up the stairs. I made it to the top landing but he was faster. He caught me by the hair and dragged me back toward the stairs. He was yelling that he'd cut my throat if Sarah called the police.

He laughed. He said, "Do you know how quick I can kill you? I can cut your throat in two seconds and you will be in a puddle of blood before anyone can get here. You'll be dead. You are so stupid. No one can help you," he taunted.

Pushed ahead of him, I stood at the top of the steep stairs, his hand rolled tightly in the hair on the back of my head. As I took a step down, he grabbed harder and the pain covered my head. He grabbed tighter and slung my head to the right, blasting me against the wall. He lowered his voice, which was dripping with contempt: "Be careful now. You don't want to hurt yourself." I hit so hard, I almost fell. He was holding me solely by holding onto the hair on my head. I took maybe two more steps down.

This time it was harder. *BANG!* And again, the voice of mockery: "You need to be more careful. You might hurt yourself." My head was pounding before I could reach the bottom stair. He clinched again and used his leverage to force my head into the wall. "You are just so clumsy," he mock-chided me. "You need to work on that." He was enjoying inflicting this pain and fear. He had no empathy for me, the person he said he loved.

Sarah, at the stairs while running back toward the other room, bravely shouted: "I called the police."

He didn't seem to care. He dragged me past Sarah, into my downstairs bedroom. He threw me on the bed, pulled my pants off, and raped me. I was paralyzed with fear, and did not have the strength to fight him.

Soon, I could hear the police at the door. I heard Sarah let them in and tell them he was in the room with me. They knocked. They knocked harder. JJ finished, stood, and zipped his pants as I jumped up to try to get myself together.

Ashamed, I was trying to straighten my clothes and then just standing there, watching and listening to the exchange between him and the police, who were growing more impatient each second, banging harder yet again on the door.

JJ opened the bedroom door and walked into the dining room with the police. "What's the problem?" he asked insolently. Tossing a look and a pointed thumb back my way, he said, "I was just in there talking to my wife." They looked at me and could see my condition, all eyes sympathetic but assessing.

One of these uniformed officers said he wanted JJ to come with him outside to talk. He reached out and tried to grab him but JJ resisted. There was a scuffle that filled the small space around the dining table. I backed up as far as I could, but I still wanted to see. The three deputies all fought hard to subdue him. JJ twisted and turned, and they grappled to hold the viper. There was no holding him without exerting full force. I just stood there and watched in disbelief.

They handcuffed him and walked him outside. One came back in and took my report. Yes, he was my husband. Yes, I had filed for divorce. I had no idea what was said outside, but they let him go. We were married. I had no restraining order. He drove off without a single charge. We were amazed.

After hiding for weeks, I was at my wit's end. I decided to call Paul at work. After numerous tries, I finally got him on the phone one morning, because I really didn't want to leave a message. He answered in his usual business voice, but quickly lowered his tone when he realized it was me. He was okay but, he said, everything was crazy in his life, too. He asked where I was and I told him. He said he would try to come by and see me, when he could, but he thought they were following him everywhere.

"*They?* Who are they?" I asked him. "Why are you being followed?" I wanted to know what was going on. I was curious. I could tell he wasn't his usual self, which I really should have expected. The man had just lost his wife, and I didn't know how he felt. There are many unhappy couples, but that sure didn't mean one spouse wanted the other to suffer or die. I felt insensitive that I had called him during his own troubled time. But he was the only person I knew, outside of my own circle of friends and family, who could help me or advise me. He said he couldn't talk then, but he would come over to Sarah's as soon as he could to talk with me in person.

Paul showed up one morning soon after my call. He parked in front of the townhouse and called the phone. I answered and he said he was outside. I walked across the room, opened the door, and there he was in his new baby blue station wagon. When he got out of the car, he looked like a pale, whipped pup.

Inside, I tried to hug him, as much as a friend as anything else. Southerners always hug people who have suffered loss. It conveys concern and honest caring. It was not a sexual hug in any way. But what I felt was a bundle of nerves. His body felt rangy and tight, fully conveying the tension he was under.

Sarah was with me, and she wanted to hear what was happening to him. Paul sat cross-legged on the floor in front of us, his head down in either sadness or defeat, and maybe both. He shook his head and picked at the carpet with his fingers. He talked without looking up.

Paul said he had to be real careful, because they were following him—he just knew it. He was adamant that they were trying to pin the murder on him in some way. He discussed timelines and distances and said they were actually trying to find a way he could have left his family long enough to drive home, murder his wife, and get back without being detected.

The whole thing was now developing into a scary, depressing situation. I was confused and couldn't understand why he was still under this kind of scrutiny, but I also knew I had no experience dealing with crime or criminal behavior. I had never received so much as a parking ticket, so this was out of my league altogether. What I did know was I felt sorry for this man, and I did not believe he had anything to do with his wife's death. He had been so good to me. No one could have convinced me that he had hurt the mother of his children. In none of the many stories he had told me, he had never shared any information that led me to see him as either the aggressor, or that he had retaliated with force against her. According to his tales, she had been a spitfire hellion, spun up on phenobarbital, and would stop at nothing when angry.

We eventually got around to talking about me and JJ. Sarah was pretty animated in reliving her recent contact with my husband. Paul seemed shocked at the way JJ had reacted to my leaving him. I had shared my problems with Paul in the past, but I had never given him the gory details.

Paul was concerned for me, and we both recognized it was not fair for Sarah to have to endure this kind of fear in her home. I acknowledged I couldn't stay there while awaiting my divorce court date. Paul said he sure wished I was not going through this separation at the same time he was dealing with the loss of his wife. He was not in a position to help me; he had the weight of the world on his shoulders.

Everyone would want to make a connection between the two, I realized, but there really was none. My marriage to JJ had been bad for years and I wanted out, but there had been no agreed-to plan to leave when I did. I had to leave—I couldn't take it anymore. No matter what was happening in Paul's life, my decisions were my own, and not based on anything other than the fact that my marriage to JJ was beyond repair. Paul soon left the apartment, but from that time onward, he would call me just to see how I was doing. I started making arrangements to leave Mobile.

I tried to think of the most remote location I could find and afford—one where I could hide for a while. I gathered up my children, crossed Mobile Bay heading east, and checked into an out-of-the-way motel in Malbis. Malbis was a Greek Orthodox settlement with a lovely church, plantation, monastery, and motel which boasted a Greek restaurant. A lot of truckers knew the place, but it was not somewhere we had ever gone, or a place where JJ would think to look for me.

I requested a room in the very back of the motel, where my car would not be seen by passing traffic. There was a door that opened to the courtyard, filled with flowers and a big swimming pool. Nathan and Jamie were happy as long as they had a pool to enjoy, while I tried to figure out how to get through the next two months before my court date.

No matter how inexpensive the place was, motel bills added up. A friend offered up a condo in Destin for my use. It was empty, and they were not going down to use it for the summer, so they loaned it to me. It was a Godsend. I thanked them then and I thank them again now for saving my life. It was as if my children and I were on vacation in Destin. We had a minimal amount of money, but I felt safe. I told no one where I was staying, not even my mom. I would not run the risk of JJ finding me again.

In mid-August, I had to return to Mobile. I met Sheryl at the townhouse, and I told her all about my problems with JJ. I also told her about Paul. She hadn't met him and I really wanted Paul to meet my beautiful niece. I told Paul all about her and he said he was ready to get out of the house. There was no reason he could not take me and Sheryl to dinner. He said he would bring his son, Mark, so Sheryl would have someone her age to talk with. We all went to the Grand Hotel, at Point Clear, where the food was known to be fabulous.

We did just that. It was fun. Mark was sophisticated and polished. Sheryl was tall, beautiful, and adorable. She certainly had not been exposed to all the finer things of life, so both of us were like school girls enjoying the special place and attention. We had a lovely evening. Neither Sheryl nor Mark seemed interested in starting a friendship after that evening.

The cat was now out of the bag, since we had been seen out in public together. So we thought it would be okay for Paul and I to spend more time together. I didn't like the situation for either of us, but I didn't create his crisis and he did not create mine.

He picked me up one morning, and I just rode with him for the day. He checked on his stores while I waited in the car. We ended up at the Colonel Dixie store located right in front of his home office. We were sitting in a booth, waiting on our food, when I saw JJ's car fly past. JJ was perusing the lot and saw us sitting there. I told Paul that JJ had just parked and was coming in. Paul immediately stood up, grabbed my hand, and led me behind the counter, through the employee door, and through the kitchen. We exited the back door and got into his car. We quickly exited the parking lot. Looking behind, I could see JJ just entering the door on the opposite side.

We narrowly escaped a confrontation, with an outcome that could not have been anything but bad. As we left, Paul said he had no intention of trying to deal with JJ or act like an idiot school kid. He said he had had both his elbows and arms broken, where they were pinned back together after accidents in his life. He was not stupid enough to fight a young, somewhat insane, disgruntled husband. I was glad he had the presence of mind to leave and take me with him.

Chapter 25
Airmont

663 Montcliff Drive, Airmont Subdivision.
Photo taken by me after the house had sat empty for over a year.

N
ews of our mid-August evening out with Mark and Sheryl spread like wildfire in our community. I didn't like that, for either of us. But, as far as I was concerned, gossip was just that—gossip.

One of the days we were out together, Paul asked if I would I mind going by his home to pick up something (I cannot remember what). We drove into his neighborhood, where straight ahead was a fabulous two-story Georgian colonial. On the right was the Leverett home, with well over an acre of manicured yard, which was dappled with huge oak trees. The big horse-shoe drive circled to the front door, and another circle extended to the back entrance. The house was built in a U-shaped pattern that left room for a covered patio and a fountain in the center of the courtyard. In the back was a very large, open carport that could easily accommodate two cars side by side. It was a drive-through, and the driveway continued on down the hill and back into the street. It was an easy family entrance to the back door, with no need to turn around. On the right side of the carport was a complete efficiency apartment for a maid or caretaker. I didn't want to go in, and I told Paul I preferred to wait for him in the car. He insisted I come in to see the house. I felt very uncomfortable being there.

From the carport entrance, you entered the laundry room, passed a half-bath, and then came to the kitchen with a breakfast table. The scale of the place astonished me. The entry from the back door to the opposite end of the kitchen must have been seventy to eighty feet. As soon as you entered, the kitchen cabinets started running the entire length of that room. I had never seen so many cabinets. *This place must to have been decorated by someone on LSD*, was my first thought. I was trying to be nice, but I said something to the tune of, "Whoa."

Envision a long room, ceilings twelve-feet high, with brightly painted, apple-green cabinets, and a painted white decorative piece of picture molding in the center of each door. The counters were white-gold hard Formica on one side. The wallpaper depicted a white trellis with huge, bright-green leafy vines, gigantic red strawberries, and big yellow and blue flowers, all in primary colors.

I walked slowly past the little half-bath, and I saw bright, sunny yellow towels with green frog appliqués on each one. As I passed the bath, I was standing in the kitchen, looking at an iron-legged breakfast table painted in apple-green and covered by a glass top. It was a patio table recruited to serve as the kitchen's focal point. *What a hoot!!* The mansion was wild. I had to giggle a little to myself.

As we continued, off to the right of the kitchen was a lovely study. It contained a big dark-pine Ethan Allen roll-top desk, a wall of bookshelves, and lower cabinets. The seating area was lost, because on all four walls, all you saw were huge deer heads, mounted from the shoulders up, stuffed fish, wildlife photos, and ducks on plaques. In the far corner was a basket-type arrangement, with duck heads hanging out, lantern wicks, and marsh grass overflowing from the container. "Unusual" may have been a better word to describe the place, instead of "plain old weird." The walls were a deep, dark, federal blue. I was thinking that it could double as a taxidermy showroom.

The study adjoined the breakfast room and kitchen.
Jamie envisioned the poor deer watching us eat venison for dinner.

Another large open doorframe allowed you to enter an oversized formal dining room, with wainscoting, and more bold blue and white floral wallpaper blasting your senses. A ten-foot, built-in china hutch was filled with fabulous crystal and china. Next to the hutch was a door that lead to an upstairs room—Paul said it was Mark's bedroom.

We continued from the dining room into the biggest, most formal living room I had ever seen. Being a poor girl, the sheer size of the room was astounding to me. The living room had a crystal chandelier, at least five feet across, a white carved marble fireplace, two nine-foot, blue-and-white Sheridan sofas, and two matching, high-back velvet chairs that sat in front of the bay window, with an antique table in the middle.

A figurine caught my eye—porcelain blue birds on brown twigs, with a lovely little nest and tiny blue eggs. The living room had an ornate European-style desk, china cabinet, and an étagère with shelves filled with carefully chosen figurines. The impact was stunning. I found the room both tasteful and beautiful.

We then stepped into the grand foyer. It was almost a pie shape from the front double-doors and sidelights. My vantage point was from the family entrance, not the front doors. The foyer floor was covered with 20" black and white checker-board tiles. A big burgundy and gold antique Chinese rug was in the center, with a tea table directly under an enormous chandelier. A burled-wood Bombay chest sat against the wall with two upholstered chairs. An antique grandfather clock ticked loudly as we walked through. A sideboard with an ornate, gold-framed mirror was on the left, and the opposite wall had a period antique high boy. The walls were covered with a pale green and white silk floral pattern, with a muted stripe of flat, then shiny, cream color. Cream-colored opaque silk drapes were pulled, but you could see the courtyard as we walked through. From the front door, it was amazing.

We were now going to enter the bedroom side of the house. There were no halls. From the foyer, through double doors was a den with a fireplace and a huge brass chandelier. The room was filled with heavy Ethan Allen pine furniture with red upholstery and again a taxidermy work of art—an 800-pound elk that dominated the room. The den must have been 25 x 50 feet.

At the far end of the den were two doors that opened directly into children's rooms, each with their own baths, and each with perfectly coordinated wallpaper, bedspreads, and drapes. Even the shower curtains were in the wallpaper-matching pattern. It was obvious that no money had been spared when the decorator was selecting the bold and colorful décor.

Paul reached over and took my hand as we walked into his bedroom, which was where his wife had been murdered. Though the room was fully furnished and put back together, it felt cold and empty. There were light blue walls, big chairs, and two dressers, side-by-side, all in the same Ethan Allen dark pine. I just stood there and looked around, trying to make sense of it all—trying to make a connection between what I was seeing and the man and woman who had shared this room. A little out of place was what looked to be a simple, handmade, contemporary bookcase headboard backing the king-sized bed. The headboard held reading materials sitting in a stack.

Over the bed was the ugliest brown and beige picture of oversized ducks. The ducks looked like they had been on steroids. A diminutive lady's chaise lounge sat in front of the big bay window. The sheer draperies were pulled, but the heavy beige draperies were open. They were so heavy they looked as if they were framing a stage instead of a home window. The bath was just one large room, all in white; white tile, white marble, white toilet, white sinks, white plantation shutters to let in a little light, and gorgeous, real gold fixtures like none I had ever seen.

I was not sure why he wanted me to see the closet, but that was next. It was as big as a bedroom, and yet another door within the closet opened to a very large, cedar-lined closet. The closet smelled of cedar and dust. It was all stuffed to the ceiling with clothes, shoes, boxes, and more stuff.

I really didn't have much to say, because I didn't know what to say. It was interesting, but it was not a welcoming house. The house possessed this bigger-than-life, cold, austere feeling. Everything was oversized and dramatic. I was uncomfortable and ready to leave. We walked back into the kitchen.

Paul told me the house had been pretty much the same before Liz's death, though they had changed some things in the bedroom, like the carpet and mattress, etc. He said they had kept the house closed while the investigation went on, though he didn't feel the police had done a very thorough job. He said that when he was finally allowed back in the home, there were two wine glasses still sitting in the kitchen that had not been fingerprinted. He seemed puzzled by who could have shared those drinks the last day of Elizabeth's life. "No matter," he said. "Come see the rest of the house."

Like a little kid, he said, "There is one more thing I want to show you." In the foyer was an elevator door. We got into the small cubicle and he closed the door, then the sliding metal shield, and pressed "2." The house had originally been built by a very wealthy old lady confined to a wheel chair. That was why there were no halls, just big rooms flowing openly from one to the next.

The elevator stopped with a jolt. The door was opened and we stepped into a boy's bedroom. It was absolutely atrocious: brown and black leopard print wallpaper, twin beds with fuzzy animal print spreads, black, brown, and beige shag carpet, and a bathroom with a black toilet, sink, and shower.

A door opened onto a small balcony that overlooked the courtyard, and an outside staircase headed up and around the outside wall. I asked Paul, "Where do the stairs go?" He led me back to the elevator. He closed the door and the slide and then pressed "R." "What is 'R?" I asked? He said it was the roof. The thing started its upward motion and then came to a thudding stop! The bang overhead scared the crap out of me and I jumped. He laughed. He said it was the cap or roof on the elevator lifting up as we exited the house to the rooftop.

We walked out onto a wrought-iron edged, flat observation deck. It was covered in green astro-turf and, to me, looked like a helicopter pad. Paul said the old lady came up here every afternoon to have her martini cocktail before dinner. It was one of the highest points in the city, and it afforded a great view of Mobile. I stood there looking out over the tree tops and turned back and saw the elevator standing in the center. When the elevator returned, the roof cap that sat on top would lower back into place, covering the elevator shaft.

"I bet your kids loved this thing," I said. He then told me that he had had to unplug the power to it when they first moved in, because his children were charging admission to take the elevator tour. It must have been in their blood—I had no doubt that Paul would sire a bunch of entrepreneurs.

We finally pulled away, and I could tell Paul had really wanted me to see where he lived. I had mixed feelings about my first glimpse into his world, and I felt my reaction was probably different than what he expected. The house was certainly impressive, and it was beautifully furnished, but it didn't feel like a home to me. It felt more like a cold museum.

You can see the door open to Mark's room upstairs and the flat roof for the elevator to pop up. Unfortunately, the photo was taken after the house had been empty for a while. It was once lovely, with barrels of blooming flowers, hanging floral baskets, and a flowing fountain. The patio had a full outdoor kitchen and built-in gas grill, a novelty at the time.

Chapter 26
The Divorce

My "little sister" Sheryl and Roy Hill. Dad is in the background.

I t was about then that I started receiving harassing phone calls. They were all from the same woman. She sounded Southern, maybe 30 to 50 years old. She also sounded as if her voice was filled with venom. She would tell me I was "in over my head," then hang up. She would also say I had better "stay away from Paul Leverett." The calls were coming over and over, and some were more menacing and angry, and included profanity-laden name-calling.

I contacted the police and the phone company, and had my number changed. Within thirty minutes of being assigned a new phone number, though, the phone rang. I thought it was the phone company, because I had not called anyone to tell them the new number. It was the same woman. This time she said, "You can change your number as many times as you want, but I will have the new one within ten minutes." I hung up without saying a word.

I discussed the calls with Paul. I described the caller, the tone, and the messages. Paul immediately guessed it was his sister-in-law. She worked for a mortgage lending company and had access to a lot of information.

I was so angry and fed up, I demanded that Paul do something to stop the calls. This woman was harassing me, scaring my children, and keeping me awake at night. I had never known Paul's wife. If her sister had a beef, it should be with Paul, not with me. I did not feel I should have to put up with the abuse, and I wasn't going to stop seeing the only person trying to help me. I was sorry for the woman's loss, but I felt she was sorely misguided in directing her anger at me.

I told Paul I wanted to confront her. I wanted to tell her that I was sorry for her loss, but she should leave me out of it. Paul, very reluctantly, agreed to take me to her place of business. As it turned out, the woman's office was only a couple of blocks from the town home where I was living. Paul and I walked in together, and Paul asked by name for his sister-in-law. We were shown to her office and entered her doorway.

As soon as she recognized Paul, she looked like someone had just pissed on the Pope's foot. My first impression was that she looked nothing like her beautiful sister. After being introduced to me, she stood from behind her desk and, as they say, "If looks could kill." Then he said something like, "Phyllis wanted to meet you and talk with you. She would like you to stop calling her home—"

The woman went berserk, going from zero to 100 in two seconds. Eyes glaring, she started yelling, "Paul Leverett, how dare you! You get out of here. Get out!" Paul turned and walked out. He actually left me standing there and I watched as this out-of-control woman screamed at him through the business lobby and out the door. I then walked out slowly and calmly. I looked around at the other people witnessing her behavior—the woman was acting like a lunatic. I was shaking my head. I really couldn't believe she would do this in a place of business. Paul was waiting in the car. "The woman is nuts!" I said to him when I quietly got into the seat.

He said, "Yes, and you need to stay away from her." I had no intention of bothering the woman. I just wanted *her* to leave me alone.

They say there is safety in numbers. I called my friends and family. Sheryl brought her new boyfriend Roy over to my place to watch TV and have dinner. My girlfriend Jean, from Grand Bay, came up to stay the day with me. Jean was known for "packing heat." When she came in and showed me the .38 she had in her purse, she looked at me and said, "If JJ breaks in while I'm here, I'll kill him." We all laughed a little, but we couldn't really imagine that would take place. Boy, were we wrong. The friendly scene—all of us sitting in the living room around the boob tube—changed in seconds. JJ was at the door. I yelled for someone to call the police. He was banging away.

Jean was sitting deep in a chair directly opposite the entry. She took out her gun and pointed the barrel directly at the door. Her arm was resting on the arm of the chair, as she sat there, stone-still, except for a little tremor in her gun hand. Jean said flatly, "Let him in."

I don't know how they got there so fast, but the cops, with lights flashing, pulled up in front. I opened the door and jumped back. Roy did an in-flight maneuver from one side of the room to the other. He and Sheryl were now hiding behind the couch, peeking over the back.

"Come on in, JJ. I've been waiting on you," Jean said sarcastically. JJ, about to walk in, looked right at that barrel. In a flash, he jumped back outside and behind the door, just as the police walked up. The police wanted to know what was going on—they were standing on the stoop with JJ. JJ's head was now peeping around the door, using the wall as a shield. Jean used this soft, ominous voice, imploring him to, "Come on in." Jean told the police, "The man keeps breaking in and it has to stop."

With the police standing there, Jean pleaded sarcastically, "JJ, come on in, please. Just take one more step inside the door." The police closed the door and asked JJ to leave. We gave the police a report. They let him go. They did nothing—just told him to stay away from me. They said he really hadn't done anything illegal, and they couldn't arrest him for just knocking on my door. They left.

Within the next few days, my Grand Prix was taken from in front of the town home. JJ had come and gotten it sometime during the night. Now I had no car. I called my mom and Paul. Paul went over to Trail Pontiac and purchased a 1974 Bonneville, two-tone brown, with brown velour seats. Mom said she gave Paul $2,500 to purchase the car for me. No one wanted to try to get my car back from JJ. From a strictly legal standpoint, he didn't steal it, since both our names were on the title as co-owners. Possession was all he needed. It was okay. The old Bonneville was just fine for me, even though the Grand Prix had been his gift to me. At that point, I was happy to have any type of transportation.

Each day passed and I felt like a walking dead woman with a target on my back. I had resigned myself to the fact that JJ would most likely kill me.

He was right. He could do it before anyone could stop him.

Paul called me and told me he was sending a friend of his, a body guard, to watch my home. I couldn't believe it, but within an hour, a licensed, armed guard was standing at my door. The agency kept a man there day and night. It was the strangest damned thing to live under these conditions—Mobile's law enforcement telling me that until he actually did something to me, they could do nothing.

I had left my home, but the violence moved with me. I remembered my mom's life. I seemed destined to relive it.

My roommate Sarah was so tolerant and brave. She had no children and was living in a parallel universe that featured her, at the center, in some kind of a time warp. She was pretty, in a sultry sort of way. That's why I call her Sarah for the purpose of my story. I did have one problem with her—she smoked. I was stressed to the max, so Sarah introduced me to the cocktail hour, Taaka Vodka, and orange juice. I was trying to keep up some semblance of a normal lifestyle for my children, but I was a robot. I got up each morning, made coffee for myself, and as always, prepared breakfast for my children.

Sarah arrived home each morning about the time we started our day. At the small breakfast table, at about 7 a.m., she would be drinking coffee, smoking, inhaling deeply, and exhaling in long, blowing sighs. The smoke left her mouth very slowly, and swirls floated gently up around her face, but it didn't seem to bother her. Her eyes were dark, and it was hard to tell what she was thinking as she just sat there, smoking and watching. I leaned over, offering her another coffee refill. As I awaited her permission to refill her cup, Sarah looked at me and quietly said, "You are disgustingly domestic."

I have never forgotten her words. I guess I *was* disgustingly domestic. It kept me busy. It gave me purpose.

The divorce court date finally arrived. JJ's words of warning that I would not live to see the courtroom had not been forgotten. My body guard, Mike, an ex-Special Forces guy, came in to take me. He was in a suit and had a "potato" under his arm. I couldn't believe it, but I needed an armed bodyguard to get me safely to court. I prayed to myself, "God, I hope he's good."

I walked into a full courtroom. My attorney was waiting and pulled me into a side room to talk for a moment. He told me all would be fine—not to worry.

When it was time, we walked back in. I saw Mom, Dad, my niece Sheryl, Roy, and my friend Jean seated in the audience. My bodyguard was standing just behind me, watching. JJ was on the other side, staring down Mike, who was carefully assessing him. You could see in his eyes he thought he might be a boyfriend. JJ recognized Mike immediately as an adversary. I looked at JJ across the room. It just couldn't be—JJ was standing there, holding a black Bible.

The courtroom was called to order. We stood. The judge, a big, handsome African-American man looking absolutely regal, walked in. Our case was the first he called. My attorney, Al Seals, read my allegations and request for divorce. Adultery, abuse, and violence were stated as my grounds for my request. It was now JJ's turn to speak. He did not have an attorney. I do not have the transcript for that day, so I will paraphrase exactly what I remember him saying.

Conspicuously holding his Bible, JJ said, "Your Honor, I want to request that you do not grant my wife a divorce. I have loved this woman more than any man has ever had a right to love a woman. I want her to come back home, and for us to enter into counseling, so we can save our marriage." The judge asked him about allegations of violence against me. I watched everyone in the courtroom almost gasp in disbelief as JJ asked the black judge. "Your Honor, you know Mohammed Ali?" He got no response. "Mohammed has 18-inch arms, and my arms are bigger around than his. Just take a look at her. If I had beaten that woman, she wouldn't look like she does today." I was both astonished and embarrassed for him.

I saw a flash of something in the judge's eyes. The judge asked again for clarification, "Did you say, before this court, that you have not been violent nor committed adultery while married to this woman?" JJ looked straight at him and answered, "Your Honor . . . Look . . . I married the girl when she was sixteen because she was pregnant."

I cringed. I didn't want this said in front of Sheryl, Roy, and my parents. I was so embarrassed. I wanted to die. I put my head down as my body began to shiver.

The judge stopped him. "Mr. JJ, you have just stood here and said you love this woman as no man should ever love a woman. And now, you stand here, in open court, and you slander her name." The judge was visibly angry, and he hit his gavel hard against the desk. The scene continued until he said he would be granting my divorce as requested.

The settlement terms were set forth in open court: I got the home, and I could live there until our youngest child reached the age of nineteen. JJ would be responsible for the house payments. I got the car (my Grand Prix), and JJ got the truck. JJ would contribute $25 per week, per child, as child support. I got custody of the children, but JJ was granted unsupervised weekend visits, every other week and on holidays.

JJ was furious and began making threats. The judge called for the bailiff and security to escort him from the courtroom.

Mike and I went out the door and down the back way. We exited the courthouse and got into the car. As soon as we pulled out of our parking space, we saw JJ whipping around the parking lot, coming toward us. He was in my Grand Prix, driving like a maniac, weaving through the parking lot to get to us.

Mike made me get down on the car floor. I wish this had been on video, because we left the court house at breakneck speed, hitting curbs, slamming on brakes, making hard turns, and flying through downtown Mobile. Mike was driving like a man in a movie car chase. He'd yell, "stay down," and he'd slam on the brakes and make a wild turn, and then floor the gas pedal. It felt like we were breaking the sound barrier through the center of Mobile. I knew we were moving at very dangerous speeds. I didn't know where Mike picked up the interstate, but within a short time we were doing 100-plus miles per hour, headed west. We exited onto Dauphin Island Parkway, with Mike pulling in behind a Ramada Inn.

It was there that I stayed in hiding for the next few days until I felt it safe to go home. My hope was that JJ would calm down once he accepted the divorce as a done deal. *Giving him some time and space should help*, I thought.

Our divorce was to be final on September 8, 1980.

As for the divorce decree, the joke was on me. I knew there was no way I could go back and live in our home. It was out in the country and thus too isolated. I would be alone there and at JJ's mercy any time he wanted to show up. Plus, I knew he would never walk away from that house without a fight. All

I wanted was to find a job in Mobile, closer to town, so I could work and take care of myself and my children.

Fifty dollars a week from child support was not going to be enough to live on, and that was if he actually paid the support. At least I had a car now. I wasn't about to try and get my Grand Prix back. Everything the judge had given me was impossible to actually enforce. The fact that JJ was granted visitation every other weekend and holidays amazed me. No one in authority, including, it seems, the judge, seemed to understand the kind of violence JJ was capable of committing.

>—!—‹›—O—‹›—!—‹

We did start talking again, by phone, a couple of weeks after the divorce had become final. He did seem to calm down and accept the situation. When we talked, he was civil and asked me questions about handling the bills and checking account that he had never had to worry about before. I put it off as long as I could, but he was demanding his right to see his children. Jamie wanted to go see her pony, and Nathan wanted to see his dad. I did not want him to come anywhere near my home, so I agreed to drop them off at his residence. He swore he was fine and he just needed for me to show him where things were. He pleaded for help, and he promised to be civil for the sake of the children. I was still afraid to go alone.

Sheryl and I drove out to his house with the children. I didn't think he would do anything in front of a witness. At first, JJ was nice. I had to go in to look at the bills and tell him what to pay and where to send each payment. Sheryl was with Nathan and Jamie.

As soon as they were out of earshot, he started badgering me, "Look, if you are going to give that shit away, then why can't you give it to me?" He grabbed me and dragged me toward the bedroom. He pushed me in, and that was when Sheryl came running down the hall. He told her to go away. Sheryl would not leave. No matter what he said, she just stood in the hall and kept telling him she would not leave and he should let me go. Somehow, because of Sheryl, I managed to get out of the bedroom and into the car. I wanted the kids to get into the car, too, but he would not let them.

JJ and the children were now standing beside the car. I had the window on the driver's side rolled down only about seven or eight inches, trying to talk to him without being exposed to him. I was trying to calm him down so he would let the children get into the car. All at once, he became angry. In a split-second, he reached into the car, through the half-rolled-down window, and grabbed me by my terry cloth v-neck sweat shirt, his hand at my chest, his fingers digging deep into my skin. He yanked me up and against the window, tearing my shirt to shreds. My bra also broke, and both shirt and bra were hanging off my body. He kept pulling and banging me hard against the window. He attacked me with such force and quickness, we were all stunned.

My little Jamie ran and jumped on her daddy's back with no thought for her own safety, screaming for him to stop. Jamie was beating him with her little fists, crying and yelling for JJ to stop. Nathan was paralyzed in fear, as he watched his mom being attacked. At twelve years old, he knew he couldn't fight his dad. A twelve-year-old boy challenging that man would have been uttering a death wish. Sheryl was screaming "stop" and was telling me to back the car up. I left as soon as he let me go. My chest was throbbing. My clothes were in pieces in my hand. Sheryl was so afraid. "I think I wet my pants," she whispered. It was horrible. We ran for our lives. I would call the police and see if they would help me get my children.

On May 25, 2011, while working on this part of my story, I wrote an email to Sheryl to tell her I was writing a book. On June 14, I asked Sheryl if she would write what she remembered of the incidents—the one in my apartment and the one that occurred at our home at Union Church. Sheryl now lives in Washington State, but we communicate often.

I was bowled over and so touched by her reply email. I was also sorry I had put her in such jeopardy. I will include the statement from her memory. It was the first time she talked of it, or wrote of it, and it has not been edited in any way. We did not discuss the events that we remembered. Here is what she wrote on June 15, 2011:

"I don't know if you got this email from May 25th. I would be glad to write down what I remember for you, right now. Some of the images seem as clear to me as if they happened yesterday. Other parts are just missing from my memory, as if it was all a bad movie that just suddenly changed scenes.

"The day you had to take the kids out to him at his house in Grand Bay, you asked me to go because you didn't think JJ would try anything violent in front of me. Wrong! I don't remember how he got you in the house, but I followed along until he took you in the bedroom. Then I just pressed myself against the wall outside the door. I don't think he knew I was there, because he didn't bother to shut the door. I peeked through the door a few times & he had you pinned against the wall talking in such a low voice I couldn't make out exactly what he was saying.

"Even without hearing his threats, I was petrified just by the intensity of his stare & body language. His muscles & veins were pumped up, bulging along the side of his neck. I didn't know if he was going to rape you or just beat you up, but he had a crazy look on his face that made me think he was going to do one or the other. It was clear to me what he was saying was very scary & I was terrified that you were trapped. I felt so helpless... too scared to run, call the police or anything else.

"I remember thinking I needed to do something, but I couldn't move. I felt bad for not going for help, but I was also afraid to leave you in there. In a way, I guess it was good that I stayed put. Who knows, maybe it would have escalated if he knew the police were coming & none of us would be here today. I truly believe he was capable of killing us all. Even now, 30 years later, my hands are shaking as I am typing this! As I was growing up, Uncle JJ had always been my idol of what a husband & father should look & act like. I thought he was handsome, kind & charming. I secretly wanted to marry someone just like him one day. All of those childish naiveties were forever changed in that instant.

"I don't know how you talked your way out of that bedroom, but the next thing I remember is being in the car. That's when he exploded in a fit of rage & ripped everything you were wearing completely in two . . . necklace, shirt, & even your bra! Somehow, you managed to drive that car away & I felt like we had escaped with our lives. I believe this was the first time I really saw his mean & ugly side. I really can't recall much about the apartment incident other than what you said. I don't know how he got in, but (Jean) whipped that gun out, pointed it straight at him & ordered him to leave. I remember being shocked & scared. I know she was scared too, because her hands were shaking. I think he believed that she would shoot him because he left quickly after that.

"I wish I could remember more details & just what he said. It was something threatening, though, like you'll be sorry for this & I think he called her a bitch, along with some other choice words. There was another time that he came there too, but I don't think he got in . . . He was outside your window & showed you a bullet with your name engraved on it . . . he was so sick."

>−•◆•−O−•◆•−<

It was Monday before I could get the sheriff to go with me to get my children back. Their position was that he had a right to visitation. I rode out there in the sheriff's car, but they were not home. The children later told me they had spent the day in an apartment in Pascagoula, where they were left alone while he worked. Without a phone or food, both were scared to death.

Jamie refused to eat, so JJ dropped her off in front of my apartment the next day. Nathan stayed for a few more days. There seemed to be nothing I could do because the judge had given JJ visiting rights. I'd have to take him back to court if I wanted to try to prove he shouldn't be allowed visitation.

JJ told Nathan to catch the school bus after he left to go to work. Nathan said he started to go to school, then turned around and went back to the house. He got the keys to his dad's truck, and at twelve-years-old, he drove the Toyota pick-up about 20 miles into Mobile during the morning traffic. He came to my apartment and knocked on the door like it was a normal thing. I was so happy to see him.

I was blown away by the fact he had taken his dad's truck to come home to me. I had to make sure he understood that he had risked his life doing such a thing. However, I was so glad he was with me and safe—I had a hard time being tough on him. His dad was playing with his head—I knew that—but Nathan was only beginning to feel the power of manipulation his dad would use on him. Nathan didn't like it, but I made him call his dad at work and tell him he had taken the truck. He didn't deserve the call, but it was for Nathan's sake, not his dad's, that I insisted on it.

Chapter 27
Another Knot

I was at wit's end trying to deal with the man from whom I was granted a divorce. My anguish was compounded by the fact that I cared deeply for a man who had lost his wife under horrible and questionable circumstances. My assessment was that because he and his wife had experienced terrible problems, he was now under suspicion that was unfounded, but the suspicion would soon pass. I believed Paul with all my heart. A man who had been so good to me I could not suspect of any involvement in such an unspeakable act.

Then again, I thought of the inhumane and humiliating things that my husband had done to me. If people only knew what I had suffered at his hands, I would probably be a suspect if something happened to him. I would never have willingly hurt my husband. I never tried to hurt him. Nor had I tried to retaliate against him. I had just tried to find some peace—something that would make me feel like a woman who was loved and appreciated. It seemed that everything I had been taught—the very beliefs that had been instilled in me—had not worked. No matter how badly you want it, it takes two to make a marriage work.

I had tried to climb out of the family life I had as a child. I had wanted better for my children. I had employed all the techniques that I thought were supposed to secure a happy family. My attempts at being a good wife, a good mom, and a good Christian hadn't given me the life I had expected. After ten years, I had given up.

When I was young, I obviously missed that critical lesson on making the right choice when selecting a life-mate. As Grandma would say, "No matter how long you stir it, you can't make chicken salad out of chicken shit."

Paul needed to talk to me, or so he said. He picked me up and took me on a drive into the country. We made some stops to drop off some of his homemade wine to old friends. He loved to take gifts to those who made it possible for him to hunt and enjoy the great outdoors that he loved so much. Depending on the perspective, Paul either wooed the people who had things he wanted, using gifts and attention, or the way I chose to see it, he loved and respected those people. They had a different way of life, and some were blessed with land handed down to them by their families.

Yes, he wanted the use of their land, but he was always thinking of them. He loved surprising them with a fresh, hot bucket of fried chicken, dove prepared with his secret recipe, or sun perch, fried crisp. I felt the good in him by watching the eyes of the people who interacted with him. His was a personality that could fill a room, or be easily singled out on a crowded field. I watched him walk up to the door and present his thoughtful gifts. I got to see, first-hand, the appreciation in those country folk's eyes. I respected that, and nothing but love and admiration filled my heart for the man.

On a beautiful September day, we ended up in a pecan orchard where a food plot had been seeded. Sitting on the blue blanket, I realized how much I loved being in the country. The sun was shining brightly and the cloudless sky was blue. We finally had a moment to relax and lie side-by-side, looking up through the trees. The shade offered a soothing reprieve from the sun. The leaves were blowing slightly overhead, the rays filtering through in flickering beats, brilliant, then blinding. I watched for the wind to change as diamonds of light quickly disappeared into dark, shaded spots. It was a God-made kaleidoscope of sparkling beauty. Here in the orchard, we were just a man and a woman, enjoying a heavenly day and the mutual comfort of our connection. We made love on the blanket, under the tree-canopy of "daylight diamonds" flickering overhead.

Lying next to me, he told me he was up against a situation he did not know how to handle. He was also very concerned that somehow JJ would make good on his threats against me. He told me he could not continue to cover the cost of providing me 24-hour protection. I knew it had to be outrageously expensive.

He also addressed another issue of great importance: Lee, his precious, youngest child, was staying with relatives whom he felt would do anything to destroy his relationship with her. He wanted her home with him, but he had to work. He said his boys were old enough to care for themselves, as long as he financially supported them through school. Lee was a different matter. He said he needed my help. He said he loved me, and no matter what anyone said, he swore to me he had not harmed his wife.

I listened closely to everything he said. He was confident that the truth would come out eventually, and all would be okay. Again, he reassured me, saying it might take some time, and he asked me to be patient. He said he felt sure he could protect me, and I would be safe, if I would marry him. "He won't bother you if you are in my house," he promised.

Marry him? Did he say marry him? I had just been divorced. I was thinking: *I can't marry him with all this craziness going on.* I asked him how we could possibly do this. He told me that people could talk all they wanted to, but since he hadn't done anything wrong, they would eventually figure it out. I believed him—I desperately wanted, and needed, to believe him.

I told Paul that I had run away from home to enter into my first marriage, and I would never do that again. I refused to run or hide. So I would not marry him unless he could marry me in a real wedding, with the blessings of his family members. Nor, I said, would I live in his house until we were married. I would not allow my children to see me living with a man without our being married first. Surprisingly, he agreed to all my conditions.

My divorce decree had granted me the house, my Grand Prix, and child support. What would I do about pursuing these things which rightfully belonged to me? Paul told me that I would not need anything from JJ. He advised me to just give JJ our house. I told him I couldn't—it was half mine. How could I walk away from the divorce with nothing?

Paul told me he would give me half of all he had if I would marry him. He said he did not want any more trouble with anyone, and if I married him, I would never need anything that I had left behind. He said he loved me, and then added, "My home is your home—*mi casa es su casa*." Because of this promise, I did eventually sign a Quit Claim Deed and gave up all rights to the home JJ and I co-owned.

I told Paul, I did not want to live in his house, or have anything to do with a house that he had shared with Liz—not now, not ever. The house had bad vibes, and I did not feel comfortable there. Then he made me this promise, "If you are not happy with the house after living there for six months, I will sell it, and we will buy a house somewhere else."

"Are you sure?" I asked him.

If I was not happy then, he again promised me, we would move.

I felt I could live with that condition. He seemed happy that I had been appeased. We now had the job of meeting each other's families, and making sure our marrying was something they could understand, or try to understand. I knew he was going to have a much tougher job than I.

I had already met Lee and Mark, Paul's youngest children, at their home. I had first met Mark in August, when we had all gone out together. He was a big guy with a sweet face and a contagious smile. Lee had the bluest eyes, a peaches and cream complexion, and thick, luxurious, light brown hair—all window dressing for a very precocious child. After I first met her, she said she wanted to come over to my townhouse, so I took her over for a visit. She looked around, and I was a bit surprised when she asked if she could go up and look at my children's clothes.

I didn't really think much about it at the time; kids were always curious. There wasn't much to look at, because it was summer, and the kids had very few things at the condo I shared with Sarah. It took me a while to understand the ramifications of a "closet assessment" launched impromptu by one of Mobile's Springhill snobs.

I had a lot to learn.

In fact, I was beyond stupid. I was totally unaware of things that would have a direct impact on my life. I had not been born under Mobile's proverbial azalea bush. I was wide open, vulnerable, and happy in my naïveté.

On meeting his children, I had very positive feelings. They didn't automatically express disdain for me, or anything negative that I could pick up on. They were very nice, and very polite, and somehow their reaction gave me confidence it would be okay if Paul and I moved ahead with our plans.

Paul's oldest daughter and his oldest son were another story entirely. The daughter, from a first marriage, was not Paul's biological daughter, but you'd never know it by hearing him speak of her. She had been adopted by Paul after he married her mother. She was now an adult, and married to a much older eye doctor in Houston, Texas. Paul's oldest son, "Little" Paul, was attending school at Vanderbilt University in Nashville, Tennessee. Paul also had an elder aunt and her husband, who lived in a small town just outside Dallas. Though a bit anxious, I was ready to meet them all.

I too had to tell my children, my mom, dad, sister, and brother that my plans included marrying a man who was under a "cloud," so to speak. I knew it was the best option for me and my children. Without Paul's help and protection, I would never be able to survive. I would not risk putting my parents, family, or friends in jeopardy again. I felt confident my family would support my decision, even if the decision did not make sense to them. How Paul broke the news to his children, I have no idea. If there was a problem at his end, he did not convey it to me.

We looked at setting a date for our wedding. The first convenient date, sixty days or more after my final divorce decree, was November 14, 1980. It was only six months after his wife's death. There were two things to consider: 1) such an early date was bad, everything was so raw, and everyone was hurting; 2) each day I was alone in the townhouse, I was extremely vulnerable to JJ, ready prey to be abused at his whim. Fear drove the decision to act more quickly than either of us wanted. Because I knew I was innocent of any connection or wrongdoing in the Leverett case, I would have to say it was ignorance on my part that caused me to underestimate the implications of such an act.

Paul made arrangements for his adopted daughter, Kathy Rhea, to come visit us at the end of October. She had very gracefully declined to attend the wedding, but would make it a point to come meet me afterward. Now in his senior year at Vanderbilt, "Little" Paul would not be able to leave school or his part-time job for the wedding, but he said he was looking forward to meeting me in the near future.

The wedding plans came together quickly. Paul took over the planning job and ran with it full force. We would be married at home—an evening wedding—and family and friends would be invited. The guest list included our family, closest friends, Paul's hunting buddies, attorney friends, his business partner, his administrative assistant, his accountant, some of the farmers/ranchers whose land he hunted, and a couple of my high school friends. In fact, one was our soloist. My sister would stand up for me and his son for him. Paul had a preacher friend who agreed to officiate at the civil ceremony. Paul planned almost every detail. All I had to do, it seemed, was show up.

Toward the end of October, we prepared for a visit by his adopted daughter, Kathy. I was very anxious, but Paul had a very cavalier attitude about it. He conveyed to me, by his actions and words, that she "owed" him a lot. He had taken care of her, educated her, and treated her like a princess. For example, at a party, she'd danced like she was in the movie *Dirty Dancing* in its final scene, ending up face first on someone's concrete patio. Paul spent thousands restoring her perfect smile to its former radiance. Whatever that relationship had been, he honestly felt she had no right to criticize him for mistakes he had made. I listened closely. I really didn't ask for clarification or explanation, but by the things that were said, Paul had been at her side for a lot of her trials and tribulations.

Paul and I were in the kitchen at his home when the door opened and Kathy arrived for our first meeting. Paul and I were ready to greet her and we had planned an evening at one of the nicest restaurants in Mobile, The Pillars. We thought it would be a great place to talk and for me to get to know her. As she entered, flashing a wide, white, toothy smile, she walked with her hand extended to Paul. Paul walked toward her, hugged her, and then turned to introduce her to me. She said hello and I said about the same, followed by me saying, "I have been looking forward to meeting you." The usual first-meeting stuff.

Her smile was as radiant as her mom's. It was such a different image, though, because her ivory-white skin was framed by black hair pulled severely back into a very elegant bun, but somehow it seemed harsh for such a pretty young woman. After meeting her, I could envision how dramatic the difference had to be for those who had known her mom with black hair, and then saw the bleached blonde in the photo that appeared in the Pensacola News Journal after her death. Most anyone would have to have done a double-take to make sense of the very different image. Some said they did not even recognize the photo of Elizabeth in the paper, and they had known her for years.

Diamond in the Dark

Kathy had on a lovely dress made of a soft, crepe de chine. I recognized the luxurious fabric and complimented her on how pretty the dress was on her. Her reaction was unexpected. She began to preen, rubbing open palms around her very ample hips, slowly turning around to model the dress from all angles. "Albert Nippon, $298," she said.

She looked at me, awaiting my recognition of the designer's name, and to see how impressed I was with the amount she had paid for the dress. *Talk about deer in the headlights.* I didn't have a clue who Albert Nippon was, nor did I understand the distinct air that this prissy young woman projected. I thought, *Mom would call this little lady "high falutin."* I had honestly never seen anyone make such a display.

She looked at me and asked if I was familiar with Albert Nippon. When I started to say no, Paul made it abundantly clear he was irritated at this line of conversation, and that he was ready to leave for dinner. As Paul started herding us toward the car, Kathy insisted that I should try one from "his" new line. She knew it would look very nice on me, she said.

The night was interesting, the conversation light and non-memorable. I was taken with the mannerisms and the polished diction of this woman and her very affected feminine ways. She carried herself as though she was a queen, and seemed to believe she was one. I watched and wondered, *How on Earth does she have the nerve to carry this off?*

The dinner was fabulous. We had appetizers of stone crab with a Dijon mustard sauce and my first French wine, Pouilly Fousé (it was divine), a salad, Beef Wellington (the specialty of the chef), and beautiful, incredibly decadent desserts. Paul and I ooh'd and ah'd over the spectacular presentations. We shared, laughed about, and enjoyed all the courses. His daughter ordered the most expensive items on the menu.

I watched as each plate of hers was taken away, virtually untouched. This behavior would have been considered sacrilege to the great food god where I grew up. I was intrigued at how the act of ordering the most expensive thing on a menu, and then waving it away uneaten, seemed to reinforce a self-appointed aristocratic status. I felt a subtle, condescending attitude, directed toward me, for both enjoying the lovely dining experience, and actually eating the food.

Silly me. I was hoping I could make a good impression, and that Paul's daughter might even like me a bit. I was operating under an emotional over-load, dealing with my own daily problems and fears, to the point where it skewed my ability to distinguish genuine behavior from the calculating wiles of this little lady. I was in that proverbial situation of "not seeing the forest for the trees." I honestly felt that if I were myself, she would see I was a good and decent person. I made allowances for any behavior I didn't understand, knowing she had to be in pain and still grieving for her mother.

I certainly understood and accepted that Kathy would not be able to attend the wedding. I respected the fact that she had made the effort to come meet me beforehand. But I also thought that by the way all the children conducted themselves when in my presence, they were fully accepting of the fact that their parents' marriage had been over long before tragedy struck their lives. I made that assumption because I never saw a flicker of grief, a single tear surface of its own will, or a mention of "this is all too soon."

None of his family ever asked, "Why so soon?" I would have answered them if they had asked. They did not. It didn't even seem to be an issue. Not once did Paul's children show any disrespect to me, talk rudely to me, or sulk or distance themselves from me. From all surface behaviors, we got along just fine.

The day after the dinner, I was invited back to Paul's home. I was to bring my children with me, so they would also have a chance to be together with the people who would soon become their step-family.

The first meeting was polite and cordial. My sweet country bumpkins were natural and unassuming. Their eyes were big, as they took in the high ceilings and the bright colors of the unique kitchen. The treasure of the evening was Jamie and Nathan walking into the small study off to the side, adjoining the kitchen. Jamie eyed the taxidermists' work. The largest animal in that small room was a white-tailed deer, stuffed from the shoulders up, with his long neck, proud face, and huge brown deer eyes pointed toward the kitchen. His antlers were reining high over the antique sofa. Jamie kept staring at this very realistic, glassy-eyed deer. She finally asked Paul, in a child's timid voice, "Mr. Paul, what did you do with the rest of him?"

Paul looked at her, looked up at the deer, then back at her again, "Well honey, we ate him." You could see the wheels turning in Jamie's head as she looked at the deer, turned, and looked toward the breakfast table that could be seen from where we were standing. After what seemed like a very long pause, Jamie asked, "You ate it in front of him?"

>─┤◄▸──○──◂▸┤─◄

That evening, we were talking a bit about the county fair. Each year, at the end of October, the Mobile Interstate Fair came to town. My kids were excited and animated, begging for us to take them. We gave in to their pleading. Paul bowed out, so it was left to me and Kathy to take Lee, Nathan, and Jamie. There had to have been one more person with us, but I can't remember if it was Mark or not. I know there were six passengers in my car, including me, because Paul's oldest daughter sat in the center of the front seat, right next to me.

It was cold that night. None of us was dressed properly for the temperature drop, but the kids were having fun and did not want to leave. We stayed, and they all seemed to have a great time in spite of the cold. We didn't leave until around midnight. Walking to the car, we all laughed as we debated the merits of each ride. The warmth of the car was a welcome relief. It seemed strange sitting so close to Paul's daughter. I felt it was a good sign that she was willing to sit next to me. We both enjoyed the kids having fun, and she was obviously okay with me and my children.

As I drove back to my town home, I thought to myself, *What a nice evening!* I took everything at face value, and I could not see how it could be to the oldest daughter's benefit to come and spend two cordial evenings with me if she had nothing but animosity in her heart for her father. If she felt that way, she could have just stayed home.

>─┤◄▸──○──◂▸┤─◄

As we rode up into my parking space, my car lights shined brightly on the front door. There was a large window on the right side, and a dim light could be seen coming from the living room. There was a single-sized window off to the left. That was my bedroom window, and there were shrubs right in front of it. I always looked there twice, because someone could use that space to hide. I was not up for surprises that evening. All appeared to be in order. It was only a short distance from our car to the safety of our door. We went in quickly, locking the door behind us.

We were so tired and so happy to get back to our place. I was the only one who slept in the downstairs bedroom. I kissed my children good night. They too, were tired, but they were still glowing from their fun evening. I walked into my bedroom. As I walked in, I looked at my bed, which was straight ahead of me. The queen bed was positioned with its headboard backed up against the only window in the room—the window that looked out onto the parking lot in front of the town house. I always knew if someone drove up in front because the lights would shine into my room.

As I had become accustomed to do, I took out my newly acquired Smith and Wesson, snub-nosed .38-pistol, and laid it down on the opposite side of my bed, so I could reach it quickly. It was right there next to me, an arm's length away. I always made sure the barrel was pointed toward the wall and away from me. It made me feel safer. At least I would have a chance to defend myself. It gave me some peace, and my tired body was soon asleep.

The house must have been quiet, because the slight noise I heard outside awakened me. I looked at the clock on my dresser, and it was almost 3:30 a.m. I stared at the ceiling, listening intently, and again I heard something outside my window. My porch light was on, but I hadn't seen any car lights. Almost instinctively, I grabbed for my gun. It was in my right hand, and I stood up on the floor just to the side of my bed, left leg standing, right knee bent, and I sank deeply into my mattress as my weight shifted. I leaned over and opened the curtain to take a peek at what might have caused the noise. I pushed the curtain back, and stuck my face up close, so I could look outside.

Shock and fear were my immediate response, as I focused on the barrel of a gun pointed against the glass. The barrel was pointed right at the center of my face. Hot water rushed through my veins. I felt faint and I thought my legs might give way under me.

Simultaneously, I heard a voice saying, "If you move, I'm blowing your head off." The curtain moved in my hand. "Don't move, bitch, or I'll kill you now." Those words will never leave my head completely, even to this day. It was JJ standing in the flower bed, between the big bush and up against my window. The porch light fully illuminated him, and we were less than two feet apart, our only barrier a single window pane. I was paralyzed and trembling. He was laughing, and he told me he wanted me to see something. He kept reminding me that, if I tried to move, he was going to unload his gun into my face. I looked into his hate-filled eyes and knew I couldn't escape.

My options were spinning in my head. My fight or flight instincts ignited, my frontal lobe trying to take over. My hand was behind the headboard, so he didn't know I had a loaded gun in my hand. My mind told me that if I killed him where he stood, everyone would then see he was at my home with a loaded gun. If I tried to jump to the side, I knew I could not get clear of the window before I would be hit. Even if I jumped toward the corner, I was afraid the bullets could reach me. I was desperate.

He wanted me to look at what he had in his hand. He held up a bullet and he asked me, "Can you see this, you filthy whore? Can you see this?" He shoved the bullet up against the window, with the bullet in his fingers only inches from my face. "I scratched your name in these bullets, and I am going to kill you." He was speaking through lips so tight, it was as if he had no lips at all. I looked at him, and his eyes were dilated with rage. I knew him well enough to recognize the distraught, agonized look on his face. It was as if all his features were exaggerated and distorted. This was real and it was almost over.

I had two choices. I could start firing and hope to kill him. But he would most likely get off some shots with that .357 Magnum and most likely kill me. I didn't want to kill him. I decided I was not able to defend myself, even with a gun in my hand.

For what seemed like hours, he held me against that window. He wanted to kill me. If I made even the slightest move, the terrorizing threats would start again. Each time I thought he was going to pull the trigger, and this would all be over. I thought of my children upstairs. If I yelled, they might see this. I didn't want my children to see me die or dead.

All of a sudden, JJ started fidgeting. He was looking back and forth, juggling the bullets in one hand and continuing to hold the loaded barrel pointed at my face. We had been here for what seemed like hours—I couldn't look at the clock, because moving my head brought more threats. There must have been someone or something that caught his eye, because he leaned back a little and glanced toward the end of the building, then quickly back at me. Just as quickly as he came, he turned and left. He vanished from my view and I ran out of my bedroom and into the hall.

I was so afraid he would come back—maybe kick in my door—that I hurriedly called the police. I told them he had held me at gun-point at the window for over an hour and then disappeared as fast as he came up. The police were on their way. I prayed they would arrive soon.

When the police arrived, I opened the door before they even knocked. I asked them to come inside so I could close the door. I did not feel safe, even with two police officers standing in front of me. I told them what had happened and they took my report.

I listened in disbelief as the policeman told me, "Mrs. Phyllis, there is nothing we can do. You are not hurt and he is not here. There are no witnesses. What are we supposed to do? Go look for some guy and pull him over just to see if he has a gun in his car? Until he does something, we cannot make an arrest. If he comes back again, try to call us while he is here." In effect, there was nothing I could do to keep the man from killing me, and law enforcement made no bones about it. Until I was dead or wounded, there was no help coming from them.

How could this be right? No woman should have to endure this kind of torment from anyone, even if it's an ex-husband.

Only two weeks remained before Paul and I would marry. I didn't have great confidence that I would be alive then so it could actually take place. My fear was great enough that once again, Paul hired someone to sit by my door to keep JJ from showing up unannounced. Paul was the only one who took the guy seriously. He had personally experienced JJ's menacing intent the day he came into one of his stores, and he had heard the unforgettable threats issued against both of us. Paul knew my life was in danger.

In preparation for the wedding, I selected my cake—raspberry in the middle and swirled, white-mountain frosting on top. I purchased the wedding dress of my dreams, and I found the perfect dress for my sister to wear as my maid of honor.

We were to be married in the living room, in front of the fireplace. It would be very simple. Two of my girlfriends come from Pensacola—Ramona and Dale. I loved them for coming over to be with me. They had not been able to be with me for my first wedding. Ramona had the voice of an angel, and she sang beautifully at the ceremony, as I knew she would.

My dress was selected from Lillie Rubin's in Mobile. It was the classiest store we had, and it was the first time I had ever ventured inside its elegant reception area. As I walked in, the lady sitting behind the desk met and welcomed me, and escorted me to a lavish dressing room with velvet-covered chairs and a crystal chandelier. The mirrors were huge, and the gold molding must have been six-inches wide. I had never seen such opulence in a ladies' boutique before. Personal service was their specialty.

A middle-aged sales lady came in and asked me what I had in mind. I described my dream dress to her: something formal, not white, but a cream or pastel. I wanted elegant, simple, beautiful, and flowing. She listened intently and looked at me only for a second. She asked, "Are you a 6?" She looked satisfied as I acknowledged she was right. She turned and walked out the door saying she would return momentarily.

After a few minutes, the lady returned with a dress. I couldn't believe how beautiful it was. A pale, salmon-pink under-slip went on first. The same color fabric dress went over the top. It was so sheer it looked almost like a negligee. She helped me with the slip, and then the dress fell gracefully over it. A Victorian collar with a soft ruffle stood up around my neck. The sleeves were full and nipped back in, with the same style cuffing as was used in the collar. The many vertical tucks ran down the front of the dress with delicate details of ribbon accent. I felt like a princess. It was the most beautiful garment I had ever worn. I didn't need to see anything else. The dress was less than $300, but to me, it could not have been more special if it had been a custom-designed Vera Wang today.

My sister's dress was a print, with lavenders and pinks, that would look nice with my dress, and I knew it would flatter my sister. I looked everywhere for that perfect dress. I was at wit's end to find her something special. I had actually looked in all the better stores without success. I was about to give up when I walked through Montgomery Ward. It was there, just waiting for me. It cost less than $50 and it looked fabulous, so I bought it.

Jamie, Nathan, and me, just before the wedding.

On the day of our wedding, things got hectic. I dressed in the back room, and the photographer came back to take some pre-wedding photos. Ann came in to help me, just as the flowers were delivered. The bride's bouquet was magnificent, but it was huge. It had all the colors of Ann's lavender dress, and the bridesmaid's bouquet was the identical color of my dress. Much to the disappointment of the florist, I quickly switched flowers with my sister.

Paul was handling everything in the front of the house, letting guests in and coordinating with the caterer. A female friend, Regina, came to make the punch. I was not sure what the problem was, but at one point Paul came back to my room. He was upset over someone showing up "uninvited." For some reason, I just didn't recognize that implied threat. I wasn't worrying about anyone or anything that day.

The girls were pretty, all dressed and running around with the excitement of people arriving. Lee and Jamie were giggling and happy to be there, and visited my room to see how everything was coming along. They felt special to be able to come back to the dressing room and watch the whole "getting ready" process.

Until the day of the wedding, I didn't know that the house was surrounded by security guards, both front and back, to make sure no one came in to ruin our day. I was thinking all that protection was because of JJ. I had no idea that Liz's family was also considered dangerous. I honestly didn't know why I couldn't see, or accept, the level of animosity that side of the family had against Paul, and by association, me. None of them knew my situation, though I'm sure they would not have cared.

The wedding started. As I walked across the courtyard and into the side door, I was nervous but happy. Everyone was waiting in the living room. I walked through the kitchen and the dining room with Ann following me. We went single file to stand opposite of Paul and Mark, both so handsome, standing there in front of the white marble fireplace. I looked around to see my mom and dad, my children, and many friends and family from both sides. There was standing room only, and that standing room was filled with people. There must have been about 35-40 people there to witness our marriage.

One of the farmers who Paul knew came, as he said he would, "with bells on." With a cowbell in his hand, he grinned from ear to ear. It was a gesture of good-natured fun between him and Paul. Ramona finished singing her song, and the preacher went quickly through the civil ceremony. It was over in minutes.

Diamond in the Dark

We were wed, so from that point on, we would face whatever came together. I had no earthly idea what I was in for when I said, "for better or worse, for richer or poorer, in sickness or in health, till death do us part."

Paul and I immediately following the ceremony.
My beautiful nieces help to serve our wedding cake.

Chapter 28
Meeting "Little" Paul

This photo of me and Paul was taken by "Little" Paul, in his dorm room, at Vanderbilt University. It was taken within the first 20 minutes of meeting him. He was open, friendly, and such a handsome young man.

Adjusting to the "Leverett world" as Mrs. Leverett #2 was akin to moving to a foreign country where I did not speak the language. Paul and I were happy to just be with each other. I badly wanted to please him. Our personal relationship couldn't have been better. I was so eager to adapt to his way of life that I was jumping through hoops to make it happen. Whatever he liked or wanted, I tried my best to give it to him. My new husband had rescued me from the gates of hell. It was the least I could do for him.

We did not plan, nor take, a traditional honeymoon. We knew we needed to make sure everything at home was okay before we took off.

Our children were having a more difficult time of it. Mark, a young man and a freshman in college, was not at all happy to have a thirteen-year-old stuck in his bedroom. He had enjoyed a room to himself for a long time, and now Nathan was invading his space and his privacy. Mark was smart enough not to torment Nathan in front of us, but he was mean to him in many subtle ways. Both of the guys were dealing with different issues, testosterone high in the older one, and just budding in the younger. At thirteen, Nathan may have faced the toughest challenge trying to deal with his environmental changes. Nathan was not able to defend himself against the savvy, sophisticated maneuvering of his new, older step-brother.

Lee and Jamie seemed to do better. They enjoyed having their own bedrooms. Jamie went into Lee's old room, and Lee went into the guest room. I think that Lee's mom had often used that guest room as hers when family problems brewed. The girl's rooms were side by side, and they kept each other company.

Most of the time, Lee and I did well together. I knew it had to be tough for her. I did not try to be her mother, but I did try to be a friend and kind caregiver. The thing that was always foremost in my mind, when it came to her, was that I would always try to treat Lee the way I would want someone to treat my daughter if something happened to me. There was never a cross word between me and Lee. If I did have to ask her to do something, or stop doing something, she was very good at listening to me. What she wasn't good about was cleaning up behind herself. I knew she was big enough to know not to make such messes for someone else to clean up. But that seemed to be a totally abstract idea for her.

One of the first times I had to talk critically to Lee was when she placed in the living room a framed photo of her mother that could be seen when everyone came into the main foyer. I was sad, but I took the photo back to Lee in her bedroom. I calmly told her that I knew she loved and missed her mom very much. She was welcome to display, in her room, as many photos of her mom as she would like. I would gladly help arrange something for her, if she wanted me to, but we would not display them in the living room. It was hard, but I could not give in on that one.

Cooking for all of them was also a challenge. Their mom had been an excellent cook, and they weren't too gracious about their new choices. I thought they just missed their momma and her cooking. Who would blame them? I understood, but it still hurt my feelings because I was really trying to meet all their needs equally.

Before our marriage, Paul had hired a cook, Lula, who came in on Monday, Wednesday, and Friday afternoons after she got off work from a private club in downtown Mobile. She would prepare big meals, so I didn't have to cook seven days a week. She was a very heavy African-American lady, who somehow reminded me of my nanny when I was young. Both my children and I grew to care deeply about Lula—she was a family treasure.

I knew that I was a pretty good cook, but whatever I made wasn't what the Leverett children were accustomed to having. They liked huge portions of rare roast beef, horse radish, and gobs of sour cream. My children and I would rather have a pot roast, cooked tender, with potatoes and carrots. We all made concessions and, eventually, we made it work.

Thank goodness Paul had a sane head when it came to kids. One night we had pork chops for dinner. Lula had cooked and then left early. Mark and Lee decided to ignore our dinner. They pulled steaks out of the freezer and set about preparing their own steak dinner, just for the two of them. I quietly walked back to the bedroom and told Paul that we had two new chefs in the kitchen. I asked him if that was going to be okay. It would be a bad habit to start, allowing everyone to cook different meals. I knew I wasn't going to stay up all night to clean up after two or three separate meal times. Paul walked to the kitchen and told them that we would all eat as a family—period, problem solved.

We also had to hire a new housekeeper because the lady who had served in that capacity before, Ollie (pronounced O-Lee), would not come back. Our new housekeeper's name was Annie. Annie came four days a week and pretty much kept the house in order. She and I got along fine and she stayed with us for quite some time.

There were some strange things in that house that were of concern to me. I had never before been in a home where there was a dead bolt on the master bedroom door. The door actually had a keyed lock, too, so it could be a locked, off-limits room to the rest of the family. I thought that was crazy. "Why would you need a lock to keep family out of your room?" I asked Paul. "Couldn't you just tell your kids to stay out of your room? Couldn't you expect some respect for the privacy and boundaries of others?"

Paul's explanation was that he had to put a lock on the door because of Elizabeth, and to keep the boys from going in and taking his things out of his room while he was away. I learned that his clothes were not to leave the master bedroom. He would take his laundry to the cleaners, bring them back, and put them away himself. I guess with two boys who didn't respect his things, he would go crazy, trying to get dressed and not being able to find his belongings. I had a difficult time accepting that kind of disrespect, but that was just the beginning of many problems.

Paul said he had originally installed the dead bolt on the door because he had been attacked while taking his afternoon shower. He did not go into the details of that incident, but indicated he had been assaulted while naked and most vulnerable. In order to be able to take a shower in peace, he dead-bolted the door to his room.

There had also been an incident, he said, where he came out of the shower, only to find his daughter in his bedroom and his billfold no longer on the chest of drawers, where he had laid it. She had been startled by him. He said he could see she had something stuffed inside her pants, so he called his wife in. Lee had taken the billfold in order to give the money to her mom. Paul said her mom had sent her in to get it.

A big argument ensued, with his wife flippantly defending the behavior—it was justified, she said, as long as she felt she needed more money. I patiently listened to that story again. He had told me about it before, not long after I had met him. Now, in the context of how they lived, it made more sense. To me, it seemed to validate everything he had been saying.

We never had a discussion or a family meeting to establish how things were going to be handled within our home. Paul started giving me $250 every Friday. It was like payday. With it, I would run the house, and for me that meant I would be expected to buy groceries, clothes, recreation, and other incidentals, for myself and my children. It was plenty of money for me. We lived what I considered to be a comfortable, upper-middle class lifestyle. I was happy as a clam, and very content with the monetary arrangement.

When I inquired about how we were going to handle family business, he told me that in the past (before me), he had tried calling all the family together, at the dinner table, for family meetings. He said he had tried to explain to his then-wife and children that things were tighter because of high interest rates, and escalating adjustable rate loans for the business, thus requiring their help in cutting back on expenses. He said Elizabeth would usually throw a tantrum, or slam her hands down on the table, saying something to the tune of, "I've been cutting back all my life, and I am not going to live like that now." The meeting ended when she would storm out, leaving Paul with egg on his face.

Paul indicated he had long since given up expecting any financial cooperation from his family. How could he ask his children to help out when their mom had been adamant about not participating? When it came to finances, they thought Paul's responsibility was to provide whatever they felt was appropriate to spend.

At the time, our country was going through a crisis—interest rates had soared to eighteen percent on some loans. Times were hard for many people, but we weren't feeling the pinch, or at least I didn't think so at the time. I was a bit disappointed that Paul didn't share very much with me about financial matters. I had to learn, a bit at the time, how things really worked around my new home.

It was obvious that we were spending a lot on education, and I asked Paul about it because, without my asking, he had assumed the bills for my children's education. He just did it when I failed to receive any child support from JJ. Mobile Christian was relatively inexpensive in the private school world—both my children's tuition and fees combined were less than St. Paul's Catholic School. But the first year we were married, we had five children in private schools. "Little" Paul in Vanderbilt—$12,000 (his dad also paid for a car and provided spending money, in addition to room and board). Mark ended up at his dad's alma mater, Southern Methodist University ($8,000-plus). Lee was in the very expensive St. Paul's ($5,000), and my children were at Mobile Christian ($3,000). Our education bills mounted fast.

What bothered me was that Paul didn't even expect any appreciation for his efforts. My eyes widened as the days went by. I learned that when the kids wanted, they dropped off their clothing and school uniforms at the dry cleaners down the street. When they picked up their clothing, they signed the ticket. The same went for the gas station on the corner—simply fill up and sign. His children appeared to have no concept of how much things cost, or had any limits. Life was simple: Dad pays.

Our financial matters may have been difficult, but our morning routine was quickly established. We started each day in the same way. Paul got up, took a shower, and came in for breakfast. He showed me how he liked his eggs (one minute, soft boiled), toast, and coffee. He wanted only cloth napkins. Each morning, I made his breakfast, laid out the place mat, matching cloth napkin, fork on the left, knife and spoon on the right. He was happy.

In the evening when he arrived home, he went straight to the shower without stopping. Two showers a day, every day, and he never deviated from that schedule. He always kidded that he was "greasy," so I got used to his routine.

I walked into our bedroom one day after he had just gotten out of the shower. He was lying on his back, his knees bent and feet up on a trunk-type chest that sat at the foot of the bed. His head was hanging off the chest, as he squirted nose drops of some kind up his nose, fully expecting the most benefit to be gained by allowing the drops to drain down into his upside-down head.

What a sight! I laughed and asked what the heck he was doing. I'd used nose drops before. I would just tilt my head back, squirt-squirt, sniff-sniff, and then blow-blow. Done! I found it to be quite a spectacle—a man getting into such a silly position. The quirks continued to multiply. He also had a nose douche that was part of his twice-a-day routine. In the shower, he would fill a tiny glass vial with water, tilt his head back, and let the water drain into his sinus cavities. After some blowing and snorting, his head was clear to go. That was all done to keep his allergies at bay. It worked by keeping dust or pollen out of his head. Sudafed and Actifed were his constant companions.

The good thing about his routine was that he was always squeaky clean—that was very much appreciated by me. He just might have been the most immaculate person I've ever known.

I don't know who to attribute it to, but somewhere along the line, I heard that a person who does really quirky, strange things is usually referred to as a "nut." But if a rich person exhibits really quirky, strange behaviors, they are "eccentric." I guess Paul fell somewhere in the eccentric range.

It was December before we got a chance to go on a short honeymoon. We would leave on a Friday and return the following Wednesday. I had no input into the plan, though I was happy at the thought of getting away from Mobile, even for a few days. Paul said he wanted me to meet his son, "Little" Paul, and then we would go over to Gatlinburg for a couple of days. It sounded good to me.

I had already heard loads about "Little" Paul from an adoring little sister, his brother Mark, and of course, his father. Paul was very proud of such a fine-looking young man. From family photos, I could see a real resemblance to both his mother and father. If I had to describe him from a purely physical perspective, I'd visualize John Belushi, only taller, with a more refined look. He was a handsome guy, and Paul beamed with pride when he talked of him.

I was surprised that the driving distance from Mobile to Tennessee didn't seem to bother Paul at all—he didn't even consider flying. We loaded the car and headed north. On the way up, he told me of his time selling Scotsman Ice Machines "door to door" during the early days of his first marriage. He had pioneered the sales of Scotsman in the Southeast region. He had evidently traveled that same route many times, for he knew every exit and the best places to eat. It was as if he had the map in his head. I learned a lot about him on that trip—some things I liked, and some I didn't.

Our first stop was Vanderbilt University. Immediately after checking into the hotel, Paul got on the phone to "Little" Paul. We would go to "Little" Paul's fraternity house—he wanted his dad to see his room—then we would go to a nice dinner somewhere in town. Paul told him to choose any place he wanted to go, since he would, by now, know all the best places in town to eat. We felt confident the meal would be incredible, because one thing was for sure: The Leverett boys were slaves to their palate. Food was to be enjoyed with great gusto, with no consideration whatsoever given for calories or cost. That whole mind set was something I was unaccustomed to.

I was told "nice casual" for the dinner, so I chose a pair of brown wool slacks and white turtleneck sweater, topped by a plaid wool blazer. I really wanted to look nice for my first meeting. "Little" Paul was either twenty-two or twenty-three years old. I had never actually spoken to him because he had not made it to our wedding. I couldn't blame him. If I were him, I probably wouldn't have come either. Would he snub me? Would he be nice? The range of responses could be anything from wonderful to terrible. I was hoping for the best.

We stopped in front of his fraternity house and parked. I took a deep breath and squeezed Paul's hand as we walked up to the door. I wasn't sure whether it reminded me of scenes from *Animal House*, or if the place was just haunted.

I looked around the entry room. My first time in a fraternity house was a shock to my senses. The place reeked of rancid beer, and it looked like a herd of buffalo had been cooped up in this beautiful home for months. I looked at the furniture—it was sparse and beaten to hell and back, with knocks and scars all over the walls. Trash was on the floor. The place was filthy. Everything looked as though animals had been living there. I was disgusted with what I saw, so I edged closer to Paul, as if it wouldn't be so bad if he stood next to me. "Little" Paul soon appeared, big and bold, walking confidently down the stairs.

I recognized him immediately from his photos. He shook his dad's hand and gave him a quick, manly kind of shoulder hug. He turned and shook my hand as Paul introduced me in a very upbeat way, "I want you to meet Phyllis." Paul was beaming. I remembered thinking how nice it was that he hadn't said "wife"—no need to make that point.

Since Paul had not been here before either, "Little" Paul wanted to show us his room. We climbed the stairs, passing the wildest sights. In the rooms along the way, everything was in disarray. It was almost funny it was so awful. Not having been a college girl, I had never known that I'd missed all this craziness. I had never experienced that kind of privilege and right-of-passage into adulthood. In fact, I was so far removed from it, I had never even dreamed of people actually living like that.

In his room, a twin bed was on one side of the room, a desk and chest on the other, and miscellaneous personal things were stuck here and there. I guessed he had cleaned up a bit before we came. Sometime in the process, we took a few photos. My new stepson took one of me and his dad.

We left soon for dinner. "Little" Paul gave us a windshield tour through the beautiful and historic campus of Vanderbilt University—a fine place steeped in history, not just from an academic standpoint, but from the student culture of fraternity and sorority houses that lined the streets like monuments dedicated to the wild days of college youth. "Little" Paul also told of the not uncommon suicides that occurred because students were unable to keep up with the school's arduous academic standards. I'm sure that was thrown in for his dad's benefit.

We ended up at a big restaurant frequented by college kids. I let the guys talk and tried to stay quiet, until I got the lay of the land so to speak. "Little" Paul may have just been trying to be nice for his dad's sake, but I really got the impression he was fine with me marrying his dad. He even complimented Paul for having done a good job picking me, then *hahaha*. A guy thing, I guess.

The meal was good. I thanked him for being nice, and told him that I had been looking forward to meeting him and I appreciated his showing us around Vanderbilt. He looked straight at me and said he was glad to finally meet me. He then said, "You know it has been extremely difficult for me since Mom died." I was taken aback by the fact that he brought his mom up. I expressed my condolences. "I'm sorry. This must be really difficult for you."

He then went on to say some things I am still astounded by to this day. He was looking down as he told us, "My mom and I were not speaking when she died." He then looked up and said he had been angry with her and had refused to talk to her for months. "Now I'll never be able to talk with her again." I really didn't know what to say. I just sat there as he continued.

His last time home, he said he and his mom got into a huge fight. "I couldn't believe what Mom was up to. I had only been home for one day when I came down the stairs and entered the dining room. She and Mark were in the kitchen, so I could hear them talking. I overheard her say to Mark that she had found someone who would kill Paul for $500."

He stepped into the kitchen, and "Little" Paul asked her, "What in the hell is going on in here?" His mom then told him of a man she knew who would kill his dad for $500.

Paul and I sat silently for a bit. We looked at each other with surprise. I was in a bit of a daze—never, never, never did I expect such a disclosure to come from his son's mouth. It was surprising, puzzling, and thought-provoking. What was actually going on within that home? I wanted to know more, but I did not ask questions.

"Little" Paul finished his story by saying he had thrown a fit at the very thought of such an act.

Paul asked him who his mom knew that was supposed to do such a thing? "Little" Paul just shrugged off the question with a "how should I know?" look on his face. He said he was so angry and disgusted with the whole mess that he had not gone back home since the incident occurred. Now his mom was dead, and there would never be a second chance to make his peace with her. That was what he was left to deal with on his own. I could see in him the obvious pain caused by that hurtful memory—it was eating away at him.

I wondered if he had intended to drop this bombshell when he met us for dinner, or if he just spontaneously let it go because he needed the release. In either case, it was a bitter pill for him to swallow. I felt so very sorry for him.

Again, it seemed to give credibility to the many stories Paul had told me of Liz trying to kill him with a gun, of running him off the road, and the other physical attacks he had described to me.

What a mess!

A composite photo I put together. We took photos of each other on our honeymoon balcony at the Cobbly Nob, just outside of Gatlinburg city limits.

We headed over to Gatlinburg the next morning. On the drive over, we had a chance to talk. I asked him about "Little" Paul's comments. He told me he knew there had been a problem between Elizabeth and "Little" Paul. Not long after whatever happened in the kitchen that day, she called Paul in to intervene because "Little" Paul was speaking to her in a very disrespectful way. When Paul did try to stop the behavior, "Little" Paul revealed what his mother had said in the kitchen that morning. According to Paul, Elizabeth had been extremely angry at "Little" Paul for "outing" the conversation. "Little" Paul soon left the family home and returned to college.

Paul went back over some of the things he had told me when I first met him, but now the encounter with "Little" Paul seemed to open a floodgate of memories. We were riding along when he told me that, from 1975 on, she had threatened him numerous times with the fact that she could "arrange" for physical injury or his death at any time she wanted.

According to his story, Elizabeth had seen several psychiatrists, and neurologists, for seizures and other problems. She was always talking to her friends and expressing concerns that she had a brain tumor. Doctors had her on very strong medications like Phenobarbitol, which she took two to three times a day, Dilantin, and others. Her physicians in the Mobile area were many: Doctors Mudd, Seldon Stephens, Cope, Patterson, McGlaughlin, and George Mitchell, just to name a few.

Paul said that as she began taking the meds, she became even more jealous and paranoid in her thinking. Not just jealous of him and other women (which I reminded him, he evidently had given her cause for), but envy of his education, the fact that he looked nice in his custom clothes, his success, and his career. The jealousy became even worse when she focused on a woman who was slim and attractive. He said it was so hard because her jealousy engulfed her, which led to anger, which was deadly.

During that ride, he told me of the time she had almost pinned him between her car and his station wagon at the Springhill Kennels. He was there to put Satch (his black lab) back into his kennel after a dove hunt. The only way he had saved his legs was by jumping up and onto the hood of Elizabeth's car. She had laughed at him. After seeing Paul's fearful reaction, she had told him she was just trying to scare him. She had been very successful.

We both decided to table this conversation. It was our honeymoon and we needed to think of us—just us. I don't think any of those conversations would have come up if I had not been blown away by "Little" Paul's sad story the night before. We then made a pact: no more talk of her, since we were out to enjoy our time.

I had never been to Gatlinburg before, so I was looking forward to experiencing snow, a real fireplace, and an adult beverage or two with my husband. We stayed at an out-of-the-way place called the Cobbly Nob. We carried our bags into a warm and rustic room, overlooking a golf course, split down the middle by a swift stream, complete with soothing, bubbly water noises.

Paul built a fire, we had a drink, and we snuggled as honeymooners do. We laughed the next morning as he accused me of taking all the covers. Sleeping with him was like sleeping with a heater—his body radiated warmth like that of a hibernating bear.

For breakfast, we enjoyed fried river trout cooked to crispy perfection. It was different, it was delightful, and we savored every bite. We ventured into the very quaint German type town, and bought a couple of small souvenirs of our visit. I fell in love with a small green crystal bird. It was heavy and it fit smoothly in the palm of my hand. I held it tightly—I wanted to preserve the moment.

We entered a very expensive antique shop filled with beautiful porcelain figures, chandeliers, silver, ornate vases, and crystal. It was eye candy, and I enjoyed myself as I looked at each lovely piece. The store owner struck up a conversation with us while we shopped. He gave us a lesson in Gatlinburg history, which brought the discussion around to a large mountainside residence, built like a castle and overlooking the quaint "Bavarian" town. I found the house extraordinary, perched majestically on the side of Ober Gatlinburg. The turret jutted high into the Smokey Mountain clouds that day. The store owner said the house was numerous floors high. It featured an elevator, which was state of the art when it was originally built. I, too, found it fascinating that they had included an elevator in what looked like a centuries-old residence.

When we left the store, Paul's comment was something like: "If that had been Elizabeth, she would have told the store owner that our home had an elevator too." He said she would never have missed a chance to one-up, or impress, someone. I did not see why the store owner needed to know that piece of information. And I had no need of impressing him.

Paul then told me of Elizabeth having a beautiful bracelet that was admired by many. He said it would make him ill every time someone would tell her how pretty it was. She would not just say thank you, but add, "Saks Fifth Avenue," as she held out her wrist for closer inspection. I just could not have imagined someone doing that, but I guess that was before I had met her oldest daughter. Now I imagined it with ease.

Paul then gave me some pearls of wisdom. I have no idea if he made it up or stole it from someone else, but it went like this:

"If you can impress a person, you probably don't need them. If you need them, you probably can't impress them."

That probably runs true most of the time.

We both held up our hands and touched them together. It would be our sign not to let past experiences hurt us now.

I loved the cold weather, as did Paul. We worked up quite an appetite hiking up the mountain to experience the mist of the waterfall. That evening, we feasted on braised quail, mushrooms, and wild rice, a specialty of the warm and inviting country inn restaurant.

As we left the inn and headed across the street and back toward our parked car, a group of teen-aged boys stuffed in an SUV rounded the corner. One of them gave a whistle, and a couple of others joined in, appreciative of my winter outfit. To me, it was funny. It was funny, until Paul looked at them and slapped me on the fanny to show that possession was nine-tenths of the law. The guys howled. Paul thought it was hilarious.

I felt a fanny slap was demeaning. I was so angry—in three seconds, my blood was boiling. It was the first time I had ever turned on him. I told him in no uncertain terms, "Don't you ever slap me on my fanny again." I meant it. He knew it. I fumed for a few minutes more anyway.

It was our honeymoon and our first chance to be alone, and away, as man and wife. We had a chance to get to know a few more things about each other, with the vast majority of the experience being wonderful. Our much-delayed honeymoon ended way too soon.

Chapter 29
Road Rage

Nathan and Jamie having fun in the Airmont house during Christmas 1980.

Paul and I made it safely back from our honeymoon and slid directly into Christmas preparation. The only holiday gift that stands out in my mind was Whiz. Whiz was a well-trained western pleasure horse that was short, standing only 14.1 hands, which put him in the pony class. However, he was wide and well-muscled, and displayed quarter horse traits. He was white in color with clear blue eyes and, best of all, he possessed a gentle, sweet disposition. We purchased him and brought him to an established stable only about three miles from our home. Whiz was loved from the start, and he provided a much-needed distraction for Jamie.

Otherwise, Christmas was celebrated in a low-key fashion. Paul, my children, and I went to my mom's for Christmas Eve. Mark and Lee visited their family on their mother's side. We allowed everyone to do what was most comfortable for them, and even though we had a tree and extra holiday food, we respected the difficulty each of us would bear. Our goal was to have a nice but uneventful holiday. We almost made it.

Some time before Christmas, I pulled out of our driveway, traveled up the hill to exit our neighborhood, and turned left onto Azalea Road. At the traffic light at Azalea and Cottage Hill Road, I had to stop. As the light was turning green, I noticed unusual motion in my rear view mirror. I looked back at the face of a woman in the car behind me, whom I recognized as the sister of Paul's deceased wife. It was the same lady who, acting like an hysterical loon, had chased Paul out of her office. I thought she must have recognized me as my eyes met hers in my rear view mirror. I had only seen her that one time in her office, but the lady with the short bleached blonde hair was unmistakable as far as I was concerned. No stranger would have had a look that she had as soon as she saw me.

When the light changed, I quickly pressed my foot to the gas pedal to pull away. My intention was to just ignore the fact that she was behind me. I was thinking to myself, it would be so easy just to pretend we didn't see each other and move on. The uneasy feeling of a car too close made me look back into my mirror again. The woman had both hands on the wheel, 10:00 and 2:00 grip. She was leaning forward, her face screwed up in a wild grimace, and she was riding my bumper.

What in the heck is this woman doing? She's dangerously close to me. I couldn't believe it, but she was acting like she wanted to attack me. I sped up a bit, until I was up to the speed limit. The woman was less than a car length behind me, and her face was contorted—she was yelling and in a rage. I kept looking back at her, questioning myself: *Could she really be acting like that because she just happened to pull up behind me in traffic, or had she been waiting for me—stalking me?*

I increased my speed to about 40 mph—the speed limit was 35. The woman sped up and was again almost on top of my bumper—no more than three or four feet away. As I got ready to make my right-hand turn onto Government Street, I knew I could just veer off to the right and merge, heading west. The speed limit increased on the highway, so I adjusted my speed to just below the limit. My hope was, since I was going more slowly, she would go around me. Again, I looked back at the woman. I couldn't believe my eyes. She was rabid. She was yelling, screaming, and throwing a hissy fit.

My next idea was to speed up and attempt to leave her to her own craziness. I escalated my speed as my heart rate did triple-time. I was going way too fast, but the woman behind me was matching my speed and was on top of my bumper. I suddenly realized just how quickly this could go from bad to worse. Whatever the reason, I was dealing with a person who was totally out of control. I was not comfortable at the fast speed. I thought for a moment: *If I have to be in a wreck, it would be better to be traveling more slowly, in order to increase my chance of survival.* I slowed to the speed limit.

With some effort, I finally put my frontal lobe back in charge. She was still on my bumper, so I knew if she hit me from behind, it would be her fault, no matter what. With her less than a car length behind me, I braced. I immediately pressed hard on my brakes, in a steady, controlled, but fast stop. I looked into my mirror and watched her. She braked hard, her tires squealed, and the car swerved in an effort not to hit me, stopping within inches of my back bumper. I had actually thought she would hit me, but I had to give it to her—she stopped without crashing into my rear.

In that brief two or three seconds, at a complete stop in the middle of a busy four-lane highway, I looked back at her. Her arms were flailing and she was a true vision of tormented hatred. I thought: *The woman hates me and she doesn't even know me. She must know the problems her sister and Paul had for years. That she would attack me seems so ignorant. If she thinks Paul chose me to hurt her sister, hate him.*

I was sick of being pointed at with anger and suspicion. As I listened to conversations among Leverett family members, the one thing that kept coming up was that Elizabeth and her sister hadn't been that close. There had been a lot of jealousy and rivalry, according to accounts from Paul and the children. One was beautiful and acted like a prima donna. The other one hadn't married as well, and worked hard for a living. It was the consensus of the Leveretts, after that ridiculous attack, that Liz's sister was driven by a guilty conscience. I thought: *She must have fallen short of being the sister she knew she should have been. This scenario is a reflection of a deeper, more systemic problem.*

Uncontrollable violence was how that family dealt with anyone whom they thought threatened what they wanted. It was a known fact that Elizabeth had repeatedly attacked Paul. Her sister knew Liz had been strung out on medications, and unpredictably violent, but she must have decided that, as long as it was violence perpetrated by her sister, it was acceptable behavior.

Flash forward eight years: The Sunday, April 16, 1989 edition of the Mobile Press Register ran a feature article on the Leverett case. In that article, Paul's adopted daughter, Kathy Rhea, was quoted as she talked of her mother, Elizabeth. "Mrs. Rhea said her mother was a very religious and a very good person. She was prone to the theatrical. I remember he made her mad one time and she shot his windshield out."

In the same article, her youngest daughter, Lee, answered the question asked by the reporter, "Why did she stay with him?" Lee said, "Why does anyone stay? She was weak. She enjoyed the money. She was in love with the man. And him always putting her down and telling her she was stupid. Anybody that you'd speak to would say that she was the nicest lady."

The way these women did business was a mystery to me. Elizabeth's sister thought she would, and could, do the same violent things to me. These ladies thought themselves impervious to the law.

The only thing I regretted was that I should have gone a little faster and braked a little harder eight years earlier. After the fact, I wished she had plowed into my bumper. If she had, there would have been a police record of an out-of-control lunatic.

1981: Learning to Live as a Family

1981 brought more changes for me and our family. Both Paul and I tried hard to be good and fair to all the children. We knew they would have differences and problems, so we allowed them to work most things out on their own. Interfering at each argument or disagreement would not help them learn to get along.

My children often got the short end of the stick. They were younger than Paul's children, less sophisticated, and they did not have the home turf advantage. Nathan suffered most. He was sensitive to every slight. His attitude became even worse after any contact with his father. Nathan would tell me his dad would say things to him like, "I'm not your dad anymore. You have a new daddy now." Or JJ would threaten Nathan with total withdrawal from his life if he displayed any respect for Paul. He would tell him over and over that he had been willing to forgive me and take me back. He was intentionally leaving the impression it was I who was solely responsible for the break-up of our marriage. There was no ploy too low for him to use. If it could hurt me in some way, he'd use it. It was so despicable to see how he would play with Nathan's mind, with no regard for the effects it had on his mental health.

When Mark was not at home, the three younger children got along pretty well. I thought that was normal. When Mark and Lee were together, though, they were a force to be reckoned with by my two children. The two of them were inside one day while I was out running errands. They decided to lock Nathan out of the house. They would peek out the windows and laugh at him locked outside. Nathan was so hurt and angry, he cried. Kid crap, but hurtful nonetheless. My siblings did far worse things to me growing up, but they were my siblings, which made it something I took in stride. In a new environment and with new people, these small hurts festered into memories that affected Nathan's lifelong perspective.

Paul had been accustomed to his wife running the home and caring for his children, so he was relieved and more than happy to let me take the lead on Lee's day-to-day care. Mark was self-sufficient and spent a lot of time with his friends, doing what college kids do. In assuming care for Lee, I was responsible for her personal needs and school transportation. I was sure it was as difficult for her as it was for me. She had a sweet personality and wasn't mean to anyone. She was always respectful to me, and I went out of my way to deal kindly with her.

Lee and I ran into our first big issue during a shopping trip for clothes. She was growing rapidly and needed new jeans, so off we went to the mall. I let her lead the way to stores where she was accustomed to shopping. I went into sticker shock, though, when this fourteen year old showed an expectation for $70 designer jeans. In 1981, that seemed to be an exorbitant amount to me for a pair of girl's jeans. She assured me that her dad did not mind spending that, and that no matter what she and her mother had bought, her dad had never made her return anything. She told me, in a matter-of-fact manner, the strategy they had used on Paul to obtain whatever expensive items they wanted.

She said she and her mom would buy them, go home, and Lee would gleefully model the items for her dad. "He would never make me take something back that I loved." I thought that was not such a great thing to teach a child—how to manipulate someone for expensive items that you really couldn't afford. In fact, it was mind-boggling, but now the story of her mom sending her in to get money out of Paul's wallet began to ring more true. According to the stories I listened to, it appeared Elizabeth acted more like a spoiled manipulative child than a mother and help-mate for her husband.

Lee introduced me, however reluctantly, to the world of teenaged fashion, upscale shopping, and in-store charge accounts. Even the youngest Leverett was well-versed in how to request the check, sign, and leave with bags in hand. There were accounts in places where I didn't even know they had personal charge accounts. I struggled with it, and just couldn't relate to the idea of considering only designer brands—Izod, Lacoste, Ralph Lauren—polo shirts just to have the signature gator or polo pony on them. Calvin Klein jeans, at three or four times a regular-priced pair, blew me away. I had grown up in homemade clothes, and an expensive pair of jeans to me was a great pair of Levi's. Paul's kids would have died before wearing Lee or Levi jeans.

I made repeated, futile attempts to encourage Lee to consider other choices. I watched as the same pair of designer jeans was washed every night, and the same pair worn over and over. Getting ready for any event would mean the logo shirt, paired with designer jeans or khakis, the right shoes (Sperry topsiders, no socks), the hair so clean and shiny, and the Clinique makeup applied perfectly, before walking out the door, sparkling with the air of a privileged life.

After the kids had gotten ready and left looking so fabulous, I would walk into the bathrooms. It was like nothing I had ever seen before. Two or three clean towels on the floor, soiled clothes everywhere, shoes, make-up scattered and left open, toilets unflushed, and personal hygiene items thrown on the floor. I would open a drawer and find a saucer with a half-eaten sandwich, stale and disgusting. I never ceased to be amazed at the wake of clutter and refuse left behind, as those beautiful, dazzling, and well-coifed people walked out laughing and strutting.

Paul always looked nice, even though he wore only casual clothing most days. However, I soon learned those casual shirts with his initials on the pocket were expensive custom-made shirts from a New York tailor. I started paying attention to the brands acceptable to him, like Pendleton, Burberry, Brooks Brothers, Timberline, L.L. Bean, Orvis, and other mail order houses with no direct outlets in Mobile.

The interesting part of all that was that Paul seemed not to notice that I was sorely lacking in high-quality clothing. He didn't take me shopping or attempt to bring me up to their family standards, which he probably should have done. The huge closet that we shared was as big as a small bedroom. Ninety-five percent of the contents were his clothes, many with tags still hanging on them. I had a real shock when I told him I needed to buy some clothes. I was having trouble dressing appropriately when going out together or with family. He gave me $250, which most likely was the cost of one or two of his shirts. I was surprised, but looking back, I thought it might have been an indicator that money was not as plentiful as everyone thought. I did not complain and continued to shop the sale racks to acquire the items I needed.

No matter what I purchased, it was scrutinized by Lee, the resident fashion police. If it was a really nice item, the comment would be something like, "Yes, my mom had one just like that," or "My mom had one like that, but she didn't really like it so she gave it away." I knew it was her way of saying she missed her mom, and all nice things reminded her of her mom's things. Even though it sometimes aggravated me, I reminded myself of the unspeakable grief the child had to be suffering. She was so good at hiding it most of the time. It was always surprising when it would surface in unusual ways.

Jamie was enjoying her new horse as well as making friends at Bit and Spur Riding Stables. The Bit and Spur was one of those stables dedicated to English riding, with a few hunter-jumpers in the mix. The old sisters who ran the barn had never married and they provided a horse heaven for young women of Mobile, most of whom were from very affluent families. If you walked to the big double doors of the barn and shouted "Jennifer," most of the girls in the barn would come running.

Jennifer seemed to be "the" name of the season, and that included the daughter of Paul's business partner. The partner's daughter was riding a hunter-jumper of excellent breeding, which also happened to be a very expensive mount. When I made that observation, Lee told me that there had been a lot of animosity over Paul's partner's opulent lifestyle. Indeed, Elizabeth had been most resentful of how much better the partner's family lived.

I asked Paul about that and he quickly told me how Elizabeth had resented that whole family. Paul's partner had left his first wife for a newer, younger model. The new family was perceived to live at a much higher standard, and that was a real sore spot for Elizabeth, according to Paul. She would be angry at Paul for "holding out" on her. If the partner's family could afford something expensive, she'd ask, why couldn't they? Paul said he would try to explain the expenses of the new house, furniture, and education, plus the stress of the economy. All of those explanations were viewed with skepticism and contempt and dismissed as mere excuses. Paul alluded to the fact that Elizabeth had planted the seed, in the minds of her family and other contacts, that Paul had hidden bank accounts, maybe even foreign, and that he was deliberately concealing that wealth from them. He laughed and shook his head at the idea of hidden wealth.

Paul did not share a lot about our finances. I had my allowance each week. Mark, too, had an allowance. Paul paid the local bills that came in. He sent money to "Little" Paul. And that was about all I knew. I did hear, on a couple of occasions, that the Colonel Dixie company was "paying interest only" on some of its loans. That was a new term for me, so I asked about the business. He gave me a few pearls of wisdom: The company made more money on its real estate than from selling hamburgers and fried chicken. They bought blue chip land on U.S. highways and put in stores. The stores paid for salaries and improvements. When sold, the land brought in larger sums of money that made everything else worthwhile. I bought the explanation and let it go at that.

As I tried to warm up to my new surroundings, I saw a couple of things I wanted to change. I was now the lady of the house, so to speak, so I needed to make some things more suitable to me. Some very small aesthetic alterations, I felt, would make the house easier on the eye. The first place I wanted to change was the laundry room, just inside the back door. Hanging on the side was a white lattice-type window-box for plants. The colorful wallpaper, with the big green vine and over-sized red strawberries all spilling out over the top of the container, was so overwhelming.

I decided to refill the container with less greenery and took out the strawberry vine. The next time I came back through the room, Lee had thrown my greenery away and replaced it with the retrieved strawberry vine. It was a little thing, but clear in its meaning—nothing was to be changed. I talked with Paul about it, and that conversation resulted in no assistance. I just let that one go.

The second time I made a change was to move the big ugly brown duck print from over our bed in the master bedroom. Since the master bedroom walls were a lovely light blue color, I simply exchanged the big ugly picture with the beautiful print, over the den fireplace, by a well-known artist, which captured a wildlife scene of mallards in flight over a marshland. I loved the mallard print and it matched the blue bedroom. I thought it looked much better than the big ugly ducks.

Paul came in, looked at the new bedroom picture, turned to me, and said, "Put it back." That was it: "Put it back." I seethed with anger for days, but I did not say anything. I managed to suck it up, but it made me hate the house even more. I knew that six months would not make a difference to me. I wanted to leave that house as soon as possible—I would keep Paul to his word.

One thing I had always wanted to do was learn to play tennis. Paul gave me a membership to a local racket club, and I took lessons at Skyline Country Club. It was there that I met my new best friend, Mary Ellen. Mary Ellen and her husband obviously had some money, as indicated by his new black Mercedes sedan, and her 450 SL convertible Mercedes in a blue-gray color and black top. Mary Ellen's husband was quite the athlete, spending much time at Skyline playing tennis, golf, and cards in the club lounge. It was there that Paul often encountered his partner, sitting with his group playing cards or out playing golf. Paul worked and constantly monitored all 12 or 13 stores. The partner, it seemed, had a lot more time for club activities.

I continued to drive my old brown Bonneville, which was just fine with me. However, as people I met came to know that I was the woman who had married Paul Leverett, "the millionaire businessman," many came out and asked me why the guy wouldn't buy me a car. I didn't have any real explanation, other than I hadn't asked for one and he hadn't offered.

I loved tennis. I played three days a week, sometimes more. I left the house each morning, usually after the housekeeper arrived. I enjoyed the matches, came home, and showered. Many days, I would meet Paul at home for an afternoon rendezvous of love and intimacy. It was our time, without being under the snooping, watchful eyes of children. Other afternoons, I filled my time with shopping, lunch with the girls, or a workout at the French Riviera Spa. I was probably in the best shape of my life.

My new friends, especially Mary Ellen, were fun, and I enjoyed the stimulating conversation of well-educated, smart women. M.E., as we called her, taught me a lot about entertaining and how to enjoy the good life. We were great tennis doubles partners and won our first year of city league tennis, in our beginner flight. We were playing well for "newbees" at what they called the 3.5 level, with a 5.0 the level for very good club players. We had so much fun playing at different clubs in our area over the season, and we managed to win all of our matches. Our record of success required us to move up to the 4.0 flight the following season. We laughed and basked in the glory of small silver victory cups.

As it turned out, the following year, we were humbled beyond belief, and we were lucky to even win a single game. The 4.0 ladies beat us soundly. It was fun social tennis for me, and it was still exhilarating to be there playing each week. I think M.E. did eventually move up the ladder after I laid my racket down.

It was my new world—going out for lunch while still in my tennis togs, brandishing trophies, having smooth, tanned legs that walked with a bounce of happiness in each step. We traveled about in M.E.'s Mercedes, me with long blonde hair and she with dark, rich hair in a Dorothy Hamill cut. The wind would blow our hair, we'd stop, M.E. would give her shiny hair a shake, and it would fall smoothly and naturally back into the perfect wedge. I looked like a wild blonde who had barely survived a wind storm. I soon learned that either a pony tail, or a hat, was needed to keep from looking a mess when I reached my destination. I haven't been much of a convertible fan since.

M.E. lived in the Sugar Creek subdivision, a classy new executive-type area with fabulous homes, rolling hills, and wooded lots that I loved. M.E. and I had started looking at homes for sale in her area, and I couldn't wait to share my finds with Paul. The six-month deadline had passed many months prior. I didn't want to live at 663 Montcliff Drive when I moved in, and that did not change. The timeline for the promise kept being moved back for one reason or another, but mostly because Paul didn't want to leave. He loved that house, and I knew I'd never be comfortable there.

To me, it was just a big, incredibly beautiful house, for somebody else. He kept asking me to be patient and wait until the financial situation was better, at which time he would happily go with me to look at the homes in Sugar Creek. I didn't feel I had any right to complain, but I did feel a bit let down at how things were turning out with the house promise.

I would still have to say, life was pretty good for all of us, since there were no great problems in our home. Even Lee and Mark talked openly about how nice it was to live without constant drama and fighting. It may not have been ideal, but with family strife and violence non-existent, all of us were enjoying a much-needed reprieve. It was good, because we needed to gather strength before the onslaught to come.

Chapter 30
The Grand Jury

Me and Bubba Marsall at a party at our home.
Doesn't he look just like Hitchcock?

When the phone rang, my son Nathan was the one who answered. JJ asked to speak with me for a moment. Nathan handed me the phone with that "Oh crap!" look on his face. I rolled my eyes as I took the phone and placed it against my ear. My normal reaction to him would be something like, "Hello JJ, what can I do for you?" I listened as he said, "You know you are in a lot of trouble."

"Why?" I asked him. He told me investigators had come and asked him questions about me, and that I had better get out of that relationship because they were after me. I had to admit that that development did scare me a bit, but I felt more comfortable when I told him that I had not done anything wrong, so I wasn't worried about them asking questions about me. He said that they wanted to know what kind of person I was, and they had talked to lots of folks in the area where we lived.

I could not imagine how anyone could or would tell them something that was not true. I then asked him what he had told them about me. I knew he had a chance to make up stuff and tear me apart with lies. "I told them that the woman I knew and loved would never have any part in hurting anyone," JJ said.

That actually made me feel good. When the chips were down, he didn't lie and slander me. I took him at his word. *What could I do?* Maybe they would go talk with my preacher, at my home church there in Grand Bay. Maybe they would talk with my neighbors, all of whom loved me. Maybe they'd talk to the people I worked for—they didn't want to lose me. I just couldn't think of anyone who would have a reason to say bad things about me. The conversation ended when I told him I had no reason to change anything in my life and thanks for his concern.

For my birthday in October 1981, Paul bought me a new 20-gauge Remington automatic shotgun. He decided it would be best if he took me to a skeet range so the instructor could work with me on gun safety and shooting. Paul thought a trainer would do a better job and be more objective in teaching me how to safely use my new gun. He told me I would need instructions and a lot of practice to get the hang of shooting.

The trainer was about my age and pretty nice looking. He taught me how to safely hold my gun while not shooting, how to load, how to aim by keeping my weight forward, and how to unload when finished shooting. He carefully and slowly explained the process of how I was to prepare for the clay pigeons to be released. I was to swing through and squeeze the trigger ahead of the bird (clay pigeon). As each clay pigeon was released, I would swing through and the clay would splash in the sky—again and again. Paul was slapping his pants leg and laughing with delight at the end of the first instructional session. I had hit about 32 of the 38 or so pigeons.

The trainer told Paul not to mess me up with any more lessons, and we laughed all the way to the car. Paul was so proud of me, and I must say I loved to see the delight in his eyes. We hunted a lot that season. I did not do as well in the field as I did on clay birds. Someone forgot to tell me that doves do not fly in a straight line, nor always at the same speed. Doves are masters at darting, swooping, changing speed, and flight paths, all in less than a blink of an eye. Plus, I was very intimidated, because I was the only woman among many men, all scattered around, waiting patiently for the dove shoot to begin.

Paul was an incredible shot, so he had a dog that would go out and pick up the birds for him. I watched the masters—Paul, Leroy, Abb, and others, who could shoot one, two, three, birds at one set (the gun holds three shells before reloading)—and knew I was lucky to get one bird every now and again. At the end of the shoot, the guys would all come to my stand and circle around to laugh (good-naturedly, of course) at all the empty shells. I replied by saying how much I enjoyed shooting my gun while saving all the birds for them.

Paul's regal, ten-year-old dog Satch was as black as coal, and he epitomized the perfect hunting dog. Paul was training a new young dog named Tom, so he brought Satch over to sit with me and fetch my birds. That way, the old boy wouldn't have to work quite so hard. I thought how neat to have a dog that would run and pick up my birds. I liked him next to me for company, and the grand old fetcher made me look like a real hunter.

Satch sat quietly on our stand as I talked to him and patted him on the head. He seemed to be annoyed and impatient with me. It was obvious he was there on business. Therefore, my attention did not impress him, nor sway him from his mission. The birds were beginning to fly. Satch was sitting, but sitting as if he was on a hot plate. Looking skyward, his eyes combed the sky, and I could see the combustible tension that was straining from within his body. Satch was ready! The birds were flying as I stood and swung through their projected flight path, leading just a little. I fired, and continued swinging through. Satch leapt off the ground, looked at the sky, looked up at me, then back at the air.

No bird had fallen. I'd missed. Satch turned and looked straight at me with a wrinkled brow, like "What happened? I was ready." This same scene played out a couple more times, and I felt totally humiliated by that grand old dog. Satch had no birds to pick up, and he would stare at me as though he couldn't understand my problem. When I finally shot one, he jumped up about ten feet, because he was so excited to get a chance to retrieve. How funny he was when he came back toward me, the bird covered in wet dog slobber from Satch's soft mouth, his tail wagging and happiness all over his face. *What a hoot!* I told Paul I needed to get a lot better before I'd let Satch embarrass me like that again.

As the holidays approached, I received a subpoena to appear before a grand jury. I didn't even know what a grand jury was, so I couldn't help but be afraid. *Why did they want to talk to me? Why were they calling me?* Paul took me in to see Bubba Marsall. Bubba was a local attorney who had made a name for himself by representing local criminal defendants. When I went in to see him, I thought he looked just like Alfred Hitchcock. He possessed the same big belly, red face, and protruding bottom lip.

Reba McIntire's song, "The Nights the Lights Went Out in Georgia," summed up the situation in the deep South of Mobile, Alabama. "Don't trust your soul to no backwoods Southern lawyer." That should have been the first thing to pop into my head. I didn't like him. It was a gut reaction. But Paul thought he was great.

There was nothing I could tell them. I did not have any information about what had happened to Elizabeth Leverett. I did not even know there was an official investigation of Paul. As far as I knew, he had not been named a person of interest. And if Paul was a person of interest, then why, as his wife, would I be called to testify about anything? Paul Leverett had saved my life, time after time. He was my husband, I loved him, and our life together was good.

I didn't know anything, but I still didn't want to go before a grand jury. Bubba didn't think I should have to go either. I was a nervous wreck.

As the week passed, Bubba came back to us after negotiating with Mr. Galanos, the District Attorney for Mobile. This was how it was put to me: Mr. Galanos wants to get your testimony before the grand jury. I would be answering questions pertaining to time frames before our marriage. I still didn't want to testify. I didn't want to say anything they could twist or use to hurt the only man who had ever been good to me. There was and is a really good reason why wives should not be compelled to testify against their husbands—it's a scenario fraught with danger. Whatever they were digging for, I did not want to help them. I was not a factor. I truly believed that. If they had suspicions about anyone, they needed to look at someone other than me.

The message sent to Paul and me through Bubba was that if I refused to testify before the grand jury, then Galanos, Mobile's District Attorney, was going to charge me with contempt of court. Galanos said he would then have me arrested and I would have to defend my right not to testify. He told Bubba that he would drag me all the way to the Supreme Court to support my obligation to testify. Paul said to me that we could take that route, but it would be extremely expensive and time-consuming, so why not just go ahead and talk with them?

What the heck! I reluctantly agreed to testify. Why should I put us through the expense and heartache? I was the first person I was aware of to be called to appear before the grand jury. My expensive preparation and advice from the great guru of law, Bubba, was pretty basic: "Answer the questions and tell the truth." I could have figured that one out without the fee.

In early December, Paul received a formal, typed letter from his adopted daughter Kathy. Here is the content verbatim. It was dated December 4, 1981. It was written on letterhead from:

RHEA AND ASSOCIATES, INC.
INTERIOR DESIGN

Dear Dad:
I just wanted you to have a copy of my company's brochure.

I plan to be in Mobile the evening of the 16th for a Christmas Party given by the Jeffreys. I have several business meetings planned for the 17th and 18th in Mobile, but if you have time, maybe you and I could have lunch.

I'll be staying with the Jeffreys the night of the 16th, but I'd like to stay and visit with you and Phyllis the 17th and 18th. The 19th I'll spend with Grandmother and the 20th I fly to Florida to meet Ken. I'll see the kids in Houston on the 22nd. Paul, Lee, Ken and I will be in Mobile the 31st. Ken and I are going with the Jeffreys for New Year and we will stay at their home.

I hope you like the brochure.
All my love to you and Phyllis,
Kathy

Elizabeth Leverett, Project Designer, Jeanette Rhea, Interior Design, L.M. Smith, Fabric Coordinator

The letter's last line was most interesting. Note the people and/or the business positions.

At the time, Paul questioned why Elizabeth was listed on the letterhead as a part of Kathy's new business. He said that Elizabeth had never mentioned anything about going into business with Kathy, or that she would even hold a figurehead position. He found it curious because normally that would have been something that Elizabeth would have boasted about to everyone, had it not been a secret kept from him for some reason. Maybe the two of them were planning their escape from their respective husbands.

Kathy's visit took place as requested. We welcomed her, and we all had a very nice dinner together. Paul went to bed early and left me and Kathy talking in the den. Kathy asked if I'd like to sit on the patio to chat, since it was a very nice evening for December. We did exactly that.

Kathy and I sat in the two big rockers outside and it was girl chat time. We talked about many things, and somehow Kathy got around to talking about her mom and dad's relationship. She told me that she could see how good he was to me. She said it was nice that there seemed to be peace in the house. Then she talked of Paul cheating on her mom, and of her mom being physically abused by him. That was the first time I had ever heard anyone say that.

I told Kathy I had a hard time believing he would do such a thing. I certainly could not imagine him raising a hand to me, because he had been so good to me. The whole conversation was troubling. I was not sure what she expected or wanted me to say. And why would Paul not care if I sat on the porch talking to Kathy, if he thought she would tell me things that would so upset me?

Another interesting thing Kathy told me that evening was that she knew her mom had been getting telephone calls from John McBroom (Elizabeth's first husband and Kathy's biological father). John had been calling Liz at home in February and March of 1980, wanting her to meet him. Kathy said her mother was killed on what would have been her mother and John McBroom's wedding anniversary. That really amazed me and made me wonder what had been going on between Liz and her ex. Kathy seemed to be wondering about that herself. According to Kathy, her mother left on two or three weekends, completely alone, and would not tell anyone where she was going.

For every bad thing I heard about Paul, it seemed, there were equally bad and suspicious things I heard about Elizabeth. I didn't say anything to Kathy that night about all the gossip I had heard about her mother. One friend of Liz's said Liz often put on wigs to change her appearance when she was out and about with "others." There were tales of Elizabeth going out with a judge from Mobile, and of another local public official she met at a party, when she was supposed to be going to dinner with a friend. There were numerous accusations against Elizabeth's moral character, with accusers providing names and places. However, I had no way of knowing if it was truth or gossip. To me, jealousy might have been running wild on both sides of Elizabeth and Paul's marriage.

When our late night chat was over, I went to bed. Paul was asleep. I woke him up and asked him if he had ever beaten Elizabeth. Of course he said no. He totally dismissed the accusation as if it were bullshit, turned over, and went back to sleep. It was much later that night before I could stop trying to put it all together and go to sleep myself.

For my grand jury appearance, Paul and I met Bubba at his office and walked to the courthouse only two blocks away. I went in and was seated next to one of the assistant district attorneys, Mr. Harrison. He was a man who could best be described as a nondescript cold fish.

Someone made a note for the record that Mr. Harrison would be asking me the questions. I sat facing the jury panel. I remember men and women, young and old, black and white, all staring directly at me as I told them who I was, where I lived, and who I was married to. I tried to answer each open-ended question truthfully and to the best of my knowledge.

I think the first question was something like, "How and when did you meet Paul Leverett?" The question came from Mr. Harrison, but he did not look at me. He kept his eyes trained on his list of questions and left me to answer directly to the blank faces of the panel. I explained how I had met Paul in one of his stores while working for the insurance company. I told the panel of selling him insurance for his daughter Lee, and of doing an executive work-up for estate planning purposes. That work-up, I testified, had required numerous visits to his office, and Paul had given me and the guy from the home office a tour of the warehouse and kitchen, as he did for just about anyone who walked in his door.

I also told the grand jury of our friendship, how Paul had helped me on numerous occasions with cups, ice, and other donations for my children's school. I said I felt comfortable calling Paul for advice and assistance, and that I did so. I had no idea where the questioning would end up, so I didn't open any conversation subject that I didn't have to.

The questioning was long and very uncomfortable. Mr. Harrison would ask his question and then just sit, looking down at his papers and let me run with it. What surprised me was that he didn't really probe about any details of our relationship. I waited for specific yes or no questions, but he kept with "just tell me about this or that" kinds of requests and then wait while I tried to respond.

I told him that Paul had proven to be a good friend and a man I greatly respected. He was a person I could count on for help. He was also willing to help others, because he had employed a friend of mine who needed work. I told them of my family moving to Texas, and the break-up of my marriage due to JJ's behavioral choices. I had gone back to JJ after returning to Mobile. JJ and I had continued to have problems. I can't remember if he asked me about the time surrounding my surgery in March of 1980, and my being in the hospital for a week, then home over six weeks in recuperation.

But I did tell the panel that, after a terrible domestic violence incident in my home, I left JJ in mid-June 1980. I told of seeing Paul in July. In August, I said, I was flattered and happy when Paul asked me out for an evening. We had gone on a double-date, mid-August, along with Mark (his son) and Sheryl (my niece).

Mr. Harrison then asked me, "Were you associated with Paul Leverett during the months of April, May, and June of 1980?" I thought a moment and really did not see how my knowing Paul, and being friends with him, would automatically make me be "associated" with him.

"Associated" is pretty vague and ambiguous, and to me, it seemed like he was asking if I had some "business" or other interaction with him during that time that was beyond the scope of what I had already told him. I said "no." I braced myself for more invasive questions, but he did not ask any. I knew that I had not been involved in any particular business dealings with Paul during those months. My mind had been on trying to live through my own difficult situation.

When I was released from questioning, I rejoined Paul and Bubba, who had been waiting in the side room. Bubba said something like, "They sure kept you a long time." It seemed to me he was more concerned that he had to wait on me than on what I had been through or what I might have said. I was in the room well over an hour, and the experience was so intense, I thought my head was going to explode.

What was in my heart was the fact that Paul and Elizabeth had problems that were full-blown horror stories. Their nightmare had started years before I knew who Paul Leverett was, and I was clearly not the cause of their problems. I never sought to hurt or damage anyone, and Paul never gave me the impression I had had any impact on his relationship with his wife. Their problems stood alone, and if he was in trouble, I knew it was not my fault.

My goal in testifying was to be sure that, if they had a case against Paul, I would not deliberately let them wrongly use me to reinforce it. There was a good reason why wives are not supposed to testify when a district attorney launches a fishing expedition against their husbands. Being threatened by a D.A. to testify is potentially the prelude to disaster. I knew it. I also knew that I loved Paul and believed in him. He was my husband.

"Little" Paul, Paul, and I at Christmas." Little" Paul's hand is on my left shoulder. From all they did and said, I believed my relationship with his children to be good.

Christmas 1981

In 1981, we had a nice Christmas with our separate families. "Little" Paul came home for the holidays and stayed with us. Gifts were exchanged between all of us. I selected a beautifully produced book on interior design for Kathy. All the children got whatever they wanted. Paul, however, really, really screwed up by buying me a mixer/blender/food processor. I was angry at him, but he never knew. It wasn't worth making a fuss (at least he did give me a present), but he sure needed advice on what to give me in the future.

The kicker for that holiday visit was that "Little" Paul borrowed my car while he was in town so he could visit friends and relatives. I still had the old faithful Bonneville. It wasn't much, but it was my car, and he seemed pleased that I would loan it to him. Liz's family, the Smiths, would be happy to have their niece and nephews visit with them, I assumed. When he came home, though, my trusty Bonneville had deep gashes, and long key marks, along both sides. The gashes were all the way through the paint and into the metal.

"Little" Paul was so angry and disgusted at being connected to them. He told me he knew that while visiting his mom's family, they had keyed my car. That was probably the best indication that they had zero ability to think objectively about anything. At least the car was old, so I didn't even have it repainted.

Every time there was any involvement with the other side of that family, even when doing them a favor, I ended up being trashed. To me, it was funny that sometime after the first of the year, I heard that a new car had been purchased for the leading offender-in-chief, the family's self-appointed persecutor. I also heard that that new car ended up with some nice, deep, and long scratch marks after being parked in a crowded parking lot. I am happy to report that I never had any more vandalism done to my car.

1982: Starting all Wrong

The beginning of January 1982 brought in not only the new year, but a wave of turbulence and emotion. Kathy made good on her word, and brought her older, snooty husband for dinner. On arrival, Kathy sparkled like a diamond with her sophisticated beauty. Her doctor husband was pretentious, dull, and unattractive. We welcomed them, as best we could, and talked of positive things throughout the evening. It was an exercise in politeness, especially after he mocked my accent. They appeared to enjoy the food and left soon after.

As they left, we said the perfunctory Southern thing of, "I do hope you will come back soon." I didn't mean it. I almost choked on the words. I had a dark feeling, like snakes had been in the house. I don't think I ever saw the man again, which was fine with me.

No matter what was going on, I continued to carry on each day in a very normal fashion. After all, I had been doing that all my life. I was well-prepared for catastrophe. I had been in training since early age to face life-and-death situations, then get up and go on as though all was normal. I continued playing tennis every week with M. E. and Jane Palmer, my two best Catholic friends, and Ilse Klein, my elder Jewish opponent and friendly mentor.

Paul and I were going to church together at Cottage Hill Church of Christ, and occasionally we would go to his home church, Independent Methodist. That was the church that Paul had donated five acres to, and the very same one where Elizabeth had stood and voted against him. I stood next to him and felt such a warm, inner peace. His deep baritone voice was soothing as he sang. I stood closer to him, pressed my arm against his, and prayed that our marriage would not be torn apart by outside forces. My love was stronger than ever for this man who gave me love, closeness, and security.

New subpoenas started arriving in February. My mom was to appear before the newly convened grand jury, and so was my friend. This was a different grand jury from the panel that had heard my testimony. I knew my friend would be fine—she could handle the pressure—but I was so afraid for my mom. She was very upset, having never testified and not knowing what to expect. We tried to calm her and let her know things would be alright, no matter what they wanted to know. As Bubba said, "Just tell the truth."

At the beginning of March, Mom gave her testimony. She felt better after it was over and so did my friend. Both thought it had gone well.

Sometime around 4:30 p.m. on March 12, 1982, Paul responded to a knock at the front door. I was in the kitchen and heard him talking with men. I rounded the corner and one of the men asked, "Are you Phyllis Leverett?"

I said, "Yes." I was then informed that I was under arrest for perjury, etc. I can't remember exactly what was said after that, because I panicked. *What were they saying? I'm what?*

This was the curious thing about the situation I found myself in. I asked the men if they would like to come into the living room and have a seat. Don't ask me why I was showing these men, who came to arrest me, the same courtesy I would show any guest in my home. As soon as the words came out of my mouth, I had no idea why I had done such a thing. They declined my offer. It was then explained to me that I would be taken downtown to be booked. Paul, using a somewhat angry voice, said something to the tune of how ridiculous it was for them to come to our home. "You know you could have called us and we would have come down to the station to have her put on the docket," he said. Those were all foreign phrases for me. "Put on the docket?" *What was that?*

Paul asked them if there was any reason he couldn't drive me to the station. They gave him permission to do so. I was still stunned and felt everything was happening in slow motion. "I'm being arrested for what?" I asked them.

"What did I lie about?" I received nothing but blank stares.

I realized that I was dressed in very casual clothing. I asked them if they would give me a few minutes in order to change my clothes. They told me it was okay. They would wait in the living room. As I walked out, I saw them looking around at the splendor of the house. Its beauty and opulence was out of the norm for them, and it was obvious those officers were impressed.

Changing clothes was like dressing a mannequin. I was stiff, numb, scared, and silent. I selected a tailored gray skirt with pleats in the front, a white, oxford cloth shirt, and a navy blazer—clothing I had purchased with the big $250 Paul had given me for new clothes. I must have looked like a typical suburban yuppie as I returned to tell the men I was ready. They followed Paul's car as we drove to the station. Neither Paul nor I talked much on the ride to the police station. I tried so hard to be brave. Paul tried to reassure me by saying I would be out in an hour. He told me that while I had been changing clothes, he had called Bubba to meet us at the station. I felt like I was the star in a black and white, Fellini movie. It was all very surreal.

On arrival, for my first and only experience of being arrested and booked, I entered the dark and seedy docket room. I turned and saw a holding cell filled with more than a half-dozen people. I looked at the men in the cell. My whole body went into recoil. I knew I would not be safe locked in with those men, even if it was in plain sight of the desk. At about the same time, Paul asked one of the deputies to find me a room to sit in while he took care of my bond. My bond was $2,500, maybe $5,000, I really can't remember. It wasn't a lot of money, and Paul thought he would be able to get me out quickly. I never said a word, but thank goodness the man led me into a small interview room adjacent to the holding area. I thought I would be left alone there while Paul took care of posting my bond.

The room was dark, rancid, and dismal. I was sitting facing the door, in a straight, hard, wooden chair. All of a sudden, a man in a suit appeared at the door. He entered and headed straight toward me. In two or three steps, he was standing so close to me that I felt the rough fabric of his suit brush against me. Without hardly tilting my head up, I was looking straight into the man's face. He was really short. *Oh my God!* the inner voice of my mind shouted. *Please, not a man with a Napoleon complex.*

He leaned down so he could put his face within inches of mine. His back was to the door, so no one but me could see his mouth or hear what he said. He was so close, I felt his breath as he whispered directly into my face, "If you don't tell me everything you know, I'm going to see to it that you go to prison for fifteen to twenty years. Do you understand me?" Satisfied with himself, he straightened up and backed off a bit. He had a smirk of meanness and power on his face and in his eyes.

I asked him, "Why am I here? And what was I supposed to have lied about?" His attitude was surly and he continued his questions. I told him I didn't have anything I wanted to say to him. He asked another question, and I looked at the wall, as if he was not in the room. To say he was angry would be an understatement. He was livid. I continued to stare at the wall without saying anything to him. That was my strategy since I didn't know what the heck to say or do. I was woefully unprepared for Galanos' intimidation techniques.

I don't know what happened inside me, but at some point, my fear quickly changed to indignation. He had no right to threaten me like that.

I looked straight ahead at the wall in front of me. I made my face as expressionless as I could. I refused to look at him, nor did I acknowledge his "huffing and puffing" presence. When his questions received no response—not even a glimmer of reaction to his threats—his anger got the better of him.

He turned, told the deputies to take me back and book me, and stomped out.

The next step was to the fingerprint room and to have my mug shot. The guy in the mug shot room did his job slowly and methodically. He was sympathetic and nice. He rolled my fingerprints three times, for each finger, and took a long time. While fingerprinting, he would say things like, "You don't look like you should be in here." As he stood me up for my photo, he asked me sweetly, "Why did you do this?" I just looked at him and told him, "I didn't do anything and I don't know why I am here."

I'm sure I was being watched and baited, but at the time, I stood straight and hard against the manner of their treatment. I shouldn't have been there, and I wasn't going to cry and act stupid. No matter how fearful I was, and believe me, I was terrified, I didn't want them to know they had gotten to me. I instinctively knew things were going to get worse before they got better.

Chapter 31
"Not One Scintilla"

Dressed for Mardi Gras

fter my arraignment, we went about our business each day as if nothing unusual had happened. We even attended a Mardi Gras Ball that season. I felt like I was in a bubble just floating through the days. I didn't do anything to prepare my children for the possibility that I could go to jail, maybe because I couldn't believe they could send me to jail. I had listened to the charge and I read the papers. I knew I had not lied. Looking back, I probably should have been making preparations, but I didn't.

The night before my case was to be tried, we went to bed as usual. I loved my husband, and we would face my trial day together. He never tried to forecast the outcome. He never said anything to indicate he'd throw himself in front of the firing squad to save me. From the beginning, I had assumed his innocence, so I never thought he'd come rushing in one day to tell me the truth in order to save me. It just wasn't a possibility. In my heart, I knew they weren't really after me—they wanted to use me to make a case against Paul, that he killed Elizabeth, who wouldn't divorce him, in order to get her out of the way and then marry me. I would fight to the end to keep them from putting me in that position. There shouldn't be any way they could connect dots that simply weren't there.

For the trial day, I wore a very conservative dress, put my hair up, and wore very little makeup. I had read an article that said most jurors would make up their minds the moment they looked at the accused. Evidence might sway them one way or the other, but they would form an opinion within minutes, maybe less. I certainly didn't want to walk in looking like some femme fatale.

The drive into downtown Mobile went by like a blur, with each of us quiet, lost in our own thoughts. We met the attorneys at Bubba's office. I had both Tom Johnston and Bubba Marsal on my team. They expressed confidence but did little to nothing to prepare me for questions. They said, "Tell the truth. Period."

On the first day, the prosecution, led by Chris Galanos, said they were out to prove that I had lied when denying I had been "associated" with Paul Leverett during the months of April, May, and June of 1980. Their entire case was about that one direct question Mr. Harrison had asked me during my appearance before the grand jury.

Before a different grand jury, Galanos had questioned my mother. She had truthfully testified that during the time frame in question, Paul had interacted with her and the detective hired to watch JJ. That was their entire case. And it was impossible to prove because I had no part in that detective's work—ever— nor had I wanted my mom to hire anyone. Whatever they did had been strictly between the two of them.

The testimony was clear that my mom had met with the detectives. Paul had also had conversations with the detectives, acting on Mom's behalf. Mom wasn't too good at the business side of it, so "Curious George" had stuck his nose in. He was always up for getting involved and helping out. The detective agency was in Mobile, and my mom lived in Grand Bay, which was about 25 miles or more from their offices. The two of them—Mom and Paul—were both seen as interested parties in the outcome of the investigation. I thought Paul might have picked up the report and taken it to Mom in Grand Bay in order to save her a trip into town.

Paul was interested in the report because he knew JJ had been terribly abusive. Since JJ had threatened to kill her for helping me, Mom wanted to prove to my dad, once and for all, that I had a Biblical basis for divorce. As I stated before, it had all been a moot point for me.

At my trial, a parade of detectives and witnesses took the stand. I cannot remember if my mom was put on the stand again or not. I'm sure she was, but I have no recollection of it for some reason. That day was like a day spent in hell, so I'm sure I blocked my mom's testimony from my memory. I do remember breaking for lunch. Paul, Tom Johnston, and I went to the Captain's Table, which was located on the Mobile Causeway. It was very difficult for me to sit with those two men and chat. They acted as though nothing was wrong. I couldn't eat—my life was in the balance. It was a rude awakening for me to sit and watch life go on as usual when I realized I could go to jail for saying "no" to that one question.

Day two of the trial was even worse. My parents stood in the hall outside the courtroom. There were a lot of people waiting for me to walk through, so the judge had given Bubba permission to bring me in and out the back way (the chambers the judges used), so I would not be subjected to the masses.

I had a chance to put on character witnesses. My friend Mary Ellen took the stand, and she displayed both poise and confidence. She and I had been friends and tennis partners for well over a year. Her words rang true when she was asked her opinion of me. "In my opinion, Phyllis is the epitome of a Christian woman." Even I thought that was over the top, but her delivery was so sincere, she pulled it off (I had not ever represented myself as being the epitome of anything). Jane testified to similar feelings, but more within the range of reality. If I had to nominate someone who I thought was the epitome of a Christian, Jane would have been my choice.

My next door neighbor, Diane, must have been nervous. She was one of the nicest people on Earth, and her daughter was a good friend of Lee. They were in and out of our home quite often and were excellent neighbors. When asked by the prosecution what she thought of my reputation, she replied, "I didn't know she had a reputation." I think she meant that she didn't know anything bad about me, but the prosecution moved to strike her testimony, because she said I had no reputation. It all would have been hilarious if I had not been on trial.

I was the last to testify. The questions were geared to establishing my connection to that damned bunch of detectives. No, no, and no, I did not have anything to do with them! One of the last questions to me was long and rambling. It had about five parts to it. One part was what did you think of Paul, why would he help you, and do you really expect the court to believe that Mr. Leverett would help someone without anything to gain? It was so long and convoluted that it would have been hard for anyone to answer, and Bubba objected to it for being so broad and all-encompassing . Judge Braxton Kittrell looked at me and said, "Overruled." He then looked straight at me, nodded, and said, "I'd like to hear her answer to the question."

I told them that I had admired Paul Leverett. I had found him to be a good businessman with an outstanding personality. I had seen Paul help many people. I said an empathetic "yes" to whether I believed he would help someone without the expectation of receiving anything in return.

The word "associated" was discussed as being too vague, and how one's interpretation of its meaning would directly affect one's answer. Galanos asked me the same question again, "Were you associated with Mr. Leverett during the months of April, May, and June, of 1980?" There was a pregnant pause. If the testimony had been televised, it would have been the perfect time for a commercial break. However, in real time, my answer was again "no."

In closing remarks, both sides had a chance to roll through the whole scenario again, each putting their own spin on it. When the prosecution rested its case, the matter was ready to go to the jury. Did the jury fully understand that the whole thing rested on that one point—the definition of "associated"? My future was hanging in the balance over that single word.

I looked at the jurors. I knew in my heart they would likely find me guilty, not because of the information presented, but because everyone wanted some sort of answer, or justice, in connection with that horrific crime—the murder. I was the first person dragged before the angry masses. Would they look at the actual case, or would they make their own justice? I was afraid.

Judge Braxton Kittrell, brandishing his gavel, demanded the attention of the court. He looked straight at Chris Galanos and the prosecution's table. The judge appeared angry, and sounded as if he was issuing a reprimand. He said he had listened to all the testimony, and he couldn't believe the grand jury had indicted me. It was his use of a phrase I had never heard before, in everyday conversation, that caught my attention. But I somehow knew its meaning. With a tone of chastisement directed at Galanos, the judge said, "You have presented not one scintilla of evidence to prove your case."

Not one scintilla. The words had my ears ringing. What was happening?

The court was stirring in response to the judge's words. What was coming? Was Galanos being reprimanded for this courtroom charade? It was obvious to everyone who understood the law that I had been offered up as cannon fodder in a thinly-veiled attempt to flush out the D.A.'s main quarry.

The pit of my stomach was in cramps. I looked up at Judge Kittrell. The judge said the case was dismissed for insufficient evidence. I had been tried and acquitted because there was *not one scintilla of evidence* presented against me to prove the prosecution's case. The jury was dismissed. I was free to go!

My body trembled. I lowered my head until I could gain some control. Tears filled my eyes without warning. My husband and my attorneys hugged me as I cried, "Thank God it's over."

Paul and I walked out of the courtroom into the waiting crowd. Like a buzz of bees, word of the dismissal had already spread among the court community. I felt I was in the middle of an angry hive—they were all crawling around me. I found my mom and dad, hugged them, and told them I was okay—it was over. I saw the tears in my dad's eyes. He later told me he had been so proud to see me walk out of that courtroom, my head held high and looking like a queen. I guess my indignation at being connected in any way to such a heinous deed had shown through loud and clear.

Paul and I continued through the crowd and out the courthouse doors. We walked as quickly as we could. "No comment, no comment" was repeated over and over. We continued down the sidewalk—only one more block and we would reach the safety of Bubba's office. I kept looking straight ahead, and I said quietly as we walked, "I can't believe it's over."

We could hear one lone photographer running behind us, trying to get our photo. He ran ahead and turned around. He pointed his camera in our faces. We kept our pace. The photographer was walking backwards, trying to steady his camera. Then his heel caught the edge of a bulging oak tree root that had cracked the sidewalk. He tripped, and his camera flashed as he almost crashed into the ground. Paul and I couldn't help but chuckle at his calamity. We asked him if he was okay and he said yes, so we just kept walking.

The next day, the big photo that made the Mobile Press Register was of Paul and me holding hands, walking down the sidewalk with big smiles on our faces. The caption read, "The Leveretts, Happy Again." Our smiles at the tripping photographer had been used to make us look like we were laughing at winning my legal case. I was sure people read that caption with nothing but disdain for me, and for us.

The reporters seemed to grudgingly report the actual outcome of the trial. They would run through all the terrible stuff connected with the Leverett murder case, and in one sentence say my case had been dismissed due to lack of evidence. There was only one article that quoted the judge's "not one scintilla" of evidence conclusion, or that Chris Galanos was chastised by the judge for such a woeful case. In all the articles written, there was only one that quoted Chris Galanos as saying, "I was never under any suspicion of being connected to the criminal case."

If you are skimming through this, go back and read the last sentence again, please. Only once was there something redeeming in the many published articles as the Leveretts' high-profile, local soap opera, continued. Unfortunately, there was no end in sight.

Chapter 32
First You Make A Roux

The Chef and I.

After my acquittal, I returned to my happy, busy life without missing a beat. However, I would never be the same. I would always carry in my heart that experience—of being arrested, hauled before a grand jury, threatened, and tried before a jury of my peers. It has never left me. My gratitude and respect for Judge Braxton Kittrell have never waned. He rescued me by realizing I wasn't the person the state should be hammering. He recognized the prosecution's motive of using me to "draw fire," and I thank God that Judge Kittrell was man enough to take the case away from the jury before it was forced to make a decision.

By the time the trial was over, summer was upon us and the kids were out of school. Jamie spent most days at the stable with her horse. Lee was busy doing her own thing, which often included spending time at her aunt's home. Nathan was in Virginia with his dad. Mark was the proverbial college boy. Paul worked, and I took care of our family.

Occasionally, we found time to relax and take some sun up on our deck. Paul loved to bask in the rays and, in his five-dollar fold-out lounge chair, thoroughly enjoyed their full benefit. Paul's legs were so muscular, and he had the butt of a twenty-five-year-old. He looked good for a man of his age. I thought he was handsome. *Period.* In all the times we spent "sun worshiping," I never saw Paul in any type of swimsuit other than the classic boxer type. While sunning, he'd roll up the legs of his suit and max out, the sun hitting him full on. He looked so European, with his dark sunglasses and ever-deepening tan.

I never saw him put himself on display. This was in direct contrast to a story I read that said he wore a bikini, strutted around, and flirted with women, which I frankly can't imagine. Some less fortunate people just can't stand it when someone else looks good in an outfit, and Paul looked great!

Our weekends included our date night. Saturday evening might be at the Casbah Restaurant or The Pillars, or being entertained at a friend's home. One particular evening was different. Paul took me to the restaurant inside the local Hilton Hotel. We had never eaten there before. He told me that a man named Billy Goins had tried to see him at work, but Paul did not want to talk with him there. I didn't know the man, had not heard his name before, and it really didn't make much of an impression on me at the time.

What did make an impression was that the man walked up to our table while we were dining that Saturday evening. Paul introduced me to him, excused himself, and followed the man out of the restaurant and into the lobby area. I became a bit agitated at his long absence but quickly forgot it when he returned and we resumed our meal. I do not recall his explanation; however, I did remember this clandestine meeting with a man I did not know.

We enjoyed having company and friends stop by. I noticed Bill McEvoy coming by the house more often than usual. He'd stop by in the evening, many times right at dinner. He didn't stay and eat with us, but Paul would go and talk with him. I assumed their talks were for instruction on odd jobs that Paul had him take care of out at the leased hunting grounds. It seemed there were always field preparations and maintenance jobs to be done year round.

At the beginning of our marriage, Bill came by our house only for the purpose of picking up buckets of seed. The seed was kept in our storage room, which had an entrance under our carport. Bill had a key to the storage room, and I never once questioned his trustworthiness, for Paul surely would not have given him a key to our home otherwise. Other than picking up the seed, I would see him out in the fields when we were hunting.

Bill McEvoy was always reserved toward me, and I never got the feeling he liked me very much. I couldn't understand his attitude, unless he felt Paul might be jealous of him. He was handsome, younger than Paul, and in Paul's employ. The way he acted toward me just felt odd. *Oh well. I still enjoyed the company of his wife and precious little boy when they came with him.*

We entertained our friends and family with special dishes we prepared. My specialty became "Riverboat Duckling." I basted it with a fresh ginger and sherry glaze, then served it with a black Bing cherry sauce. It was truly fabulous, and I always got rave reviews from our guests. I served that dish one night when the McEvoys were at our home, and they were wowed by the beautiful presentation.

Paul's favorite recipe was his famous "Duck Gumbo." The making of the gumbo was quite a production. Paul really got into technique, and the whole process was treated with such flamboyance that I was convinced no one else could create the dish like he could. When he told me he would be making duck gumbo, I asked him, "How do you make it?" I was trying to envision ducks in a stew, which was not evoking good thoughts.

He looked at me and said, "First you make a roux." If you are going to make anything really good, you must spend time creating a base that will give it both body and flavor.

A huge pot was brought out of storage. Next, the onions and garlic were chopped. I was allowed to chop, wash, and clean up, but not to stir. He guarded the pot as if it was gold. He started his roux in a black iron skillet with oil, bacon drippings, seasonings, and flour. He stirred for a long time over low heat until the concoction achieved a rich, dark brown color. He let it cool a bit, then added all the additional ingredients to the big pot. He added tomatoes, okra, bell peppers, sausage, a myriad of seasonings and, of course, the ducks he had killed—large mallards and other smaller varieties. They were frozen, and he would just throw in the whole duck. We laughed as unappetizing duck lumps were thrown in to be slowly cooked beyond any recognition to their original form.

The stew would simmer for the next 24 hours, until all the meat had cooked away from the bones. The bones were removed, leaving the thick brown stew. The roux, I was told, was responsible for pulling it all together.

The aroma filled the house as Paul's special dish simmered. He would even get up throughout the night to stir and keep it going. I found his watchful attitude so silly that the next morning, I told him not to worry, that I had already stirred it when I got up. He looked at me and ran like wild fire into the kitchen to check on the precious molten goo. I eventually had to tell him I hadn't really stirred it, after all, so he could calm down. By that evening, all the laughter subsided as we poured his gumbo over fluffy white rice. It was a delightful, spicy, culinary extravaganza that was appreciated even more after watching the love and attention that went into its making. The whole certainly turned out better than the sum of its parts, and all because of Paul's TLC and that wonderful rich roux.

After the feast, the excess gumbo was carefully ladled into containers, kept cold in the cooler, and delivered throughout the countryside to each of his friends living in small farm houses near quaint, long, dusty roads, which were often in need of repair. A bottle of his homemade wine and a quart of his special gumbo would be presented as if it were frankincense and myrrh. His gifts of love, and labor, were in appreciation for sharing their land with him. His happiness was contagious—the farmers loved him.

The hot days of summer were passing, and I just kept rationalizing that all would eventually become normal. Our bad dream was all just going to go away and they would stop looking at Paul as a potential suspect. I was optimistic that they would get to the bottom of the real story and then he would be removed from all suspicion.

In August of 1982, The Mobile Press came out with a new story. A man by the name of Ricky Allen Prewitt had been arrested for the capital murder of Elizabeth Leverett. All the known details were in the paper, and it even included my name as being the person Paul had married not long after her murder. The way it was all tied together upset me terribly. I was glad they had found her killer, but why were they again invoking my name? I called the writer of the story.

The reporter who had written the piece was very easy to get on the phone. I politely told him who I was. Then I cited for him the dates, pages, and paragraphs in the Mobile Press where District Attorney Galanos had been quoted as saying I had never been suspected of having anything to do with the crime. I said that now including my name with Prewitt amounted to libel because it appeared to me they were intentionally attempting to lead people to the wrong conclusion. After that, the paper's treatment of me was better. I would still be mentioned on occasion, but not in the same light. They needed to get it right, and it seemed they did try for a while.

We read the papers each day, and our lives were affected by being the stars of Mobile's local soap opera. There was so much erroneous information being printed. Paul received calls from Bubba to meet him. Paul would leave the house to go to some undisclosed location, to talk with Bubba where there was no chance of being overheard. It was crazy. Paul would leave quickly, saying he was "going to the graveyard" because the matter was of "graveyard importance."

"What's of graveyard importance?" I asked him. "A secret taken to the grave," Paul said. These clandestine meetings continued for weeks at the request of Bubba. Paul would never disclose to me what was discussed.

Ricky Allen Prewitt went on trial in January of 1983. During the trial, the newspaper published a photo and story on the front page. Paul, Lee, and I (I cannot remember if Mark was there) were in the kitchen when the paper was being read. I saw the picture on the newspaper's front page, and looked more closely at the face of a so-called key witness, identified as Hilton Robinson. I recognized the man immediately. I told Paul and the others that I had met that man years ago when I had bought my first house in 1970. He had been a realtor. I had thought he was a creep then, and obviously my opinion was now confirmed. Lee walked over to look at the paper with me. She looked at the man and she said, "I know him too." I thought she was kidding, or trying to be a "know it all," to act big.

"How do you know him?" I asked her.

"He owns that antique store up the street. My mom and I used to go in there all the time."

Lee went on to say that Robinson knew her mother well, and that she and Robinson were very friendly with each other—he even called her mom by her first name. Then Lee walked over to a curio cabinet in the dining room. On the shelf sat a small silver service on a silver tray. Lee picked up the tray and service, and brought it into the kitchen. She said that the man in the photo had given her mom the silver service.

We were blown away by this. I told Lee to go to her room and to write down all she remembered about her mom with that man—when they went to his store, how often, and any other details. I told her I did not want to question her or for her to read the paper until she had documented her encounters with the man. My number one concern, at the time, was not to taint or color her memory of that man in any way. But I did want it documented. *Wow!* we thought. *Elizabeth knew Hilton Robinson well enough that he had sent her a silver service.* That was something that I thought the authorities should know.

Lee wrote down her recollections on a piece of paper and brought it to us. I kept a copy of her story (this is exactly as she wrote it), so I will quote it as written On January 14, 1983:

"One day my mother (Elizabeth Leverett) picked me up from school (Arnold School) when I got out early. She and I went to a store off of Highway 90 near Skyline Country Club. It was an antique china shop that looked like a flea market. We looked around at silver sets and painted china. A man by the name of Robinson helped us look around the store. He was a very ugly man with weird hair—his hair looked like it was plastered on his head. My mother and I joked about him after we left the store. He was about 6 ft 2 in., graying hair, light complexion. We stayed in the store for about 15 min. We went there twice. I know my mother went there more without me, just with other people.

"2nd time we went back Mr. Robinson helped us look around. He called her by name. I can't remember if my mother bought anything though. My mother received silver from a friend of hers from his shop.

"The way I recognized this man was during the trial of my mother's death his picture was in the Mobile Press Register and I knew he knew my mother."

The newspaper story, which I read quite carefully, indicated that Robinson was being held in federal prison for stealing and transferring stolen property across state lines. The additional information I heard was that he was a fence, or pawn shop owner, who would take teens and drop them off in neighborhoods, let them steal, and then pick them up. He would pay the kids and fill his shop with very upscale home merchandise—silver and such. He would then take the stolen property to New Orleans to be sold in shops there. My original assessment of him, 11 years earlier, was even more accurate than I could have ever believed. Robinson was a dishonest creep.

Robinson apparently had called the Mobile D.A. to let him know he had information on the Leverett case. Robinson had possession of Elizabeth's large diamond and was willing to relinquish it for a deal, which he apparently got. He told authorities he kept her diamond in the tip end of one of his ties, in a dark corner of his closet. As per his directions, they found the diamond at his home just where he said they would find it. Now he was willing to say, or do, anything to get himself out of prison, which was just what he did.

The Mobile Press quoted Galanos as saying, "There were a lot of holes in Robinson's story to start off with, but there always are." We were pretty sure the DA's investigators provided Robinson *whatever* the prosecution needed to make the case work. We believed Galanos wanted to make a case so badly, he would do anything.

Robinson told the court that Prewitt had brought him the diamond, and he gave Prewitt a $1,000 loan, so Prewitt could get out of town, all on the same day Prewitt said he killed her. According to news stories, Prewitt also told Robinson he had been paid $10,000 to kill her, and that sum was to be paid him by Paul Leverett. The kicker was Bill McEvoy had been some kind of go-between on the whole deal. It was wild, and I just couldn't believe someone would kill someone for money, then have to go a mile down the street for a loan to get out of town—so much for strategic planning. Nothing made sense to me. There was just no way Paul could be so stupid as to be involved in such lunacy.

What did make sense to me was the conversation that I had with "Little" Paul the first time we met. He had told us his mother was soliciting Mark's help in having Paul killed. She had actually obtained a price of $500 for his contract murder, according to "Little" Paul's memory of that conversation. I thought the D.A., knowing all this, would surely ask Robinson if he had known Elizabeth Leverett. Maybe the D.A. would want to know that Robinson had sent her silver as a gift. Maybe he would want to know Robinson had seen the big diamond on Elizabeth's hand, and maybe even coveted that diamond for himself when Elizabeth had indiscriminately flaunted her wealth in front of him, as she was prone to do with every person she met.

I also thought the D.A. would want to know she may have discussed with him a contract for her husband's murder? Those unasked questions could have elicited more questions, and deeper investigations, into the motives of these criminals. It seemed to me the prosecution only asked questions that furthered its theory of the case.

Ricky Allen Prewitt was found guilty of the capital offense of murder, and as a sentence received life with no parole, having obtained a prosecution deal to escape the electric chair. There were also rumors he was going to get a new identity so he would not be targeted in prison. Judging by the photos, he was a tall, thin man with dark hair. He looked sleazy. He looked like a murderer.

The case continued, and Paul assured me each day that he had no connection to any of this. According to Paul, the lies were designed to implicate him so they could save their own tails. Paul seemed utterly confident the lies would not be believed, and would certainly not be proven true. Would a jury believe a case built on nothing but the testimony of criminals, all of them given deals to cooperate?

Chapter 33
A Good Tennis Morning

Reward is offered in Leverett killing

By TOM JENNINGS
Register Staff Reporter

A state reward of $10,000 has been posted for information leading to the arrest and conviction of the killer or killers of 45-year-old Elizabeth Smith Leverett May 30, 1980.

Gov. Fob James Wednesday signed a state proclamation offering the reward for the arrest and conviction of the person or persons responsible for the brutal slaying of the attractive wife of Mobile businessman Paul Leverett, part owner of the Colonel Dixie restaurants in Mobile.

The reward also noted that a diamond ring worn by the murder victim and valued at $16,000 as taken from her after the homicide. McLarty said informatiore-

Montcliff Drive, no concrete evidence exists to link the victim with the murderer, said detectives.

An autopsy revealed that Mrs. Leverett suffered multiple gunshot wounds of the head, neck and left hand and stab wounds in the neck and chest.

Investigators said Mrs. Leverett had left a beauty parlor about 3 p.m. on the day of the murder. She later was spotted in a shopping center parking lot, they said. Her body was found in her home by her husband shortly after 5:30 p.m.

City plann

My tennis game was really "on" the morning of February 4, 1983. I played with my usual group and left the court victorious, feeling really pumped. The phone was ringing as I walked in the door at home. Paul was on the phone to let me know he would be coming home to pick me up. We planned a ride to check on some stores and then lunch. I headed back to take a shower and change into casual clothing. I wanted to be ready to go when he arrived.

It never took me long to get ready, so it was only about thirty minutes later that I was dressed and back in the kitchen. The phone rang yet again. I answered and immediately recognized the Scottish voice of the secretary who worked for Colonel Dixie. Her voice was very clear, but apologetic, as she delivered to me the news that Paul had just been arrested. He had been picked up at the local gas station, at the corner of Azalea Road and Cottage Hill Road, where he always filled his car. His car was still at the station, and he had been taken by the deputies or investigators to be booked downtown.

I all but blacked out. I don't remember what I did after hearing the dreadful news. I don't remember anything about the first few days after his arrest, except the horrible stories in the paper. Every day would become a new test of survival for me, my children, and for Mark and Lee.

Paul was not granted bond, so he would not be coming home. I would stand strong and loyal to him, because I knew he could not have, and would not have, committed such an unconscionable thing to the mother of his children. Not only that, I had to present the new situation to our children. I wanted them to believe in him too.

I soon had to learn the process of visiting someone in a jail. They kept Paul in solitary confinement (for his benefit, I was told). Paul would write to me and tell me what to do, who to go talk to, and who could help me deal with the problems ahead. I waited for the allowed phone calls and for my letter or letters each day. Paul was optimistic. He kept telling me not to worry, that there was no way they could convict an innocent man. I wanted to believe him, so I did.

I learned quickly who our real friends were. Some "friends" paid lip service to us, but were not necessarily believers in Paul's innocence. I started recognizing those of his friends who had been close to us, who would continue to say they were our friends, versus the ones who merely wanted access to the latest scoop. After all, we were now the hottest story in Mobile. My brother, in Washington State, was following our story on national news programs. The story was hitting the big time while we were all just trying to survive.

Once a week, I would go to the jail to see Paul. After the requisite check-in and search, I would be escorted to his cell. Paul was in solitary confinement, in a cell that looked like it was about 6'x 8.' It was so small and had only one small glass window where I could see him through the door. The opening where your voice could pass was much lower, so I'd have to bend over to speak to him and then stand to see him. Most of the visits were about reassuring me that things would be okay and what I needed to do next.

It was only after his arrest that he made arrangements for me to be able to pay the bills. Until that time, I did not know where the mortgage payment went, nor did I know how much it was. I was just at the beginning of trying to make sense of what he had been juggling financially. It wasn't pretty.

As Paul always did in any situation, he immediately began making friends at the jail. He started making some connections for things he wanted or needed. He would call me and say, "I need you to go get a bucket of fried chicken and take it to (the side door, back door, or some location), and give it to (so and so, who had been appointed the receiver). I was struggling with the money, and it was often very difficult for me to leave what I was doing, or head out at night, to go get something and take it all the way downtown to the jail. I didn't want to do it, and I honestly did not know I was doing something wrong. I took the bucket of chicken to someone who would open a side door. I did not go in, or even know who took it in. I finally got an excuse not to deliver anything after I got a call from someone downtown who said I was bringing contraband to the jail, and if I didn't stop, I would be arrested. It was a relief not to be put in the position of carrying out these secretive deliveries of fried chicken to jail guards.

Paul's children stayed with me. We got along well, and Mark and I tried to plan what to do as best we could. Lee and Jamie were just too young to understand everything (I thought), so all we could do for them was try to protect them. Lee and Jamie clung to each other for support. By then, Jamie looked up to Lee as her big sister. Jamie suffered greatly because of the absence of her beloved step dad. She cried for her "Daddy Paul" to come home.

I tried going to church. I needed to feel the strength it gave me. I went to the Sage Avenue Church of Christ at the time. The preacher there was very good to me and sympathetic to our families' pain. However, I quickly learned that most people were not able to give anyone the benefit of the doubt. We were all weak Earthly creatures, and even though the Bible gives repeated examples of how not to be judgmental, that was not the way it was in real life. People, in general, and especially those at the church, chose to believe all the bad things they heard. I was struggling, and I finally gave up trying to seek support from people who only knew me from what they read in the paper.

My family was also divided. My mom was always on my team and so was my dad, but they had no experience to draw on to help me. I went to my parents' home to talk with them and try to reassure them by telling them why I believed Paul to be innocent. I told them of the case, and the numerous problems I was struggling with each day. Dad looked at me with sadness and said, "Your problems are just too big, I don't know how to help you." He got up and walked out of the room. He didn't mean to hurt me. He just didn't have the resources or wisdom to offer assistance. Other members of my immediate family stayed away because they wanted no involvement with me or my problems. Their answer was to stay out of it. They felt it best to allow me to suffer alone, so they pretended it wasn't happening.

My dear niece, Sheryl, was young and inexperienced but so full of love. She helped me so much by simply loving me, loving us, and being there for me. My Aunt Ina was also there for me. A strong lady, she had known adversity in her life.

What I learned was that adults—the ones who had been fortunate enough to have little or no adversity in their lives—were the most judgmental. Those who had met challenges before were wiser, and more willing to reach out, in spite of the adverse publicity. The children who loved me did not have the ability to turn that love off because of something they read or heard. Their innocence and youth protected them from believing the worst, and their loyalty to me grew even stronger.

Paul's partner in the Colonel Dixie business was also the president of the company. He had an obvious loathing for me, and he reeked of it from the moment I walked in the door. At the time, paychecks were picked up at the office, so I had no choice but to go there in order to get Paul's check. I would deposit it in the bank and then have to go back to Paul's office to pay the bills. It was as if everything everywhere had to be left just where it was because, after all, Paul was coming back. At that time, I was picking up a $2,500 check the first of the month. After all the bills were paid, there was very little left over for anything, much less to pay attorneys. *What would we do?*

Every day the press talked of the "wealthy businessman" or "the million-aire" defendant. It might have been on paper, but cash was in very short supply. All the cards had been stacked against Paul, and they were about to tumble.

My meetings started with Bubba Marsall. I didn't like him, and I tried to convince Paul to let me hire Jerry Spence from Colorado. We probably could have had him for the same money we had to pay Bubba, and we would have had much better representation. One of the first sessions I had with Bubba was a "how are you going to pay me?" meeting.

Paul had told me to offer him some land he owned out toward the hunting lease. It was a forty-acre parcel, which Bubba agreed to take at appraised value as a down-payment for his services. The forty acres were probably worth about $80,000—it was a start. For the $80,000, I got to meet with Bubba very briefly. He would always start by telling me how he was working on Paul's case day and night. According to him, he thought about Paul's case twenty-four hours a day.

I would always have my notebook or scratch paper ready for when I'd finally get my 15 minutes with Bubba. I would raise questions about information being fed to me by Paul, or by others—leads that we thought should be pursued. You might have guessed that I soon broached the subject of Elizabeth knowing Hilton Robinson, and that Lee had been the one to tell me of their relationship and of the mysterious gift of the silver service to her mom. Bubba had me bring him the silver service to use as evidence.

Bubba actually appeared to get angry with me when I told him about "Little" Paul's disclosure of his mother toying with the possibility of having Paul murdered. Bubba waved it off as nonsense. Bubba would not put credence in Elizabeth actually discussing that with her younger son. *Why on Earth would her son say such a thing if it was not true?* I asked Bubba questions like, "What if she had tried to have Paul murdered and it went awry? What if Hilton Robinson had put Ricky Allen Prewitt up to killing her so he could have that big diamond?" Robinson wanted her ring, and he was the one in possession of it after she died, so how could you believe him when he said Prewitt had brought it to him for a loan to get out of town? I had so many questions, and so much information, but he would not consider any of it as the basis for a viable defense.

The same answers would be given to me each time I would go in to see him. He would say that we could not slander a mother who had been murdered. If you slandered her, then it would make Paul look worse, and it would give him a motive for the murder.

I didn't see it that way. In my opinion, if no viable alternative was put forth, how could you create reasonable doubt with the jury? And to me, there was plenty of reasonable doubt. Bubba and I didn't agree, and I didn't want him to be Paul's attorney. But we were locked in. There was now no money to hire anyone else.

Paul called me at home one evening. It was one of his regular calls. He told me that a guard at the jail had come to him and talked to him on his own. According to Paul, the guard told him that he worked as a security guard, part-time, at the Creighton Towers in Mobile. According to Paul, the guard wanted him to know that he recognized Elizabeth from a photo that had appeared in the paper. He went on to tell him that Elizabeth was a regular visitor of a man who lived at the Towers. The man she visited traveled a lot, and when he was in town, Elizabeth would meet him and spend the afternoon with him in his apartment.

I was very excited about this new contact, and according to Paul, the man was willing to testify to the fact that he had seen her visit the man on a regular basis. Paul and I felt that his story was relevant to showing that Elizabeth may have been participating in some things that could have put her at risk. We didn't know if it could have played a part, but it was certainly worth finding more about what she had been doing with her days, and what she may have been planning for her future.

My next visit with Bubba came after spending a long time in the waiting room first. Finally, I was shown into his inner sanctum. I started going down the list of things that made Elizabeth seem to be a very unstable person. I started with her visits to numerous psychiatrists, all the meds, running away with the kids with a sack of onions for food, secretly going into business with her daughter (as if they had been planning a new life after Paul was gone), her purchase of a gun, with a tag still hanging from the trigger, shooting at Paul in his place of business, her running into Paul with her car, the fact that Liz had been friends with Hilton Robinson, and the possibility of other, illicit marital affairs.

"Bubba, there is so much here, and it's not being looked at!" I shouted at him, not out of anger but frustration. Bubba was angry and slammed his hands on the desk. He told me he didn't want me to launch off on that tangent again. I stopped what I was saying, and he told me again that he/we could not say anything negative about her, because it would not help Paul's case.

I asked him what we were going to do, because all they kept pushing in the paper was that another woman (implying me) was Paul's motive. I told him again that I was not the motive for anything. If—and I repeated, *if*—Paul did such a deed, it was not for me or for any woman. Such a deed could only be contemplated to advance someone's own despicable desires, and I did not think he had done, or would do, such a thing. I asked him why he would not help Paul show that there were other possible motives, other suspects, and other possible scenarios that should be considered by a jury.

From my perspective, Bubba was obligated to show such evidence to the jury. "Why am I being held up as his motive?" I wanted to fight back, but Bubba would not help me. I wanted to tell the world what I had heard from Paul and others. Bubba wouldn't hear of it. I asked Bubba again why he refused to explore any other avenues. "Why, Bubba? Why do I have to be slandered and maligned because I love a man who loved and protected me?"

His eyes glared at me and he said, "You are the kind of woman men kill for." I couldn't believe my ears. I stood up, because I was getting ready to walk out of the door. I felt as though he had slapped my face. Those words ricocheted in my head like a bullet in a steel tub. *What an insult! How dare he say that to me?* Shaking my head, I stopped to ask him why he would say such a horrible thing to me.

His voice softened. His answer sounded to me like a problem he was having. It wasn't me or anything I had actually done. This fat, ugly man was looking through me. He finally told me, "You are a curvaceous, slender, voluptuous blonde. You are what men want. Some want it enough to kill for it."

I was not prepared to hear such a thing, but now I understood why he would not even give Paul a chance by suggesting another scenario. He had bought into the same press. "Bubba, it's just not so," I said as I walked out. I had put up with as much of him as I could stand for the day. The thought of Bubba Marsall looking at me in that light actually made me a sick. *How could he defend Paul when he believed what everyone else was saying? How could I make him see it just was not so?*

Chapter 34
An Expensive Trip
To Montgomery

Paul in his jail whites.

F our months passed with agonizing slowness, Paul in solitary confinement, the children and I in our own hell. We held together as a family
pack, us against the world. The case was front page news almost every
day, which made it difficult for all of us. I saved every paper, with every article
filled with everything they knew, every new tidbit each day, and every journal-
ists' spin on the same information. By the time they were setting the trial date,
Bubba made the request to move the trial, because area residents had been
so saturated with, so tainted by, all the information that had been published.
Bubba asked me to bring all the papers I had saved. He would use them as evidence when he made his motion to have the trial moved. I dutifully took them
to Bubba, and as with every other thing I provided, I never got them back, no
matter how many times I asked.

Paul's trial was moved to Montgomery, Alabama. The good thing was that maybe, just maybe, we could find a jury there that had not been influenced by all the news. Since my brother in Washington State had been following the case, I wondered how Montgomery would be any better. If a Montgomery resident was so out of the loop in current events, would that also be a person who could help make up a true jury of one's peers?

During the four months waiting for the trial to start, I often was a "gopher" for Paul to gather anything he needed. Each evening, we talked on the phone, so I could ask him where things were, who had to be paid, and how I was to pay them. We knew that our conversations were being monitored, but I didn't care. They even allowed me to go to the jail for the purpose of cutting his hair. I knew it had to be a setup, but that was the one and only time I had a chance to touch him, to talk to him, without a barrier between us. I showed up at the jail with a comb and scissors. They brought Paul to a small room just behind the docket counter. They left us alone, with the door cracked a bit, but it still provided the illusion of privacy.

I leaned down and kissed him softly on the neck. We talked quietly and reaffirmed our love for each other. I felt sure they were taping everything we said, but I didn't have any need to say anything about the case. I didn't have anything to hide. We were ready to go to Montgomery for trial.

Bubba assured us he would make liars out of Bill McEvoy, Hilton Robinson, and Ricky Prewitt once he got them on the stand. That was his big plan—he'd cross-examine these guys, and the jury would see they were lying.

Meantime, a new guy came on the scene. It was yet another person neither I nor Paul had ever heard of. Steve Hart was a convicted robber, then incarcerated in Memphis, Tennessee. And guess what? He too was a friend of Hilton Robinson, and he was saying that he had information on the Leverett case. Hart said that he felt compelled to come forward to authorities and say that Robinson had approached him to help with a job—robbing a very wealthy businessman's home for the purpose of acquiring a very large diamond, plus other items.

That new information had come to Paul via Bubba. With Hart coming forward, they now had another witness who put Prewitt and Robinson together much earlier, and for the purpose of planning a robbery of Paul's home. Steve Hart said he had been solicited by Robinson to help with the robbery.

In my heart, I just knew all that new info would help clear Paul. When they heard all the plotting of these known criminals, the jurors would see Paul didn't do it. I prayed that Paul would be freed to come home. I steeled myself for what was to follow. I had to be strong. I also had to come up with more money for Bubba.

The only thing we could do was give him a deed to more land that Paul owned, or give him a lien on a store. There was a piece of land that Paul had put "Little" Paul's name on as a gift many years before. "Little" Paul agreed to transfer the land. It was a big thing that he gave that up for his dad, and I truly appreciated his easy willingness to sign it over to Bubba. The land had been a gesture of love from his father—a gift made during good times.

As April 28th approached, Mark, Jamie, Lee, my mom, and I headed to Montgomery for the trial. We drove Paul's station wagon, and I rented a room in the outskirts of town. I did not want to stay in the city center and be caught up in that zoo of photographers and harassing crowds. We were being depicted as wealthy people, and I didn't know how I was going to pay for two motel rooms, food, and other needs.

Kathy, the oldest daughter, joined us at the motel. She was obviously not happy with the less than first-class accommodations. Her first question was why we were staying so far away from Montgomery's center. She stayed in the room next to me, sharing it with her brother and sister. She, being the oldest, gathered them under her wing. I felt really uncomfortable with her, but that was their family. I did not know what they discussed, but I was sure she was guiding them in a direction I didn't think they should take.

I was not happy when I found out that Judge Byrd, the one who would be trying Paul's case, was not a criminal law judge. He was a civil case judge and was low man on the totem pole in Mobile. His first criminal case would be Paul's capital murder trial. Galanos wanted a judge to be "in his pocket," and one unfamiliar with criminal proceedings would work best. It kept getting worse.

When the trial was to begin, they spent a good deal of time selecting a jury. I found out that there is a fine art to selecting a sympathetic jury. I listened closely to the confusing "attorney-speak." Both the defense and prosecution attorneys took turns questioning the prospective jurors. I learned that the procedure of jury selection favored the defendant more than the prosecution because the defendant's attorney could question and strike/or dismiss two prospective jurors who did not appear to be favorable to the defense case, versus the prosecution's strike of only one juror that it did not see as favorable to its case. But, with a recent rule change, now it was one strike each, which made the process quicker and much harder for the defense to select a sympathetic jury.

My clothing, make-up, and hair style were all carefully chosen to keep me from looking like a woman who would inspire envy. I wore no makeup. I also wore ugly, unflattering, cheap dresses. And I put my blonde hair in a bun. The last thing I wanted was for someone to look at me and then use me as a reason to convict Paul.

Mom, Jamie, and I slipped into the courthouse through a back door. Mark, Lee, and Kathy entered through the front and were confronted by an onslaught of people and photographers. Kathy was wearing a designer dress and opera pearls, and she was dripping with diamonds. It made a statement. I felt her diamonds might be brilliant, but her heart just might be black as coal.

I was provided a room, just behind the courtroom, where I could observe Paul's case being tried. The room looked like a conference room with a big table and chairs. It was a blessing. I stayed there for much of the trial. I was just out of sight, but still able to hear some of the testimony in the next room. At least I did not have to sit in the courtroom. Bubba did not want me in the courtroom, nor did I want to be there.

The second day of the trial, they brought Paul down the hall as they guided him into the courtroom. I was able to position myself so that he walked right past me. He was shackled—it broke my heart to see him that way. He wore his suit, and I thought he looked extremely gaunt and tired. As he walked by me and his sad eyes met mine, he said only one thing: "I am filthy."

Later, I learned they would not allow Paul to shower. This was the same man who took two showers a day, scrubbing from head to toe, and now he was being denied a shower. He said he could see the showers from his cell. He begged to be able to bathe, but they would not let him.

I am not going to try to solve this case with my story. But I need to put into words what was happening that kept me believing in Paul. There was always something being introduced that I felt helped substantiate his side, or at least show there may well have been a different scenario entirely than the one the prosecution was pushing.

From the backroom, I could not hear everything, but when Bill McEvoy testified about Paul soliciting him to find a person to kill his wife, I felt chills go down my spine. Bubba was supposed to slaughter him with his cross-examination and make Bill out to be a liar. It didn't happen. Bill stood firm in his position that Paul had used him to find a killer for his wife. Bill had a received a plea agreement for his testimony. Rather than be charged with capital murder, he was allowed to plead guilty to conspiracy to commit murder. For that sweet deal, he received a guaranteed ten-year sentence.

My question was: If you had a capital murder charge that could mean the death penalty in Alabama, and you could "sell" your testimony for a short prison sentence, wouldn't you take the deal? I knew Bill McEvoy would have agreed to say anything to reduce that charge.

The testimony depicted Paul as moving money around, borrowing money, and trying to juggle his debt. His salary at Colonel Dixie had been cut in half during that time, interest rates were sky high (18 percent), and it could have been he was caught up in keeping a lifestyle he could no longer afford. For every point the prosecution made, I felt there could have been a more than reasonable response based on the facts. In the four months since Paul's arrest, I could see that his financial picture was nothing like what the papers were reporting. I knew the lifestyle of Paul's family could not have been maintained much longer. I didn't know how he had kept it up as long as he did.

Prewitt testified to the brutal, unconscionable murder. The testimony was so hard to listen to that I didn't know how friends and family could bear to hear his story. Only a cold-hearted animal could do what he did. He said he entered the house with a key given him by Paul. He waited for her, confronted her, shot her, stabbed her multiple times, and then cut her throat. Then, he said, he took her car and left it at the shopping center, a couple blocks away from the murder scene. (*The same place the lady from Las Damas had seen Elizabeth wave as she walked over to talk to a man standing near her car. My question was; Why, if you just committed a crime, would you only drive two blocks and then get out of the car? Why wouldn't you keep driving?*)

Prewitt said he took the diamond ring directly to Robinson because he couldn't find Bill. They popped the diamond out of the ring, Robinson took the diamond, and then gave Prewitt $1,000 to leave town. He was to get more money later. Paul was supposed to have paid up on the contract by leaving the remainder in a truck at Robinson's store. The coupe de grâce for Paul was when Prewitt testified he had been paid $11,000 instead of the $10,000 he had agreed to. Prewitt said he was told the extra $1,000 was "for a job well done."

That was very damning testimony, and it certainly got the attention of the otherwise somnolent jury. Several of the jurors slept through important parts of testimony. One pregnant girl kept being excused for sickness, and most of the other jurors didn't seem to be up to the task of sorting out the complexities of the testimony. The whole mess got more sickening with each person who took the stand.

Galanos used every trick in the book to give the jury the wrong and slanted impression of what had actually happened. During Paul's testimony—and yes, unlike most murder defendants, he did testify on his own behalf—Galanos asked him if Elizabeth had ever filed for divorce. Paul said no. Paul said she had filled papers only for separate maintenance, not divorce. However, Galanos kept pushing that it was for a divorce and Paul was lying. In his closing argument, Galanos admitted the papers had been for separate maintenance, but the impression he created of "Paul the liar" had already been created.

Galanos also introduced a "manufactured" mug shot of me. It was not a real mug shot, but he put it into evidence as a photo of Paul's present wife, Phyllis Leverett, Exhibit #47. Galanos knew that he had not even been able to make a *prima facie* case against me—Judge Kittrell had tossed it out and reprimanded him for his theatrics—but Galanos still used a manufactured mug shot to influence the jury.

There were plenty of current photos available of me. He chose to use a modified photo, and created a mug shot to make the jury think I was some ugly, low-life criminal. They were ahead of their time in Photoshop techniques. Galanos knew that was misleading the jury, but he did it anyway. Paul's "crack" attorney never objected to the use of the manufactured mug shot.

I found out later that, in preparation for the trial, Galanos had tried to use that composite mug shot in a mock lineup to get someone ... anyone ... to say Paul and I had been seen at Colonel Dixie at the time of Elizabeth's death. An employee, Cynthia Jones, said she had seen Paul, in the middle of the day, with a blonde woman, and he was just talking to her in the parking lot behind the Government Street store. No matter how hard Galanos tried, she did not identify me. I had no idea who Paul was talking to, but it sure wasn't me.

It was confirmed through many statements that I read, after the trial, that Paul had casual relationships with numerous blondes—in fact, five different blonde women in the Mobile area evidently admitted to having had affairs with him. That was an interesting tidbit for me to hear, because if

Galanos knew he was involved with so many women, why was he trying so hard to single me out to take the blame? *The real reason?* Galanos didn't care about the truth. He just wanted to win at any cost.

Galanos also managed to allow the jury to hear a very distorted version of an incident in 1975, when Paul and Elizabeth were separated. Elizabeth evidently went to the airport with Mark and Lee. She asked the ticket agent if her husband would be able to find out if she was departing on this flight. She told them she didn't want him to know, because he might try to blow the plane up. That totally far-fetched figment of Elizabeth's imagination was used to discredit Paul, as if he had actually done such a thing. Even the FBI agent testified that Paul was never under suspicion for that.

However, the impulsive, vindictive nature of Elizabeth, paired with the unethical tactics of Galanos, meshed seamlessly to create one more jab at Paul's character. It was encouraging when Bubba woke up long enough to object to this totally fictitious charge against Paul, even though Galanos had again prevailed in planting yet another misleading, prejudicial seed.

A bit of background: The day of the murder, Elizabeth was supposed to get her hair done, then pick up her outfit to wear that evening to Mark's graduation. Paul was supposed to have taken Mark, Lee, and Mark's girlfriend to lunch. Paul then took Mark to pick out his new car, and they all went for a tour of the stores, and to the Army/Navy store to get a pair of jeans—all to fill time while waiting for the new car to be made ready for Mark to pick up at 5:00 p.m. When Lee and Paul finally arrived home, Lee went in first, but did not find her mother dead (thank God). Paul came in, minutes later, and discovered the body.

The police were called, and a family member came and picked up Lee. It was late afternoon, and Bubba Marsal just happened to be driving down Azalea Road that Friday on his normal route home. Bubba saw all the emergency vehicles at the Leverett home. Bubba, knowing the family, whipped in to see what was up, and he was there when the investigation began. Paul and Mark were taken in and tested for gunpowder on their hands. They were both found to be clean.

The D.A. made a big deal out of Bubba being there, as though Paul had arranged it, but it was so obvious it was coincidental.

During the trial, a woman named Mary Williams testified that she had been with Elizabeth at the hairdresser that fateful day. She said that she ran into her again, a short time later, at a shopping center parking lot as she entered the Rexall Drug Store. It was in that parking lot where they found Elizabeth's car after the murder. Mary Williams said she waved at Elizabeth. Elizabeth threw up her hand and waved back. Ms. Williams said she saw Elizabeth walking over to talk with a man standing near her car and, according to her testimony, never saw Elizabeth again. As soon as she heard Elizabeth had been murdered, she called to report that she had seen her about 3:00 p.m. with a man in the parking lot.

Prewitt testified that Paul gave him a key to get into the home. However, the patio door was unlocked, and the night chain had been previously broken. There was no need for someone to need a key to gain entry. Prewitt readily set out, in horrific testimony, all the horrific details about the bloody murder of Elizabeth. He said he drove her car to a gas station where he washed up, because there was so much blood.

The fingerprint man testified that, in his opinion, the car had not been wiped clean. How did Pruitt get into that car, all bloody, drive it to the shopping mall, park it, and leave it, with no one seeing him, and without getting any blood in the car? Lieutenant Richardson testified there were no blood stains in the car. He also said the clothes Elizabeth picked up from the cleaners were still hanging in the back seat. One could assume she most likely would have taken those clothes into the house when she went in, since she was to wear them that night. There were so many holes in all the stories.

My daughter Jamie was called to testify, and she said she loved Paul like a father, in a tearful and innocent attempt to help the man she then called her

"Daddy Paul." I had stayed out of the courtroom until they put Jamie on the stand. As I listened to her testimony, my heart was ripped open. I heard the sadness in her young voice. I came in for her, and then couldn't bring myself to leave. I sat in the back and listened until the end.

Lee, Paul's youngest child, also testified. She said she had witnessed the marital fights, and had seen her dad both threaten and abuse her mom. Her testimony certainly had an impact. Yet again, Bubba, in his effort to remain sensitive to the dead victim, dropped the ball. He did not ask Lee if she had been in the car with her mom when her mom tried to kill her dad. She wasn't asked any of the hard questions about her mother's crazy behavior. Bubba let her go because she was young and, in his eyes, it wouldn't help to ask a child those questions. I didn't agree. He should have pulled out of her the mutual violence that had taken place in that home. A good attorney could have done that with a little tact while still allowing the child to tell her stories in her own words.

Lee did testify to her mother knowing Hilton Robinson, visiting his store, Robinson calling her mother by name, and Robinson giving the silver set to her mother.

Galanos got in a really skewed Exhibit #47, the manufactured mug shot of me. He made a production over the mean and ugly woman in the mug shot who had made Lee write a memo on that day she recognized Hilton Robinson in the paper. It was as though I was doing something really sinister, when the opposite was true. I wanted Lee to write what she remembered, without interference from anyone. Again, our "sleeping" counsel did not object.

Paul's youngest son, Mark, testified that McEvoy already had keys to the house. Mark did not offer derogatory testimony about his father. In all the statements Mark had made up until that day, it appeared he believed in his father's innocence, the same as I did.

Twenty-seven people traveled 260 miles to Montgomery, at their own expense, to testify to Paul's good character. About 30 people were willing to give statements on his behalf, all to his trustworthiness and good character.

>━┥◆┝━○━┥◆┝━<

During the closing arguments, Chris Galanos managed to point at me and say I was the reason Paul wanted his divorce. I just looked at him and shook my head, no. *I couldn't very well jump up and say no. He had already shown* that jury the papers where Elizabeth and Paul were legally separating, or filing for separate maintenance in 1975, years before I ever met Paul. Their marriage was a terrible mess, with settlement proposals being made and rejected. Paul obviously had numerous affairs along the way. They had succeeded in destroying that union on their own.

During all this, Bubba was "so polite." That fat Southern boy just sat quietly and allowed Galanos to complete his entire closing remarks without objecting to a single thing he said.

Bubba was sick the day of his closing argument. To me, he looked bloated and red-faced. His wife handed him medications throughout the morning. He lost his voice and had to stop to take water several times. He started his closing remarks with some grandiose statements about man being able to go into space, walk on the moon, and do great things. I thought he was trying to tie it in to the fact that, even with the progress of mankind, we still needed the wisdom and judgment of the human mind to listen to evidence and render fair, impartial verdicts. Somehow, he seemed to get off track, and try as I did to follow his logic, he just wasn't making much sense.

While Bubba was attempting to give an eloquent and profound summation, Chris Galanos was making every possible distraction by moving around big chalk boards or anything else that would take the jury's attention away from Bubba. Galanos was very successful in distracting the jury. Bubba's big moment was a miserable bust. The judge was finally ready to send the case to the jury.

Here is the Galanos-written charge from the grand jury that had issued the original indictment against Paul: "Paul Leverett, whose name is to the Grand Jury otherwise known as stated, unlawfully, intentionally, and with malice aforethought caused Elizabeth Leverett to be killed with a pistol and / or a knife pursuant to a contract for hire, to-wit: a contract or promise to pay Ricky Allan Prewitt the approximate sum of $10,000 in United States currency to kill Elizabeth Leverett. The said Ricky Allan Prewitt, pursuant to said contract or promise with Paul Leverett, did unlawfully, intentionally, and with malice aforethought kill Elizabeth Leverett by shooting her with a gun and/or stabbing her with a knife in violation of 13A-5-31 (a) (7), Code of Alabama, against the peace and dignity of the State of Alabama."

The judge charged the jury and gave them the offenses to consider. The jury was given three choices:

Find the defendant guilty of capital felony as charged in the indictment;

Find the defendant guilty of murder as charged in the indictment;

Find the defendant not guilty.

As we departed from the courtroom and were walking down the hall, Bubba sidled up to Kathy. He was walking along beside her and I overheard him saying, "This is the worst I've ever seen. It's bad. The jury is not on our side."

I thought: *Why the hell is he telling her that? I'm the one paying him Paul's money to defend him, and he did a piss-poor job.* That so-called great attorney had dropped the ball so many times it was pathetic. For his approximate $125,000 fee to mastermind Paul's defense, about all he did was get a couple of those guys on the stand and say, "Liar, liar, pants on fire." Now he was running to Elizabeth's daughter, trying to make excuses. I was livid, yes, but I was even more scared.

When we received word the jury had reached a verdict, my heart almost stopped. I positioned myself in the conference room, where I had waited most of the week. As the courtroom filled, I could stand in the hall and see Paul sitting at the table. I watched as he stood to hear the verdict.

On May 2, 1983, Paul Fawcett Leverett was found guilty of the lesser charge of murder. His face remained solemn as the verdict was read. He turned to look at me, and as we made eye contact, he mouthed the words, "I'm not guilty."

Tears were welling up inside—I tried not to cry. There was noise in the courtroom, but I can't remember too much about it. It is another of those black holes in my memory, where my brain was once again doing its best to protect me from the pain.

This time, we all held hands and walked out the front door.

The cameras were flashing. No matter.

It was done.

I obviously had not been the only one who did not feel that the prosecution had proven its case that Paul had paid for the murder of Elizabeth Leverett.

In the State of Alabama, murder for hire was a capital offense punishable by the death penalty. The entire case presented by Chris Galanos and team was to show that Paul Leverett had solicited Bill McEvoy to find and hire a killer. Bill found a killer, according to their story, and Prewitt carried out the murder. The killer, Prewitt, had given the ring to Robinson, for money, and then received full payment later, according to them. However, the testimony was all so contrived, bought, and paid for, from criminals jockeying to better their plight. Galanos wanted the big fish, Paul, and he did whatever was necessary to get him.

In the end, the jury was not convinced, and they could not, and they did not, find him guilty of hiring someone to commit that murder. There was not any evidence that was reliable enough to convict him of murder-for-hire beyond a reasonable doubt.

But the judge had given them another option, and the jury took it. No one on that jury had enough guts to stand up and say, "There is no evidence to prove the case, so we are going to acquit." Instead, they found Paul guilty of the lesser-included offense of murder.

There was never any evidence during that trial that indicated Paul had anything to do with the murder itself. So they found Paul not guilty of hiring her murderer (the only thing he could have been guilty of based on the evidence), and found him guilty of something he couldn't have done (which was to actually murder her). *Is that a conundrum or what?*

I believed that if Paul was guilty of that crime, he should have been executed. There was no way that a guilty person should have walked away from that courtroom with less than the ultimate penalty. No one deserved to die the way Elizabeth Leverett died.

Ricky Prewitt, who described his unconscionable acts of murder for monetary gain, walked away with life without parole, and possibly a new identity within the system. Bill McEvoy, who said he set it all up as a joke on Paul, walked away with a conspiracy charge and ten years in jail. Hilton Robinson, the star scum-ball, bought his way out of prison by hanging on to Elizabeth's diamond, the ring he had wanted so badly, using it to gain his freedom and launch Chris Galanos into the big time.

Funny how it all works—every time I hear the song about the night that the lights went out in Georgia ("That's the night that they hung an innocent man, Don't trust your soul to no backwoods Southern Lawyer, cuz the judge in the towns got blood stains on his hands"), I think of Bubba, the "backwoods" Southern lawyer, matched up against a district attorney hungry to make a name for himself.

Bubba had thrown Paul "under the bus" for some reason. There was financial gain for a few, but the collateral damage to the family left behind was incalculable.

The Trial Was Over

How do you describe grief—deep, hard, unspeakable grief? I am sure it would be worse when a person loses a child, but other than that loss, I can't imagine anything worse than Paul's conviction. I had completely lost control over my future, with no way to plan anything. I had no idea what would happen next.

What I did know was I had to get my family back together and take them home. We managed to get back to the motel. My Aunt Ina had arrived some time during the day, and wanted to take me away, somewhere just me and her, for a dinner together. Mom was able to stay with Jamie, and I went with Aunt Ina to a hotel restaurant in Montgomery. It was good to have her there with me, and it was good not to be the one to keep everyone else together, for just one evening.

We were seated in a lovely, soothing, and warm dining room. It had the feeling of an Old World lodge, surrounded by wood paneling and soothed by soft candle light and linen-draped tables. It was a precious time with me and my dear aunt, who cared enough about me to make the trip, and to rescue me for just these brief hours from the wave that had overtaken me.

Talking to her was easy, and the glass of white wine was gradually allowing me to relax and let go of my guarded control. We talked and I didn't have to think, "Is this room bugged?" "Do I need to protect a child?" or "Can my statement be twisted to hurt me?" It was just me and Ina.

I looked past her and, to the left of the room, there sat Detective Bob Eddy. He was one of the detectives who had worked so hard to seal my husband's fate. We made eye contact. I looked at Ina. I told her the detective who had framed Paul was sitting behind her. We both turned and looked at him, causing his table companions to ask him, "Who are those two ladies at the table?"

He stood up and walked toward us, and we asked him to join us. I had a hard time putting into words what I was feeling. I told him that he had no idea what a mistake he had made. While trying to get those words out, the tears welled and spilled from my eyes. Aunt Ina told him he had done the wrong thing, and Eddy immediately became defensive.

He looked at my aunt and said, "I've been threatened before." I remembered that phrase exactly. I knew that was wrong, and immediately set out to stop that line of conversation. I told him that no one was threatening him. He needed to understand he had made a terrible mistake—he had helped to convict an innocent man. My grief was so deep and so apparent to anyone. I had just lost the only man who had ever been good to me. Paul had protected me and given me a good life, and now he was gone.

Detective Eddy looked at me for what seemed like a long time. I regained my composure as he spoke to me quietly. "Just like Elizabeth," Eddy said, "you are also a victim of this crime."

"*A victim of a crime?*" Is that what he just said? I shook my head no, Paul didn't do it. Eddy was quiet, but his belief was firm. Eddy believed Paul to be guilty of the crime. I didn't. I couldn't. It just couldn't be. Eddy said he hoped I'd be okay, and then he excused himself and returned to his table and his friends. We tried to complete our meal without looking his way again.

Me? Just another crime victim? Those words resonated within my subconscious long after the conversation ended. For me to accept the notion that I was yet another victim of this heinous crime, I would have to believe that Paul was guilty. I was not ready to even consider that possibility.

We drove back to Pensacola in what seemed like a funeral dirge. Lee and Mark were with me. Kathy had left to go back to her Houston home. I could feel the tension, and I knew that Kathy would continue to pursue whatever was left, because her mom was dead, and Paul would be gone for a long time. I wondered, "What can I do to prevent everything from collapsing?"

When we arrived back home, I called Lee and Mark into the living room. I told them that I knew there would be people, and especially lawyers, trying to tear us apart. I asked them to please tell me what they wanted, so attorneys would not have to be involved. I could sense its coming, much like a person with arthritis can anticipate the rain. Just as sure as the sun shines, and rain falls, I knew that Kathy would be hiring attorneys. I didn't dislike her for that. I just intuitively knew that action was going to make things harder for all of us. Over and over, I tried to stress that they should work with me to figure out what to do next. I warned them: Once attorneys are involved, we lose the chance to work this out in everyone's best interest.

Nothing was said by Mark or Lee that indicated they were ready to start anything. Mark and I talked about how we could work for Colonel Dixie and keep everything going. He was such a sharp kid. I felt like we were friends with a strong bond. I told him I was willing to learn to manage a store, fry chicken, flip burgers, whatever. At first, I thought maybe Mark and I could manage. But no matter what they said, it soon became apparent the external pressure that would come from Elizabeth's family and Paul's partner would override anything we tried to do.

Chapter 35
Saint Clair

Leverett faces 10 years
to life for wife's murder

MAY 3 - 1983

By ANNE REEKS
Press Staff Reporter

Convicted of murder Monday evening in the hire-killing of his first wife, Mobile businessman Paul Leverett faces 10 years to life in prison at sentencing June 10 in Mobile County Circuit Court.

The well-heeled co-owner of a chain of Mobile fast-food restaurants remains in jail, where he has been held since he was arrested Feb. 4 on the capital felony charge of paying another man $10,000 to kill his first wife, Elizabeth, nearly three years ago.

The 45-year-old suburban matron was shot twice in the head and her throat was cut in the bedroom of the Leveretts' luxurious Montcliff Drive home on May 30, 1980.

IN AN APPARENT compromise verdict, the jury in Leverett's Montgomery County Circuit Court trial bypassed the capital murder charge and found Leverett guilty of the lesser included offense of murder.

The six women and six men of the jury

reached their unanimous verdict after about 3½ hours of deliberation at the conclusion of a six-day trial, which was held in Montgomery instead of Mobile because of pretrial publicity here.

Mobile County Circuit Judge Robert L. Byrd Jr., who presided over the trial, will sentence Leverett June 10.

Leverett, co-owner of the Colonel Dixie fast-food chain, can look forward to the prospect of being paroled in seven to 10 years even if he is given the maximum sentence.

Leverett was denied bail pending trial on the capital charge, and if the judge sentences him to 20 years or more in prison, he will not be eligible for release on bail pending appeal.

His attorney said that until sentencing it is too early to say whether there will be an appeal.

SHOULD LEVERETT win reversal of his conviction on appeal, he could not be retried on the capital charge, a judicial source said,

Please see Page 5, Col. 1

AP photo
GUILTY — Mobile businessman Paul Leverett leaves a Montgomery courtroom Monday night after his murder conviction.

THOUGH THE TRIAL was held businessman as the one who paid

W*hen Hell Was Brand New* was the title of the book Paul said he was going to write. Given the circumstances, I could see why. The Saint Clair Correctional Facility was a new medium security prison located in Odenville, Alabama, about twenty-five miles north of Birmingham. That was where they sent Paul after his June 8, 1983 sentencing. Paul received a life sentence for murder, the lesser included offense to the capital murder-for-hire charge. The capital offense would have put him into the death-penalty range. At 49 years of age, a life sentence would give him the possibility of parole at around 65 years of age. Plus, he was very optimistic about his chances of having his conviction overturned on appeal. Paul was the eternal optimist, so he embraced all the appeal's positive aspects. I, on the other hand, did not share his optimism.

I pulled out my map to locate the prison. The route there would become so familiar that my car could just about reach it on auto-pilot. My life would wrap around my visitation time with Paul. I would be able to see him, one time each week, for about three to four hours. The visitation schedule was organized by using the first letter of the prisoner's last name. Visitors would fall into schedules 1, 2, 3, or 4. On a rotational basis, the schedule changed each week. For example, if I visited Paul from 8 a.m. to 11 a.m. on Saturday, the visitation time on the following Saturday afternoon would be from 1 p.m. to 4 p.m. The third week visitation would be on Sunday at 8 a.m. to 11 a.m., with the last rotation visit on Sunday afternoon from 1 p.m. to 4 p.m.

In order to see Paul for the 8 a.m. visit on either Saturday or Sunday, I would have to be parked in the line of waiting visitors at Saint Clair's outer gate by no later than 6:30 a.m. Sometime around 6:30 a.m., they would open the gate, allowing all of us to drive in, park, and enter the in-process area. We lined up to make sure that our names had been cleared for visitation—the inmate had designated, by their signature, that they wanted a visit from the person showing up—and that the visitor's identification matched.

The officials held to the letter of the rule. They really got off on being able to turn a wife, mom, dad, brother, or sister away because the inmate had not put the person's name on his visitation card for that week. Over the time I visited, I saw numerous relatives and friends, who had driven for hours, or in the area for only one day and be unable to return any time soon, turned away, crying, because they were not allowed to see their loved one.

The searches were horrendous. Visitors had to have on underwear (bra and panties—you had to have both), and basic, non-revealing outer garments (pants and shirt, or a dress or skirt). No jackets, zip sweatshirts, or additional outerwear allowed. They would run their hands through your hair and under your arms. They'd cup your breasts with their hands (sometimes it felt like they were fondling me) to make sure nothing was in your bra, and then run their hands basically all over you before you were cleared for a visit. Since no coats, or additional clothing, were allowed into the visitation area, everyone would just stay inside on cold days, or they could choose to weather the cold, until their teeth would chatter, then run back in to warm up. You could carry in one pack of cigarettes, and one transparent bag of change for the vending machines.

Even after the arduous in-processing, we often had to wait an hour or more before we would be escorted through the locked doors, down a hall, and into an open room with stationary tables and seats. The tables were square, with a seat on each side. The room was used as a cafeteria on some days. One long side of the room was nothing but glass, which overlooked a walled, totally empty, courtyard open to the sky above. There was only one way into the courtyard, and that was from the tabled area.

After everyone was inside, counted, and doors secured, the prison guards would open the flood gates for the prisoners to come into the room to see their families. Lots of hugs and kisses before people settled in for their visits. If anyone left the area, they could not return. There were restrooms inside, but if a female visitor had to use the restroom while there, she had to endure another intimate pat down by "Helga, Queen of the SS." I tried not to go.

For those early morning visits, I would have to drive up to Birmingham the day before. Getting a hotel or motel room every week proved to be very expensive, but I had to do it. The trip up was a four and a half hour drive from Mobile to Birmingham. I would get a room, and then be up by 4:30 to get dressed and drive to Saint Clair before 6:30 a.m.

For the afternoon visitation days, I could sleep at home, then get up early and drive five hours straight in order to be at the front gate by 11:30. I'd process in, wait, have my visit, and leave. No matter the time of my visit, as soon as it was over, I would start the five-hour drive back home. On afternoon visit times, I would be in for a 14-to 16-hour day in order to see my husband. I was well aware that anyone I told about the inconvenience of trying to visit him would most likely be delighted. It was punishment for him, so I guess that was the intention.

In the beginning, I would cry just about all the way home. It was so painful to sit with my husband, hold his hand, exchange a peck or two, but that was it—it was torture. My body would want to respond, but we could not allow it. Each week after our visit, I so stressed I was a nervous wreck. For those who wanted incarceration to be painful for the offender, just know it was. The pain also extended to all of the offender's family, so everyone paid, one way or the other.

During my many hours in the car alone, dealing with my pain and frustration, I practiced making my case for allowing conjugal visits. Believe me, I understand the many arguments for not giving that privilege to inmates, and I agreed with 99 percent of them. But I had needs too, like most of the wives who visited. In my imaginary plea to those imaginary, judgmental women, I would say to them, "It is okay. I understand he has to pay the price, so, since you don't want me to have a conjugal visit with *my* husband, then I'll just have sex with *your* husband." I was so angry and in so much pain. I didn't act on any of my internal conversations, even though the imaginary fights were very vivid in my mind.

While gathering evidence, handling Paul's affairs, and meeting with attorneys, I probably had at least two hits a week from horny, married men (many Mobile, and a couple of Montgomery, attorneys; bankers; insurance agents, etc.), all trying to take advantage of my lonely state. I'm sure most were truly altruistic in wanting to help ease my pain.

A Polaroid shot that someone took during one of my visits to St. Clair.

Back to Saint Clair: If the guards saw anyone attempting too much intimacy, the visitor would be immediately, and without discussion or ceremony, escorted to the door. If ejected, they would not be allowed to return during that visit. That being said, there were some who had connections with guards—for those few, the guards chose not to see what was going on. Visitors intuitively knew to keep their mouths shut and stay out of it.

I witnessed many strange things over the first year and a half following Paul's incarceration.

Conjugal visits were definitely not allowed in Alabama state prisons. But I knew the guards had to be on the take when I watched a strange looking woman being processed into the facility for visitation. She was tall, thin, black-haired, and had on what looked to be a gypsy skirt. It was well below the knees, and as full as gathers could make it. If she whirled, it would have stood out straight around her. She also had on high-heeled shoes.

Week after week, I would see the same pathetic people showing up to see their loved ones. That "lady" got everyone's attention, because no one had seen her before. After everyone was settled in for their visits, I turned and saw the woman and her inmate in the courtyard. It was a nice day, so there were quite a few people outside. Most would stand along the walls. They would lean up against them, stand close to their visitor, and talk.

There was something strange about her scene. I looked more closely at them, and out of the corner of my eye tried to figure out what the heck was going on. The woman was standing with her back against the wall, leaning back with her legs slightly spread. The man had his back to the center of the courtyard. The full skirt of the woman camouflaged the fact that she had the front center front hem pulled up to the height of the inmate's penis. The remainder of the skirt flowed down in a normal position around her. The man was moving and having intercourse with her while standing among the other couples around them.

Paul and I looked at each other, rolled our eyes, and acknowledged what was happening. My eyes darted around the room. There were many people who knew what was happening, but everyone seemed to be trying their best to pretend nothing out of the ordinary was going on. Soon, it was over, with the guards pretending to be none the wiser.

A second disturbing incident was a woman who visited her husband with her two children. They would position themselves at a corner table, the inmate with his back to the wall. The mom would sit to his right, on the side next to him, with the two kids opposite. I learned that mom would have a condom in her hand and apply it discreetly. With her body leaning forward, and an elbow propped on the table, she faced him. In that position, she was able to pull off a hand-job without detection.

It was so demeaning to be there, but it was more than that. Among the crowd, Paul and I stood out like sore thumbs. The guards liked us, and recognized we were different. We were polite and obeyed the rules.

Paul was very proud of me visiting—an element of prison life not readily apparent to the outside world of the law-abiding. If you had a family that could put money into your account, brought you money for snacks during visitation, or had a wife or girlfriend who was pretty, the inmate gained some respect from the other prisoners. Paul immediately went to the top, as far as other prisoners respecting him. They all knew Paul was well-educated by the way he carried himself and by the way he spoke. They liked the big contagious grin he flashed to everyone he met. Word got out that he was visited every week by his young, blonde wife. He also received money for cigarettes. Paul never smoked, but cigarettes were used in prison in lieu of money. He bartered for better food, additional laundry services, sinus meds, etc.

During our short visits, Paul would tell me of the horrific things that happened each week. Much of it was because it was a new system, new guards were always being trained, and everything centered around a new building that had been cheaply thrown up, at great expense to the taxpayer.

In the beginning, my visitations were what kept me going. Each and every week, it was like a trip to Mecca, to spend my brief visitation charging my brain with new information and new instructions needed to get me through the week. For well over a year following Paul's incarceration, I dutifully made my pilgrimage to that prison. In a fourteen-month period, I missed only one weekend, when I was so ill I could not make the trip. Looking back, I really don't know how I did it. I was like a mouse on a wheel, running like crazy, not able to figure out how to make the wheel stop or how to jump off.

Paul's letters to me arrived every day. He begged for sexy photos of me. I did make a very uncomfortable attempt to find a friend to take some photos of me at the pool. It was my big attempt at "cheesecake," which was not my forte. However, he loved it.

My "cheesy" attempt at cheesecake.
The photo was taken next to M.E.'s pool by Jimmy Langston.

He would write words of love and sadness, followed by ideas he thought might help in his appeal. He would discuss with me financial matters that boggled my mind. Bubba had gotten his $125,000 fee paid in cash and in mortgages. The store liens were to be paid as soon as we could complete the sale of Paul's shares of stock and real estate holdings in the Dixie Company. He and Dick Moore owned the stock 50-50, with Moore being the President, and Paul serving as Treasurer.

Their Grand Opening of Colonel Dixie, as co-owners;
Dick on the left, Paul on right.

As I began putting all the pieces together like a puzzle, one of the first things that reared its ugly head was Paul's relationship with Moore. Moore arrogantly referred to Paul as his employee. That seemed strange, considering it was a 50-50 business. I looked back through records and files. Minutes from the Board of Directors meeting in September 1979 (the year before Elizabeth had been murdered) showed they had voted to reduce the salaries of both Paul and Moore by more than one-half. Their salaries of $5,700 per month were reduced to $2,500 due to economic conditions, slowing business, and rising interest rates.

I also discovered the reason Moore was not impacted as severely as Paul. The business had started with Moore approaching Paul, yet, to adjust for Moore's special expertise, it was agreed that he would retain 1 percent of all gross sales, in addition to his salary. That extra 1 percent was enough to keep Moore in a much better financial position, and the reason Paul's family could see a difference in Moore's lifestyle vs. theirs. That being said, the press kept describing Paul as a wealthy businessman, a millionaire, a whatever. It was laughable to me. Yes, property holdings had a high value on paper, but those values were offset by big liens and other obligations. Paul paid a home mortgage of about $900 a month, plus paid the kids' education bills. It all worked as long as Paul was there to keep it going.

From the end of 1979 on, Paul started pulling money from savings his mom had left him. He also began borrowing from Colonel Dixie, or selling property, or selling shares of property, to raise money. He was also receiving additional income from some property he was renting out.

Seeing his financial shortfall on paper made me believe him even more when he said the juggling and borrowing of money from 1979 to 1980 was all part of trying to maintain the family lifestyle until the economy came back and his salary could be restored. The prosecution used that fact to help prove he borrowed money to have his wife killed. There seemed to be no way to win; his best defense could also be used as the prosecution's best argument.

My job was to deal with the here and now. I soon found out that Merchants National Bank held the first mortgage on the house. The deal we made with them allowed me to borrow about $20,000 as a second mortgage on our home. The bankers liked Paul and they really were trying to help us. We were betting on the sale of the company, and on the sale of the house, in the very near future. Merchants Bank was willing to loan Paul and I the money to make principal payments on the house for two years. It was a loan that gave us two years, guaranteed, that the house would not go into foreclosure. Surely within the next two years we could sell the house, and pay off mortgages. Surely within two years . . .

Chapter 36
"Is That All There Is?"

Wendy (Jamie's friend) on her Arabian, Marshall, and Jamie on The Whiz.
(Photo taken by me at our rental house at Cottage Hill.)

A
s soon as we could, we hired the Howell, Johnston, and Langford law firm to work on Paul's appeal to the appellate court. The law firm of Kilborn and Redditt was working on negotiating a sale price for Colonel Dixie stock and real estate holdings. Even with the buy-sell agreement in place, there was much to be worked out. The value of the 500 shares of stock was established at $500 a share at the beginning of 1983. Then I found out that Paul had taken out promissory notes with Colonel Dixie totaling about $55,000. That money, plus interest and attorneys fees, would be deducted from the proceeds from his shares of stock.

The real estate was another matter. Only a good real estate attorney was going to be able to put the deal together. Each of the ten stores had to be appraised. One-half of the store value and one-half of the mortgage debt belonged to Paul and Moore. For Paul's defense and appeals, he assigned his attorneys one-half of his one-half share as payment. Or, in a couple of circumstances, he gave a $10,000 lien on one store, and a $15,000 lien on another. Since Moore was buying Paul out, the title companies had to work out how they could insure clear titles back to Moore after the purchase was completed. It was a test for the proverbial New York lawyer. As a country girl, I was in way over my head.

But I had to try to understand. I dug deeper into Paul's desk and files. I found a drawer that held every bank statement from his checking account dating back several years. None had ever been opened. That was so peculiar that I decided to balance his checkbook. He actually had $10,000 more than his balance in his check register reflected. I asked him, "Did you know you had extra money in your account?" He didn't. From his habit of padding every check he wrote when he entered it in his register, he had, over the years, accumulated an extra $10,000. Paul seemed to be suffering from *calcuphobia*—always err big and you'll be okay.

Since he didn't know he had the money, I told Paul that I was taking it. I was really in fear of what each day would bring. I told him, "I need to put this found money away in order to have something in reserve. Otherwise, your attorneys will consume every dime you have." I actually put the cash money into a safe deposit box, which helped make me feel somewhat better.

I received a call from Chobee Slay, a loan officer from the 1st National Bank. He said he needed to talk with me and would like for me to come in to the bank, or if that was uncomfortable, he would drop by the house. I told him to come by the house. He had been a hunting buddy and good friend of Paul's.

When he arrived, I invited him into our study, the sitting room right off our kitchen. After we sat down, he explained that Paul had done business with him for many years on a gentleman's hand-shake, "my word is my bond," sort of basis. Paul often juggled money to keep things going, so it was not unusual for Paul to accumulate a bank debt of almost $100,000 in unsecured loans. Chobee was left holding a bunch of signature loans that Paul had been keeping up through interest-only payments.

After seeing so many zeros, my mind went blank and my mouth dropped open. Chobee was here with his "hat in his hand," he said, to ask me what I (I repeat, *what I*) intended to do about the money *Paul* owed the 1st National

Bank. The bank told Chobee to figure out how to get their money. He was really pitiful in his humble demeanor. I got the feeling his career was on the line that day.

I had been taking a crash informal course in creative financing. I asked Chobee whether, if we gave him a third mortgage on the Airmont house (appraised value $380,000), that would satisfy 1st National and remove the noose from around his neck? Chobee grabbed the lifeline I tossed him. He asked me, in the most incredulous voice, if I would actually give them a third on the house. I really didn't mind. I figured that Paul had borrowed the money, and it needed to be paid back. The equity in that albatross of a house was the only thing I knew I could give him, and so I did.

As I walked Chobee to the door, he said to me, "Phyllis, when I left the bank to come here, all the members of our board told me I was wasting my time, and bet me that I would not be able to get any security for the loans. No one is going to believe this."

I don't want to sound like I thought I was so wonderful in signing a third mortgage to Chobee. Number one, it was the right thing to do. They were Paul's honestly incurred debts, and justly due for repayment. Number two, I didn't care about that damned house, and I didn't want it.

After Chobee left that night, I walked around the house. I had never wanted to live there. I knew that Mark had to go back to Dallas to finish school, and even though I would take care of Lee, I knew she would most likely want to live with the big sister she adored in Houston. Paul understood when I told him I wanted to leave the house. He actually agreed with me, that it would be best if I did not stay there.

As far as I was concerned, it could be mortgaged to the hilt and, worse come to worse, the bank could have it. Paul knew I never wanted to live there, and under the circumstances, living there would be unbearable for me. I was more than ready to leave, and as they say, ready to "shake the dust from my shoes" as I walked out the door.

In the aftermath of the trial, I continued to allow our children to have their friends come to visit. They needed their support systems and I tried to be welcoming. I also felt that children in the house kept it from feeling like it was dying, and it badly needed resuscitating. Jamie, the youngest, was 12, Nathan 15, Lee 16, and Mark, the oldest, was almost 19 years old at the time.

Diamond in the Dark

All of Jamie's little girl friends were infatuated with the good looks of her big brother Nathan. Lee's friends were infatuated with the handsome young college friends that Mark brought through on his way out for the evening. To me, it all seemed a healthy, age-appropriate phenomenon. All of them seemed to be respectful, empathetic, and supportive. While the children were occupied with more positive energy, I was assessing and planning the next, best course of action.

With only a $2,500 a month income, plus some rental money still coming in, I figured I would be able to live alright if I didn't have to maintain a huge house. During the summer, our air-conditioning bill was astronomical. In the early 80's, a $350-$450 power bill was unheard of by most, but that was just one of the myriad of problems that had to be factored into the equation.

The stress was getting to me. I worried all the time and I started to lose weight. I wasn't sleeping and I couldn't eat much of anything. My stomach cramped, growled, and churned. When I did eat something, it would be even worse. Anyone around me could hear rumbling that sounded more like a tsunami moving toward the shore, causing everyone to look around the room trying to discern where the noise was coming from. It was very embarrassing.

The next time I went to Kilborn's office to discuss the sale of the company and other matters, I sat in the chair across from his desk. I felt small as I looked across this huge brown span that separated me from the tall, graying, and handsome older man. As he would candidly give me his opinion, I at times would almost double over from stomach cramps. He asked me if I'd eaten, and I told him it didn't help—eating just made things worse. He shook his head and apologized for what I was going through, as though it was his fault. He was a nice man. He told me to call him Ben.

Ben told me to get prepared for the additional lawsuits that would most likely be following soon. He had heard through the grapevine to expect Paul and Elizabeth's daughter to sue for the children's share of everything. I told him I had tried from the start to head that off, and I had actually asked them to work with me, to tell me what they wanted before getting attorneys involved. He looked down, shook his head, and gave a warm, low chuckle. "I don't think you can stop them," he said.

I asked him what he thought they would get if they sued their father. Paul was appealing the case, and maintained he was innocent. He looked at me and said, "They may take everything, and that's including the kitchen sink."

That was certainly encouraging. I intended to be proactive on this one, and I told him of my plan to find a different place to live and a job, so I would be able to care for my children regardless of the outcome. I talked to him more like he was a counselor than a real estate attorney. He was in agreement that going to work would be a good thing to do, but working in Mobile was most likely going to be difficult in the aftermath of the trial. Everyone knew the Leverett name now, and everyone had an opinion. He knew the wounds were still too fresh, and I was not yet in any condition to take on anything else. I had "Paul business" of some kind that had to be attended to every day. I was non-stop busy and mentally weary.

Later that week, I had an appointment with Jimmy Langford about Paul's appeal. I dragged myself in to one of Mobile's only high-rise office buildings. When I entered, I was greeted by their very slender, "knock-out" secretary Deborah. Deborah had long, dark, curly hair, coiffed to perfection. She was wearing skin-tight jeans (not unusual), three-inch FMP's (Fuck-Me-Pumps), and a blazer—the girl should have been in *9 to 5* with Dolly Parton and Jane Fonda. She not only looked great, but she was a very nice girl.

Tom Johnston, me, Paul, and, the Lady Helen. Both Tom and Lady Helen became my very good friends.

Tom Johnston, the other partner, just happened to be walking through the office. He saw me and waved his hand for me to come into his office. Tom was a gruff old sort (it was suspected that he had purchased his Scottish title as the 13th Baronette of Caskeben, along with his wife's title, the Lady Helen), so I followed obediently.

Sir Johnston was on his side of his desk, and he barked out marching orders in no uncertain terms: "Don't ya ever come down heah looking like this again. They'll beat ya down if they can. From now on, ya fix ya-sef up. When I see ya ag'in, you better have ya hair done, a new outfit, and some real nice high heels on. D'ya hee-ah me? You hold ya head up high, and forget about what people say. The only thing they know is what they read in a paper. I'll be waitin' to see ya next time." He smiled at me, winked, and then waved me out the door. He most likely laughed when I closed the door behind me.

The first thing I wanted to do was to get out of that big house. I needed to be in an environment where I felt more in control. If I moved out, the bank could have it. It was amazing luck when I found a house for rent on West Cottage Hill Road. The house was an old brick ranch, about 2200 square feet, and had a double carport and outside storage/laundry room. There were three bedrooms, two baths, a large country kitchen, beautiful hardwood floors, a breakfast bar, a den, a foyer, a huge formal dining room, and a living room in the front of the house. I knew those rooms could store a lot of furniture.

The clincher for the deal was that the house sat far back on the property, and a white rail fence surrounded the front two acres and lined the driveway all the way back to the house. It was private. It was made for us. The house was in fair condition, and the pasture would allow me to save several hundred dollars each month because I could move Whiz to our house instead of paying for his expensive board. Jamie could ride across the street and through the woods to the stable where he had been kept. I knew she would need to keep in touch with her riding friends. I rented the place for $550 a month.

Now came the job of preparing for the move. I felt so alone. I spent every night packing china and crystal into huge packing boxes. I would just pack it, label it, and store it. I would keep out only what I needed to keep house in my new environment. The Airmont house was filled from top to bottom with stuff Paul and Elizabeth had collected for years, including stuff Paul had inherited from both his mom and his aunt (enough china and crystal for three families), and more stuff they must have bought just to be buying.

Paul had three large cedar wardrobes in the storage room, and they were packed full of very expensive hunting clothes, rainwear, boots, and jackets, many with price tags still hanging on them. Paul had nine Remington 12-gauge 1100s. I sold or gave them away. I gave things to my family, put antique sofas and chairs up for auction, and I donated beautiful, antique rugs to the Daughters of the Confederacy for their beautiful antebellum mansion in Mobile.

As Paul directed, I sold a lot of miscellaneous furniture to friends who were trying to help me. Ms. Lamar Barnett and her son, Jim, helped me immensely. Ms. Barnett purchased things from me, and paid a fair price for them, because she knew the money was going to Paul's defense. She believed him to be innocent, so she did everything a good friend could do, and I truly appreciated her help.

During the actual move-out process, everything was hectic. Abb's moving van was at the front door when one of Mark and Lee's best friends stopped by to see them. Such a nice, handsome young man, he was taken aback by the move, and sad when I told him Mark and Lee had already left. He asked where Nathan, Jamie, and I were going. He seemed genuinely concerned about all of us, and he said he wanted to stay in touch. *How nice*, I thought. He asked if I would mind if he dropped by to see us some time after we got settled into our new place. I was so busy, and I wanted to be nice, so I said, "Sure, we'd love to see you anytime." It was normal Southern hospitality to tell someone to stop by and visit ("Ya'll come see us"). I waved bye and turned my attention back to the job at hand, not thinking of it again.

Elizabeth had a porcelain bird collection and other personal effects that I packed carefully in large moving boxes. I let the children know they were there, and they came and got the things I left for them. "Little" Paul took the large picture of the ugly ducks that hung in the master bedroom. There were also photo albums from the family that I delivered to Elizabeth's sister's home (I left them on the porch). I couldn't bear to throw them away. I thought I would never get the house, attic, and storage emptied. It was a nightmare, and I almost worked myself to exhaustion. Paul knew I could not keep it all up. He wrote a letter instructing me to move, sell items, do whatever I needed to prepare for the war ahead of us.

My old Bonneville was still a great car, but I knew it would not hold up in making the weekend trek to see Paul. I was putting about 700 miles a week on the poor old thing. I wanted a safe, reliable, economical car, so I chose a Honda Accord. I traded my car in, added some cash from the things I was selling, and bought the Accord. I could have bought a much more expensive car with a prestige name, but I didn't need it. I did need dependable transportation.

No matter what people said, I now believed Paul would win on appeal. But we both realized we were in for the long haul, and there would be no quick or easy fix for any of our problems. I became ill with all the stress. A doctor who had seen me before now welcomed me to his office with genuine kindness and concern. I had lost weight, and was down to 114 lbs., which for me was skinny.

He checked me over, asked me how Paul was doing, listened to my woes, and wrote me a prescription for something to help me with the stress, anxiety, and insomnia. It sounded like a miracle drug. I was ready to try almost anything. Then the doc left me with these final pearls of wisdom. Looking me straight in the eyes while touching my shoulder, he said sweetly, "Honey, what you need to do is get laid."

I left his office with my script for Stellazine clutched tightly in my hand. I truly expected it to be the miracle that would ease my pain. That night, I took one pill as directed. I awoke to what I still remember as an "out of body experience." An outer voice, coming from another entity, would speak to me softly. The voice would say, "Pick up your arm." I dutifully thought about the command, and maybe five seconds later, I would slowly raise my arm. Since I had never been a drug user, the experience was surreal. It took me three days before I felt normal again. I flushed the Stellazine down the toilet and made a pact with myself to face everything head on, without the benefit of drugs. I would be strong. My husband was innocent, and I would have to stay strong and clear-headed to put up the proper fight.

The first offer for the business came from Moore in letter form. He threw out the number of $750,000 for the whole thing, which was much less than offers they had received from some independent businessmen prior to Paul's arrest. The lesson was that offers are higher when businessmen know a company is thriving. Once they smell blood in the water, things change quickly. Moore's intention was to seize the moment and buy Paul out at a distress price.

Ben told him to submit the offer as a formal "Offer to Purchase" that was specific to each asset. That meant the shares in one sale, the real estate holdings in a separate package. Each store could be appraised with present market value indicated, any liens subtracted, and the value of Paul's half-share indicated for each one. Some stores were very profitable, while some were either just holding on or losing money. All factors would be considered in the final offer.

With Mark back in Dallas, Lee with Kathy in Houston, and me now living with my children in the rental house, I felt as though I was "hunkered down" and prepared to face the enemy. And I *was* ready, at least as much as I could be.

Every month I received the $2,500 from Colonel Dixie. I would write out checks for my rent, my car, insurance, utilities, and put some aside for gas to see Paul each weekend. With whatever was left, I made minimum payments to all the creditors that Paul had been paying since before Elizabeth died. None of the debts were incurred after I came on the scene. They were all bills run up by the Leverett family—a glaring reminder of the excesses in which they had all indulged. There were bills from Penney's, Sears, Metzgers, Kaysers, Gayfers, DH Holmes, Rafael's, and on and on. I was determined to pay some on each one, until I could pay all of them off.

August is miserably hot in Mobile. I was at home alone one afternoon when I heard a knock at the back door under our carport. I could see a somewhat familiar face through the clear glass insert. It was the young and good-looking man who had tried to visit the kids on moving day. I opened the door to him as he stood on the steps. Smiling, he said he just wanted to stop by to say bye to all of us before he headed off to college, and to find out how we were settling in. As he stepped into the kitchen, and I closed the door behind him, he asked if Nathan was at home. I told him no.

A breakfast table filled the kitchen space, and I asked him if he wanted some ice water or tea. He took the ice water, and we sat in the kitchen talking about the crazy Leverett soap opera, when the phone rang. I remembered excusing myself to go answer it, as I was expecting a call from Ben, my attorney. I again excused myself, my hand over the phone and whispered, "I'll be back in a minute." I left him in the kitchen, walked back to my bedroom, and closed the door to conduct a private call. I was only on the phone for a minute or two.

As I opened my bedroom door, I was already formulating my apology for leaving a guest to take a phone call. I stepped out of my bedroom and headed back into the den. It startled me to see this young man standing at the end of the hall, leaning one hip against the side, and his muscular arm extended and his left hand on the door frame. I thought it was a joke and I'd be able to laughingly push him out of the way and go back to the kitchen. I tried to walk through, but he wasn't moving. I pushed again, but he pushed back.

It took a few seconds for me to realize he was serious. I couldn't believe what was happening. I had no interest in this young person—he was a friend of our children. He was making it clear that he wasn't going to be pushed aside. I tried again by telling him to let me by, that he needed to leave, that it was not funny. He was much taller than me and very strong. He looked down at me and just kept pushing me back, with both of his hands hitting my shoulders. I'd fall back and he'd come a step closer.

Nathan's bedroom was the first door on the left. It was a very small room, with only a twin bed and a dresser as furnishings. Even with that, it seemed the room was full. As he pushed me back down the narrow hall, we were at the door of the small room. He grabbed me by both shoulders, lunging hard against me and pushing me into the room. It was like a tackle that made me fall backwards onto the bed. It wasn't fear that I felt—it was more like disbelief. The kid tore my shorts off along with my panties. I looked up to see the handsome face of someone who could have any young girl he wanted, and he was bearing down on me, his jaw set in determination. I couldn't win.

The somewhat humorous and bizarre thing was that he hardly got the thing out of his pants before it was over. I had steeled myself for what was coming, and then it was over. When I realized the guy had ejaculated within probably five seconds, I said, "Is that it?" For him, it had to have felt like a slap in the face.

He didn't say another word. He stood up and straightened himself up as he turned and walked out of the bedroom, straight to the back door. I stood, pulling my clothes back on and running behind him, screaming at him, "You have no idea what you have done."

I didn't know what that was supposed to mean to him, or why I said it. What did he care? I followed him to the back door and stood and watched him almost run to his car. He got in, backed up, and sped down my drive.

I was alone again. Paul had been gone since February, and I had not even considered letting anyone get near me. I closed the back door and ran to my bedroom. I locked my bedroom door, locked my bathroom door, and then I showered until I felt I had practically rubbed my skin off. Tears mingled with the hot water until the water ran cold.

In the days that followed, I contemplated what would happen if I reported the crime. He should be punished for what he did, but I knew I could not report what had happened. For me, with the trial of Paul so fresh, no one would believe me. "Why was he there?" they'd ask. The papers would have a fine time with me. I knew there were many who would revel in the fact I had been raped. Some would think I deserved it. For me, it was just one more thing in a life that I couldn't/wouldn't tell anyone about.

>─┤◄►─•─☉─•─◄►┤─◄

My next visit to Paul became the hardest test I had ever endured. I was gripped with anguish and fear that he would see the empty black hole that rape had left in my heart. He would know just by looking at me. The doors would open, the prisoners would walk in, each to their waiting family. He would walk toward me as always, look at me, and see my pain. How could he not?

The amazing thing was he didn't. He didn't notice anything. The voice within me was screaming for recognition, but he didn't hear. We talked, we exchanged our usual declaration of love, and we kissed goodbye. To him, I was unchanged. It was one of those double-edged swords. I didn't want him to know what had happened to us—to us—this invasion of our intimacy, but I was hurt that my excruciating pain was imperceptible to him. The long drive home always gave me time to think. I listened to the radio without hearing it. The brain does interesting things when you least expect it. Out of the blue, I remembered a song that I had heard years before. At the time I first heard it, I thought it was the dumbest song ever, and I had not found the music to be particularly appealing, but for some reason the melody had stuck. That day was the reason.

Peggy Lee's lyrics burst from my lips:

> *Is that all there is?*
> *Is that all there is?*
> *If that's all there is, my friend, then let's keep dancing.*
> *Let's bring out the booze ... and have ... a party ...*
> *if that ... is all ... there is.*
> *Then let's keep dancing.*

The song I couldn't understand before, I now embraced. It was mine. Peggy had given it to me to help me get through the high hurdles of my life. It became my mantra. Singing it gave me strength, not necessarily to face what was coming, but to accept what was mine to bear.

I never saw that young man again. He went away to college, and I would bet most anything that he has raped again.

Chapter 37
Hold Everything

I took this photo of Nathan at 16 and the one of Jamie
at a show jumping Whiz. The kids helped keep me sane.

September brought the annual meeting of the board directors of Colonel Dixie. Paul assigned his proxy to me, but, with indescribable arrogance, his partner refused to recognize or accept it. Not only that, but as president of the company, he canceled my family's health insurance.

October was a big month for birthdays in our entire family—all three of us born within six days of each other. My son turned sixteen (he looked like Tom Cruise); Jamie, a beautiful new teen, turned thirteen; and me, thirty-three.

Nathan spent most nights during the week at his dad's house, which was only about seven miles away from our rental house in Cottage Hill. He appeared at my house each morning for breakfast before going to school. I called Nathan my "floater." He went back and forth at will. On the day of my birthday, Jamie was with a friend and Nathan was with his dad. It was so strange—no one needed me. The loneliness of the day hit full bore as I spent the day alone. It was the worst birthday of my life.

We soon received a formal, particularized "Offer to Purchase" from Paul's partner. It was less than we wanted, but we weren't in much of a position to bargain. We accepted it and moved toward closing, which was set for November 15, 1983.

That day, we met around the table to start the closing process. It was a solemn group with my attorneys Ben and Tom, on one side, and the closing agents, Paul's partner, and his attorneys on the other. The papers were being laid out when a man walked in brandishing a court order, the effect of which was to stop the sale of the company. *The reason?* A lawsuit filed by Paul's children. The guy should have had on a cape. It was just like in the movies, where at the last second, he saves the day for the children. Turned out to be a *ka-ching$$* payday, but only for the attorneys.

The children followed with another suit to remove Paul as the administrator of Elizabeth's estate. The oldest two children filed the suit, without anyone representing the younger two children. They alleged that Paul, knowing he was a murderer, should have removed himself as the estate's administrator. Paul's argument was that he was innocent and had no reason to remove himself. The kids' suit lost. *Ka-ching$$, ka-ching$$.*

They came back with another demand, wanting Paul removed from the estate and to be replaced by Mark Leverett, the younger son, since Mark had reached the age of 19 and was a legal resident of Alabama. Mark was finally made the Administrator of Elizabeth's estate in January of 1984. *Ka-ching$, ka-ching$$, ka-ching$$$.*

Meantime, the Airmont house remained vacant with a "For Sale" sign standing in its yard. It had been appraised for $387,000, and we were hoping it would sell quickly for a reasonable portion of that amount. However, the lawsuits put a stop to all sales until those suits could be resolved. It just sat there, a beautiful, empty house, with no one to care for it.

The hardest weekends were the ones when I had to spend the night in Birmingham. An area in Oxmoor had numerous hotels and motels right off the interstate, so I would just pick one and make a reservation. One evening, I arrived late, had dinner at a local restaurant, and headed to my room to get some sleep.

I was in bed only for a few minutes when I heard a loud bang at my door, and then another, louder bang that rattled the entire room. Terrified, I rolled over on the floor next to the bed, grabbed the phone, and called the front desk, "Someone is kicking in my door." I was frantic. I yelled loudly, "I have a gun—I've called the front desk!" The noise stopped. I sat on the floor, my heart pounding.

After that incident, I booked at hotels with entry from an interior hallway. I've always wanted to know who tried to get into my room that night. If those doors had not been heavy steel, whoever was beating and kicking at the door would have gotten inside. I really couldn't help but wonder if someone was after me personally, or if it was just a random incident. It left me with the feeling I was a target on someone's list. Not a comfortable feeling while in a big city alone.

A friend of mine, who knew of my trips each week, was concerned. She introduced me, by phone, to a close friend of hers who lived in Birmingham, hoping we would hit it off and she could provide a room where I could sleep on those every-other weekends when I stayed overnight. It was a God-send for me. I met Margaret and Marianne (not their real names) at their condo/apartment. It was a very nice area and I was delighted to make the connection. Our first meeting was interesting. My intuition told me, in no uncertain terms, that these two ladies were life partners.

Margaret was a professional and Marianne the sweet, feminine compliment. They made me welcome in their home for months following. I had a key, and the girls were so thoughtful. They'd leave me a sandwich plate in the fridge or some other dinner they made for me. They partied on the weekend and I arrived late on either Friday or Saturday night, had the meal they so sweetly left for me, slept in their guest room, and departed before the night owls got up the next morning. They were wonderful.

Margaret eventually was hired into a better job, so they moved from the area. I bought their second car, a burgundy Trans Am for Nathan—it would be his first car. Wherever those two ladies are today, I thank them for their many kindnesses.

>—I—‹◆›—O—‹◆›—I—‹

Diamond in the Dark

In January of 1984, all hell broke loose. The Mobile Press was again my first source of information. Paul's two oldest children had launched a civil suit against their father for the nice, round figure of 200 million dollars. Yep, you read that right: $200,000,000. I actually found the sum ridiculous and laughable. I didn't blame them, but they could have gotten their Mom's full share of the business had they just been willing to talk with me. I had told them that from the start. After Paul was convicted, they circled the wagons, closing off all communication with me.

I was struggling to pay the bills, pay the attorneys, pay taxes, and pay insurance, knowing full well that the assets were woefully short of anything the kids were imagining. They bought the press that Dad was a millionaire and their mom's belief that Paul was holding out on them, hiding all that money he had somehow ferreted away. *What a joke!* I knew full well nothing good was going to come from this tangled web. However, I would not be deterred in my goal to help Paul prove his innocence, stand by him through his appeal, and preserve whatever could be salvaged in case he gained his freedom.

I didn't think there was another place where we could be attacked, but I was wrong. Paul's partner now launched a suit against Paul, all of Paul's attorneys, all of the children, and the children's attorneys. *Ka-ching to the fifth power!* The partner wanted to be able to consummate the sale of the Colonel Dixie stock and/or at least force the sale of the real estate assets. It was now, officially, a true "cluster fuck."

My meeting with Ben regarding the suits was comforting. We talked about each suit, possible outcomes, Paul's appeal to have his trial declared a mistrial, the children suing for 200 million, etc. We chatted about the future possibilities and the decisions that Paul and I would have to make. I posed to him a carefully worded question in order to extract from him his true personal opinion of the situation. "Ben," I asked, "if you were me, what would you do?"

He looked down for what seemed a long time. He looked up at me and said, "If I were you, I'd hang myself." I sat there staring at him. I knew there was no malice in his words—he was being honest. It did take me a few seconds to make sense of his remark and appreciate its true meaning. I knew he wasn't advising me to hang myself, but he was just expressing his inability to handle such an overwhelming number of attacks. His life had been a blessed one. His family was wealthy, and high up there in Mobile's social circle. His grandmother had been the Queen of Mardi Gras, his mother Queen of Mardi Gras, and now his daughter would be the same. He had no experience dealing with the seemingly insurmountable problems that were coming, or had come, in my direction.

It was somewhere around this time that I stopped caring what the outcome of the suits would be. The money was not a driving issue, since I had already accepted the fact that all Paul had worked for would be lost. However, I was pinning my hopes on his appeal. I dreamed that if Paul's case was ordered for a retrial, and he had another chance with another jury, he would walk away, free to start over somewhere else.

Stress was winning, and my attitude continued to change. I started to refocus on my life apart from the Leverett family. I needed to take care of myself. Paul had already been gone over a year when I started classes to learn the real estate business, and by April of 1984, I was a licensed agent working for Century 21 Real Estate Company. I also went to insurance classes and was licensed in property and casualty.

While in Montgomery for pre-test classes and the exam, I met one of the most handsome men I have ever seen in my life. "T-Bone" was 6'4," and about 240 lbs. of gorgeous man. He also possessed a great record from his years of playing football for Auburn. I said, "WAR DAMN EAGLE." He was five years younger than me and one of the nicest men I have ever known. We formed a friendship that would last for many years.

I was not in love with the man, but he was such a great guy that I felt lucky to be in his presence. "T-Bone" was single, never married, no attachments, hard worker, hard player, and a real gentleman. He never asked me questions, and I don't think he cared a rip about my problems, or maybe since he didn't have any, he didn't even think about those things. He became my escape, even if it was just for a short time.

My trips to Saint Clair now were broken up with a stop in Montgomery for dinner, an afternoon softball game with his league, or a fishing trip to Lake Martin. We became lovers and I enjoyed the relationship without intending it to go any further. It was good for me because I thought any relationship in Mobile would have been a problem. It had been well over a year since Paul was arrested, and at 33, I was weak. Yes, I felt guilty, but I needed to have someone to share some time and not dwell on the horrific problems going on at home.

Montgomery was now my refuge one or two days a month.

Despite my intentions, being a Leverett followed me wherever I went. Working to build my real estate business produced interesting encounters. Not counting the "hate" phone calls that would come in from what I suspected to be venomous family members, there was one man who started stalking me. He lived somewhere off Springhill Avenue. I had seen him before as he walked up and down that avenue, and he never went unnoticed because he was so strange.

An elderly man, he always wore a suit, and he was thin as a rail. But most interesting was the tracheotomy in his throat. He used a voice box to speak. For some reason, I kept running into this man—at the supermarket, coming out of the doctor's office, and several other times—too many times to be a coincidence.

The man called me at work, where I was trying to make a living. I was immediately suspicious when I heard the gravelly voice. He wanted to talk with me about a real estate deal and to make an appointment to see me. As leery as I was, I didn't want him in the office where there might be contact with others that I didn't want to know my business. I agreed to meet him, in a very public hotel restaurant at Tillman's Corner.

When I arrived, the man was sitting by the glass window overlooking the pool. He was just as creepy as I'd remembered. I immediately set out to find out what he wanted and actually tried to be nice to him. He was asking questions about my new work at Century 21. We ordered Cokes and continued to make odd, uncomfortable conversation. Instead of asking me about property insurance matters, he looked straight at me and asked, "How did a girl like you get involved in such a mess?" My answer to him was that I really was not a part of any mess. He then threw out this statement, "I know how I can get Paul out of jail for you."

I was surprised and suspicious. I began to tell him I was not interested, but he stopped me. "Just to make it clear, I do not want your body," he said. "I have no interest in any of your body parts, for sex or anything else, but I know how to get Paul out of jail."

That I found this man "repugnant" is like calling my childhood a charmed existence. He made me sick just looking at him. My steeled gaze met him with all the presence I could muster, and I told him directly and emphatically, "I will not do anything immoral, illegal, or unethical to get Paul out of jail. Do you understand? Our conversation is over."

I felt the whole thing was a set-up of some kind, or maybe the man was just plain crazy. At that point, I stood up, grabbed the check, and walked to the bar to pay for our drinks. The last thing I wanted was for him to buy me anything, though it did piss me off that I had to pay.

I now had a circle of friends in Mobile that were very good support for me. The ones who actually knew me figured out pretty quickly that I didn't deserve what I had been through. We met every Wednesday and Friday nights, at Studabakers, a local 50's theme bar and dance place. It was great. It was patronized by professionals and others from the downtown crowd. There was a dress code—the guys wore collared shirts or sport coats—and it had an ambiance conducive to meeting people, talking, and dancing.

At the time, I was a dance-a-holic. I admit it, "My name is Phyllis, and I am . . . a dance-a-holic." Dancing saved me. It helped me burn energy and reduced my stress. It was therapy for me, and I danced until I was so tired that I couldn't wait to get home and fall into bed. Only then would blessed sleep come.

People can think whatever they want, but I needed to meet my girlfriends (#1 girlfriend, Dale). We shared conversation, laughter, and the free food bar during happy hour. We had some drinks, and I danced to forget.

I went home alone.

Paul never questioned me about what I did or didn't do. As long as I was there every visiting day, he was happy. His letters came in almost daily, and they expressed so much love, with so many words, that by the summer of 1984, I was having a difficult time reading them. How many times can you say I love you, I need you, or I will get out one day and make love to you again?

His confinement was wearing on him, too. He would admit in his letters that he had to visit "Old Doc Baggett." At first, I found this a little humorous, but over time, I could no longer take the visual on that one. Letters of love suck. No matter how much you love someone, you can't make love to a letter.

My life was like that of a puppet on a string, I went to the guru each week, giving him the update, coming home, and trying to do his bidding. It was exceedingly difficult to pull it all off, and it was mentally and physically exhausting. To show up for a loving, supportive visit, when I knew I would be going home to be alone, and then to continue fighting the battles alone, became an agonizing obligation for me.

Almost every letter Paul wrote would contain a new rumor from a prisoner who had talked to someone, who had talked to someone else, who might be able to provide a lead that the whole thing had been a robbery gone bad. Paul would want me to go talk to people, or write to people, to try to follow up on every rumor he thought could be used to help his case. The problem is that once convicted and sentenced, getting a new venue to present any new information is almost like a shot in the dark. Getting permission to talk to prisoners, people I didn't know, people I didn't want to know, was a difficult task. Prisoners have to put you on their list. A person who is not an attorney can't just go visit an inmate. I just couldn't do it all.

Soon, there was yet another lawsuit. We were notified that the children were trying to force Paul into bankruptcy. It was an extended part of the civil suit. *Ka-ching$$ to the tenth power!* They first stopped the sale of the business, which would have given Paul the money to pay all his debtors, and it would have put some money into our account that could have been attached. They had blocked everything, then they were mad because there was nothing to attach. Since Paul would continue to cling to his innocence, there was no way he would give in.

In the middle of the summer of 1984, we were in four courts at one time. Going crazy, I just had to detach. My mantra—"Is that all there is?"—would replay in my mind almost every day as I experienced each new and terrible situation.

It did end up with me against all four of Paul's offspring, face to face, in Federal court, for the purpose of defeating their attempt to force his bankruptcy. I guess they thought if he was forced into bankruptcy, everything could be sold and the money forthcoming. What my attorneys told me was that, in order to prevail, we would have to show either nine, or maybe it was eleven, creditors who were being paid on a regular basis.

We entered court with a list of all the creditors I had been paying each month. The names were written on a big sheet of poster board (*such high tech!*) that showed the court I had been paying, like clockwork, when Paul's monthly check came in (just a reminder these were all P.P. bills—Pre-Phyllis). I showed the court more than the number required, and proved they had been receiving payment. If a creditor wasn't being paid the full amount, there had been some kind of agreement made, in writing, to work out a payment.

Paul's oldest son, "Little" Paul, said his dad owed him for the land he signed back over to Paul. Paul had put his son's name on that deed when times were good. "Little" Paul had no money or investment in the land. I had asked him to sign it back to Paul to help pay Paul's attorney fees, and he did (I thought he was wonderful for helping his dad). Now he wanted to be repaid, and there was no money to do it. I said on the stand that, as far as I was concerned, Paul had added his son's name to the property as an act of love, and that Little Paul had signed it back for the same reason. If it had been a loan, it would have been stated as such.

"Little" Paul then said something very derogatory—that all his dad gave him for graduation was a handshake. He appeared very resentful that his dad had not given him enough.

It made me so angry. *What ingrates!* flashed through my mind. "Little" Paul had attended a private university, with no scholarships, and his dad had picked up the entire tab. He had been given a trip to Europe, with his rugby team, as his graduation present. I was there when his dad told him he could not afford to send him, unless it was going to be his graduation present, and the deal was struck. "Little" Paul had a ball in Europe, then promptly forgot the deal he'd struck.

The judge's words were music to my ears. As closely as I can paraphrase, the judge recognized me when he said I appeared to be the only person in the whole business who appeared to be trying to do the right thing. *Thank you, Judge. At that point, I was willing to take any compliment, and any win, I could get.*

Jamie riding bareback in our pasture on Whiz.
The pony would jump anything.

Chapter 38
Goodbye, Colonel Dixie

Jamie aboard Shawna successfully clearing a brick wall.
(Photo taken by her proud mom.)

The year 1984 was one of considerable change for me. My children kept me grounded because they required attention and supervision. I was there for them throughout the week. On weekends, I continued to visit Paul. They didn't like my weekend absences, but they seemed to understand.

Nathan played football, the "field" with all the pretty little girls, and the drums, and seemed to be enjoying life. Jamie was becoming an accomplished equestrian, successfully showing a leased horse in hunter jumper classes. She fell in love with the beautiful bay quarter horse (Shawna) that she was exercising for a college girl who couldn't get home to ride. Shawna was stabled across the street at Raintree Farms, which meant that, more and more often, Jamie walked right by Whiz's pasture en-route to ride Shawna. No longer in a pony class, Jamie had moved into the big-time with that incredible,

16-hand mare. I knew it wouldn't be long before I would need to place Whiz with a new owner, so he would be loved as much as he deserved.

It was as if I had two distinct lives: taking care of my family, and doing whatever I could to make sure Paul's cases and appeals moved forward. I continued to put money in his account so he could have whatever he was able to buy while in prison, and I wrote letters to him keeping him informed of at-home events. Gradually, I realized I needed my own life. Paul's prospects for release no longer seemed as promising to me as they seemed to him, the eternal optimist. I accepted his life sentence as a harsh and daunting reality.

My friends in Mobile, Montgomery, and Birmingham proved to be welcome distractions. I was not interested in anything but relaxing and having fun during the short times I stole away from home and business. As a teen, I had never had a real dating life, other than JJ, married way too early, lived thirteen years in hell, and finally "escaping," moving post-haste from the frying pan into a blazing bonfire, and not having the support of my family or of my church (regardless of fault). I was now officially jaded.

The escape that being a pretty young woman provided became my new salvation. It saved me from depression and gave me short-term relief from the grief and stress.

My philosophy on life changed. I reset my benchmark to something more reasonable and attainable under my present circumstances. I decided I would no longer even try to hold myself to my mom and dad's expectations. Their way just wasn't working for me. I didn't smoke, I didn't do drugs, I didn't steal, I paid my just and honest debts, I loved my family, I was not filled with hatred, and I did not have indiscriminate sex. My biggest vice was turning to alcohol when I went out with friends—I seldom drank at home.

If I had to pinpoint my new point of view, I'd say I was just like Jeannie C. Riley singing "Harper Valley PTA": "I'd be drinkin', dancin', runnin' round with men and going wild." In comparison with my life up to that point, I'd have to change that last part to "Hog Ass Wild." If I wanted to party until 2 a.m., I did. There was no one to answer to for the first time in my life.

By that time, it became apparent to me that no matter what I did, most people's opinion of me would not change unless they got to know me personally. It was easy to make male friends. I didn't tell people about my situation, but usually they would find out. More often than not, they found the whole thing intriguing. Most became sympathetic and protective, and wanted to console me with their penis. Men in the 80's were still okay with taking you to dinner and paying for it, knowing full well they were not going to get lucky. They might have other motives, but they were willing to be what I needed them to be. I had several friends who talked with me almost daily, but more and more, I was working on being totally independent. I had no strings on me, and I made no commitments.

That summer, while out one evening with my friends, we met some handsome guys who were in Mobile for business and golfing. One of the guys, who was unbelievably handsome, about 6'2," with dark hair and the sweetest smile, zeroed in on me almost immediately. We drank, talked, and danced, and then drank some more, talked some more, and danced some more. The guys were moving around that evening together, so when he asked for my number, I gave it to him. He called me the next day, and we became fast friends. He had to leave to go home, but he said he would stay in touch. He did just that.

Much later, I found out that this man was extremely wealthy, his family-owned company was a Fortune 500 company, and his name was known world-wide. That laid-back, sweet man would become yet another dear friend for many years to come. He would allow me a glimpse into the world of travel, private jets, and "living large."

Every time I went to see Paul, it felt as if he was just looking for things to keep me non-stop busy. There was always a written set of instructions for me, in which he would tell me to try and find yet another person who might be able to provide some new information. It was extremely hard for me to work, be an investigator, run to Birmingham every week, and be a mom. After well over a year of traveling to the prison each week, I finally had to tell Paul I would no longer be able to keep that schedule. I just couldn't do it anymore. He actually took the news well. He could see I was reaching the end of my rope.

><｜•＞•O•＜•｜><

The first big disappointment since Paul's trial came in October 1984. Paul's request for a rehearing was denied. We were surprised and saddened, but Paul was optimistic that his other appeals might come through.

As 1985 was looming, we received an offer and a sale date for Colonel Dixie and Real Estate. In the end, Paul's partner just about stole the thing, because everyone was suing everyone and we had to liquidate. All promissory notes that Paul had made to Colonel Dixie were paid, including penalties and attorney fees. All—and I mean all—attorneys were paid in full for every service they had provided. So was interest on carrying the debt, and attorney's fees on the attorney's fees. We ended up netting about $240,000 or so. That was cut in half: half was paid to Elizabeth's heirs, and half to Paul.

The children received one-fourth, or $60,000 immediately, and so did Paul. The remaining one-fourth, for each side, was to be paid in increments of $6,000 every quarter, until paid in full. The sad thing was their part would be divided four ways. No one came out well, except the attorneys. It had been a feeding frenzy for them.

The deal was just fine with me. Mercifully, everything was over. If the Leverett brood had just been willing to leave the attorneys out of it, they would have gotten half of about $600,000 from the first attempted sale, plus half of the sale of the house. I knew they deserved half. It was their mom's, but now, because of lawsuits, distrust, and greed, everyone suffered. I thought: *Maybe now the kids will believe their dad had not been holding out on them.* I wondered how had they come up with the round figure of $200 million? Had they ever really thought there was that kind of money?

Now, what about the house? What would happen to that great, big, fabulous, and very empty house? It had been sitting there vacant since I moved out. I didn't want it. I had moved out of there and left it for Paul's children to take possession after the lawsuit settlement. However, there were mortgages that had to be paid as well as taxes and insurance. Paul's children were not interested in using their money to help pay the mortgages and various maintenance bills until it could be sold. Because they wanted no part of the liability, they relinquished their claim to the house.

In the end, the house was transferred to me, the only one willing to pay the mortgages. Paul signed a quit claim and transferred it to me only. That would make it easier to resell, and it would be removed from claims against him. Paul knew there was nothing he could do from prison, and he certainly didn't need a house. The only thing for me to do was to accept the responsibility of the house, or walk away and let it eventually be foreclosed. I couldn't do that—I took the risk.

In all my life, I would never have guessed that would be the ending of the deal. I had not wanted the house, but I couldn't walk away from it either. What would my children do? How would they feel when I told them we would have to move back into the Airmont house? It would be just the three of us to rattle around in almost 6,000 square feet.

Nathan, Jamie, and I

My first trip back to Airmont was heartbreaking and frustrating. I walked in the back door, and as I made my way around to the bedroom side of the house, I saw the house had been flooded. The carpets were soaked throughout, the bottoms of the draperies were water stained, and they had shrunk from the water rising above the hems. A pipe had apparently broken in the house during a recent freeze, and now everything was a mess. There was so much work for me to do, I cried. I was overwhelmed. I would have to go to see Paul and with him decide what to do next.

This visit with him would be hard. I knew I would not be able to make him feel better, because everything he had worked for had disappeared. It had been a war of attrition. His life was drained from him a little at a time. The only good thing he had to hold onto each day was his ability to help others. He was serving as the assistant to the education manager at the prison. Paul was proud of teaching inmates to read and helping them with their writing and math. He felt a sense of accomplishment when those young inmates got their GED.

By the time I did get to see him face to face, he had accepted the results and finality of the sale. He held my hands in his as we sat across the table from each other. He told me again that he had given me the house when he married me. He wanted me to know it was mine now, and he was glad that I would have something. He was glad there had been assets, and that I had been financially supported while he was fighting for his freedom from behind prison bars. He was thankful that I had taken care of his affairs and his appeal, and that I had made sure he had what monetary support he needed while he was there in prison. He said he loved me. I could see he still did.

Paul's attitude changed dramatically, though, when the subject of his children came up. Their lawsuit had hurt all of us, but I saw real anger in his eyes. I saw betrayal. He called his children ingrates, and said he wanted them to have nothing he had worked for—nothing! He was as angry as I had ever seen him.

The conversation turned to Elizabeth. His eyes were almost glazed over while he spewed venom and hatred. "The one thing I regret is that I never had a chance to hit her just one time," he said as he made the motion of swinging a bat. My eyes slowly processed his verbal and non-verbal message. I froze for a moment, as if an instant replay of his deadly message scrolled across my thoughts. I felt a wave of nausea that almost made me throw up. *Did he feel that intense anger because of the outcome of events, or was that a feeling he had carried for years?* Seeing him swinging that imaginary bat frightened me.

All the way home, I tried to make sense of the terrible images of hatred for Elizabeth vs. the sweet love he had displayed to me. How could two such conflicting feelings dwell within the same person? Maybe prison life had gotten to him, and the hatred was due to his imprisonment. I struggled with the conflicts running rampant through my mind. The man I knew and loved wouldn't be capable of swinging a bat at someone. I didn't want to love a man who could do that to anyone.

My head was out of control, though, debating a bigger issue. If he did indeed murder Elizabeth, then he had used me as an expendable shield. If he was guilty, then my poor mom, dad, children, family, and friends had all been used as he pushed us forward to take the heat from him. I thought of my own trial. He had never shown even the slightest sign of accepting any guilt. If my case had gone to a jury, who knows what could have happened? Would Paul have let me go to jail for him—because of him? I couldn't countenance the idea of Paul committing such monstrous acts. I tried to block out the thoughts, but they wouldn't leave—they tormented my soul. Each day, I would go over all the reasons I believed him to be innocent, hoping to once again find the faith I had had in him just a short time before.

When I returned to Mobile, I called the home insurance company. The adjuster came to see the condition of the home. At the time of his departure, he gave me a check, told me to keep receipts, and to get the house repaired. If it was more, they'd cover the difference.

It was not a problem getting the plumbing repaired, hiring painters, a wallpaper specialist to replace the damaged paper, or carpet layers to cover the floors in beautiful new cream-colored carpet. The draperies in the bedroom were another matter. Several people shook their heads at the damaged hems, saying they couldn't repair them, I decided to give it a shot myself. I moved my ironing board next to them, let out the damaged hem, and washed the water lines off while they were still hanging in place. I hemmed them straight and pressed them down. They looked new after a week of work. That one bay window of draperies, to be replaced with like materials, would have cost about ten grand. They truly were like stage curtains, having been made from the most luxurious brocade fabric I had ever seen. I stood back, proud of my work.

I was feeling the pressure to sell the house. It was worth a lot of money, but no one wanted the stigma attached to it. It had been almost five years since the crime had taken place, and more than two years since Paul had been arrested and taken away.

As I was wrapping up the repairs and getting ready to move back to Airmont, Jimmy Langford called me. Paul's petition for writ of certiorari to the Supreme Court of Alabama had been acted upon, but our appeal, in all its arguments, had been rejected.

Our first argument had been that the judge should not have charged the jury with the lesser offense of murder, because the only evidence presented had to do with murder for hire, a capital offense. There had not been enough evidence to prove that charge, so the jury found him guilty of something in which there was no substantiating evidence—the lesser offense of murder.

Our second argument had related to the use of "bought" testimony. All the witnesses who had testified against Paul were already in prison, and/or they had gotten deals to reduce their charges. They all received something for their testimony.

Our third argument was that the conviction had been based on hearsay testimony that was improperly allowed. The prosecution led the jury to believe the airport bomb incident (the one hatched in Elizabeth's fertile mind) had been a real scare, and it was introduced only to prejudice the jury.

Our fourth argument had centered on proof that some jurors were sleeping during the trial, and thus missed important testimony.

Our fifth argument was that the prosecution kept using a manufactured mug shot of me every chance they had to bring my face to the jury's attention. There were many photos that could have been made available to them, but Galanos chose to make up a mug shot in order to prejudice the jury. Galanos never told the jury that there had been no case against me, nor did he tell the jurors he knew I had nothing to do with the murder. Bubba never objected, so the court found this to be no basis for overturning the conviction.

I'm not an attorney, so all this is in layman's terms as I understood the situation at the time. No matter what the argument was, the appellate court rejected it. Paul's big hope was gone. I thought of all the money and time that had gone to trial and appellate attorneys, but in the end, Paul was back at square one.

Is that all there is? Is that all there is? If that's all there is, my friends, then let's keep dancing . . . Let's bring out the booze and have a party. If that . . . is all . . . there is.

I sang Peggy Lee's song loudly and repeatedly. I was numb from pain and disillusionment. Singing helped. It filled the otherwise imploding void in my chest.

Of course, every time there was any development in the case, the Mobile Press would jump on it, filling its pages with the whole story regurgitated all over again. The evening news on TV led with Paul's case. If Nathan didn't get in another fight, it would be a miracle, because he usually ended punching someone's lights out after every new press development. If some guy was stupid enough to rag him about his mom, he might get more than bargained for. I, too, had endured enough of the local press.

I felt numb and lost. I called my fireman friend so I would have a sympathetic adult to talk with. I was invited over to his apartment, where he was ready and willing to "console" me. He made us a drink. Relaxing after dealing with negative press was something I had not yet mastered. I needed to be held and loved. Maybe that would make me feel better. Lying next to him on the couch, I felt I was capable only of quietly going through the motions—an enthusiastic partner, I was not.

As a loving, concerned, and attentive person, he got up from the couch and said, "Hang on. I'll be right back." A little confused, I listened as the pots and pans in the kitchen started rattling. I heard a drawer open and slam shut. Soon, he reappeared in front of me. He was standing with a metal pot and a big metal spoon in his hands.

I was trying to figure out what the heck he was doing. He put the pot in my left hand, then he pushed the handle of the long steel spoon into my right palm. I was lying there, holding the pot and spoon, looking up at him with a puzzled face (*What do you want me to do with this?*), when he said, "You're too quiet. If you don't mind, bang on this and let me know how I'm doing?" I laughed so hard I almost fell off the couch. I probably needed the laugh more than anything else.

Nathan, Jamie, and I finally got settled back into the Airmont house. It looked good, because a lot of the excess stuff—pictures, dead animals, etc.— were gone. The house looked fresh and clean, but kept its original elegance, because I had saved all the best items. It was now my house, along with the care and upkeep. I was busy every day, and the prospect of weekends, which most people look forward to, became a source of dread.

I knew I had to visit Paul. I knew I had to talk with him again, in person, about his appeal being denied, and what would be next. I didn't want to go. I had not gotten over the previous visit with Paul, when I saw a side of him I had never seen before. Reading his letters each day became increasingly difficult—many went unopened. I couldn't face the same non-stop declarations of undying love and devotion. The neediness in the letters seemed to drive me away and often made me angry.

No matter how much I had loved him, there was no longer a way to carry on a relationship. I was so hurt by his actions, I couldn't get past them. Paul was 51 years old, facing life in prison. I was 34 and in my prime. I realized how unrealistic the goal was of sticking it out until he could get out of prison. Everything was different. I was different. He was different. The world kept moving, and we were both moving in different directions.

Somewhere along the line, as I tried to resolve the conflicting information I had accumulated over the course of years dealing with the Leverett mess, I decided I had to get answers. I wanted to just talk to Bill McEvoy, look him in the eye, and ask him if he had told the truth at the trial, or if he had participated in some sort of unjust conspiracy to convict Paul in order to save his own hide. He had bargained for and secured a ten-year sentence. Maybe he would tell me the truth now that it couldn't hurt him.

I wanted some kind of closure, to know if Paul really was guilty or not. I knew Paul would never admit guilt. He knew I would turn my back on him if he did so. I decided to find Bill, go see him, and ask him. It was something I felt compelled to do.

Nathan quickly turned the guest house into his band room, where he and his friends practiced for hours. Jamie had gotten the big bay horse for Christmas and was fully engaged in the horse community. Her riding had improved dramatically, and all her little girlfriends were horse lovers too. I needed to be home with her, especially on the weekends when she was showing her horse. She was showing, and winning, much of the time. I decided that, given the risk, she shouldn't be jumping a horse without her mother being there with her.

I needed to get away from Mobile. My cousin came to stay with the children, and I went on a trip to Jackson Hole with my Fortune 500 friend. We traveled in a little pack of friends. I was finally able to vacation with normal, fun people, and not connected or interested in my crazy life. It was the best medicine I could have gotten. It allowed me to feel healthy and normal again. It helped me to realize I had something in the future waiting for me. Getting completely away cleared my head, or maybe it was the mountain air.

I had stayed and fought the dragons with Paul, right through the Alabama Supreme Court across-the-board loss. Almost all his assets had now been used to pursue his legal cause. Now he started sending me letters suggesting several new ways to hire attorneys and to keep fighting. "With what?" I asked him.

In the spring, I had a very low offer for the home. It was about half what the house was appraised for, so I had to turn it down. It was still early in the game, so I tried to hang on a little longer. Surely someone would come along who would be willing to pay something close to what the house was worth.

It was during the summer when I finally found Bill McEvoy. I wrote a letter, got an answer, and made arrangements to drive to Thomasville, Alabama, to meet him. He was at some type of place where he could actually meet me in the town, and I did not have to go to a prison. It was a little surprising to find him so quickly in that position. He had received his ten years, but he was able to meet me in town, alone. *Go figure.*

"Hard" was not the word for this meeting. I had pulled out all the records of Paul's trial I could find. It was like studying for an interview: What to ask, what to look for, how to formulate the questions, and about what? I had not been able to stay in the courtroom during the trial. I heard only bits and pieces of the testimony, but certainly not all of it. The part about money changing hands was all new to me and very confusing. Paul had been in such dire financial straits during that time, most of which could be attributed to his huge cut in salary. He had CD's and money that his mom left him, so he'd borrow money waiting for those to mature instead of withdrawing it with penalties. He was not a good financial manager. That had been readily apparent when I had started looking at his books.

The document I found most interesting was the Pre-Sentencing Report. I had never read it before. I was reading it now with a wholly different perspective. Now I was ready to consider the possibility that Paul had been lying to me all along. It was an idea I had never truly been able to accept. <u>Note</u>: Much of what's in this report, which I excerpt below, is false or wrong. It was poorly written, with names misspelled, etc:

STATE BOARD OF PARDONS AND PAROLES
Montgomery, Alabama
REPORT OF THE PRE-SENTENCE INVESTIGATION

Name: Paul Fawcett Leverett Date: June 9, 1983
Mobile County No. CC83-334
Montgomery County No. CC83-553-B
White Male—Age 49 5'8"—170 Complexion: Fair Hair: Black
Color of Eyes; Brown
Offense: Murder Date of Arrest:2-4-83 Bond: Since Arrest
Address: 663 Montcliff Drive, Mobile Alabama
Trial Judge: Robert L. Byrd, Jr. Attorney: M. A. Marsal
D.A. Chris Galanos DOB 1-23-34
SSN Not Available
Criminal History—FBI NO. None
Subject has the following record in Mobile County District Court, Mobile,
Alabama:
Case #31148, Allowing another to operate a vessel without fire extinguisher

aboard a vessel

    Case #51043, Speeding

    Case #TR-57801. Speeding

    <u>*PRESENT OFFENSE:*</u>

    <u>*Mobile County Circuit Court Case # 83-334;Murder.*</u>

Leverett was indicted by the Mobile County, February 1983, Grand Jury for Capital Murder, On March 4, 1983, he was granted a change of venue and the case transferred to Montgomery, Alabama. The case number there was assigned as83-553-B. On May 2, 1983 Leverett was found guilty by jury in Montgomery County, Alabama, and the request was made for Pre-Sentence Investigation. The case was reset for June 10, 1983.

The facts in this case have been summarized from the Mobile County District Attorney's file.

On May 30, 1980, at approximately 5:39 P.M., Mobile Police Radio Operator received a call from Paul Leverett. The call was dispatched to Car 329 and J. Stokes in Car 327. Officer P. Brazell was in Car 329 and J. Stokes in Car 327.

Mobile Police Sergeant Joe Connick, III, was the first car to arrive at the scene. 663 South Montcliff Drive, Mobile, Alabama. On arrival at the home, Officer Connick was met at the back door of the residence by Paul Leverett. Mr. Leverett showed officer Connick the master bedroom. Elizabeth Smith Leverett was lying on the floor with blood about her upper body. She appeared to Officer Connick to be dead.

Officer Connick requested that Paul Leverett go back to the kitchen and sit down. Mr. Leverett stated that he had checked on some wine, along with his son, before he entered the home and found Mrs. Leverett. Officer Paul Brazell arrived on the scene and was assigned to stay in the kitchen with Mr. Leverett.

Officer Connick returned to the master bedroom and noticed a pillow with what appeared to be bullet holes and gun powder, laying on the bed and a club with engravings on the floor.

Lieutenant Vince Richardson of the Mobile Police Department arrived on the scene and joined the investigation. He observed nothing appeared to be disturbed in the bedroom or the entire house. Mrs. Leverett's left hand had been moved from the original position and a diamond ring taken from her finger. The left hand had a bullet hole through it near the thumb area. A large pool of blood was on the brown throw rug beside the bed, where the hand had been lying. The gold guard from the missing diamond was approximately one and a half foot from the right hand on the carpet. Mrs. Leverett's blue and white polka dot blouse was unbuttoned in the front and on the sleeves with the sash untied. She had blood about her face, neck, and her shoes. Doctor Leroy Reddick arrived with his assistant, Jim Small, and Bryan Delmas along with Police Identification Lieutenant Long. The investigation was conducted by Dr. Reddick, Jim Small, and Delmas. On the bed was a pillow, from a chair near the center of the room, with two bullet holes with powder residue, along with blood on the other side. Mrs. Leverett's pocketbook was in a chair just inside the doorway in the bedroom. The contents disclosed her car keys. Further investigation revealed that the side door leading to the patio was discovered to be unlocked. No forced entry could be located to the house. Sergeant Bolton advised Lieutenant Richardson that the automobile belonging to Mrs. Leverett was missing. Lieutenant Richardson suggested that a canvass of the shopping center at Cottage Hill and Azalea Road be made. A short time later Sergeant Connick advised Lieutenant Richardson that the car had been located in the Cottage Hill Shopping Center. No keys were found in the vehicle.

A canvass of the area was made but no one had seen anything unusual. One neighbor recalled having seen Mrs. Leverett leave the home. She understood that Mrs. Leverett went each Friday to Las Damos Beauty Salon at approximately 1:00 p.m.

Paul Leverett went with the officers to the police department, however, he did not give a statement. He did, through the advice of his attorneys have his hand tested along with his son, Mark. They were negative for the traces of nitrate. Paul Leverett did state that a black and maroon van with Texas tag had been seen around the home about two weeks prior to the homicide.

Further investigation by Mobile Police revealed that Mrs. Leverett was at Kelley Cleaners at about 3:00 p.m. the day of the homicide, but her whereabouts after that time were not known.

Mrs. Leverett's body was transferred to the University of South Alabama Medical Center, where she was pronounced dead on arrival.

In 1982 Hilton Robinson, white male, who serving a prison term in the Federal Penitentiary, Tallahassee, Florida, gave information to unravel this case. Further investigation by Mobile County District Attorney's Office later implicated Ricky Prewitt, Bill McElvoy, and Paul Leverett.

The following information is a summary of the dates and action taken in this case:

In October 1979, Paul leveret approached Bill McElvoy, white male, regarding getting some to kill Elizabeth Leverett. Later in October 1079, McElvoy conspired with a white male known as 4,000 up front W. McCloud, to rip off Leverett, and the price for the killing was supposed to be $10,000 up front and $10,000 after the murder. In October 1979, Leverett made a partial payment of $2,000 to McElvoy. McElvoy gave McCloud $500 of the amount and kept $1,500. October 23, 1979, Gaylord Lyons borrowed $20,000 from First National Bank for Paul Leverett. On October 29, 1979, Paul Leverett cashed a Cashier's Check for $20,000 that he had received from Gaylord Lyons. November 1979, Leverett makes the next payment of $8,000 for the murder of his wife. November 15, 1979, McElvoy purchases a 1974 Corvette for $4,000. In February 1980, Leverett gives McElvoy $300 to locate and retrieve money from the first hired killer. Later during the month McElvoy goes on a fishing trip with the $300 he received from Leverett. March 1980, McElvoy purchases a motor and outdrive from Carr Marine for $5,018.06 with the $6,500 he had received from Leverett. April 23, 1980 Leverett secures a $20,000 loan from First National Bank to repay the $20,000 he had borrowed from Gaylord Lyons.

In April 1980, Leverett met with Ricky Prewitt in the SunRay Parking lot located on Airport Boulevard in Mobile. They discussed arrangements for the murder of Elizabeth Leverett. There was a second meeting in the same parking lot the latter part of May 1980 to set a date for the murder to be May 30, 1980. Prior to May 30, 1983, Leverett met with Ricky Prewitt at the Pub Restaurant and exchanged Chip Construction Company check in the amount of $2,500 for cash. It was on this date that Leverett gave the keys to his home and to Mrs. Leverett's car. May 30, 1980, Elizabeth Leverett was murdered by Ricky Prewitt. On June 7, 1980, or thereabouts, Leverett made the remaining payoff in Hilton Robinson pickup, which was located at Robinson's place of business. This had been done as per instructions from Ricky Prewitt.

During the period of time April 1980 to the death of Elizabeth Leverett, there was several banking transactions by Paul Leverett at First National Band and Merchants National Bank. This would account for the total of $11,000 that Ricky Prewitt claims Leverett paid him to perform the murder.

SUBJECT'S STATEMENT:

I interviewed Paul Leverett in Mobile County Jail on May 12, 1983 and again on June 7, 1983. On each occasion Paul Leverett stated that he did not murder his former wife, Elizabeth Smith Leverett. Paul Leverett stated that he only knew Bill McElvoy and had had no dealings whatsoever with Ricky Prewitt or Hilton Robinson. He further stated that he had never heard of Steven Hart. Paul Leverett described the events of May 30, 1980. He stated he took his son,

Mark, to lunch and was going to buy him a car that day. Mark was graduating from S. Paul's School and he wanted to give him a nice present. He said after they ate lunch, they went by Ward's Army Navy Store and then by one of the Colonel Dixie Restaurants. They went to the bank and then from there they went home and found Elizabeth Leverett murdered. Paul Leverett stated he called the police. He claims he had no dealings whatsoever with her murder in any shape, form or fashion.

The document then goes into some of Paul Leverett's personal history, like father/ mother/ dates of their deaths/siblings.

SUBJECT:

PAUL FAWCETT LEVERETT was born on January 23, 1934 in Dallas, Texas. He stayed in Dallas, Texas until he entered the US Air Force. The subject was reared by his parents. He stated they provided him with the necessities of life. His father was employed at a poultry processing plant and his mother at Westinghouse. Paul reported that he had lived in Mobile, Alabama, since 1956.

Paul Leverett married Elizabeth Smith Leverett, the victim in this case, on February 28, 1959 in Pascagoula, Mississippi. Elizabeth had previously been married to a man by the name of McBrennen. They were married in 1952 and divorced in 1954. One child was born to Elizabeth in her first marriage, and that was Cathy. Cathy was later adopted by Paul Leverett. According to Paul Leverett, he met Elizabeth in November 1956 while she was employed at Brookley Air Force Base in Mobile. Three children were born to Elizabeth and Paul Leverett. They are: Paul Leverett III, now 24 years of age and residing in Dallas, Texas. Mark Leverett is 20 years of age and attending Southern Methodist University. Lee Leverett is 16 years of age and is a student at Davidson High School in Mobile.

Subject married Phyllis Brown [married name deleted]on November 15, 1980 in Mobile, Alabama. This was eight days after Phyllis had received her divorce from [xxxxx]. Phyllis Leverett and her step-daughter, Jamie and Lee, are residing at the Leverett home at 663 Montcliff Drive in Mobile.

HEALTH:

Paul Leverett denies the use of illegal drugs. Paul stated he has never received any psychiatric treatment. His general health is reported to be good, however, he does occasionally suffer from sinus problems.

EDUCATION:

Paul reported he graduated from Southern Methodist University in 1955 with a degree in Marketing.

EMPLOYMENT HISTORY:

Subject is 50% owner of Colonel Dixie Restaurants in Mobile, Alabama, and had been so employed for the past almost twenty years. His partner is Mr. Richard H. Moor. Prior to this time had sold Scotsman Queen Icemakers in the Mobile area. He reported that his present wife, Phyllis has power of attorney.

ECONOMIC STATUS:

As stated above, subject has 50% interest in Colonel Dixie Restaurants in Mobile. He does not know what will happen with the company in the event he receives a prison sentence. Leverett stated he has been buying his home and payments are $860 a month. He could not recall whether the mortgage was for 25 or 30 years. Leverett stated he had had to sell off several pieces in Mobile, that he owned or had interest in, in order to pay his attorney. The home is up for sale at this time.

MILITARY:

Leverett reported that he served in the US Air Force from 1955 to 1958.

CHURCH, CLUB, AND COMMUNITY ACTIVITIES:

Leverett reported that he had attended First Independent Methodist Church in Mobile and Sage Avenue Church of Christ. He had also been to a Missionary Baptist Church some. Leverett reported he was a member of the Mobile County Wildlife Association.

REPUTATION:

It is my understanding that approximately 25 people testified regarding subject's reputation at the trial in Montgomery, Alabama. The court has knowledge of their sworn statements. They stated he had a good reputation.

REMARKS:

I was shown a Diary which allegedly was kept by Elizabeth Smith Leverett, the deceased victim in this case. The Diary covers a period of time from January 2, 1975 through April 21, 1979. Throughout this period of time Elizabeth felt that something was going to happen to her. She talked about some of her husband's girlfriends throughout the Diary.

On May 12, 1983, I talked with Mrs. Phyllis Leverett, the present wife of Paul Leverett. She had requested the interview. Mrs. Leverett stated that she does not believe that Paul Leverett had Elizabeth Leverett killed. She denies having any relationship with him prior to the death of Elizabeth Leverett.

On May 25, 1983, I talked with Mr. and Mrs. Dewey George. Mrs. George is the sister of the deceased, Elizabeth Leverett. Mr. and Mrs. George stated that Paul and Elizabeth had had a good many marital problems over the years. The *children would call their grandmother, Mrs. C. L. Smith and advise them of what was taking place. Following the death of Mrs. Elizabeth Leverett, Lee, the youngest child, stated with Mr. and Mrs. George for approximately four months. Mrs. George stated that she felt Lee was still very upset over the death of her mother.*

On May 31, 1983, I visited the Colonel Dixie Company Headquarters. There I talked to Mr. Richard Moor, who is president of the company. He stated that he had been in business with Mr. Paul Leverett for approximately 20 years. He stated for the first fifteen years Mr. Leverett was a very good employee: was a very good person to be involved with in the company. He stated that for the last few years thought that Mr. Leverett had used the company headquarters as a place to arrange hunting trips and have contact with other women. Mr. Leverett was supposed to be in charge of personnel and training. Mr. Moore stated that Mr. Leverett had a different set of friends than he and his family. He felt that someone was apparently bribing Mr. Leverett over the past few years. He stated that Mr. Leverett had spent a great deal of money in the past few years. He further stated that he actually had to cut Mr. Leverett off from borrowing money from the company. He stated that Mr. Leverett owes the company about $55,000 plus interest. Following the arrest of Mr. Leverett, a loan officer from first National Bank went to see Mr. Moore at the company. He advised Mr. Moore that Mr. Leverett had approximately $120,000 in unsecured loans. Mr. Moored state that he had continued to pay Phyllis Leverett while Mr. Leverett is confined in the jail. He pays her a total of $5,000 per month.

On June 8, 1983, I talked with Mark Leverett, son of Mr. Paul Leverett. Mark is 20 years of age and a senior at Southern Methodist University. He had requested that I talk with him regarding this case. He is upset because criminals were used to convict his father. He was aware that his mother and father had some marital problems, especially five or six years ago. He sated that his father was running around with another woman at the time. However, they had reconciled, she dropped her action regarding divorce and things seemed to have gotten better. He stated that in the recent years they did have some sporadic trouble; however, he did not feel that it was of a very serious nature. Mark stated that he does not believe that his father committed the crime.

PROBATION PROGRAM:

In the event that probation is the decision of the court, Paul Leverett will reside at 663 Montcliff Drive in Mobile, and continue his employment with Colonel Dixie Restaurants.

Signed and dated in Mobile, Alabama, on this the 9th day of June, 1983.

William H. Cobb
State Probation and Parole Officer
WHC/ep
End of Report

I made the contact and drove to Thomasville, Alabama, to meet with Bill. We talked. It was an interesting experience to meet with him. He had mixed feelings about me. I felt it, and I could hear it in his voice. I needed honest information. My life hinged on what he had to say. He probably wondered why the hell I'd come to see him, and most likely didn't trust me. However, he was humble in his demeanor. He was thinner than I remembered, but still a nice-looking man—a man you would never guess to be in his situation.

There wasn't a long time to talk, so after the perfunctory "How is everybody?" questions, the conversation became much more difficult. I told him of Paul's appeal being denied. I told him of ending up with that damned house. We talked of our children.

When there was no more small talk, I trudged into the real reason for my visit. I laughed at him and reminded him about how distant he had always been with me. Taking a deep breath, I finally just asked him outright if he had really done the things he said on the stand. I asked him why he had turned on Paul. Was it to save his own hide? He hemmed and hawed. I could tell he did not want to answer me directly. Who knows? Maybe he thought it was a set-up of some kind. I then asked him a really stupid question, "Why didn't you tell me what was going on?" He finally looked up at me, eye-to-eye, and his response was in such a flat voice that his answer speared me like a cold knife. "I thought you knew," he said.

Nothing else was important. His answer, "I thought you knew," kept ricocheting in my head, as though it was intent on finding a vulnerable place to penetrate, to sink in. I was still resistant. I had wanted to talk to him because I thought he would tell me the truth, but what he said was much more subtle, unguarded, spontaneous. Whatever happened between him and Paul was not shared with me that day. I needed to end the conversation, but his flat, bare statement felt like a knife thrust into my chest.

Chapter 39
Three and You're Out

A wedding photo with husband #3.

During the summer of '85, my visits to Paul were few and far between. No matter how hard I tried to cope, my depression increased. Something was wrong, but I didn't know what to do. I battled fatigue, cried a lot, and stayed in my room with draperies drawn shut. Nathan was very concerned about me. He would come to the door of my bedroom and ask if I was okay, but there was nothing he could do to help. I wanted to give up. Other than driving a bit recklessly on my trips, I never made a plan to kill myself, but I didn't care if I died or not.

Paul knew I was drifting from him. He had never before worried about what I did, but he recognized there was a problem. I couldn't bring myself to write to him. His letters would plead for me to write, plead for me to come see him. He appealed to me in every way he could as he felt me slip away. Paul could be very tenacious and persistent when he thought he was losing control. I was just too sick. Even he couldn't manipulate me into action.

The doctor put me through several rounds of antibiotics for a sinus infection, then bronchitis, but nothing worked. Some of my symptoms were similar to tuberculosis, and I grew worried when my doctor sent me for chest x-rays. The x-rays cleared me, but the infection lingered until shots of steroids jolted me back after two months of real illness.

Paul finally reached me by phone. I told him I had been very ill. He said he, too, had been sick, and he needed for me to do something for him. He said he would send me a letter with instructions. Making small talk was difficult, and saying "I love you" was even more painful to do—I was glad for the call to be over.

The letter arrived as promised. It was filled with "I love you's." I don't quite know how to describe my reaction. I was trying to pull away while his endearments kept clutching at my arms, my hands, pulling on me, until I was ready to scream.

He asked me to bring some cash on my next visit. His instructions were, "When you come to the gate to line up, there will be some guys who will meet you. I want you to give them $50 in cash." The fix was in to get him whatever he needed inside the prison. Paul said he told them how to recognize me (*that was a scary thought*), so not to worry, they would know me and my car.

I was blown away by his plan, but not in a good way—it seemed to be designed by an idiot for an idiot. There was no way on Earth I was going to meet some "guys" I didn't know, with cash, in order to get contraband delivered to him in prison. I could not believe he would ask me to do it. It could put me at great personal risk. *Traveling alone to Birmingham, then to the middle of nowhere in front of that prison entrance, meeting strange people, giving cash to some guys who most likely were criminals?* I thought: *You gotta be fuckin' crazy.*

That was it—the last straw to be placed on an already staggering camel—and I fell.

PHYLLIS BROWN

A full length shot, my Casablanco outfit, and my "head" shot. I was doing girl stuff, and trying very hard to feel better about myself. (Photos by Shelia Slepian.)

I tried not to answer the phone, I wouldn't read the letters, I tried to shut Paul out. I had to replace that void with something. That summer, I got a job working with Fonger Modeling Agency, to keep me busy and to learn a few things along the way.

The modeling agency was a school for young girls to learn some manners, a little poise, make-up tips, and how-to's for dressing appropriately and walking on a runway, etc. The agency also represented a few boys. The studio provided professional photos, with head shots, accompanied by three modeling poses, which served as a business card. What a delight it was for me to work with that group. We assisted ladies' clubs to put on fashion shows, and produced shows on executive dressing for job fairs. We represented Gayfers, a department store, in its television and print ads, plus took part in other events. My son Nathan was in some local magazines, though he found the whole *shtick* a bit girly. He was so handsome that I wished he had stuck with it. (*Just to put any such notions to rest, it was not a dating or escort agency, nor were "massages" offered.*)

By the time the kids started school again in the fall, I was ready to face the music. I planned my trip to see Paul in September, the script practiced over and over, as I rehearsed asking for a divorce twenty different ways. I was going to file, no matter what, but it would be easier if he was in agreement. I wanted, and needed, to be free to rebuild my life.

My reasoning was that I could spend the next twenty years as his wife, while all requests for parole could be rejected, or anything could happen such that he would never make it out of prison. I talked to him as I had never talked to him before. I told him that I knew he would never admit to being guilty of the crime, but I also knew that whether he was guilty or not, I didn't deserve to spend the rest of my life paying for what had happened in his family. I pleaded for him to understand.

Paul was such a smart man that he quickly figured it out. And no, I was not going to spend every last cent left to hire more attorneys. If I did that, then I would not be able to hang on long enough to sell the house. I asked him to please give me a divorce. Sadly, he agreed and said I could have everything—indeed, he *wanted* me to have everything. But he had one request: He wanted me to keep the name Leverett.

I filed for divorce on September 13, 1985. Paul signed without any problem—the divorce was final on October 2, 1985. Without me or anyone asking, Paul followed up with a personal letter that he had witnessed and notarized by a prison notary. In it, he said he wanted me to have all his possessions. He wanted me to have his mother's jewelry, china, crystal—everything he had inherited, all his worldly goods. The letter appeared to me to be a way to protect me, as much as he could, from his children or any other claims on his estate. He certainly didn't need the house, china, or crystal.

With the divorce final, my luck started changing. I got a job at Rafael's, an upscale clothing and fur store. I worked hard, loved retail sales, and my commissions were good.

Down to my last $12,000 in savings, my break came when the house sold in November 1985. It went at a distress sale price, but I was able to walk away with enough money to buy a nice house in Daphne, Alabama. I had given up a car, a house, and five acres of land when marrying Paul. At the end of my marriage to Paul, I ended up with a car and enough money to buy a house of about the same price as the one I had walked away from when I divorced JJ. *Touché!*

I didn't completely abandon Paul. I did, however, cut my personal ties with him. I wished him no harm, but my ship had now sailed toward a different, beckoning horizon.

At Paul's request, I gave in and hired Dan Turberville, a criminal attorney in Birmingham, Alabama, to look into the problems at Paul's trial. I went to Birmingham several times to give Turberville information, and to hand-carry the transcript of Paul's trial. It had cost hundreds of dollars for the transcript in hard copy. It read like a bad play. Dan initiated some type of action for Paul, basically claiming that Bubba Marsall had provided ineffective counsel. If Dan had represented Paul, I would bet just about anything he would have been acquitted. Anyway, Dan took on the job for a little of nothing. He thought the case was a colossal failure of the legal system.

Dan took me to dinner one evening so we could talk of all the events before and during the trial. He told me of a case he had just won, where they had the robber's photo, clear as day, taken while he was in the act of robbing the bank. He won an acquittal for his guilty-as-sin client. I asked him how he could represent people he knew to be guilty. He said it was his responsibility to make sure that people were given their constitutional rights, treated as innocent until proven guilty, and the rules obeyed during law enforcement's quest to put a suspect in jail. He was an interesting person, though a little too left-leaning for me.

Paul and Dan developed a relationship that continued long after I was no longer paying anything for his defense. I think Dan was a good guy who genuinely believed Paul and was upset that he had gotten a raw deal.

The lovely little town of Daphne lies "over the bay" (as the locals say) on the Eastern Shore. The house I found was on a hill, a corner lot, four bedrooms, two baths, a large den that opened onto an old brick patio, a small entry foyer that led to a formal living room and dining room, all neatly fitting into its 2,200 square feet. I fell in love with it as soon as I walked in the back door. The breakfast room was papered in blue-and-white gingham-checked paper, the windows covered with white Priscilla curtains, with white wood cabinets and a red brick floor. It was cozy. Lake Forest was a nice neighborhood. It had hills covered with beautiful trees, and a lovely club house. I made an offer of $89,000 for the house, and they took it. I would now be able to shake the dust off my shoes and leave Mobile.

Yet again, I packed up everything to leave Airmont. That time in my life was growing dimmer in my rear view mirror as my future was looking brighter. There was so much work for me to do, but I was accustomed to work. I was trying to save money by doing as much as possible by myself. I remembered a conversation with a guy trying to get me to go out with him. He had complained to me, "You know, it's easier to get laid nowadays than to get a home-cooked meal."

I told him that was quite charming, but I didn't want to do either one for him. Anyway, the reason I thought of that was because I had found men to be more than happy to buy drinks for the ladies, or spend a lot of money on a nice dinner. But ... to find one who would mow your grass? Now that was special.

One of my male friends helped me pack, carry boxes, clean, move, mow grass, and get settled in. He was the first man I met who didn't hesitate to stand by my side, and he seemed willing to fight my battles with me. I moved from that $380,000 house to an $89,000 house, yet it made me so happy. That pretty, painted brick home was mine. It was the first home I had ever chosen and purchased for myself—and I loved it.

The guy who helped me move was doing all the right things to get close to me. He lived in Pensacola, worked at Naval Air Station Pensacola, and had come to Mobile to drill with the Alabama National Guard. He was a helicopter pilot who often invited me to join the fun when his drill group gathered after work. That crazy group provided side-splitting laughter, the likes of which I hadn't enjoyed in a long time.

He had graduated from the Naval Academy and served, according to him, honorably in the Marine Corps for eight years. He was one of those great big braggadocio guys from Pittsburgh, part of a large, tight-knit Jewish family. He was full of himself, and I fell madly in love with him. He was like no one I had ever known. One of the first questions I asked him when we met was, "Are you married?" He said he wasn't.

Meantime, I worked each day at Rafael's in Mobile. I did some modeling on the side that included some television commercials and print advertising. At 35 years old, it was good to be on my own and living well.

Eventually, someone told me, the guy I was dating was not single. When confronted, he said he was married, but in the process of divorce and had been separated from his wife. I was so upset that he had lied to me.

A clip from a Rafael's Mardi Gras ad in the Mobile Press Register, 1987.
(Photo by Jackson Hill Photography)

That he had already asked her for the divorce, which was in the process—at least that much was true. Here was the telling part of the conversation that went right over my head. He said to me, "I asked her for a divorce, and I thought she would be devastated." He went on to say that when he asked her, she turned and gave him this incredulous look, and according to him, she asked, "YOU! Want a divorce from ME?" If you are smart enough to listen to what people say, you can often avert danger, heartache, shame, and sorrow. I, on the other hand, seemed to do my best decoding of these little gems well after I paid the price for my stupidity.

This time I had genuinely tried to do a better job of selecting a partner. I had wanted to find someone who was educated, someone who had a proven track record of responsibility (eight years in the Marine Corps), someone who had a religious background (he was Jewish), was clean, and possessed good social manners. He was good at presenting well in all those areas.

I should have known better. I ignored another bad sign. My children hated him. They were teenagers who had been through a lot of bad experiences. He was a rigid military guy who tried to back me up by reinforcing the rules I laid out. When it was just me and him, it seemed wonderful at first. I should have run away from him like a wild Indian—run as fast as I could run. I didn't. He and his wife did get an amicable divorce.

In October of 1986, I could no longer stand to carry the name of Leverett. I petitioned for my name to be changed back to my maiden name, Brown.

By 1987, we were planning a wedding. My fiancé liked that I was featured on Sunday full-page Mobile Press Register ads for Rafael's. The Rafael's girls were coveted positions in the Mobile area. I had pulled myself out of the Leverett problems, to the point where I was now a featured model of one of Mobile's finest stores. I felt like saying, "So there, Mobile, talk all you want. I am doing just fine."

My Court House Wedding Dress

In May 1987, I married again. At first, we planned a beautiful wedding to be held at the Country Club of Lake Forest. I had ordered a silk-beaded gown from New York that the Rafael's buyer brought back just for me. We had formal wedding photos made, with the photographer giving the bride-to-be a lot of attention. The groom-to-be became pissed and petulant, not being the center of attention (yet another sign for me to run). The wedding plans were ditched when he decided to follow his long-time dream, and took a flying job with Airborne. Starting at the bottom of a cargo airline, he wouldn't know his schedule far enough out to plan a real wedding with out-of-town guests. We drove to the courthouse in Crestview, Florida, for a ceremony officiated by a notary. Not very glamorous, but we were happy for the day.

To start, I loved his family and enjoyed meeting all of them. Like all families, they had issues. For my first visit to Pittsburgh, my new husband took me to the cemetery where his parents were buried. We stood next to their graves, he held my hand, and he introduced me, "Mom and Dad, this is Phyllis. She is the woman I love and I wanted you to meet her." Isn't that sweet? I was touched by the sentiment ("touched" being the operative word—in retrospect, it was a bit nuts).

Because of his respect for education, he encouraged me to go back to school. I did, and I received an Associate of Arts in Mass Communications. I made one "B," in algebra, so I finished with a 3.98. Algebra was always hard for me. While attending school, I was nominated by the staff to the *Who's Who of American College Students*. I was so proud. Several of the women on staff also came to me and said the college wanted to sponsor me to run for Mrs. Alabama. The contest, with a swimsuit competition, would be held in Birmingham, Alabama. I sweetly demurred, for a number of good reasons. *What a hoot!*

The College Relations Director was also my English instructor. As we say in the South, she took a liking to me. She found out about my background with modeling and commercials by reading a paper I wrote for her class. I had described positive experiences, so she offered me a spot in a television commercial for the college. The 30-second spot targeted adults, hoping to inspire them to come back to school. The commercial ran for five years. They paid me $100 for about 30 minutes of work, but I would have done it for free.

The president of the college offered me a job as College Relations Director when my English instructor said she wanted to go back to just teaching. She recommended me, and I was hired. *Wow!* Now I had a real job that had the potential to help me, both now and in the future. I helped create new commercials, newspaper ad campaigns, and radio and billboard ads. College registration increased, so they were very happy with my work.

The school had a great baseball and basketball program. Their all-girl cheerleading team was dynamite. The squad coach had to step aside for a year (severely pregnant with twins), which gave me the chance to work as the cheerleading supervisor/ stand-in coach. What a great time I had traveling as chaperone to games and other competitions. That wonderful team of girls—plus two boys who were catchers—won the 1989 National Cheerleading Championship, All Girl Division, that took place in Dallas, Texas.

I got to be with them for the win and counted it among my most incredible life experiences to have accompanied such a talented group of young people to their three days of grueling competition. They loved me and I loved them. My new husband also tried to love them—carnally.

There were not many jobs for modeling, so I was very happy when Sheryl (my beautiful niece) and I were featured in several jewelry store commercials that ran for several years. The modeling thing was strictly a hobby which I enjoyed very much. It was a diversion to my real job. The biggest joy were the commercials I did for a mobile home business in West Mobile. They were as fun to make as they were funny. Everywhere I went with my new husband, people would recognize me from either the TV commercials or the Rafael's ads. With me on his arm, he strutted like a peacock. "Narcissism" was not yet a word in my vocabulary.

>—‹•›—•—O—•—‹•›—‹

Being married to a fledgling pilot was all new to me, especially one who commuted from Daphne, Alabama, to Wilmington, Ohio for work. He'd leave from the Mobile Regional Airport, take a hop to New Orleans or to Birmingham, and from there to Wilmington before he started his own flights. It was one hell of a commute. He had been a helicopter pilot, so they started him flying the safest, slowest thing they had. I listened for two years to how much he wanted to move from the lumbering old C-131 twin-engine plane to the world of jets—after all, jets were much more glamorous and had the cachet he needed. Finally, his big chance arrived, so I accompanied him to his initial school in Wilmington, Ohio.

His younger brother and family lived close by the school, so we planned a month-long visit with them while he completed his DC-9 training. I stayed in their home while everyone else went to work or school. One day I decided to do a nice thing and make dinner for everyone, preparing something they might not normally have in Ohio. My husband and I decided on Cajun red beans and rice, with sausage and cornbread. It was a New Orleans specialty, and we thought it would be a nice surprise for our hosts. My husband's obese brother refused to eat it, sulking silently in the living room. I found it hard to believe an adult would react that way to a dinner.

One morning, I got up early to have a cup of coffee with my husband before he left for the day. The coffee was made in the kitchen, so I poured a cup at about the time the brother entered the kitchen. He actually grabbed my cup, poured it back into the pot, looked at me, and said, "No one gets coffee until my thermos is filled!" I had never encountered such ignorant rudeness before. However, I didn't bother his coffee again.

At the end of two weeks, my husband, a self-proclaimed "stellar performer," had decided the school was just too tough for him. *"I don't have enough study time. It's unfair. It's too hard. Waa, waa, waa!"* My words to him were, "Do what you need to do." I would not make that call for him. Given how long he had wanted to fly jets, there was no way I'd ask him to quit. He asked me to go with him to turn in his resignation from the class. I was dumbfounded by his quick decision to quit something he had worked so hard for, and wanted so badly, but I agreed to go with him.

I accompanied him into the training director's office. We were sitting across the room from the guy behind the big desk. My dear husband, red-faced and sweating, gave him a spiel that went kind of like this: "I really am sorry to have to come in here like this, but my wife [*finger pointed at me*] wants me to quit [*audible gasp from my side of the room*]."

I couldn't believe my ears. Never would I have expected the man to go into the director's office to quit (because it was too hard, whine-whine), and then have the nerve to point at me, his wife, to take the blame. His more-than-minor character flaw was glaring.

The director looked at me. I could read the look on his face. He was thinking the same thing I was. He turned back and looked straight at my big, moronic husband. Without missing a beat, the director politely said he was sorry he was leaving. My husband told him, "Don't worry. We'll mail you any paperwork we have to sign." I was embarrassed, but more embarrassed for him. After leaving, he told me he really thought the director would try to talk him into staying. From what I witnessed, the manager was ready for him to take a hike.

The good thing was, he got his old job back at Naval Air Station Pensacola. That job required traveling back and forth to Pensacola (50 miles), one hour each way. After resuming work there, there seemed to be a lot of distractions in Pensacola that kept him from coming home on time. I started having flash-backs to my Texas experience with JJ.

My husband was still drilling with the National Guard. The final kicker was the lipstick all over his dress shirt that he had taken with him on his required two-week Guard duty in Panama. Jealousy ensued, as did fighting. I fought him harder than I had ever fought anyone in my life. It was a third marriage for me, and I didn't want to strike out again. I was ready to kill myself.

Crying hysterically, I called my sister. I needed to talk to someone before I slit my wrists. She was on her way out the door to some event with her family and couldn't talk. When I hung up the phone, I somehow found it sobering that she didn't have time to listen to my sob story. I loved my husband madly, but jealousy, mistrust, and his constant lies were, as he put it, "my problem," and a problem I needed to learn to deal with myself.

My problem had a name familiar to many—a broken heart.

To cut his long commute, we moved to Pensacola and built a house there, and I applied for a job on the Navy base. I knew I had minimal qualifications—armed only with my newly acquired Associate of Arts degree in Mass Communications. I held my breath, went into my best professional demeanor, and readied for my interview. At the initial introduction, it was apparent the hiring director liked me. The female marketing manager handed me a written scenario, ushered me into the lobby, and instructed me to write a press release. The press release was no problem. Then I went through an hour of interview questions before a committee of five. They liked my portfolio of articles and commercials I had created for the college. They seemed impressed that I had been the College Relations Director.

Then the Marketing Manager threw her "hardball" question at me: "If you have a $100 budget to decorate for a BBQ at the Officer's Club, what would you do?" I thought: *You are kidding, right?* I looked at her. No, she wasn't kidding. I gave her my answer, and then listened to ten minutes of what she had done meeting that not-so-hypothetical challenge. She had taken one look at me, and her feathers had gotten ruffled by the competition. I felt I was competing with her for the job.

The Navy Commander ended the interview with, "Tell us about the funniest thing that ever happened to you." My mind raced through my "card catalog" of memories. I thought of my experience with my fireman. I thought of being handed the metal pot and spoon while lying on the couch. I kept thinking of falling off the couch and laughing until my sides hurt. That one incident would not leave my mind, nor allow me to think of anything else. After a very long pause, I finally told him that it would be inappropriate for me to share my funniest memory. His eyebrows went up in surprise. No more questions were asked of me.

I was hired as a Public Affairs Specialist for the Morale, Welfare, and Recreation Department. I started work at Naval Air Station Pensacola on January 2, 1991.

Chapter 40
Military Life

Skiing at Keystone, and me at an Officers' Club costume party.

S tarting my new job the first working day of 1991 gave me a chance to see how some of the old Navy worked—"Hide your daughters. The sailors are in port." The demographics of Naval Air Station Pensacola (NASP) seemed quite different from that old cliché. Mostly, they were new college graduates, the cream of the crop, and they arrived in Pensacola to receive their flight training. NASP is known as "The Cradle of Naval Aviation." It is truly the "birthplace" for our naval aviators, and carries with it quite a legacy, if you are lucky enough to belong to the elite aviator club.

The upshot of all that was I began my new career working with officers— young, healthy, testosterone-filled aviators. Some were women breaking into their inner sanctum. I worked at the club, which was patronized by flight instructors, flight surgeons (my favorite one was a female, Doc Debbie, or "Fists"), and commanding officers from both Navy and Marine commands. In addition to the schools, there were quite a few civilian support commands like NADEP, the Naval Aviation Depot, which was on base to refurbish aging aircraft. These commands were usually headed by an active duty Navy Captain or Marine Colonel (for those not familiar, captain and colonel are the same level, just different services). My husband worked at NADEP. The enlisted personnel on the base held down support positions.

My first assigned task was to build business at the failing Mustin Beach Officers' Club (aka: O'Club), by planning big-theme parties, hiring live bands, coordinating fashion shows, and putting on other events. The club's cocktail lounge was called the "Ready Room." It had been the scene of lunchtime lingerie shows featuring scantily clad models. I refused to continue that tradition. The International Swimsuit Show had also been a favorite, though considered very risqué. There were changes that needed to be made in order for the business to be more profitable without resorting to tasteless female nudity.

Before the end of 1991, the Navy started shunning those events as inappropriate conduct thanks to the Tailhook scandal. It took me a while to assess what our target audience wanted. I used surveys and focus groups, and evaluated past records, etc. When I asked the 90–95 percent male population what they wanted in order to use the club more often, it always came back to the same: girls, preferably naked ones, cheap booze, and more girls. It was my job to find a politically acceptable alternative.

Apparently, the girl who had worked in my position before I was hired left with a cloud over her head. That explained why my initial training included many warnings of what not to do. An example of the don'ts were: Don't visit a commanding officer's house during his lunch hour, even if you are "innocently" filling his wife's closet with balloons for her birthday (cough-cough); Don't do coke during business hours (we are not talking Diet Coke here), as it seemed to produce strange behaviors; Don't get your manicure on company time, especially if you use Uncle Sam's money to pay for it.

I wasn't told why I received such specific words of warning. My guess was that, over years of employee turnover, they may have faced those issues before.

It was a very unusual occurrence (like never) for a Commanding Officer of a training command to summon someone as low on the food chain as me to their office for a meeting. In the chain of command, there were numerous levels between me (at the bottom) and a particular commanding officer, like a Navy Captain. Had I not been a civilian, my position would have been the equivalent of an Ensign. Word around the base was that the Captain had not wanted to lose my predecessor, which made him very truculent toward anyone filling that position.

Within two weeks of starting employment, I was ordered to the Captain's office, with no information or way to prepare. I was responsible for event coordination and marketing at the O'Club. My boss was a Navy Commander, which is one step below a captain. Under normal circumstances, a captain would have given direction to the subordinate commander, with those orders flowing down the chain of command until they would have eventually reached me.

I showed up at his secretary's desk at my appointed time, looking smart and confident. The Captain's Executive Officer (XO) came out and escorted me into the spacious office overlooking the base airport. There was a huge conference table in the center of a very palatial military office. After the initial introduction and some cordial small talk, the Captain said something to the tune of, "So, you're the girl taking XYZ's place." I said I really didn't know anything about my predecessor, but I had been hired as the new Public Affairs Specialist and special events coordinator.

The Captain took the time to show me, on a large map spread across his conference table, how many people were under his command. I listened intently, and I was impressed with his responsibility. He continued his instructions to me with, "You need to know what your predecessor did to keep us happy. First, you will need to come visit my office, every week, to tell me what you are planning at the club, and while here, keep the candy jar on my desk filled." The Executive Officer (XO) added, "Yeah, and make sure the waffles at Sunday brunch are round instead of square." The responsibility for the brunch menu for Sunday, a day I did not work, actually fell to the O'Club's professional chef.

The Captain took back control of the discussion. "When we arrive at the club for happy hour, it is your job to make us feel welcome and special." He then reiterated, "Remember that my influence is over several hundred young aviators—if you don't please us" (as my illustrious predecessor had done), "then my aviators won't be supporting the Officers' Club."

The meeting actually lasted about forty-five minutes, with him giving me my marching orders. As I left his conference room and started heading back toward my office at the other end of the base, I started to see red. His words had been patronizing, sexist, and downright insulting. When I arrived back at my office, both the Marketing Manager and the Commander of the MWR Department were anxiously waiting to hear what the Captain had wanted to discuss with me. Their eyes bulged when they heard the threat he had made—if I didn't "please" him, he'd boycott the club, and instruct others to do the same. And if that happened, that would cost me my job.

I fumed for the rest of the day, getting madder each minute. By the next day, I had drafted a letter to the Commanding Officer of NASP, setting forth my complaint against the Captain. I blasted the guy, quoting the ridiculous instructions he had given me, especially the remark about round waffles, and lodged my grievance over the treatment. I knew the letter would either set the ground rules for what kind of crap I would be willing to put up with, or he would fire me. The one thing I knew for sure was that I would not fall into the trap of "taking care" of anyone or anything. I would handle reasonable job duties, which would not include filling candy jars.

It took a couple of weeks before I received a letter from my Commanding Officer, saying I had misunderstood what the captain had said to me. He had discussed the situation with the captain, and he could assure me it wouldn't be an issue again. The ground rules were established. Word soon got around that I wouldn't put up with sexist nonsense just because of rank. I was so new I really didn't fully understand how powerful the man was. I didn't care. After only two weeks on the job, so what if they fired me?

I am happy to say things got better. I grew to love my job. It proved to be fun and challenging. Friday nights were considered to be the biggest night for partying, so I was there, every Friday night, trying to create an atmosphere conducive to aviators having fun. I filled that club, and it rocked with music, dancing, and great free food. My position gave me an opportunity to converse, one on one, with the most-senior officers on the base. Most seemed to like me and appreciated the good times being had by all. There was one fly in the ointment, though. My big, boisterous husband didn't like my job at all. It was my first initiation into living inside a rank structure. I was oblivious to the culture of the military and didn't fully understand the underlying problem for a long time.

My husband was a Warrant-Officer-03, who had given up his commission when he joined the National Guard. Though he was a pilot, he was in the lowest officer category. I knew he had been a Marine Officer during his active duty, and he was a very good Huey helicopter pilot, so I mistakenly saw him as being one of their peers. For those who haven't had the pleasure of working in the very competitive arena of pilots, it is a huge f****ing deal to them.

As in the movie *Top Gun*, jet fighter pilots rule. Commanders of jet fighter pilots rule even more. In that arena, Warrant Officers and National Guard helicopter pilots ain't shit, even when they hover. I was oblivious to this at the start and just couldn't understand why he was so intimidated at the O'Club. I was often pulled into the commander's circle of friends; my husband was subtly shunned.

Our problems multiplied and our fights became brutal. My position at the O'Club had elevated me to the aviator leadership's club—their clientele was my job. He was no longer able to be top dog, with me looking on with admiring eyes, as was the case when we were with his guard buddies. Unfortunately, in the O'Club crowd, he was greatly diminished and his ego couldn't bear it.

Getting to the divorce stage arrived far too soon. I was so in love with him, trying so hard to make the marriage work, and I was blind to the issues. He insisted I stop working on the base, because I did not need to be in his "fish bowl." He wanted to have anonymity, to flirt, and do as he pleased, without everyone knowing his wife. He actually said that.

I refused to quit.

>-!-‹›-•-O-•-‹›-!-‹

Nathan and I at his wedding.

Nathan came home and announced he would be getting married to his high school sweetheart. She was a beautiful little girl, about 4'11" tall. They had been living together, in Birmingham, for the previous two years. We were all happy. We felt they were a good match, and were delighted they would be married in the Creekwood Church of Christ in West Mobile.

The wedding showers began. At one, the cute, perky little bride-to-be opened a large box containing a complete set of copper-clad pots and pans. Her comment was, "Nathan is going to love these." I don't think she intended to do any cooking.

We all showed up, appropriately attired, for the wedding. The mother of the bride had done a beautiful job of preparing the church for such a solemn and special union of our children. As the church filled, I could see my ex (Nathan's father) and his wife (Nathan's step-mother) on the opposite side. I told my husband I would break the ice by going over to speak with them.

As I approached, JJ's wife was glaring at me. JJ then turned sideways, looked at me, then turned his face away. I walked up and stuck my hand out toward them, saying, "JJ, this is the wedding of our son. Can we declare a truce for the day?"He turned back again, looked at my face, and asked sarcastically, "Are you talking to me?" Then he said, "You better get away from me, now, before I hurt you." At first, I just stood there staring at him. I shook my head as I walked back to the pew—*could he really be that ignorant and trashy?*

I looked back toward his wife to see if I could spot support for that type of behavior. She gave me the smuggest look, and nodded her head, fully backing his threat against me right there in the church on our son's wedding day. It had been more than ten years since our divorce, but nothing had changed. The wedding reception was about the same. They stood on one side of the lovely brick courtyard, we stood on the other, both sides respecting the stupid, imaginary line he had drawn down the center. It was awkward but we survived.

As we were all getting ready to leave the reception, my sister and her husband were experiencing some type of car problem. We offered to take them home, or help make whatever arrangements they needed to get them safely back on the road. They declined our assistance, and told us they were allowing JJ to help them out. That didn't sit well with me.

By that evening, I had begun to ruminate about JJ's threat and his wife's approval of such despicable behavior. Their actions had distracted from the celebrating and dancing we did, and from the joy we felt. Ann's opting to accept JJ's friendship and help reminded me of something I had heard many years ago. For me to accept that my sister chose to continue a friendship with a person she knew to threaten and abuse me was like "eating snake." The more I tried to chew it, the bigger it got, until I had to choke or spit it out.

I just about choked to death.

My marriage wasn't getting any better. We were fighting all the time, mostly over jealousy issues—my jealousy, he said, not his. We separated, then went back and forth many times. One of the times we were together, he didn't come home until 3 a.m. I was furious. He slept on the couch, I in our bed. The next day, we argued all morning. That night we decided to try to talk as we were lying in the bed next to each other. He looked at me and said he had something to tell me. He then admitted he had "messed up" the night before. He actually admitted to having sex with a woman he had run into at a bar.

My reaction was not of anger. I was numb, and I was speechless. It is one thing to think the person you love may be cheating on you. It is quite another to hear a full confession of infidelity. I was a zombie for days.

How could he do this to me? To us?

He enjoyed the power he had over my emotions, because he knew I didn't want to fail at marriage again. I resorted to seeing a counselor, located on NASP, for military personnel and their families. I was hoping that a marriage counselor could help us get back to where we were in the beginning. Each week, I'd go to my appointment and tell her about everything: the screaming, the violence, his cheating, and the irrational behavior.

The counselor always gave me such great insight into different perspectives and dealing with troubled relationships. After seeing the counselor six times, she told me she would have to refer me to someone in town. I had used up all my allotted government counseling appointments. I didn't want to start over with a new counselor. She reassured me that she would do a "warm handoff," meaning she would brief my in-town counselor on my situation and the methods she was using for my treatment.

She said she had been using a treatment method for victims of domestic abuse. "You are a victim of domestic abuse. I don't think marriage counseling will help you or your marriage." In fact, she said she feared for my safety.

A potential victim? Oh no, not again. I was a strong, competent, and capable woman, I kept telling myself. I hadn't been seeing myself in that light,

I had been trying to make my marriage work. I didn't want to fail again. She explained that I had been enduring a pattern of abuse directed toward me for the self-aggrandizement of my husband. She explained the criteria for a narcissist and for narcissistic behaviors. They are happy when they can play the hero—it builds them up. They are interested in surrounding themselves with people they can bully and control.

But if I did not acquiesce to the narcissist's demands, it was not uncommon for violence to ensue, usually in the form of the silent treatment (for days). If that didn't work, then he resorted to yelling. If that didn't work, he would get sick. When all those things failed, he started breaking things and throwing a fit.

Oh my God, I was literally back to square one. I had tried hard not to duplicate my mistakes in selecting a husband. No matter what, though, I found myself back in the same situation again.

I demanded he leave our home while we worked out the problems. My idea was akin to a time-out. I couldn't forgive him.

He called me weeks later and asked me to meet him in a restaurant just outside the front gate of the Navy base. I did. We sat and talked, and I listened to him as he persuaded me to try again. He wanted us to go to counseling. As we continued to chat, he started glancing at his watch. I ended the conversation and said I would think about what he had said.

I knew it was strange that he kept looking at his watch. I followed my hunch. Knowing the local downtown pick-up joint was in full swing on Wednesday nights, I decided to take a drive over. I was curious to see if he was there. The popular waterfront spot was the Beef and Ale House, aka "the Beef and Tail." Yep, there he was with another woman. They were in a booth, his arm wrapped around her, the two so close you couldn't get a knife between them.

Smiling sweetly, I walked up and said hello. The woman came back with a smile and a hello (she had no idea who I was), while my surprised husband just sat there with a blank look on his face. I asked the pretty woman, "Are you enjoying having a drink with my husband?" Her face went from smile to frown in half a second.

I reached and picked up the bottled beer that had just been set down in front of him. I raised the beer high, turning the bottle upside down, pouring all the contents directly on top of his head. It played out like a movie in slow motion. He didn't move. The beer poured out in a nice stream, falling with rhythmic splashes off his balding head. The foaming beer ran down his face, shoulders, and onto his lap. He reached for a napkin, dabbing at his red, flushed face. The crowd in the bar started cheering loudly for me.

By now, we were the place's featured spectacle. I sat the empty beer bottle down with a thud as I directed my attention to the stunned woman. I looked at her and said, "Don't go out with him again until his divorce is final." I quickly left the premises. I realized he had finally succeeded in reducing me to the lowest common denominator. I was ashamed that I had allowed him to drag me down to his level.

I cried all the way home—my heart was broken. The marriage seemed destined to die a slow and very painful death. I thought I would die along with it.

> *I liken that marriage to getting off heroin.*
> *I tried it cold turkey, but would relapse into the ecstasy of the moment,*
> *I tried desperately to recapture the feelings*
> *As the bittersweet taste of a decadent dark chocolate*
> *No matter how I savored the flavor that should sate*
> *It soon dissolved, leaving me empty and wanting.*

We had enjoyed many, though sporadic, good times during our relationship. We both loved to ski, ride horses, play tennis, and more. During our last attempt to make up, we took a ski vacation to Keystone with a bunch of his friends. My counselor advised me not to go because she was concerned for my safety.

Our first argument started on the slopes when I refused to take the lift with his friends to ski a double-diamond black trail. I am not (and never have been) that excellent a skier. I would stick with my intermediate blue ski runs, thank you very much. I really didn't care if all the others were heading to the top. I was not going. I encouraged him to go ski with his friends if he wanted. I would be happy to ski alone until they came back down. He said he would not go with them because I wouldn't go. He became so angry, he seemed about to explode. He yelled—wait, no, not yelled. He stood in the middle of a busy ski run and bellowed, to high heaven, cursing me out for not going to the top of the mountain.

It was truly astonishing and pathetic that a man would stand and curse God and me in the middle of a mountain of skiers because I refused to go up to a black diamond run. I am sure people could hear his rage for miles. I was embarrassed for him.

Why on Earth would he be so upset at me for not going on a black slope? I was obviously not able to ski that run. I often had difficulty negotiating tough, intermediate slopes—for me, it would have been suicide. My crazy thought was, either he was going to suck it up and try to show off for his friends, or maybe he planned to push me off a cliff. I'll never know for sure.

We all met for drinks at the end of the day. A beautiful girl, there with one of the other guys, decided she would make spaghetti at their condo for everyone. She walked over to our car and took off her glove. She reached into the car and rubbed her hand around my husband's neck to let him feel the cold of her hand. I questioned the intimacy of the act.

During the après-ski banter at the bar, I learned the evening was to include some skinny dipping in the condo hot tub. I got really quiet. For them, it was all fun and games. For me, that was it. I was out. Not on a bet would I jump into a hot tub with a bunch of topless people, or in the buff—not then, not now, not ever. This became a huge deal and caused a heartfelt defense of my personal boundaries. He was so angry, the steam was coming from his ears.

I ended up flying home with a black and blue jaw from where he slapped me repeatedly after he took his 245 lb. frame, sat it on my chest, and pinned me to the bed. Lying on my back, I could do nothing but spit right into his face, so spit I did.

On the flight home, I pulled the turtleneck of my shirt down and exposed the dark bruises that were now readily apparent down the side of my jaw and neck. His comment was, "If you love me, you'd make up a story that you fell skiing." *I should cover for his hitting me?* No way. I felt it was my badge of courage for defying him.

When we returned to Pensacola, he returned to his apartment and I returned to the home we had shared. I went in to see the counselor and told her what had happened. Her knowing words expressed how glad she was that I had made it home safely.

Our divorce was in the works. We awaited our court date to make it final. As we sat in the judge's chambers to complete our self-mediated divorce, he asked the judge not to grant the petition. He had changed his mind, again. When he thought the judge wasn't listening to his plea, he became angry. Like flipping a switch, his attitude changed. He told her I had spit in his face when I was angry. He left out the part that his fat ass was on top of me, with my hands pinned down. I just sat there looking at him. Florida is a no-fault divorce state and the judge doesn't give a rip. In order to be in her court, we were supposed to be in agreement on the settlement. I was concerned that she was going to deny ruling on the case because of his last-minute antics.

The female judge cracked her gavel and ended the session. She said she could feel the anger and tension from an out-of-control man. She said, "I do not feel safe in this room." She removed everyone and told the bailiff that we could reenter, after a sufficient number of guards were in the room to protect her from my husband's wrath. When we reconvened an hour later, she granted me a divorce. With a clearer mind and in hindsight, I know he had coveted my Airmont house. At the time, I must have looked pretty good to him, and we became the envy of his National Guard group. In fact, at one time, he actually said, "You were so pretty, I thought *you* would be enough for me."

This photo was taken on Perdido Key Beach, in front of our condo.
It was the best I could do. I was not enough.

Diamond in the Dark

My omniscient viewing-glass hadn't worked. When we married, I had actually believed he loved me, and I thought it would be good for us to start afresh. He had been deep in debt, so I let him use part of the money I received from Colonel Dixie to pay off his used 280Z Datsun. He had lived in my house, and I had supported him, while he made his big attempt at becoming a jet pilot. He left our marriage financially better off, his retirement intact, his bills paid, and with $15,000 of my money. I felt victorious that I had finally beaten the addiction. Although I had relapsed several times, I had finally prevailed.

The next day, he showed up on base, driving a brand new red Corvette, purchased, in part, with his divorce settlement.

Is that all there is? Is that all there is? If that's all there is, my friends, then let's keep dancing. Let's bring out the booze and have a party, If that . . . is all . . . there is . . .

Chapter 41
Finding My Bearings

Lanee Michelle, my first grandchild, and Jamie's wedding photo.
(Both by Olan Mills and printed with permission.)

Working on a Navy base with active-duty military and seasoned civilian workers, I soon realized I had entered a totally different sub-culture of American life. I intuitively recognized the new lifestyle as the gateway I had been looking for, in order for me to change my up-to-now destructive life path. I submerged myself in the culture, and worked hard to understand the military mind set. I learned the rank structure, the insignia, and the language of military acronyms. I knew I needed to refocus, because in my own eyes, I was an official, proven, dumb-ass-loser, with three marriages to prove it.

My strengths were directed at doing a good job for my director, and keep business, business. I set new guiding parameters for my life: care for myself indefinitely, never again trust a man to keep commitments, work hard to pay off all debts, assure my ability to sustain "aloneness," and enjoy my life and relationships with family and friends without expecting anything in return (*that way I wouldn't be disappointed*). My new barometer for intimate rela-tionships, if any, was an initial question I'd always ask myself, "Is this person someone I really like, find sexually attractive, *and* someone I feel sure really likes me, finds me interesting, funny, and sexually attractive. Plus, when I see this person the next day, will I feel comfortable that we still are friends?" It was amazing how that test weeded out most suitors. *Oh yeah!*

And did I mention, never expect any man to actually keep a commit-ment after the newness wears off?

One of my favorite events each year was to coordinate a team-building day for admirals. Team building was always set for the last day of their week-long conference. I would do my best to create an environment that tested skills and teamwork, and provided a lot of laughter, for 80-plus Navy leaders of our nation. The day was taken up in contests, beach run relays, beach volleyball with a few twists, and raft races. The grand finale: Each team was allowed twenty minutes to construct a paper airplane with provided materials. Which team's plane would fly farthest? The tension reached a fever pitch, and competition was intense, as some used questionable techniques, like including a few rocks in the plane's nose (*cheating*), or anything else they thought would give them a winning edge.

They had a great time even though I busted them for "stretching the rules." I loved coordinating the games for them so they could just have fun. They loved it too, and year after year, they asked me to take care of their much-deserved play day.

One participant in that group was a good-looking rear admiral. He called me every month for a year. We chatted and laughed, and I looked forward to him coming back the following year. He made an interim visit, for a weekend, and he accompanied me to a dinner theatre I had arranged for the O'Club. We had a nice time. He was so polite as he sat through what was a very mediocre play. We said our goodbyes at the door.

The next time he came to NASP, he asked me to dinner. He picked me up at my home.

Our destination was Scottos for a lovely Italian meal. Conversation turned to family and friends. He did not wear a wedding ring and, from all indications, he was not married. I finally had to ask, "Are you married?" I did not think he was—he had never mentioned a wife or family. I had talked of my children, but he never chimed in.

As he solemnly revealed to me he was married, I glared at him. "You are married? What is your problem? Why are you out with me?"

He said, "No problem at home. I love my wife. I just really have a weakness for beautiful women."

There was no way I was prepared for his answer. He could have said, "We are never together and we have drifted apart," or "We are unhappy and we are headed for divorce." Maybe, "She hit menopause and no longer wants sex." But no, I was looking into the eyes of the G. D. enemy—yet another prick concerned only about himself.

I took a sip of my wine. I leaned toward the center of the table and whispered, "Let me clarify what you are saying. You love your wife, but you are out with me." He seemed to have no qualms in expressing his weakness.

My response was emphatic. "You are a real son-of-a-bitch." I thanked him for my dinner, and for the evening, and asked if he would mind driving me home, or if I needed to take a cab. He drove me home. We had little to say, and I never even kissed the man (and, under other circumstances, I would have liked to).

Please give me credit. I was finally learning the nature of man. It makes no difference if they love you, or if they don't. They want "different" stuff. It's not me, and it's not their wives. It's them.

And he was so good looking.

Damn!

My son called me in July 1992. He wanted me to know that my daughter (his sister), who was living and working in Mobile, was expecting. *Expecting what?* Much to my chagrin, Jamie had dated one guy from high school to college. She had dropped out of college, much to my disappointment, and was living in Mobile with roommates. It just so happened I was at home with a male friend when I got the call. I really did fall apart at the thought that my daughter was pregnant with my first grandchild. I wasn't prepared. OMG! What would I do? I cried out of deep, all-engulfing sadness.

My friend reached out, his arms encircling me as I sobbed. I asked him, "What am I going to do?" She was having a baby, and at the time, I didn't know how to handle it. The deep racking sobs touched his heart. "You're going to love her," he said.

How simple was that? Nothing else really mattered. I was going to have a grandchild. No matter what, I was going to love my child and the one she carried. A dear, male friend was the one to put that life-changing event into proper perspective for me.

My next move was to go to Mobile, load up my child, with child, and bring her to Pensacola. The following four months, we prepared for "our" baby, our beautiful, unbelievable, incredible, first baby girl. My friend was out of my life by then, but I will never forget his words of wisdom. What will you do when a unexpected baby is coming? "You're going to love her," and I did, with all my heart.

My at-work tasks grew in many ways. I would know that a new challenge was heading my way when my new director would come to me and ask, "How would you like another opportunity to excel?"

I coordinated the official Navy Marathon three years in a row. Those winners went on to win a place in the Boston Marathon.

I served as the base liaison for the International Bill Fish Tournament, which brought in boats from all over the world.

Each year, as part of the MWR team, I worked on the homecoming show for the Blue Angels. It took place in November, and was the last show of the season. I gained sponsorships, and I helped make sure that the 100,000 to 150,000 people who showed up had great choices to eat, starting with the volunteer-manned concessions. All the MWR staff (my buddies) did their part, and we worked hard to meet the needs of the air show: parking, programs, bleacher seating, food, souvenirs, etc. The military handled the actual flight show, but MWR's staff set the stage for Naval Aviation to do its thing.

In 1993, I was invited to a party at a Commanding Officer's home on base. Captain and Mrs. Spence Robbins were hosting. Barb Robbins was known for her beauty, grace, charm, and matching outfits. You know—the perfect woman, whose every outfit has matching earrings, necklace, shoes, and purse. She was always so nice, which made it so easy for our department to assist her with anything she needed. Though always dressed to the nines, she was never pretentious.

Barb and I became good friends, which was interesting because her husband had graduated from Annapolis with my last ex (#3). Barb invited me to their annual Halloween Party. I was a bit gun shy, because at the last party I went to at one of the officers' homes, a civilian woman told me, point blank, "You are too nice looking. Don't ever come to a party again without an escort."

I hated the implication. However, she was right. Everywhere I went alone, married guys would wait until their wives were in the other room, or wherever, and throw me their best pitch. There was no way for the wives to know, but at that point, I was impervious to their husbands' crap. The wives liked me but still saw me as a threat.

I wanted to go to the party, but I would not go alone. I called my ex, with whom I had long since been divorced. I told him I needed an escort to a Halloween party at the home of Captain and Mrs. Robbins. It would be held at their home on "Admirals Row" (North Avenue). An invitation to anything on North Avenue was coveted in Pensacola, especially among non-military. When I told him it was at the home of his old classmate, Captain Spence Robbins, he said, "Sure. Why not?"

The week before the party, I applied for a new job at the Navy Hospital. It was a Public Affairs position, which made me dream of moving to the hospital to work with a different team. No one knew I had put in my application, but I was hoping I would get a chance to move and expand my skills.

At the party, my ex-husband in tow, I arrived as a Viking princess. My black leather and fur bustier was cinched tightly around my twenty-four inch waist. My breasts were covered with real fur cups, so very little cleavage showed. It was handmade to fit perfectly. My long skirt was of washed denim, my boots of tan leather with fur added around the top, my natural blond braids hanging long, all topped off with my horned Viking hat. A sheepskin vest, with the soft shearling fur turned out, complimented the costume, which I have to say was beautiful.

We arrived on time. The magnificent home was decorated from stem to stern. Our hostess met us at the door and highly recommended that we get in line for the palm reader clairvoyant, who was upstairs to give us a reading of our future. I wasn't sure I wanted to know my future, but what the heck? We positioned ourselves in a line that ran up the staircase to one of the upper rooms. It was early, and only a couple of people were ahead of us.

Diamond in the Dark

We would have a glass of wine and wait our turn for our fortunes to be told.

On the stairs, there was a man waiting in line. We talked, exchanging our humorous expectations of what the soothsayer might say. I looked at the man in the Middle Eastern *jalaba* (or robe). His eyes were brown, and so dark that the light made a sparkle. He was trying hard not to stare at my leather bustier. I found him intriguing, dark, and handsome—very handsome.

When it finally came my turn, the clairvoyant took my hand. She said that she could see me in the middle of a lot of doctors. She immediately tried not to alarm me, patting my hand, and began, "You are okay. You are not in an accident." She seemed concerned. "Are you a nurse?" she asked. I told her no. She shook her head. She sat still, as though she was hearing voices, or at least trying to hear voices. She kept shaking her head slowly and said, "I see doctors all around you. You are not sick, and you are not hurt, but doctors are everywhere." She seemed confused. My time was up. She wished me luck.

Since I had applied at the hospital, I was hoping she had foreseen my getting the job. It was plausible, and I wanted so badly to go to the hospital to work.

I came back to the stairs, and my ex went in for his reading. I stood on the stairs, waiting for him, but continued to talk with the very handsome man. We had a great conversation, filled with laughter and flirtation. He knew I was with a date. I could see he was alone. His eyes sparkled as he looked at me. My ex returned from his uneventful reading, and we left to re-enter the party downstairs.

Then we chatted with lots of guests, but eventually ended up crossing paths again with the handsome man with the dark, sparkling eyes. I liked his feel and presence. He moved to several different places around the big house, seeming to position himself so I'd keep running into him. Finally, my big ex acknowledged the obvious attraction between me and the man. He looked at him, then at me, and asked, "Who is that guy?" I really didn't know anything about him, other than his first name (Bob) and his rank (commanding officer of a place called NAMI), which he had told me stood for the Naval Aerospace Medical Institute.

Back at work on Monday, I tried to get my friend and supervisor to find out if anyone knew the new commander and if he was married. After days of inquiry, no one was able to give me any information on Bob.

As always, at the first of November, our department was preparing for the 1993 Homecoming Air Show. I was working at the show that Saturday morning, when across the tarmac I spotted the same guy I'd met at the party. He must have been at least fifty yards away, surrounded by spectators, but I saw him and he saw me. We immediately started walking toward each other.

I found our conversation to be stilted, and our reaction to one another curious. The fact that we were definitely attracted to one another was obvious. I was enjoying talking to him, when a tall woman with dark hair walked up and said, "Bob, we need to go." He turned and said he had to leave. I watched him walk away with the woman. *The son of a bitch is married*, I thought.

The year 1994 came in like a lamb for me—quietly—and even though I was dating a nice man, also named Bob, I had not forgotten the man from the party. The first weekend in '94, I ran into him again at the O'Club. We talked. I was at work, so I excused myself, telling him I had to get back to work. He stopped me by saying that we had run into each other twice, and he would like to get my phone number. I gave it to him.

He stopped me again. "I don't want your work number," he said. "I want your home number." My answer to him was that I did not give my number to married men. He had a strange and questioning look on his face, and said, "I am not married."

"You aren't married? Are you sure?" He confirmed he was indeed not married. I gave him my home number.

I hope I get some credit here for finally verifying, ahead of time, the man's marital status.

We had dinner together a couple of times. The first time, I was so sick with the flu, I should have stayed home. I ended up not eating, and was in the restroom barfing most of the evening. He took me to his house and put me in the guest room (alone), because I was too sick to drive the twelve miles to my house. He was a good sport about the whole thing, but I didn't think he'd ask me out again. It can't have been very romantic going out with a woman who throws up all evening.

To my surprise, he did ask me out again. I looked forward to our second date and the opportunity to make a better impression. He took me for his favorite meal, sushi. I had never eaten sushi, so he ordered for me. He ordered the roll he liked most—a spicy eel roll. Again, I spent most of the evening in the restroom, thinking I would barf from the incredibly nasty taste of the sushi. Yet again, I figured that was the end of it.

I was now dating two Bobs. Bob #1, whom I had been going out with for several months, had made friends with my daughter and her boyfriend, Michael. Bob#1 had the ability to make them feel comfortable. He once brought in oysters, so they jokingly started a campaign to keep the guy around.

Jamie and Michael preferred to invite Bob #1 to their January wedding. It was okay with me—it was their wedding. They were married in the small, All Faiths Chapel at Naval Air Station Pensacola. Jamie's brother, Nathan, was the best man. Another friend was a groomsman. Jamie's maid of honor was Kerry, Nathan's wife, and the other maid was Michael's cousin. The church was beautiful, the music was extraordinary, the bride was radiant—there was just one little problem. The father of the bride, JJ, who had agreed to come to her wedding, and had accepted the honor to give her away, didn't bother to show. I am still not sure why I was surprised. He didn't call before, and he didn't call to apologize after it was over. He simply left his only daughter standing at the front of the church, waiting for her dad.

Nathan escorted his sister down the aisle. When asked, "Who gives this woman to be married to this man?" Nathan proudly spoke his only line, "Her mother and I."

Jamie and Michael might have made their preference known, but my thoughts were mostly on Bob #2, who had already exhibited an extremely high tolerance for sick women. He was a caregiver. After the wedding, Bob #2 called and asked for a third date. That request was for a Saturday afternoon BBQ. I declined, because I had my grand-daughter for the day. To my surprise, he said, "Bring her with you."

When I arrived at his home, his patio had a baby swimming pool filled with warm water, toys, and balls, all spread out just for my Lanee. I was bowled over by the fact that the guy who had no kids had prepared for *my* baby. I was hooked. Bob #2 quickly moved up the line, and now was ahead of Bob #1. In fact, for me, he became my only Bob.

Me and my little bathing beauty, Lanee.

As they say, the rest is history. We dated, we laughed, we enjoyed dinners and military functions, plus we attended several weddings that spring. Once we started getting close, there was no deviation from the pattern, and no games. There was never any, "I need more time," or, "We need to date other people." It was natural. We just liked being together, and we made that happen as much as possible.

Bob was single, a Navy Captain. In military terms, he was an 0-6. He had arrived in Pensacola during June of 1993. He had gone through a divorce the year before. He was a physician taking care of our pilots—a Flight Surgeon, as they call the position. He was the Commanding Officer for the Resident Naval Aerospace Medical Institute (NAMI), which prepared flight surgeons to serve as doctors in the fleet or aboard Navy ships. And he was such a gentleman. We fell in love. I didn't expect it. He didn't either.

Before our relationship went too far, I knew I had to tell Bob about all the problems I had left behind. I felt uncomfortable that the man was so squared away and so accomplished, and I had such a tainted background, especially the Leverett disaster. I asked him to come over to my house, where I told him my long story. I even gave him an "out" by saying I would understand if he was not interested in continuing our relationship. He didn't care. He had no concerns about anything, or anyone, in my past—the past was the past. *What a find!* I was such a lucky girl.

However, I told him that if he had any political aspirations, he needed to leave in a hurry. He laughed and assured me he would never run for political office. He took my hand and we started our journey together.

Chapter 42
A Bitter End

Paul's last recorded wave goodbye.

Jamie was now married, so I had my home back to myself again. It was wonderful having her live with me for a while, and even better to take part in the birth of my grand-daughter. Living alone had its positives, privacy being important for me. Usually if my phone rang, depending on the time of the call, I could pretty often guess who the caller would be. There were only so many people who had my home number.

My phone rang one Saturday afternoon. I answered it fully expecting to hear Bob's voice. It was not. I listened closely, but I didn't want to hear. The voice was clear and unmistakable—Paul Leverett. He was calling from prison. His smooth baritone voice took me back to another time—a time gone by, a time better forgotten. He waited patiently for it to sink in that it was him.

There had been no time for preparation. I am sure I sounded pretty cold when I asked him what he wanted. My question obviously took him aback, for he said he just wanted to hear my voice and let me know he might be up for parole in a few months. I could hear a thinly-veiled excitement beneath the normal cadence of his tone. He wanted to know if I would be there for him—be there to help him if he got out.

I almost passed out. My spine stiffened. I was clear and my voice resolute. I told him that I would not, could not, no matter what, reenter our relationship. Life had taken me in a different direction, and there was no way I would be pulled back into dealing with the Leverett "curse." I just couldn't even consider getting involved in any way. I asked him if he realized how hard it had been, getting to a point where that curse did not dominate me, my family, my entire life. I tried to make him understand that there just wasn't anything left in me for his cause.

I knew I had to stop him now, because if you gave Paul a chance, he would suck you in, give you jobs, get you working for him, and then, before you knew it, you were hooked. He had a way of making you feel beholden to him, and he never forgot if he did something for you.

No. No. No. Not for all the world would I go back. By the end of the conversation, which was short, he knew I meant what I'd said. But the call worried me. It ate at me for days. In my mind, I played through forty imagined scenarios for his possible release. I reminded myself that he most likely would not get paroled the first time he was eligible. That would be exceedingly unusual for a high-profile murder case like his, with the victim's family still in the courtyard screaming "To the guillotine!" He had only been in prison a little more than ten years, but as the eternal optimist, he was trying to make plans to survive once he was out. My mind allowed me to think of little else for days.

My greatest fear was of him, standing in front of me at my door. OMG! What would I do? As much as I didn't want to deal with that entire disaster again, my conscience was telling me I could not turn him away if he was out of prison with nowhere else to go. I knew that if he did come, I would try, at a minimum, to help him get on his feet. I didn't want anything but good for him. I just didn't want his new life to include me.

I followed up with a letter that reflected that sentiment. I wrote: "I wish you well, but don't dream of a life with me when you get out, because I won't go back."

Captain Bob Hain and I began dating in January, and by March, we were dating only each other. May was the big training month for Bob's command. The Aerospace Medical Association met every year for the docs to get their Continuing Medical Education Credits (CMEs). That year (1994), the event was to be held in San Antonio in May. He asked me to join him for the weekend. I flew out on Friday and flew home on Sunday. We had two nights and a whole day together. The Riverwalk was lovely.

For Saturday, Bob had a special evening planned at a fabulous restaurant he remembered from visiting San Antonio another time. I dressed in my most flattering outfit, an expensive and very feminine dress made of a creamy white silk with a beautiful floral pattern. The neckline was crossed over with a fitted waist. There was no cleavage showing. It wasn't too short. It wasn't too tight. It was a perfectly fitted dress for an evening out with Bob that might also present an opportunity to be with others from his Command. I wanted to look my best for him.

We had such a lovely time. The wine was good, the food fabulous. I didn't know what he was thinking when he suddenly asked me this hypothetical question, "If you were going to go out with someone for money, what would you charge?" *What*? *What did you just say to me?* I was aghast.

My eyes narrowed and my ire grew. I quietly glared at him in total disbelief. I was angry. I was confused. I was hurt. I asked him, with more than a little obvious irritation, "I got dressed up for you, and this is what I get? Why would you ask me such a question?" I shook my head in disbelief, that after all the time we had spent together, he would say such a callous, stupid, insensitive thing.

He got my drift. I gave him the "eat shit and die look." He apologized, and he made some excuse that I looked so beautiful (he was trying to recover from the blunder), he just didn't know what to say, so he said something really stupid. We did get past it for the evening, but it would be much later before I would figure out the meaning of what was almost a show-stopper for us.

He really doesn't want to admit it, even to this day, but he was looking at me and asking me a question based on a somewhat apocryphal story about Benjamin Franklin. Supposedly, Ben Franklin asked a pretty lady of the Parisian court, a courtesan, if she would go to bed with him for a million pounds? She looked at him, batted her eyes, and said, "Why yes." Then good old Ben was said to have asked, "Well, would you go to bed with me for five pounds?" The quite shocked and very beautiful lady replied, "What do you think I am, a whore?" Ben supposedly replied, "We've already established that. Now we are just haggling over the price."

I guess you can say he used a test question to bait me, and I passed.

I didn't get a chance to tell you about Dr. Bob's past. He had worked for eight years at Kaiser Permanente, in Beverly Hills, California, 90210—there he became Dr. Gucci. He had been a surgeon there, with, as he says, "a connection to the lesser lights of the film industry." He was cool, funny, and extremely forgivable. Bob described his Hollywood friends this way, "You know in the western where you see the bad guy? And the bad guy has a gang that you can see in the background. You know, the ones sitting up on the hillside, silhouetted in the distance? Well, those are my friends."

He ran with a wild group there. He was friends with Stan Kamen (Goldie Hahn's agent), Karen Black and her friend Lee Purcell (his girlfriend for a while), and an agent friend, Michael Selsman (Marilyn Monroe's agent.) Evidently, he also worked his way through a number of starlets on the agent's list.

That night in San Antonio, he had lapsed into a Beverly Hills frame of mind. He's a very smart man, and it didn't take him long to figure out that, with me, he would have been better off to have just stuck his foot in his mouth. It was amazing how quickly he came to understand me, and then he proceeded to stake his claim.

It might have been a rocky start, but the rough spots were soon over. We spent a lot of time together. His home on Pensacola Bay was beautiful, but so was mine. He would sometimes spend the night with me, but because he lived closer to town, I would usually stay with him on the weekends, returning home on Sunday afternoon. To my amazement and happiness, I found that he enjoyed "The Far Side" comics, and that he liked horses. I thought: *It just can't be true.* I have finally found a man with a quirky sense of humor, whose immediate comedic responses kept me entertained and intellectually challenged.

We were with friends one evening when the conversation turned to horses and riding. They told us of a company called FITS Equitour that scheduled rides all over the world. We located the company and booked a ride, in Vermont, called the "Sugarbush Tolt"—a genteel ride, on Icelandic horses, through the winding Sugarbush mountain area. They used the mountain trails for horseback riding during the spring, summer, and fall. These were the same trails used by snowmobiles during the winter. The week-long ride would start at the Mad River Inn, a charming bed and breakfast that was so picturesque, you would want to pinch yourself just to make sure it was real.

Each morning, we would have a lovely breakfast, dress for a day of riding, then depart for the stables to mount up for the day. Our luggage would be moved for us to the next bed and breakfast destination. We would ride, laugh, enjoy Vermont's countryside, picnic, or have lunch at a local restaurant, remount, and ride again until late afternoon. It was pure, exhilarating happiness.

We celebrated Bob's 54th birthday, August 24, at one of the inns. I sent ahead for a special cake and Champagne to be shared with our group of nine riders. Our unforgettable week ended with a feast of three-pound lobsters, cooked up special for us, by the Mad River staff—a wonderful memory well worth holding on to. I think that week gave both of us a glimpse at what life together could be.

They look like ponies, but they are small, sturdy Icelandic horses.

Bob had a lot of formal and official responsibilities as a Commanding Officer. I didn't get too carried away with all the pomp and circumstance, but I loved attending the functions on the arm of my handsome captain. He was invited to so many parties and official ceremonies, and he often traveled to great places for conferences or training. The good thing was he didn't seem to want to go to any of them without me. I knew that would eventually come to an end, but that didn't keep us from having the time of our lives.

The usual stint of time was about three years before commanders have to move on to their next command. I knew he would not stay in Pensacola forever, so I determined to keep everything in proper perspective, but in what I consider my best description of that time, I felt like "Queen for A Day" for two and one-half years. Happiness filled our lives, and our relationship flourished. As much as I enjoyed the "moment," I knew it wasn't mine, but I loved riding in his "parade."

We were planning to celebrate my birthday in October 1994, when I would turn 44. I was at my home when I received a call from my girlfriend Dale, who still lived in Mobile. She told me she had some bad news, and just blurted it out: "Paul is dead. He was killed yesterday up in Greensboro, Alabama."

I was speechless. I didn't want to think of anything bad happening to him, I didn't want him to die, and I certainly didn't want him to be a victim of murder. With real sadness in her voice, Dale gave me the information she had. She had been with me during those first years after Paul was gone. She knew how hard it had been for me. Dale had been a good friend, but her total dislike for my third husband, and now ex-husband, made it difficult to maintain the bond we once held dear. After moving to Pensacola, our friendship became merely a good memory.

Monday, October 24, 1994 Pensacola News Journal front page story under "crime":

FOUR KILLED AT ALABAMA PRISON RANCH; DIRECTOR, WIFE, FOUND BLUDGEONED

Associated Press, GREENSBORO, AL—An inmate at a state prison cattle ranch killed the director, the director's wife, and two inmates before setting fire to the director's house Sunday, prison officials said.

Charles A. Farquhar, 74, director of the prison ranch named in his honor, was bludgeoned to death inside his brick home on the ranch property, said State Department of Corrections spokesman John Hale. He said Farguhar's wife, Doris, 68, also was bludgeoned to death in the home. Authorities said one of the inmates was shot to death in the house and the other was found shot to death on the carport. They were identified as Clifton D. Martin, 44, from Lawrence County, and Paul Leverette, 60, from Mobile County. Hale said Kelvin O'Neal Washington, 27, from Tuscaloosa County, was arrested in the slayings, which occurred during the early morning hours. A motive in the slayings was not known, Hale said. Washington was an inmate at the west Alabama prison ranch, serving a 20-year sentence for a 1984 conviction for assault with intent to murder a police officer and theft.

Washington was still on the prison property when he was taken into custody, authorities said.

Hale said it appeared that Farquhar had gone out for his usual walk when Washington went into the house and bludgeoned Mrs. Farguhar to death. Hale said Martin and Leverette had gone to the house to report for work and were shot to death upon returning from his walk, and then the house was burned down.

Hale County Coroner Kevin Crawford said the bodies were burned beyond recognition and he was unable to make a positive identification. The bodies were turned over to state forensic scientists, he said.

On Thursday October 27, 1994, the Pensacola News Journal ran an Associated Press article on page 5c. This is an excerpt:

GREENSBORO, AL—The sons of slain warden Charles Farquhar and his wife, Doris, took time out from burying their parents to praise the efforts of two inmates killed while trying to help the couple.

In a statement, the Farquahars' two sons, Robbie and Andy, described Martin and Leverett as "kind and considerate people." Martin and Leverett died of shotgun blasts while apparently trying to help the Farquahars after they had been attacked in their home.

"We believe in our hearts that they lost their lives out of concern and compassion for our mother and father," said the sons' statement issued by prison system spokesman John Hale.

It was later announced that Paul would be buried in Mobile, at the same cemetery where Elizabeth Leverett had been buried. I was a bit surprised that his family chose to put him there, but I guessed that was where his children decided he should be.

I attended the funeral. His children were all there—"Little" Paul, Mark, and Lee. Lee hugged me and made an interesting comment to me. "Boy, you have blossomed," she said while looking me up and down. Kathy, his adopted daughter from Elizabeth's first marriage, was not there—maybe her designer dress was in the cleaners. J.C. Smith, the black man who had been Paul's helper, was there, and I got a big smile and warm hug from him.

Lamar Barnett came with her son, Jim Oswalt. Lamar wasn't speaking to me. I'm sure she wasn't happy that I had decided to leave Paul after I had lost confidence in his innocence. I was just no longer willing to bet my life on it, or give up my life for it. I had a lot of respect for Lamar. She had been such a good and loyal friend to Paul, and I was sorry she didn't understand me or my decision.

Jimmy Langford was there with his wife. He was Paul's attorney, whom we paid handsomely for his unsuccessful appeal of Paul's case. He didn't appear to be interested in talking to me, but that was okay. I assumed, from their reactions, that they all thought I should have given my life up for Paul and been content to be a poor prison visitor for the rest of my days. Paul knew how I felt, and that was between me and him.

One funeral attendee was a former judge who had departed the bench under a cloud. I don't remember what he did to lose his judgeship, but I do remember he was dynamite on the dance floor.

As I scanned the crowd, I noticed a woman who stood off to the side. She had very bleached blonde hair, was overweight, and might have been an attractive woman when she was younger. The lady was carrying long-stem red roses and was giving them to people as they walked by. Someone told me she had been visiting Paul in prison. I walked over to her and introduced myself to her. Her eyes acknowledged that she recognized my name. I thanked her for coming, and from the look in her eyes, I was sure she had loved him. It somehow made me feel better knowing he hadn't been alone during his last months of life.

I was surprised by how many people showed up for him. It may be more accurate to say, I was surprised that anyone showed up, especially his children. It was a mercifully short service. We all huddled by the grave side while the family preacher said a few words. His eulogy started by depicting some happy times of their family's life. He spoke as if Paul's life had not progressed past the time of his marriage to Elizabeth. The preacher reminisced, looking down at Paul's children, as if they were frozen in time, having never left the '70s. It was the craziest damned scene.

I envisioned the whole picture as: A preacher blocking the view of Paul's cheap casket placed front and center under the funeral tent. An unseen guest, the wife he was supposed to have murdered, lying six-feet-under, somewhere nearby. His adopted daughter conspicuously absent, but his three biological children sitting stone-faced, in ugly, metal, fold-up chairs, that had been placed directly in front of the preacher. We stand behind them—Jamie, his only step-daughter, and me (his second wife)—completely invisible. Behind us, standing in the sun, are a cadre of Paul's loyal friends. And, off to the side, like a bad anecdote, stands the heavy blonde woman with the red roses.

Chapter 43
Four to the Fore

One of many military occasions we enjoyed.

Bob and I traveled to Brussels in the fall—my first trip to Europe. It would be the first of many. Each year, this international group, AGARD (Advisory Group for Aerospace Research and Development), meets in a different NATO country to discuss medical issues and problems all the represented countries might face in times of conflict. The meetings last for an entire week, usually starting with a welcome from the hosting town's mayor, immediately followed by an elegant reception, most often at the local castle. There are luncheons, formal dinners, awards, and a grand banquet night for the newly-named fellows of the organization. It is quite the fraternity, comprised mostly of medical doctors, much to the chagrin of the engineers who were growing among their ranks.

Bob loves to make fun of the painstaking slowness in which real progress and decisions are made by this group. As he would say:"The United States would be discussing their idea of what medical aid would be dispatched to the injured or wounded soldier in the field. It would include everything up to and including helicopter flights with a medical team treating in flight. One of the smaller, poorer countries would say their affordable plan was to include a home first-aid kit with a tourniquet and two band-aids. Since compromise would be arduous and almost impossible due to the vast schism between rich and poor militaries, the most predictable outcome would be to table that discussion until the next meeting (controversial subjects were always in dire need of more study and contemplation). However, they were able to decide quickly on the best place for all to dine that evening. *Hear, hear!*

I loved Bob's story of a very irate and passionate person who held the meeting floor for over 30 minutes, ranting and railing about some subject that no one cared about or seemed willing to debate. Everyone waited patiently for the speaker's fury to abate, until he finally yielded the floor back to the chairman. The chairman, moving on without missing a beat, calmly said, "Recognizing the kind gentleman, Mr. X from the country of [fill in the blank], we thank you for those kind remarks. If no one else has an opposing view, let us adjourn for dinner and meet again tomorrow at 0900."

Some of the guys, bored with the snail's pace of progress, freelanced to come up with a "tongue in cheek" logo for the group. The end result was a large plate filled with baked beans and large sausages, a knife and fork crisscrossing the plate, a glass of wine placed to the side, and words in italics that read, "Nice to meet you." It was funny, but it somehow summed up the difficulty, even futility, of compromising on much of anything except good food and drink.

It was the season of my debut to all of Bob's international colleagues and friends. I was charmed by the intellectual presence of this very accomplished group. Bob listened as I gave him my take on the fabulous world he had long taken for granted. It was so special. *He* was so special.

Regardless of what anyone thought of me or of our relationship, most everyone was polite and seemed to genuinely welcome me as Bob's girlfriend. He didn't really care. He and I were single, in love, and enjoyed living large. I didn't contribute anything to his professional status, but he was enjoying life more.

Diamond in the Dark

We had Thanksgiving dinner together and invited some of our closest friends for the feast. The two of us, entertaining our friends and visiting guests, became the norm. I was acting lady of the house for these evenings, even though I continued to live in my own home. Bob was very appreciative of my ability to "work a crowd."

We had been dating for almost a year when the holiday season of 1994 came around. December's weather was cool and clear as we walked the white sand beaches of Santa Rosa Island, then continued our drive east to San Destin. We picked up tiny shells, holding and examining each, and keeping only the most perfect ones. We held hands, drank wine, and left our footprints behind in the deep white sand as the sun set on the horizon.

Bob, my Jewish boyfriend, watched as I turned the white shells, ribbon, and glitter into sparkling ornaments that would adorn our first table-top Christmas tree. The tree was beautiful, small but meaningful in our relationship. We celebrated our first Christmas season together with an exchange of gifts, and we enjoyed happiness throughout the following week. I could feel we were close to the point of talking marriage, but I waited for him to bring up the subject.

Romantic times came and went, with nothing being said about a future commitment to each other. I was more than a little confused. I thought we were both in the same place about our relationship. I finally decided, reluctantly, that I must have misread the signs.

With the holiday over, it was time for me to go back home and get things ready for the first work week of 1995. Bob asked me to stay, but my answer to him was that I had a home—I couldn't just stay with him all the time. I gathered my things from the guest room and guest bath. I always made sure I took my things home when I left.

The following evening, Bob came to my house for a dinner together. I was standing in my kitchen, wearing a big floppy sweatshirt, baggy, comfortable pants, and sandals. As usual for Florida, it was not at all cold. While I was making dinner, I sat a small bowl of smoked tuna dip, from Joe Patti's Seafood Company (a Pensacola landmark), on the counter. For those who have never tasted smoked tuna dip, I can bet you're envisioning something just short of cat food. This dip was made fresh from smoked tuna, and it is delicious. Bob stood at the counter, munching away, not seeming to notice that I had not gone to so much trouble to get ready for his visit.

He asked me again why I would not continue to stay with him at his home. I told him yet again that I had a home and I would not live with him. Jokingly, I added the fact that he did not have enough closet space for me. We laughed. He had one walk-in closet off his master bathroom, and one regular closet in the bedroom itself. He followed my observation with, "If you'll come live with me, I will let you have the big closet." I had to laugh.

"You mean you're willing to give up your closet?" I teased. "You must be serious to make that offer." I kept laughing at him. But he was serious. He said something like, "You can do, or have, whatever you want, if you would come and be with me." Then he threw in what amounted to the last dash of salt to the simmering pot. "I guess I'm talking about marriage."

I looked at him and asked him if he was serious. When he said he was, I turned off everything that was cooking. In silence, I poured both of us a glass of wine and told him we needed to sit and talk. I couldn't believe it. We had been through such a lovely holiday together, but he had not seized his many opportunities to pose the question to me. No, he waited until life was back to normal, me in my sweat shirt, no makeup, totally unsuspecting, and he virtually proposing marriage over the damned tuna fish dip. *How romantic!* I've never let him forget it.

As we sat and talked, I reminded him of all the negatives that I had to deal with in my life. I reminded Bob of the child I would most likely be supporting for the rest of my life. I wanted him to understand that my obligation to her would most likely never go away. He assured me he was fine with that. Then I told him that if he had any aspirations of running for public office, I would not marry him. I knew that with my connection to the Leverett family, I couldn't be vetted for any kind of public office, nor did I want to be in that arena. Yet again, he said he had no intention of entering politics. With those things out of the way, we talked of all the changes we'd have to make for our marriage to take place. We talked for what seemed to be hours.

At the end of the conversation, we were lying, side-by-side, on the couch. I reminded him that he really hadn't properly proposed to me. Then, as only Bob could do, he cleared his throat and said, "Phyllis—" He stopped abruptly, looking at me with an inquisitive face, and asked, "What is your middle name?"

"Anita," I said with a laugh in my voice and joy in my heart.

"Anita," he repeated. Again, he readied for the moment, deliberately cleared his voice, then said, "Phyllis Anita Brown, will you be my wife?"

I laughed at his stilted, humorous delivery. It was so Bob. I said, "Yes, I will be your wife." We were happy, but I still couldn't believe he hadn't proposed to me earlier, when romantic situations had been so blatantly obvious. *Whatever.* We were both ready to make our commitment to each other—it was our time.

Chapter 44
The Smokies

Me, "Marrying Sam," and Bob

I
n January 1995, Bob and I had a wedding to plan. We sat with dry Chardonnay, pen, and paper, to begin the task of making a guest list. Our
thoughts went back to a wedding we had attended at the big Naval Air
Station Chapel just after we started dating. The wedding was extremely formal,
with all the men in either black tie or formal military attire. The bridesmaids,
about eight of them, were dressed in deep royal blue bridal satin. It was a
sight to behold, for each maid must have been at least fifty years of age. The
youthful-looking dresses started at about size W-16, and went up from there.
(I am not making fun. The whole "picture" was incongruent with anything
you would normally expect for a wedding of two people in their fifties). The
procession continued. The ring bearer, and the flower girl, followed the string
of satin-dressed maids. The crowd stood in hushed silence as the large bride,
fifty-ish, red-hair coiffed around her shoulders, made her appearance wearing

a formal, white bridal gown, with a train dragging six feet behind her. Her dad walked her down the aisle, braving the course without the use of his walker.

Their choice to officiate at their wedding ceremony was a man who catered to married couples wanting unique weddings. In fact, he specialized in sky diving weddings by parachute (on the way down), or undersea in their scuba gear, with vows bubbling to the top. The procession lasted far longer than the ceremony. We stood for the bride and never sat down. They were man and wife in about three minutes. All that planning, money, and stress—all those bolts of blue satin—and in minutes, it was all over. (The marriage lasted about the same length.)

We thought of other weddings we had attended—the effort, the family stressors, and all the hoopla. Bob was a commanding officer, so he said he wanted to invite his executive officer, a Navy captain and a dear friend, some of the other commanders, and his department heads. After contemplating that thought for a few minutes, he decided he might need to extend the invitation to his entire command, for fear of offending someone if they were left out. I knew that I did not want to spend my wedding reception meeting people I didn't know and would never see again. We continued with our list of friends, family, and co-workers. In about 20 minutes, the list was at 100 people and climbing rapidly.

I gazed at the list, poured more Chardonnay, and stopped the speeding train with a pull of the emergency brake. I could envision the whole thing barreling forward and out of control. On one thing we did agree. We did not want our wedding to be a "dog and pony show" to impress and entertain the masses.

We sipped and talked. What did we really want? We decided we wanted an intimate, fun, relaxed union, for us and only a few witnesses. Our guests would be selected on the basis of their ability to contribute to our joy and happiness for the occasion. We started a new list. Who were our family and friends? Who could be invited to our wedding that would be truly happy for us, despite our deviation from all conventional rules? Family or friends still fondly attached to our ex's, for whatever reason they chose to hold on to them, would not be asked. My Southern Christian parents and relatives, who were appalled at liquor, music, dancing, and wedding in the same sentence, were nixed. We loved them, so we would do a reception on our return for those opposed to drinking, feasting, and celebrating.

We knew we couldn't be married in the base chapel—he a Jew, and I a Christian. We decided our wedding would take place in the cool of the mountains, where no one we knew lived. We would transport the "chosen" ones on a tour bus, along with catered food and a good bartender. On a Friday morning, we would meet at the Mustin Beach Officers' Club parking lot, load on the bus, and head north to the Smokey Mountains of Tennessee. The Rockies would have been better, but it created a logistical nightmare.

Because of my love for the mountains, Bob agreed to a garden wedding overlooking the mountainside behind the Park Vista Hotel in Gatlinburg. Me, as Southern as a biscuit, and my sweet Jewish doctor from New York, would share a civil ceremony to unite us (hopefully) into blissful matrimony. Bob said he really didn't care where we married or who officiated, as long as it was legal.

We had twenty people attend and witness our union. It was joyful and crazy, but quite civilized and beautiful. By late Saturday afternoon, June 3, 1995, the garden was filled with flowers, the three-piece band played quietly from the gazebo, and the bride on the groom's arm entered the awaiting group via the garden path. The groom wore black pants and a white dinner jacket; the bride a creamy white Chantilly lace, heavily beaded, tea-length dress. We swished past the sign, "Please don't feed the bears."

We exchanged the vows we had written. "Marrying Sam," as he was known, was a retired judge. He was tall and handsome with a full head of white hair. I had made a special trip up to meet "Marrying Sam" before the wedding, to emphasize the civil union and give him our vows. Everything was going really well, and as planned, when the dear old man got a little off track. I knew I was in trouble when he started admonishing Bob to love me as Christ loved the Church.

I took a big breath, squeezed Bob's hand, and whispered, "I swear I told him." I expected to see Bob turn and flee like Wiley Coyote through the woods. However, without missing a beat, Bob said he would love me. At last, Sam asked Bob if he would take me, to have and hold from that day forward, for better or worse, for richer or poorer, in sickness and in health, for as long as we both shall live?

There seemed to be a very long and pregnant pause as the groom contemplated all the questions, then Bob said very clearly and emphatically, "I will, I will, I will, and I will." We were pronounced man and wife, followed by some shouts of "mazel tov" from the happy gallery.

Our marriage was followed by a lovely reception, a sit-down dinner, an abundance of Champagne and other adult beverages, music, singing, and dancing. It ended when one of my guests (who never fessed up) ordered a round of Tequila shots. It was around 10:30 p.m. when some of our younger guests headed to town, as the bride and groom headed to the bridal suite for the rest of the evening. The next morning, Bob and I agreed that there wasn't much dignity in admitting we had seven marriages between us; he with three and me with four. Neither Bob nor I was particularly proud of that fact. However, we wholeheartedly agreed it had been the best of all our weddings.

Jamie, me, and Bob; I thought my flowers were exquisite.

As usual, I felt guilty for anything really wonderful happening to me. I kept waiting for the imaginary hammer to fall on my head, because I couldn't believe I was that happy. I made every attempt to play down my exceedingly good luck in finding such a wonderful man so late in my life. It was pre-9/11, and I believed the statistic that it was more likely for a woman to be shot by a terrorist than to get married after forty. Since then, I think the odds have improved for being shot.

As I sat in the National Museum of Naval Aviation, at the Change of Command ceremony when Bob left that position and a new Commander took over, it finally hit me. It was the first time I had read my husband's short military bio. It was in the ceremony's program. I was so impressed with the things he had accomplished, and it was hard for me to believe that he was my husband. He is special, and I am so happy he chose me.

It flew in the face of many who prophesied the relationship wouldn't last. Some said Bob was too staid; an intellectual, and, I, a dumb blonde, or maybe a gold digger out for gain. One of his best female friends took him to lunch just two days before we would leave for our wedding trip. She expressed her concerns and counseled him to secure a pre-nuptial agreement. That still raises the hair on my neck. That being said, some of my friends, who thought I was special, said they didn't see what I saw in Bob. Many got us both wrong.

Bob handled my quirks pretty well. He accepted my expectation of unwavering fidelity. I was jealous of him, and didn't make any pretense otherwise—my track record with truthful, trustworthy men was running about zero for three, so can you blame me? I also had to learn how to deal with some of his OCD quirks. It was always a give and take. Whatever! It works, and it works well.

It's never too late.

In 1996, I received notification that Paul Leverett had an insurance policy I was not aware of, and I was the beneficiary of a "huge" cash payment of about $6,800. *What a windfall!* I contemplated how I would spend that money. I wanted to spend it in a way in which I could thank him for doing something good for me. I decided I'd use it to go back to school.

I had spent many hours in classes, and I probably had more credits than most people who've earned an undergraduate degree. I had two years in a business college, studying accounting and income tax preparation. I had many hours for insurance licensing in life, health, property, and casualty. I had gone to real estate school and was licensed in Alabama. I also had my humble little Associate of Arts degree in Mass Communications. But I was still short of a Bachelor's degree. It was embarrassing for me, but my education had been mostly hard knocks, with the formal part haphazard at best.

With my transferable credits, I needed a year to finish, so I enrolled at Faulkner University, a private Christian university located in Montgomery, Alabama with a satellite campus in Mobile. After I got off work, I would drive each week to Mobile, about 60 miles to the campus. I'd leave Pensacola about 4:00 p.m., and get home around 11 p.m. One weekend a month, I would go to weekend classes in Montgomery. I graduated with a 4.0 in May 1997, with a Bachelor of Science in Management of Human Resources—better late than never.

I was the first and only person in my family to finish college. So, late or not, I was proud of the accomplishment. My husband and I drove to Montgomery so I could walk with my class—none of my family came. I have two men to thank for it—Paul, for leaving me the money, and my husband, for supporting me during that grueling schedule. Thank you both!

The one thing Bob didn't expect was for me to make him a father. But, he was 57 years old when Lanee, my beautiful little granddaughter, came to live with us. My daughter was having some problems. Bob and I could offer Lanee a more stable home life, so we agreed to take her for a while. Lanee made us a family of three. We loved and treated her as our own. She would live with us for the next eight years.

At this time, I want to thank Lanee's "Fairy God Mother," as we called her. Mary Farris is our friend who kept Lanee almost every Friday night for years so that Bob and I could enjoy a date night—an alone night. It was such a precious gift to us, and it was always seen that way. We thank you, Mary. Your kindness made our lives so much better.

From the start of our relationship, Bob and I traveled quite a bit, both for his work and for mine. However, the places they sent him were usually fabulous cities in faraway places, like my favorite city, Prague. The most exotic of my work trips landed me in Canada for a week. We tried to extend our stays after business trips that took us to Europe. Bob and I loved taking adventure horse-back rides, getting out of the big cities, venturing into small villages, and riding challenging mounts through the countryside. For business trips, they would pay for Bob's plane fare, his lodging, and a per diem for the days of his meeting. All we had to do was buy my plane ticket and I could tag along. Bob would always tell me that since I didn't get a per diem, I wasn't allowed to eat—fat chance of that happening!

In 1999, I left the MWR Department and moved to the Navy's Fleet and Family Support Center (FFSC). MWR was all about recreation, fitness, and fun for the military. The FFSC, as it is called, was all about more serious services provided to military personnel and their families. FFSC offered counseling, social services, relocation help, transition help, unemployment assistance for family members, financial education with budgeting classes, numerous life skill classes, and case management for the serious issues of sexual assault, domestic violence, or child abuse. I loved it from the start, diving in to learn all about my new Personal Financial Management (PFM) position.

Within six months, I had attended several week-long schools in Tennessee, Texas, and California. After exams, I became the center's first Accredited Financial Counselor, through the National Association for Financial Counseling, Planning, and Education. I worked in that capacity for three years.

In the years to come, Bob and I became very involved in the care of my dad and my mom. They had been living in Grand Bay, Alabama for years, but as Dad's health began to fail, we were constantly running interference for him. As Dr. Bob would say, "Dad had hardening of the categories." Bob was constantly encouraging the Veteran's Administration medical staff in Biloxi to take better care of Dad, or he was calling a friend in Mobile to intervene when Dad presented at the emergency room with congestive heart failure. Bob's dear friend, Dr. Frank Pettyjohn, saved my dad's life.

It became too much to drive so great a distance to see them, so we helped them move to Pensacola. We found them a lovely home right across the street from the subdivision where Bob and I had purchased a lot for our eventual retirement home.

Dad started getting better medical care after moving closer to us. He was stoic, and seldom complained, but he had so many ailments. He was treated with many drugs, but the best was Prozac. It was amazing how he changed when he was appropriately treated for his depression and PTSD. When she needed to write a paper for a school project, my niece, Salice, became the first to start Dad talking about his WWII experiences. It was her essay, "An Unrecognized Hero," that earned her an "A" and opened the "box" of emotions that Dad should have opened long before. He actually got to be such a sweet old man. It was wonderful that, in his last years, I was able to love him again—for that, I thank God and Prozac.

Dad and I became close friends and he left me with the task of caring for Mom. It was good that the man I had often wished dead while he was putting us through hell on Earth, I now loved and treasured. It would break my heart to see him go.

After four months of being in and out of the hospital, Daddy died peacefully at home with his wife and children there to say goodbye. He died on May 2, 2002, at 78 years of age, just 28 days shy of being married to Mom for sixty years.

When Dad died, there were some things I wanted to say. I gave one of the eulogies for his funeral—I needed to speak. I have always been a crybaby at anything that pulls at my heart strings. I felt if I could rise above all that had happened, if I could speak for my dad and remain in control, it would be a milestone in my healing. It would somehow make me free if I could stand and convey the sadness of his burden, highlight the good in him that he had expressed through his strong belief in Christianity, and offer him back to God with love in my heart.

I arranged for Marines to be his pallbearers. There were eight of them there to carry his body to its last resting place. He would have been so proud. I asked the Marines whether, when I finished my talk and reading Dad's poem, they would, on cue, give him a big, Marine-style Ooh-Aah!? They were happy to oblige. Speaking from the heart and some notes I made ahead of time, I completed his eulogy without a tear. I told the audience that I wanted to read a poem that Dad had kept. Dad hadn't been big into poetry, so I knew it must have been meaningful to him. It was the only poem he had kept with his Marine memorabilia.

> My Friends,
> As young boys we would fight battles, that if we lived long enough,
> Would make some of us old before our time;
> Leaving our youth in the wake of the waves as we hit the beach,
> And others, forever fighting battles, in the remnants of a childlike mind.
> Most of us would survive and remain silent when people said that war makes men of boys.
> For we knew first-hand how many children died, on an island so long ago.
> And sadly the only thing war made of them was but a fading memory.
> Some have asked what was it like to be a boy in the body of a man?
> And I reply, "It's like a little boy lost in a grown-up world he doesn't fully understand. A world where the righteous do not always win,
> and battles don't always go according to plan."
> And so it was that we, who never planned or wanted war, were to make up the majority of the combatants.
> We did not start the war, but it was we who were chosen to finish it.
> And our lives were changed forever. Now, we that still survive fight our own kind of battles;
> And if we live long enough, perhaps we will once again know what it is like to be that child we left behind on those islands so long ago.
> —*Author, Anonymous*

I closed by saying that I believed my dad had finally been returned to the childhood he had left behind. *Semper Fi, Daddy!* The Marines stood and gave him a resounding, "Ooh-Aah!" I wished he could have been there to hear it. Maybe he was.

Dad was buried with full military honors at Barrancas National Cemetery, with my husband wearing his dress-whites, as Dad had requested. As "Taps" were played, my husband stepped forward and stood at attention and saluted. To my amazement, our Lanee, age nine, stepped forward alongside her grandpa. She stood at attention, straight as a stick, with hands to her sides. I would love to have had a photo taken of that impromptu moment. I was so proud of the way she chose to honor her great-grandfather.

It is easier now to remember my dad with love in my heart. What a travesty that, while we were all young, he never received treatment for his combat-received brain trauma and PTSD. *What a positive difference he could have made in so many people's lives!*

I made friends with Joe Delsignore, a co-worker who worked as the Sexual Assault Victim Intervention (SAVI) Coordinator at NAS Pensacola. The Navy had a SAVI program which required every person who said they had been sexually assaulted to have the right to support by a trained victim advocate. The advocates are basically trained hand-holders, and information and referral specialists, and they make sure the victim knows that no matter what the circumstances, the assault was not their fault. Victims do not have to accept advocate services, but the support is available 24/7, no matter what.

Joe recruited me to work for him as a volunteer. I went to a week of training to learn the ropes of being an advocate. It was after that training that I started standing the watch and working with victims of sexual assault, both male and female. I found there was no way to work with others without seeing my own reflection in their pain. It had to be God's plan for me, because I never once dreamed I would end up working as an advocate for victims of sexual assault.

The SAVI program opened my eyes. I started attending all the training I could find on working with victims. By 2002, when Joe took a new job and the coordinator position was posted, I was qualified and I applied for the open position. I was hired and promoted. The first year that I worked as the SAVI Coordinator, we handled over fifty-four cases on our base. Those were the ones reported. I am sure there were many more. Date rape (with alcohol involved) became our biggest problem in our eighteen-to twenty-two-year old population. I knew we had to work on educating these young military recruits that "no" really means "no."

Uncle Sam contributed mightily to my education when it came to working with victims. I worked for five and a half years with victims of sexual assault, and completed hundreds of classroom hours in training, participated in symposiums and conferences, and worked on the Joint Task Force, in Washington, D.C., to provide input from the field. I was able to give program managers insight into the actual working mechanics of the program as changes were being made. I was on the committee, and saw it change from a Navy program to a Department of Defense, all-branches-of-the-services program.

Under the guidance of Brigadier General K.C. McClain, appointed after the Colorado Springs scandal, the new and improved program was renamed the Sexual Assault Prevention and Response (SAPR) Program. I received a very meaningful award, as Civilian Employee of the Year in 2006, for my educational work in the prevention of sexual assault. The program was made available to thousands of young service members, and ended up reducing the number of assaults at NAS Pensacola by more than 50 percent.

My training was heartfelt. I knew what it was like to be raped, to be violated. What I didn't realize was how common it was in both military and civilian communities. I had dealt with assault by learning to "suck it up" and keep it to myself. What I saw and heard from so many military personnel was that attitudes hadn't changed much over the years. It was still easier to blame the victim.

After years of intense training for everyone in uniform, I heard a commanding officer say, and I quote, "If she hadn't gotten herself drunk, it wouldn't have happened to her." If you followed that reasoning, then any woman (or man) who drinks too much should also expect to be raped. It was ludicrous to justify such a crime by blaming it on the indiscretion of the victim. In all states, it is legal to drink if you are 21. It is never legal to rape.

I talked to my mom about my new job. She could not grasp the idea of putting blame on the offender rather than the victim. She had never seen it work that way. I asked my mom if she remembered the young woman who often visited my Grandma Brown. It was many years ago, during my visits with my grandma, in Gaskin, Florida. I was very young, but I remembered the girl who lived in the house just up the dirt road. I remembered the girl to be about seventeen or so. She was a little plump and not very attractive, but sometimes she would visit Grandma's house with her baby girl in tow. The little girl had blonde hair just like me, and for some reason, I felt sorry for her.

My grandma and my aunt would talk about them when they left. I listened to their gossip. They whispered that the little girl was a child of sin—born out of wedlock. Everyone thought the child's daddy was also her grandfather. I didn't understand completely, but I knew it had to be bad.

My mom remembered the young woman. She even remembered the girl's family name. But it was how mom remembered the visit that haunts me to this day. Mom said, "That girl was having an affair with her daddy. Everyone knew it was going on." The girl's daddy would get up in the morning, but before going to work, he would rake the ground all around the house (the yards were dirt, no grass anywhere), so he could tell if anyone had walked to the door or if she had gone outside. He was known to beat her if she went anywhere without his permission. Mom said, "They finally sent her away, to a woman's prison, for messin' round with her daddy like that."

I just stared at my mom in disbelief. Did she just say, "Messin' round with her daddy like that?" Mom's attitude was a reflection of her own times: A man holds his minor daughter hostage, rapes her, impregnates her, and puts her in prison. I have no idea what ultimately happened to that little girl. Mom thought that she had no choice but to go along. I didn't even try to explain to her why she was wrong. It was too late.

The stories of rape that I have heard should shame us as a community, as a society. It was not just the stories I heard from young military members reporting they had been raped, usually by their shipmates or fellow Marines, but it was the disclosures I heard from women after they found out I was a sexual assault victim advocate. I wasn't a counselor, but I became a very good listener. Many women told me of their shattered childhoods, disclosing this for the first time to a "knowing," empathetic, and non-threatening woman.

One woman just blurted out to me that her daddy had raped her. We were talking of her doll collection when she said, "That is why I love dolls and toys so much now. I finally get to be a child." I think it even surprised her that she told me. I asked her if she was doing okay. My question opened up the floodgates of emotion, and she told me more of what happened. She grew up in the country, her mom worked, and her dad was a farmer of sorts. She and her younger sister were left in the care of their father while their mom worked.

She said she always knew when he was going to rape her, or if it was to be her little sister's turn. She said, "We knew that whoever had to stay inside to do house-work, she was the one he would fuck that day." He never paid for his crimes.

She now plays with dolls as her way to deal with her loss.

Over and over, I met with promiscuous young females who had been raped, most of them in the military. Many left home to get away because they were being, or had been, sexually abused by family members. It was usually the stepdad or an uncle.

Victims should not be ashamed that they have been hurt. We have to stop looking at them as less, because they were not lucky enough to get through their childhoods without being victimized. In my opinion, there's one thing you can depend on: If you want to double, maybe even triple, your child's chances of being raped or molested, all you have to do is bring a boyfriend or stepfather into the home. Sibling abuse cannot be ignored, especially pubescent children caring for smaller, very vulnerable children. My advice, based on dealing with hundreds and hundreds of child abuse cases, is to carefully screen anyone, male or female, you allow to care for your children, no matter who they are. The excuse that they are so nice and just love kids may be the ruse used to gain access to the children. Victimizing children becomes much easier if the perpetrator earns the trust of the parents first.

Of course, not everyone is a child molester. But believe me when I tell you, it is much more common than good people want to accept. Is it worth the risk?

Chapter 45
Advocacy Changed My Life

Finally seeing the world from a new perspective.

I worked hard for the Navy, but it was my volunteer service that put me onto a path I never expected to take. I have often said I didn't know how I got here from there. My life has been a series of adversities and challenges, triggering my survival instincts until I could find a path that could give me a chance to better my plight. It seems I have always been actively en route. I just had no clear idea where I was going. My "strategy" was to keep moving because I trusted I would know what was right when I found it.

I have always been envious of those lucky young women born into healthy and loving homes. I have often wondered who would I be today if:

- I had been born to parents who had not been dealing with the aftermath of World War II, and a dad struggling with untreated PTSD.
- I had been the first child that was doted on, loved, and adored.
- I hadn't been sick, with some unidentified illness that inconvenienced everyone, especially me.

- I hadn't been molested as a child, robbed of innocence that made me feel guilty, dirty, and less.
- I hadn't been physically attractive. (The luck of the genealogical draw presented me opportunities to shine, be included, and sometimes envied.)
- I hadn't had parents that loved me, even though they struggled every day in the good-faith upbringing of their children, dedicated to provide the basis for my faith, instill moral parameters, mete out discipline, and hold me accountable, for as Dad said, "Do as I say, not as I do."
- I hadn't "screwed up" and gotten pregnant at the ripe old age of sixteen.
- I had waited, married a man who was confident, educated, and moral, and who respected me as a woman, wife, and mother.
- I had been older and better prepared to be a mother, not tearing my children's home apart to find that better/ safer place.
- I had not made so many wrong decisions. As hard as I tried to implement the plan my parents embedded in me, it hadn't worked for them, and it didn't work for me.

However, I played the hand I was dealt, and I kept trying to make it right. I know I could have been a better, more accomplished person if I had experienced the advantage of a stable home, mature, loving guidance, and mentorship. However, even though the cards were stacked against me, I must have done something right. As I look around me, I am amazed at where I am and how far I have come.

Those three benchmarks I had set as a child as indicators of true wealth had been attained: a two-story house with a grand staircase, a swimming pool in the back yard to cool the oppressive days of Southern heat, and above all, to own a horse—the biggest trophy of all. We have them all, and so much more. I learned quickly that those things were even sweeter when we shared our good fortune with family and friends.

I have also learned that the harder I work, the luckier I get. After two years of working as a volunteer sexual assault victim advocate, I was hooked. From 2002 through 2008, I worked full time as the coordinator for the Navy's Sexual Assault Prevention and Response Program, responding to sexual assault victims 24/7, training other victim advocates and thousands of military personnel on prevention and awareness of sexual assault. In 2008, I applied for, and was appointed to, the position of Education Services Facilitator. That job made me responsible for training first responders in one of the Navy's high-visibility programs, the Family Advocacy Program (FAP), which dealt with all allegations of domestic violence and child abuse. When the war on terror began, the stressors on military families increased and the need for more assistance and support to families went up exponentially. I got the job and started on my new path without looking back.

I quickly learned more about the effects of abuse on individuals, families, and children. As an educator for the Family Advocacy Program (FAP), my audiences were many and varied. FAP is mandated by Congress. It is the Navy's response to domestic violence, child abuse, neglect, and child sexual abuse within a military family. It does not set forth a legal process. It is all about assessing the situation for safety, treatment, and offender accountability.

To young military service members ages eighteen to twenty-four, I taught prevention and awareness of domestic violence, along with how to recognize and build healthy relationships. I taught instructors—the more senior people—how to identify and refer presenting problems for assistance. Commanding officers received instruction on Navy policy and regulations, along with their reporting responsibilities and avenues for treatment to restore safety. My classes for first responders, such as law enforcement, were geared toward sensitive treatment of victims, better interviewing skills, working with victim advocates, and more thorough forensic documentation. The Navy's child-care providers were trained to recognize symptoms of child abuse and neglect, and how to report all suspected cases of abuse.

I have worked with parents involved in Family Advocacy cases to help them recognize how their behavior affects their children. Most enter the required classes, refusing to see the connection between their behavior and the adverse effects that abuse or violence have on their children.

Last, but not least, are the classes for the children. With parental permission, we have taught hundreds of children that their bodies are private, they belong to them, and they have a right to say "no" to anything that makes them feel uncomfortable. They learned to say "STOP," to yell, to run away, and to tell an adult. If that adult didn't help, then tell another, until someone helps.

In order to teach or facilitate the aforementioned classes, the Navy sent me to hundreds of hours of training, classes, workshops, symposiums, and conferences. I say with all sincerity, "Thank you, Uncle Sam, for paying me to learn how to help others." As an unexpected byproduct, I was given information that changed my life.

One workshop I attended, at the University of West Florida, was called "Animal Abuse: Its Connection to Domestic Violence." The class held me in its grip. That class was the first of its kind that I had attended, and it connected how power and control over a spouse is often secured by threatening to hurt or kill family pets. Victims of domestic abuse that sought shelter often learned their animals would not be allowed refuge or safety. The thought horrified me, and brought back memories of how my animals had been threatened and abused. My horses had always been subjects of threats, made in order to subdue me.

I have trained and worked alongside Licensed Clinical Social Workers, Marriage and Family Therapists, Counselors, professional victim advocates, Naval Criminal Investigative Services personnel, and local law enforcement. As a part of assisting families, I have learned that domestic violence, child abuse, and animal abuse are often connected and far too common.

The abuse that I was subjected to by the use of guns would now, even with just a misdemeanor conviction, prevent an abuser from ever legally possessing a firearm, assuming it didn't actually land them in prison. Under today's laws, a conviction of child sexual abuse, or even exposing oneself to a child, would land an abuser on a registered sexual offender list, with all manner of restrictions and reporting requirements. I have often thought of the present and the much lower threshold required for an arrest for domestic violence or abuse, in comparison to law enforcement during the 1970's and 80's. I have felt vindicated when I have seen abusers held accountable. I hadn't been wrong then in asking for, or expecting, help.

That one volunteer job as a victim advocate changed my life and the life of every suffering soul we were able to educate, support, and help to find peace. If, as a society, we don't help, we will continue to live side by side with families where offenders continue to perpetrate their crimes. Turning a blind eye to abuse can be devastating because the effects can permeate the fiber of entire families for generations.

My mom was one of those victims. She lived for over 60 years as a victim of abuse—so long, in fact, it was her norm. Mom hated the oppression and the oppressor—she prayed for relief. As Dad was dying, I tried to get her to forgive him. We cried, we held hands, and I said, "Mom, please forgive him."

She couldn't.

The real sadness came as I saw her finally free of his domination and power. Her freedom made more apparent the crippling co-dependence that had developed over the years. My layman's observation was that my mother had learned manipulative behaviors. She had perfected them over years of being controlled and dominated. She had learned to suppress anger and to suffer in silence as she seethed for days. She wasn't allowed to have a differing opinion, nor to ever debate a situation.

Surprisingly, Dad "loved her very much," in his way, so he responded to her desires if she approached him in the right way. He turned to jelly when subjected to her subtle, sweet manipulations. Mom gently steered him, by planting seeds of thought. Any negative message she delivered was always attributed to someone else. A likely conversation could go like, "I don't know why," or "I'm not supposed to tell you, but... so and so said your drinking is a problem," or "Phyllis thinks you need to stop drinking." Never could she, or would she, address a problem directly.

After Dad died, her communication techniques stayed the same, which created family crisis after crisis. Mom went from sibling to sibling, carrying tales about what we were supposed to have said as she attempted to manipulate or steer us toward addressing issues she wanted addressed. Her "contaminated seeds" were constantly causing grief and hard feelings. She was good—we fell for it, over and over.

I describe her technique as "lobbing the turd into the punch bowl" routine. She would lob, then she would stand back, innocently watching as the punch bowl crisis began, pretending she had no idea how the turd had gotten into the bowl. Her routine continued until we were all on to her, and the family had a pact not to believe anything she said, unless it was witnessed, and until we verified the source. Our confrontation, over and over, finally got through to her that her approach was not going to work any longer. It was sad. For a while, she spoke haltingly, hesitating after each word. God Bless her soul. Freedom for her came too late—she needed to develop new skills that somehow eluded her grasp.

She lasted about five years in her home, with me, my husband, my brother, and his wife providing what was tantamount to assisted living. She was lonely. My mom could have been a poster child for the life-long effects of domestic physical, mental, emotional, and psychological abuse.

Mom finally decided she was ready to move into an Assisted Living

Retirement Community. There was nothing easy about cleaning out the family home after "cherry picking" her best things to be moved to her apartment. It was heartbreaking for me to see my mom have to give up any of her cherished treasures. She also had much difficulty parting with all the saved Mason jars, the jellies that had been preserved years ago, the cans and cans of vegetables she had bought on sale, and a staggering collection of miscellaneous Tupperware with a million mismatched lids.

Every glass, little vase, or dish that had been rooting new life in her kitchen window was precious to her. The souvenir spoon collection, from all the great landmarks in America, the copper clad kettles, the tea pots, the crystal, and the *Gone with the Wind* Collector's Edition of plates, were treated lovingly, as each was considered for rescue.

Then there were the 100 or more pieces of milk glass that she had assembled over years and years of avid garage sale spelunking. The pain that I saw on Mom's face was like what I'd see if we were taking her kidney. I tried to console her, informing her that each piece would be carefully replanted in the overflowing home of my sister, who could have been featured in the next production of "Hoarders Gone Wild."

My sister-in-law, Margaret, had skills we called on in our hour of need. My brother and Margaret showed up to help with the tough tasks that lay ahead. They were troupers, and Margaret had a special talent: The girl was able to put ten pounds of potatoes in a five-pound sack, and she made them look as neat and tidy as a fresh roll of pennies. Margaret's talent allowed Mom to have her greatest treasures surround her in her new two-room apartment, all arranged to perfection.

It took a while to upgrade Mom's house and spruce it up for sale. The market was awful. Joseph and I spent over a year making upgrades and keeping up the yard before it finally sold.

In 2008, I identified my next project: I wanted to create an album of all of my mom's most treasured photos. My hope was that it would help her remember her family for a longer time as we watched her slip further into dementia. I wanted her to have every chance to jog all that gray matter and keep it working as long as possible. There seemed to be thousands of photos for me to sort through for the album. I sat on the floor for hours trying to identify all the images.

I was feeling especially tired one day when I picked up a faded, paper-covered photo book. It was so old the edges were curled. The binder contained

3" x 5" photos, was sealed on one end, and held firmly the twelve photos taken from a single roll of film. Each photo looked like it was cut out with pinking-sheers using a zig-zagged edge. The very first photo took me back to another time and place. Uncle Bill and my dad were happily standing in front of Brown's Sporting Goods, the store the brothers started together as partners when I was a very young child. They were holding up their string of fish, each beaming with a fisherman's pride.

I flipped to the next photo. Something unexpected happened, truly in the blink of an eye. From the core of my being, my body felt like a pebble dropping into calm and peaceful water. I felt the splash, the ripple mounding high, then moving in waves of hot water to the end of each extremity, a tsunami within my body. It was him—HIM! My heart was pounding so hard, I felt it in my ears. I was looking into the face of the man who had exposed himself to me and molested me—the man who had sat in his jeans, in the position of Buddha, when he demanded I come to him. There was NO doubt. There was NO question. It was HIM!

I was now fifty-eight years old. It had been more than fifty years since I had seen that face. It was the one face I could never recreate in my mind. It had been there all along, stored neatly in some crinkle of my brain. I had been a little girl. It wasn't that the man did not know that what he was doing was wrong. He did. He just didn't care. Sexual predators of children do not care about the lifetime effects their acts have on child victims. They only consider their own needs, no more, no less. The man I saw in the photo was simply a robber of childhood innocence.

Child molesters and sexual predators rarely stop at one victim. Studies have shown they will molest many times before being discovered, if they ever are. The good thing is, there is no statute of limitations protecting child molesters or rapists.

When I looked at him, I knew he now had to be at least 78, maybe older. I asked myself: Is he still alive? Would he remember what he did to me? The strange thing was I was not interested in finding or confronting him, because I didn't want to see him. I knew if I shared my story with him, I would have to deal not only with my feelings, but his and our family's as well. It had always been so much easier to deal with my feelings alone.

The action I decided to take was the harder choice. I decided to channel my emotions toward something that would, hopefully, help someone else—those still suffering in silence and shame. If I could finally stand up and say

I had been a victim, then maybe another person could hear my story and it would give them the strength to realize they are not alone, and to help them start working toward self-vindication and inner peace.

My Uncle Bill is standing on the left and the guy on the right is HIM.
I blurred his face.

>─┼─◆>─◆─O─◆─<◆─┼─<

After a lot of praying and a lot of soul-searching, I decided to write this book. Each member of my immediate family had a different perspective on events, and clearly different reasons for encouraging me to write it. Three of them have loved me and stood by me during the unusual events of my life. They wanted to know more—they wanted to understand.

My husband thought the writing of a book would prove to be excellent therapy. He said, "No matter if you publish or not, it should help to get those suppressed feelings out and on paper." He wanted me to find inner-peace and happiness.

My daughter, Jamie, wanted to know more about the Leverett case. She had loved Paul Leverett like a father. She came away with much less trauma from that time-period than did my son. Jamie remembered many of the big events that happened, like the trials, the loss of her Daddy Paul, then ultimately the loss of her step-brother and sister, whom she had grown to love. Jamie has always been supportive and eager to read her mom's story.

For this book, Nathan was my biggest collaborator. I picked his brain about some incidents, to see from his eyes how they had played out in his life. Our conversations lasted for hours, because he had so much pent-up anger and so many unresolved issues in regard to his father. According to Nathan, his dad no longer had any contact with, nor influence over, him, but he couldn't let it go. He dreamed of a great physical confrontation that would leave him standing dominant and victorious. He wanted me to give him insight that would help him better understand his father.

When it came to the Leverett case, Nathan, Jamie, and I could never reach a unanimous conclusion. Jamie loved Daddy Paul, and continued her contact with him up through his confinement at the ranch. Jamie took her new baby daughter to Paul so he could see his grandchild. The photo she brought back from the visit showed Grand-daddy Paul beaming with pride as he held Lanee for the first, and the only, time. Jamie believes unequivocally that her Daddy Paul was innocent. She will not accept any other conclusions.

It has been over 30 years since my marriage to Paul. Depending on the day you ask me, I offer conflicting conclusions. Admitting to myself that Paul was guilty would mean our relationship was a lie, and that he had used me, my children, family, and friends. That thought was incomprehensible to me. It conflicted resoundingly with the love and protection he provided me. But, if he was innocent, I let him down by losing faith in him. He's gone, so I'll never know for sure. I choose to remember him for helping me escape the tyranny of my oppressor.

Nathan has never had a problem believing Paul was guilty. His father helped to instill hatred of Paul. The negative influence a father can have on his child has no bounds. When I asked Nathan to tell me what happened to make him hold so much anger and hatred towards JJ, the scenarios gushed like an artesian well being released for the first time. All I had to do was ask him and out poured the stories of how his dad had mistreated him and coerced his choices.

He tearfully remembered being out in the Gulf, fishing with his dad, when he was thrown into the water to be used as "shark bait." His voice was still filled with terror. He said he was left for a long time in the open water, crying and scared, before he was finally pulled to safety. Nathan said his dad thought it was a joke, and told him he needed to toughen up and stop being such a crybaby. I had never before heard that story.

Nathan said his father enticed both our children to visit him with promises of a movie night. The prospect of spending time with him, and going to the movies, would be much anticipated. Our children instead spent the evening sitting in a car outside a bar.

Nathan said he almost died of strep throat while in Virginia with his dad and step-mother. According to Nathan, he was burning up with fever, and so sick he could hardly stand. He was 15 years old, with a 104 fever, and he was laughed at and ridiculed.

Nathan tearfully asked me why, when driving down the road, his dad would, out of nowhere, reach over and put a "frog" on his leg or arm that would raise a huge "egg." Nathan's question, "Why would he do that to me?" I had no answer for such abject cruelty. I do know that it wasn't Nathan's fault.

I told Nathan that I was having a very difficult time with his revelation of all those horrible incidents. If he had told me about them at the time, I would have tried to save him. Without intending to, I had passed on the legacy of secrecy so necessary to protect an abuser.

Nathan told me that many of his dad's friends knew of or witnessed the abuse. Yet none of them would stand up to JJ—just "like the time with Sugarboy." I seized on the phrase. I asked, "What are you talking about? What about Sugarboy?" The story had always been that, after our divorce, JJ had given the pony to a family with several small children. We were happy with the assurance that Sugarboy had gone to a good home.

But now, after all these years, Nathan had chosen to reveal a different story. "What happened to the pony, Nathan?" I asked tentatively, not really sure I wanted to know the answer.

The story, as he told it, was this: Nathan's dad (JJ), Otto, one of his dad's friends, and Nathan were all at JJ's house for an afternoon. JJ decided it would be funny to feed the pony some of the red hot peppers he had grown in his garden. He picked the peppers and held them to the pony's mouth. The pony refused to eat them, but JJ held his little head in an arm lock and tried to force the peppers into his mouth. The full strength of a hysterical pony, in fight or flight mode, was something to be reckoned with. The pony fought for its freedom from his tormentor. Sugarboy reared back and managed to get one tiny little hoof up and around, making quick contact with JJ's cheek. Blood spilled from the cut. Under a rage of curses, Sugarboy was able to fight free.

However, JJ couldn't let the pony win in front of three other sets of testicles. Nathan said his dad walked away, and none of the visitors there that day could, or would, stand against him to stop the madness. His dad sent him into the house. Nathan stayed at the window, knowing something terrible was about to happen. There was silence as JJ disappeared into the utility room attached to the house. He reappeared moments later with a shovel in hand. JJ chased and cornered that sweet, innocent little pony. Vile anger spent, he beat Sugarboy to death, blow by blow, with the shovel.

I believe that pony was a symbol. JJ knew how much Jamie and I loved him. The pony was the one thing remaining that he had control over, so he violently murdered Sugarboy, beating the very life out of his body. None of the guys who witnessed the act told anyone about it.

I wanted to yell, "NO one told."

I knew that my children and I were in danger around JJ, but I will always regret that I didn't see the signs of danger looming for Sugarboy. My daughter and I have cried together, sharing our disbelief, at such a stupid, heinous act. Leaving Sugarboy alone with JJ was my sin of omission, and my burden to bear. Now that all the gates of secrecy have been opened, my prayer is that Sugarboy is running free somewhere in Heaven's pasture.

Epilogue

My Ladies' Man and I would like to wish you happiness on life's journey.

In the United States Navy, domestic abuse is defined as a pattern of abuse where the offender exerts power and control over the victim. Abuse can be physical, mental, emotional, psychological, verbal, economic, or financial, or the holding of anyone against their will who is a married spouse, an intimate partner, or a couple with a child in common.

Child abuse or neglect is defined as: Mental, physical, emotional, sexual, or psychological abuse of a child, under the age of eighteen, by a parent, guardian, or caregiver.

I struggle with defining abuse, but clearly abuse occurs all too frequently, and is illegal, unacceptable by society, and morally repugnant. Yet there seems to be so much more that we can do to assist victims and families living in abusive situations. Victims are so often unable to break the cycle of abuse because their lives depend on the support of the abuser. They stay, believing or hoping the offender will change.

If it gets so bad that they finally decide to make a final break, their chance of becoming the victim of abuse or homicide increases tremendously. Some statistics show that 75 percent of all homicides resulting from domestic violence occur when the victims attempt to gain their freedom. The victims, their children, and other relatives are often caught up in the last deadly frenzy of an abuser losing control.

Family pets may also be victims, used by offenders to control and deter a victim from leaving. I remember the situation of a woman shattered by the torture and murder of her mini-dachshund that wasn't allowed to come with her into a women's shelter.

I remember another abuse case where an entire aquarium of tropical fish was killed by the introduction of chlorine. When your own survival or that of your children is on the line, animals often end up suffering the consequences.

My appeal is for all of us, as a society, to reach out to those who are in need. If someone discloses abuse to us, be open and hear the plea, without judging the victim. We empower abusers when we make victims bear the shame for their abuse. Let us offer love and understanding to those who feel they have no way out.

We can make a stand against child abusers by reporting suspected abuse to authorities as soon as possible.

We can volunteer as victim advocates or train to be an "angel of the court"—a *Guardian Ad Litem*—to be the voice of a lonely child.

Is there room in your heart and home to become a foster parent?

We can support our local shelters for abused women and children, giving victims more time to get strong enough to make it on their own. That one last piece that could be keeping an abused person in her home may well be her fear for their animals. If you can't take on foster children, maybe you can foster the family pet until the abused person's safety can be restored.

We can make a difference if we support our community services, work together to identify and fill service gaps, better understand the silence of shame, and help stop empowering abusers who have been allowed to thrive within our midst.

And remember: "Just keep dancing."

In Memory of Sugarboy

Jamie's first love, and the only true
innocent in the whole story.

After-Book Professional Commentary on the Life of Phyllis Hain

By Bryan Glazier, Ph.D., LMFT, LMHC*

In reading about Phyllis's childhood, we can see how multiple elements may have influenced what was to come throughout her adolescence and adulthood. For example, her early bout of illness brought about criticisms from her father and family. She was often being accused of "faking" it or seeking attention because she was "spoiled."

Additionally, her three instances of sexual molestation and abuse, which resulted from an instilled fear of disobeying, may have influenced her perception of what males want from females.

The teasing she received from other girls may have resulted in her feelings of being "dirty" or "blemished."

The chaos that ensued when her father had been drinking and committed acts of violence were often the family's normal state instead of the abnormal. Being routinely threatened by her father, as well as criticized and blamed by her mother, would easily cause emotional conflict about one's self-worth or value to the family.

Children in these environments often seek out ways to escape, whether physically, mentally, or socially. For Phyllis, her way of escape was socially, as she developed friendships that allowed her to minimize the time spent with her family. Unfortunately, this did not work out in her long-term favor, as she was ill-prepared for how to handle intimate relationships.

Developmental and social research has found that children reared in the authoritarian style of parenting tend to suffer from higher degrees of aggression, withdrawal, or domination by their peers. Upon closer examination of Phyllis's story, she appeared to struggle more with the domination of her peers,

---

*Bryan Glazier is a Florida Licensed Marriage and Family Therapist and Florida Licensed Mental Health Counselor. Dr. Glazier has a Doctorate degree in Psychology, and a Master's degree in Marriage and Family Counseling. Dr. Glazier has worked in both public and private sectors, and currently works as a civilian clinical counselor for the Department of the Navy. Dr. Glazier has received training in the topic of domestic violence, and provides clinical services and training to those who have experienced it, as well as other emotional and relational concerns. Dr. Glazier is a Florida Board of Clinical Social Work-, Marriage and Family Therapist-, and Mental Health Counselor-approved supervisor for Mental Health Counselors and has served as an Adjunct Instructor at Pensacola State College.

Commentary

specifically in the area of intimate partners. For instance, she may have felt unimportant to her family, and often received personal criticisms. When she first met JJ, the initial stage was a whirlwind romance stumbled upon while out horseback riding with a friend. Phyllis was mesmerized by the handsome guy at the lake. The fleeting moment was etched into her mind until, suddenly, the "what could have been" became the "what is" as JJ showed up at her school. The relationship skyrocketed into a blissful, passionate, youthful love.

She was treated as she had only fantasized about being treated. She was taken to movies, dances, and dinners, all of which was beyond the reach of what was possible by her own family. This person—this one special person—loved her, which was proof to her that there was a distinct "specialness" about her now. JJ had chosen *her*—not someone else, but her. Further proof of how "special" she was can be seen when Phyllis describes JJ as becoming more "possessive" by dictating her dress habits, limiting her social contact with other guys, and threatening other guys. The "in love" view is about being wanted, accepted, and prized. The emptiness of approval, acceptance, and value once felt in the home was now fulfilled and overflowing because of JJ. Phyllis had become someone special.

Now, the cliché of hindsight being 20/20 would fit right here. One can see the emergence of intimate partner abuse. As the partner limits the social setting for the victim, the view of the victim is constricted into believing the abuser is simply devoted. As Phyllis put it, "We didn't care about anything anyone was saying. We had each other." The focus shifted from living her own life, to working to maintain and secure the happiness of her partner. "The best thing I could give him was myself."

Unfortunately, this often costs the victim, whether it is physically or emotionally. This is illustrated in Phyllis's and JJ's first instance of "making love." While not a wonderful physical experience for Phyllis, she was emotionally invested, while JJ, in the end, demonstrated his lack of emotional investment in an act of humiliation towards Phyllis with a simple statement, "I thought you were a virgin." The impact of this statement upon Phyllis is evident a few short lines later. "As time passed, JJ seemed to forget about his disappointment in me." JJ's simple statement reinforced Phyllis's feelings of being "less than" or "not good enough" planted during her childhood. This enabled JJ to control her because it increased the possibility that others would feel the same way about her.

At this point, the gateway to dependence is crossed, and the victim begins to work only to make the partner happy and calm, because this is just the way life is—the way it was observed in Phyllis's family of origin. Of course, this dependency creates an imbalance in the relationship in favor of the abuser, who seems to always give slightly less to the relationship but acts as if he is the only one invested.

Often, people on the outside of this type of relationship don't seem to fully grasp the complexities that make up the relationship. In reading through the dynamics of JJ and Phyllis's relationship, it is easy to see the dangers and risks to Phyllis. However, in the moment of the lived experience, the repertoire of behaviors is often focused on ensuring that the partner remains calm and content in order to survive.

Phyllis ended up in a situation in which she felt she had no choice but to run away from home and marry JJ. Her father was physically abusive, and her mother highly critical and minimally supportive, so the very possibility of sharing or opening up about a secret that would "make me feel dirty and rotten" was terrifying at the least, and more like feeling that life itself was ending. Once the decision had been made, Phyllis "gave up the reins of control and prayed he knew what he was doing" as she ran away with JJ.

As Phyllis recounts the life of the newlywed couple, one can see the multiple similarities between her marriage to JJ and what she had experienced as a child in her family of origin. As the newlywed couple began their life together, the cycle of abuse reset, and the couple, or should it be said, the abuser, JJ, acted as if the abuse had never happened. Of course, Phyllis had not forgotten the intimidation, verbal abuse, and most of all "the slap," or the more accurate description, the physical abuse.

This is a parallel to how her father would act after an episode of anger and abuse in the family home. The family would pull themselves back together, attend church, ask for repentance (until the next time), and go about daily life once again. Even the creating of nicknames and teasing was present, just as in childhood. JJ returned to his "old" habits, and began the degrading comments once again. Nicknames such as "Queen Lead Bottom" and "Ms. Round Pound" replaced terms of endearment such as "I love you." The characteristics of Phyllis's family of origin began to be reflected in her marital relationship with JJ as he began to stay out until the early morning hours, or not return home at all.

While there is no indication that Phyllis's father was unfaithful to her mother, the outcomes were the same upon return to the home. The strong-willed Phyllis confronted her husband, which resulted in JJ pushing her down

Commentary

and sitting on her, threatening to "shut her up" with a pair of plyers. As JJ mocked Phyllis, she became aware of her role to him. "He set the stage for our marriage—I'll do what I please, and if you say anything about it, I'll hurt you . . . bad."

This is a direct comparison to the alcohol-fueled rages that her father would often have upon returning from a night of drinking. The numerous times Phyllis's father got his gun out and threatened someone with it, broke furniture in the home, and spewed verbal threats at family events seem to be a template for Phyllis's future marital happiness.

Of course, the parallels between Phyllis's family of origin are not limited to JJ and Phyllis's father. Phyllis also drew upon the resources that she was exposed to in order to survive and cope with the circumstances. If you recall, Phyllis was cared for initially by her nanny, with whom she spent a great deal of time. Phyllis was introduced to things such as cooking, sewing, and "taking care" of the household. This was reinforced by JJ's grandmother, or "Granny." She furthered Phyllis's love of cooking and taking care of the home, so that is what Phyllis did.

She invested herself in what gave her a sense of peace, belonging, and comfort. She began to truly immerse herself in the caring of her children, providing her own family a nice and *respectable* home. She found an element of pride in herself through what she was able to accomplish in her surroundings. This quality of self-respect, or finding the value in one's self, is what would help her to push forward through her life. For the time being, though, it would need to be further developed.

In the course of a violent relationship with an intimate partner, it is not uncommon for the victim to want to leave the relationship, but there always seems to be something that draws the victim back into the relationship. Phyllis explains these circumstances very accurately: "I left him a couple of times over the years. Once he learned I was at a cousin's in Pensacola, I went back because I had no way to sustain the separation. I had no money, no education that gave me a real marketable skill, and I didn't want to burden friends and family." These are the type of burdens individuals outside the relationship often do not understand fully.

Of course, resolve, the outcome of developed self-respect, often puts things into perspective, which Phyllis finally developed at their ten-year anniversary. As JJ lay sleeping during the movie, Phyllis took her first step out the door— realized she actually deserved better. As she stated, "I looked at him with sheer disgust. I hated him. I actually *hated* him. It was at that moment that I decided our marriage was over. In my heart, it was over. In my brain, it was over. But I knew the break would not be easy. Nothing with JJ was ever easy."

Even with this change of mind, one has to remember that the abusive partner is not going to simply acquiesce. JJ continued to exert his power and control over Phyllis, even to the point of raping her. Many people struggle with the concept of whether a spouse can be raped by her partner, but it becomes a clearer question when you read how Phyllis describes the experience: "The only thing he cared about was having sex. He wouldn't take no for an answer. I didn't want him to touch me ever again. He held me hostage in our bedroom until I had sex with him. He would penetrate me, with my fists clenched on my chest and tears running down my face. He did not care, and in fact, he did not appear to notice."

It becomes increasingly more evident that it *is* possible to be raped by one's spouse. Fortunately, this rape became the catalyst Phyllis needed to get out or get killed trying.

This appears to be the first step in breaking a cycle she herself observed in almost two generations of her family's history. Phyllis made the crucial decision to get out, but contrary to what seems to be the norm in everyday social beliefs, trying to leave an abusive relationship has numerous complexities and consequences for the victim. When Phyllis first verbalized her desire for a divorce, she observes: "He [JJ] got angry. He would not let me leave, nor leave me alone. He kept pushing me, then tried to kiss me. He barred my exit and kept me in the bedroom. We talked and talked and talked. He would not let me leave the room. He held me captive all day."

Putting up this type of barrier simply prevents the victim from saying she is going to leave, and then doing it. In order to ensure a greater degree of success, it is almost imperative the victim formulate a plan, drawing upon whatever potential resources she believes are present. She has been through the daily cycle with the abuser, and often knows *when* to leave, just not *how to survive beyond that first step.*

In preparation, Phyllis again resorted to the skills and almost innate abilities she had learned during those years as a child around people such as her mother, and Grandma Brown, and then JJ's granny. She had witnessed her mother's tenacity in setting up her own business, working at whatever was available, and seeking whatever means necessary in order to accomplish the goal at hand. For her mother, it was the beauty shop which provided her an

Commentary

outlet, both financial and emotional, to deal with the abuse of Phyllis's father.

For Phyllis, it was pursuing an education, as well as a job that would provide a financial and social basis for her to accomplish her goal of getting away from JJ.

As previously discussed, the underlying feelings of being special and accepted were, for Phyllis, often a potential unconscious motivating drive. Once hired by the insurance company, she excelled, and in return, she received a great deal of positive affirmation of her accomplishments, both by her colleagues and by her customers. This also led to one of the most influential resources she would have in her escape from JJ and in her quest for love.

During her time selling insurance, Phyllis stumbled onto a figure who would provide her with what she believed was true love and acceptance. The relationship between Phyllis and Paul Leverett was not one of whirlwind romance, but more of a steady reliance upon one another. It was more of an emotional relationship that turned physical, a stark contrast to the budding relationship between her and JJ. In examining the relationship, Paul needed Phyllis just as much as she needed him. They each filled a void in the life of the other. Paul was reportedly unhappy in his marriage, and often felt victimized or taken for granted. Phyllis felt unappreciated and unloved in her marriage. Each of them leaned upon the other for emotional support. It was this dependence that seemed to draw the couple together. Of course, a major roadblock of Phyllis's life was in the way—JJ—and she still wanted out regardless of her relationship with Paul.

As those in abusive relationships know and many on the outside don't, leaving the abuser is not as easy as simply packing a bag and finding a new place to live. As you read, each time Phyllis left JJ, it placed another person at risk of harm, such as her mother and her friends. Phyllis faced this several times as she worked to distance herself from JJ. He would show up at her friend's apartment, looking for her, dragging her down hallways and stairways, and then disappearing once again with no consequence. Even involving law enforcement was to no avail, because during that time, without evidence of harm, nothing would be done.

In order to protect their loved ones, victims will often leave without warning or allowing others to know where they are. This is out of necessity and not personal desire. For Phyllis, it meant living in a motel in another town until the date of her divorce.

Just because a divorce is finalized doesn't mean the risk of abuse is over for the victim. As Phyllis put it, "Even after the divorce was final, I never felt safe." For example, when Phyllis, accompanied by her niece for safety reasons, went to pick up her children from visiting with JJ, there were threats of violence and intimidation. JJ "grabbed me and dragged me toward the bedroom," and after she escaped the house and thought she had made it safely into the car, "at once, he was angry, and in a split-second he reached into the car through the half-rolled-down window and grabbed my shirt. He kept pulling and banging me hard against the window." Even if the victim is able to move forward in her life, there is always the threat of violence by the abuser.

Phyllis felt she had begun moving forward in her relationship with Paul, her emotional knight in shining armor. She had her own place, and felt somewhat protected with a firearm by her bed "just in case" JJ were to show up again. Phyllis had done it—she had escaped the marriage and broken the cycle in her family history, or at least that's what she believed. A brief passage describes how the victim can quickly go from feeling like a survivor to a victim once again:

"The house must have been quiet, because the slight noise I heard outside awakened me. I looked at the clock on my dresser, and it was almost 3:30 a.m. I stared at the ceiling, listening intently, and again I heard something outside my window. My porch light was on, but I hadn't seen any car lights. Almost instinctively, I grabbed for my gun. It was in my right hand, and I stood up on the floor just to the side of my bed, left leg standing, right knee bent, and I sank deeply into my mattress as my weight shifted. I leaned over and opened the curtain to take a peek at what might have caused the noise. I pushed the curtain back, and stuck my face up close, so I could look outside.

Shock and fear were my immediate response, as I focused on the barrel of a gun pointed against the glass. The barrel was pointed right at the center of my face. Hot water rushed through my veins. I felt faint and I thought my legs might give way under me.

Simultaneously, I heard a voice saying, "If you move, I'm blowing your head off." The curtain moved in my hand. "Don't move, bitch, or I'll kill you now." Those words will never leave my head completely, even to this day. It was JJ standing in the flower bed, between the big bush and up against my window. The porch light fully illuminated him, and we were less than two feet apart, our only barrier a single window pane. I was paralyzed and trembling. He was laughing, and he told me he wanted me to see something. He kept reminding me that, if I tried to move, he was going to unload his gun into my face. I

Commentary

looked into his hate-filled eyes and knew I couldn't escape.

My options were spinning in my head. My fight or flight instincts ignited, my frontal lobe trying to take over. My hand was behind the headboard, so he didn't know I had a loaded gun in my hand. My mind told me that if I killed him where he stood, everyone would then see he was at my home with a loaded gun. If I tried to jump to the side, I knew I could not get clear of the window before I would be hit. Even if I jumped toward the corner, I was afraid the bullets could reach me. I was desperate.

He wanted me to look at what he had in his hand. He held up a bullet and he asked me, "Can you see this, you filthy whore? Can you see this?" He shoved the bullet up against the window, with the bullet in his fingers only inches from my face. "I scratched your name in these bullets, and I am going to kill you." He was speaking through lips so tight, it was as if he had no lips at all. I looked at him, and his eyes were dilated with rage. I knew him well enough to recognize the distraught, agonized look on his face. It was as if all his features were exaggerated and distorted. This was real and it was almost over."

What seemed like forward progress in her life again became a nightmare of the past. The emotional fear of certain death began to replay in her mind and her life. Fortunately, there was a difference this time. There was Paul, who seems to be her emotional refuge, because he apparently accepted Phyllis regardless of her circumstances. Paul would do whatever it took to protect her, including hiring bodyguards, providing financial help, and just being there for her, even in the midst of his own scandal.

The scandal surrounding Paul Leverett arose over the death of his wife, Elizabeth. Without rehashing all the details, some aspects of the incident reinforce the rejection and criticisms that Phyllis faced early in her life. There were allegations of Phyllis being the "other woman" in Paul's life, which led to the destruction of his marriage, as well as Phyllis being charged with perjury. Paul's own attorney made sexualized comments towards her, which could be easily compared to the criticisms she experienced as a child by her peers and her family. Remember the instances of Phyllis feeling "dirty," "blemished," and "humiliated" as a child? The scandal-related accusations surrounding her would cause those feelings to resurface, as well as cause an inner conflict over what she had been through.

Here was her emotional knight in shining armor, who had demonstrated nothing but loyalty and acceptance towards her, being accused of such a crime, and her being accused of having "influenced" it. This turmoil caused an instant flashback to the accusations of her mother during the altercation between JJ and Thom, in which Phyllis's mother exclaimed, "This is *your* fault!"

Phyllis was trying to rebuild her life once again, reaching out, showing care and compassion to Paul's children—something she felt had been missing in her own life and theirs—hoping for acceptance and love from them, but often feeling less than successful. So, once again, Phyllis resorted to the resources that had carried her through some of the darkest times in her life. She invested herself in her life, her surroundings, and her children, including Paul's this time.

She toils away at making the home an inviting, warm, and loving place as she works to bury the emotional scars of her history. She focuses on the children, working to invest herself in them, providing them with a sense of security, love, and acceptance she had always longed for, and never wanting her own children to doubt. Though legally married to Paul, and loyal, and emotionally bonded to him, she found herself, because of the scandal, once again alone.

Never one to sit back and just allow things to happen, Phyllis relied once again on her internal resources. With Paul being imprisoned, and her divorce from him finalized, her focus shifted back to survival, as she often was required to do in the past. This time was different, though, because it was not a focus on personal and physical survival, but more working towards a healthy functioning life. By this time, she knew the drill, and she set out on the journey of rebuilding herself.

As she had frequently demonstrated in the past, Phyllis knew how to take care of herself in the physical realm, but the emotional and relational areas continued to throw challenges at her. After her divorce, she began dating a man who she once again thought of as being genuine and sincere. He didn't seem like the others in the past. As she described it, "He was the first man I met that didn't hesitate to stand by my side to fight my battles," while all the others seemed to have only wanted one thing.

But not this one. He had all the "right" credentials for giving her the acceptance and approval she unknowingly desired. As she put it, "The guy that helped me move was doing all the right things to get close to me. He invited me often to join the fun when his drill group gathered after work, and that crazy group provided side-splitting laughter and fun like I hadn't experienced in a long time . . . And he was one of those great big braggadocio guys from Pittsburgh, part of a large tight-knit Jewish family. He was full of himself, and

Commentary

I fell madly in love with him. He was like no one I had ever known."

Now, one would think that with everything she had been through, slightly more caution and guardedness would be in order, but you have to remember that we often get blinded by what we want to see, and fail to see what we should see. By now, I'm sure you can see the pattern developing, but if not, let's take a quick refresher. A lack of emotional connectedness and supportiveness during childhood may promote an unconscious or unknowing innate drive to seek out these behaviors later in life. We can't say that Phyllis had not learned anything from her previous experiences, because she did initially inquire about him being married, which he dutifully denied. And when informed by her friends that he was not officially single, she confronted him about it.

Unfortunately, although he met the criteria she believed would make for a better partner—educated, strong religious background, well-groomed, and well-mannered—she continued to be blinded by her quest for love. Phyllis again put her heart all in, longing for that feeling of being loved while ignoring those signs and symptoms around her telling her to beware. This time it was her children, as she put it in her story: "I should have known better—my children hated him. They were teenagers who had been through a lot of bad experiences. He was a rigid military type who tried to back me up and reinforce the rules I laid out."

Phyllis is again off to another wedding with the unconscious drive of again thinking this marriage would fill the void. And as history has a tendency to do, another reminder of the past emerges. Signs and symptoms fly around as if on banners behind airplanes that you just barely miss as the plane passes behind the buildings, or the billboard that you catch a glimpse of but whose words you can't quite make out.

The fantasy wedding at a local country club, the wedding dress of silk imported from the grand city of New York, and the formal wedding photos with the bride as the star—everything seemed perfect and enchanted. Well, everything except for the groom's pouting about not being the center of attention during the photo shoot, and his choosing to chase his dream job in the midst of planning and having a wedding. So, off to the courthouse for the ceremony she goes—more signs of the past.

During her travels to competitions with the all-girl cheerleading team that she loved so much, her "husband also tried to love them"—still more signs of the past. Another sign was his reaction to the positive publicity Phyllis got from to her modeling exposure. "With me on his arm," she writes, "he strutted like a peacock." Now, please don't misunderstand; it is easy to miss signs. As mentioned before, they sometimes seem to slip right by.

One by now would expect the past to rear its ugly head again. Phyllis described how her new husband, "my husband, the self-proclaimed stellar performer, decides the [jet-flight] school is just too tough." As we have observed, just like her mother and her grandmother, Phyllis was often loyal to a fault. Because her husband asked her to go with him, the unexpected [to her] happens, and in return he thanks her by telling the manager of the school, "I really am sorry to have to come in here like this, but my wife [finger pointed at me] wants me to quit." It is almost as if one wants to say, "Hi there, Blame! Haven't seen you in a while. Welcome back," and back with a vengeance it came.

She had feelings of being embarrassed at that moment, and then "I started getting flashbacks of my Texas experience with JJ. The kicker was the lipstick all over his dress shirt that he took with him on his National Guard two-week required duty in Panama." The patterns of the past were back: the frequent arguments, the jealousy, the leaving and coming back together. The only difference this time was that Phyllis had more resources than she previously had, and she sought the services of a professional to help make the marriage work.

As a psychotherapist, I often find the presenting symptoms—what people initially pursue counseling for—to be interesting, but the root issue is usually something greater. For Phyllis, it was during this time that someone other than her actually said the words she had been dreading and denying. Those dreadful words were from her counselor. "She said she had been using a treatment method for victims of domestic abuse. She said, 'You are a victim of domestic abuse. I don't think marriage counseling will help you or your marriage.' And the denial began, "*A victim?* Oh no, not again. I will not be a victim again. I am a strong, competent, and capable woman, I kept telling myself. I wasn't seeing myself in that light. I was just trying to make my marriage work!"

As is often the case in therapy, most of the work is completed outside of the office setting. Those words of the therapist rang incessantly in Phyllis's mind, as the clouds seemed to part and the epiphany occurred: "Oh my God, I am literally back to square one. I had tried hard not to duplicate my mistakes in selecting a husband. No matter what, here I am, back in the same situation again." And as she had seen so vividly in her past, when her mother was loyal to her father through all the anger and rampages, Phyllis, too, was going to make the marriage work, in spite of the concerns expressed to her by her therapist, and despite her own acknowledgment that she was back in the past.

Commentary

Reminded of the criticism of the past, Phyllis finds herself working hard to prove the past wrong, trying to believe that she was worth something and not to blame for everything, and continuing to work on her marriage. Well, as predicted by the counselor, things did escalate on a "reconciliation" ski trip, in which Phyllis, attempting to exercise her own personal boundaries, ended with a trip souvenir in the form of "a black and blue jaw from where he had slapped me repeatedly after he took his 245 lb. frame, sat it on my chest, and pinned me to the bed."

Fortunately for Phyllis, the divorce was already in the process, and she was able to escape this blast from the past, although it did cost her, physically, emotionally, and financially.

Now, by this point in the book, many readers were probably thinking, "Is she kidding me?" or "What is she doing still picking these types of guys to marry?" I offer not an excuse but an explanation. Researchers in the field of social and developmental psychology have found that many people who experienced trauma would, almost compulsively, expose themselves to situations reminiscent of the original trauma, although they may not make a connection between their current actions and the historical trauma they experienced.

So, maybe, just maybe, Phyllis continued to gravitate towards these types of individuals in order to unconsciously repeat the horrible events of her childhood. *Probably not.* What person would ever deliberately put themselves in those types of situations?

A more plausible explanation may be that the individuals she chose presented, at least on the outside, as the exact opposite of what she had experienced as a child. Each person appeared to give her love and acceptance, and had, as she put it, "the correct credentials" to be successful. Each of the individuals she had married to this point were outgoing, larger than life individuals, who worked hard, made great money, and seemed to be adored by others. Of course, what one sees behind closed doors is another story.

If there is a common thread present throughout the life of Phyllis, it is in her resilience. By this time, she had demonstrated the ability to pull herself out of nothing and create a sustainable lifestyle. After marriage number three, as if a significant change was beginning to occur for her, she set a few more long-term guidelines and rules. As Phyllis writes, "I set new guiding parameters for my life: care for myself indefinitely, never again trust a man to keep commitments, work hard to pay off all debts, assure my ability to sustain 'aloneness,' and enjoy my life and relationships with family and friends without expecting anything in return (*that way I wouldn't be disappointed*). My new barometer for intimate relationships, if any, was an initial question I'd always ask myself: 'Is this person someone I really like, find sexually attractive, *and* someone I feel sure really likes me, finds me interesting, funny, and sexually attractive. Plus, when I see this person the next day, will I feel comfortable that we still are friends?' It was amazing how that test weeded out most suitors. *Oh yeah!"*

Of course, on the surface, these changes do not seem to work perfectly, as again she seems to use the same old criteria for a potential partner as she did before: attractive, successful, and interested. One of the key differences is that she seemed more cautious this time around, as in the case of an admiral she went on a date with. While flattered by the attention and the sense of acceptance and approval he seemingly gave her, she did not allow these things to dictate her emotions surrounding the relationship. Once he proclaimed his intentions, she quickly removed herself from the situation. As she reflected, "Please give me credit that I am finally learning the nature of man. It makes no difference if they love you or not. They want 'different' stuff. It's not me. It's not their wives. It's them."

Several theories in psychology surrounding families and the ability to adapt are based on how families use the resources they have surrounding them, whether they be physical, emotional, or social. In applying that basic concept to Phyllis, one can see how she continued to evaluate the resources she had surrounding her and worked to overcome whatever stress, or hurdle, may have been before her. As she prepared to become a grandmother, she focused on those principles of doing what it takes to make a better life—one in which she is self-sufficient and not dependent upon anyone else to fill the voids of love and acceptance. She excelled at work, although this continued to bring those age-old criticisms to the fore, as, for example, when she simply appeared at a function at an officer's home without someone escorting her. The criticisms came more in the form of, "You are too nice looking. Don't ever come to a party again without an escort." Again came the blame for attracting the attention of males, especially married ones.

Another flashback to the past was being blamed for actions that clearly fell beyond the reach of one individual into the responsibility of others. And as always, Phyllis would accept the criticism and apply it to her life as another means of not wanting to offend others. This is evident in her preparing for the next party invitation. In order to protect others, she reached out to her ex-husband, the "narcissistic," "it's-my-wife's-fault-I-have-to-quit" ex-husband.

Commentary

Again, research has shown that when individuals face external dangers, whether it is an issue of pain, fear, fatigue, or loss, it often will drive them to seek care. The issue takes shape when healthy forms of support or comfort are not available. Victims will usually return to what is known. Often, this means a past abuser.

For Phyllis, there may not have been the risk of physical harm in this "need-an-escort" situation, but there was a risk of emotional and reputational harm. She had been through several instances in the past in which she was criticized because of her physical appearance, and this resulted in enormous stress upon her and her family. After all she had been through, her adaptation response was "nope, not this time." So, she reached out to the ex-husband in hopes of protecting herself once again.

Remember when Phyllis said she was changing? Well, the party she attended with her ex-husband became the turning point for her and her life. During the party, she struck up a conversation with another male, Bob, whom she described as "intriguing, dark, and handsome—very handsome." She wrote, "I liked the feel and the presence of the man." While the initial reaction of you, the reader, at that point, was probably, "Here we go again," subtle changes seemed to have happened with Phyllis. While she was attracted to him and flirtatious, Phyllis didn't throw her entire self into him. She seems to have been more cautious and inquisitive than she had been in prior relationships. She asked around, sought out information, and attempted to use the past as a learning experience to prevent future mistakes.

There were other differences as well this time. She refused to give her phone number to him until he assured her he was single. After their two first dates went awry, she didn't panic or appear to have an emotional meltdown because she may have "lost him." She persevered and remained focused on her own life. She seems to have set boundaries, as when she was initially unable to enjoy an afternoon with him due to her granddaughter.

Another notable difference was that he actually behaved differently than the other guys had. When she was ill, he was attentive and allowed her to stay *alone* in a separate room of his home, with no expectations. He made accommodations for her granddaughter, despite not having his own children. These details provide contrast from Phyllis's past choices.

A final major difference from her past relationships was the ability to stand on her own, not requiring someone else to fulfill her. The turning point for her, whether she was consciously aware of it or not, was when she was up front and forthcoming about her past. She knew the potential consequences of telling him about the horrors she had experienced throughout her life. As she states, "I told him my story. I told him I would understand if he was not interested in continuing the relationship."

This part right here seems like the completion of Phyllis. She no longer seemed to need acceptance or to be loved by someone. She seemed, for the first time, to have placed all her cards on the table and said, "This is who I am, and this is why." While she hoped for the best, she knew, consciously or unconsciously, she would be okay. No more feelings of being dependent; no more feelings of self-blame or criticism. She was emotionally whole. "He had no concerns about anything or anyone in my past. He was perfectly okay disregarding the issue. He held my hand and we have walked together since."

So, what is the point of all this so-called analysis of Phyllis's life? There are actually three points that I hope have been drawn out through this process. First, your family and history *do* influence your life. Your family—that system in which individual members have the ability to influence one another as well as the entire system—does have the ability to influence you throughout your life. As you can see through Phyllis's life, there were times when these influences may not have been readily noticeable or apparent to the individual, but that does not mean they were not present.

That being said, these familial influences do not have to define your life. Just because you experienced a horrific childhood or trauma does not mean it has to define you as a person. Remember all the negative situations Phyllis went through? Through them all, there was frequent evaluation of who she was and what she truly desired in her life. This often motivated her to seek out changes in her life, and you, the reader, have the ability to accomplish the same.

The second point is the need for advocacy, or what the Merriam-Webster Dictionary (2011) defines as "the act or process of providing support for a cause." Phyllis's life could single-handedly promote the cause for greater awareness and resources for the destructive issues of PTSD, sexual abuse of a child, family violence, alcohol abuse, and intimate partner violence. Several times during her life, Phyllis reached out to individuals, family, and community officials (law enforcement) seeking assistance. Each time her needs were diminished, criticized, or ignored altogether.

But the problem is out there, as are the resources to deal with it. A simple internet web search for family violence indicated a total of 21 million links,

Commentary

and a search for domestic violence returned 39 million links. The resources are available, but often it is not necessarily the lack of available resources, but more likely the lack of individuals hearing and willing to help that keeps individuals from getting to those resources. Furthermore, the resources must be more diligently present throughout the entire process, which, as can be observed through Phyllis's life, may be a long, long time.

The third and final point has to do with resiliency. Resiliency is one of those psychological buzzwords that focuses on one's ability to "rebound" or "bounce" back from adversity. If there is a key idea to emphasize through all the trauma and craziness that was Phyllis's life, it is the idea of resiliency. Resiliency is not a simple thing that one does one day, but more of a process that requires the individual to take a personal inventory and find that drive within themselves to push through whatever life is throwing at them.

Whether that is having a chaotic family, including violence, being sexually abused or molested on repeated occasions, being physically and emotionally abused by one's partner, or something else, resiliency is finding that core being of who you are and empowering it to move you forward, one step at a time, one hurdle at a time, until you are back—back to who you were, but better.

Because now you've shown yourself what you are capable of. You are no longer a victim who just suffers through all the pain, agony, and criticisms.

You are a SURVIVOR.

References

Babcock, J., Green, C., & Robie, C. (2004) Does batter's treatment work? A meta-analytic review of domestic violence treatment. Clinical Psychology Review, 23(8). 1023-1053. doi:10.1016/j.cpr.2002.07.001

Babcock, J., Waltz, J., Jacobson, N., & Gottman, J. (1993). Power and violence: The relation between communication patterns, power discrepancies, and domestic violence. Journal of Consulting and Clinical Psychology, 61(1), 40-50. doi: 10.1037/0022-006X.61.1.40

Boss, P. (2002). Family Stress Management: A Context Approach. Thousand Oaks, CA: Sage Publications.

Bowen, M. (1966). The use of family theory in clinical practice. Comprehensive Psychiatry, 7(5). 345-374. doi:10.1016/S0010-440X(66)80065-2.

Coleman, F. (1997). Stalking Behavior and the cycle of domestic violence. Journal of Interpersonal Violence, 12(3). 420-432. doi: 10.1177/088626097012003007

Cumsille, P., & Epstein, N. (1994). Family cohesion, family adaptability, social support, and adolescent depressive symptoms in outpatient clinic families. Journal of Family Psychology, 8(2), 202-214. doi:10.1037/0893-3200.8.2.202

Dekovkic, M. & Meeus, W. (1997). Peer relations in adolescence: Effects of parenting and adolescents' self concept. Journal of Adolescence, 20 (2). 163-175. doi:10.1006/jado.1996.0074

Edleson, J. (1999). Children's witnessing of adult domestic violence. Journal of Interpersonal Violence, 14(8). 839-870. doi: 10.1177/088626099014008004

El-Sheikh, M., & Buckhalt, J. (2003). Parental problem drinking and children's adjustment: Attachment and family functioning as moderators and mediators of risk. Journal of Family Psychology, 17(4), 510-520. doi:10.1037/0893-3200.17.4.510

Fergusson, D. & Lynskey, M. (1996). Adolescent resiliency to family adversity. Journal of Child Psychology and Psychiatry, 37(3). 281-292. doi: 10.1111/j.1469-7610.1996.tb01405.x

Hawley, D., & DeHann, L. (1996). Towards a definition of family resilience: Integrating lifespan and family perspectives. Family Process, 35(3), 283-298. doi: 10.1111/j.1545-5300.1996.00283.x

Hobfoll, S. E., & Spielberger, C. D. (2003). Family stress: Integrating theory and measurement. In P. Boss & C. Mulligan (Eds.), Family stress: Classic and contemporary readings (pp.142-157). Thousand Oaks, CA: Sage.

Johnson, M. & Ferraro, K., (2000). Research on Domestic Violence in the 1990s: Making Distinctions. Journal of Marriage and Famiyl Therapy, 62(4).948-963. doi: 10.1111/j.1741-3737.2000.00948.x

Johnson, P. (2001). Dimensions of functioning in alcoholic and nonalcoholic families. Journal of Mental Health Counseling, 23, 127—136.

Lavee, Y., McCubbin, H.I., & Patterson, J. (1985). The Double ABCX model of family stress and adaptation: An empirical test by analysis of structural equations with latent variables. Journal of Marriage and the Family, 47,(4), 811-825. doi:10.2307/352326

Lin, P., & Chen, J. (1994). Characteristics of a healthy family and family strengths: A crosscultural study. Retrieved from ERIC database. (ED377101).

McCubbin, H. I. & Patterson, J. (1983). The Family Stress Process—The Double ABCX model of adjustment and adaptation. Marriage & Family Review, 6(1), 7-37. doi:10.1300/J002v06n01_02

Mounts, N. (2002). Parental management of adolescent peer relationships in context: The role of parenting style. Journal of Family Psychology,16(1), 58-69. doi: 10.1037/0893-3200.16.1.58

Neal, J. & Frick-Horbury, D. (2001) The effects of parenting styles and childhood attachment patterns on intimate relationships. Journal of Instructional Psychology 28, (3).

Olson, D. H., Sprenkle, D. H., & Russell, C. S. (1979). Circumplex model of marital and family systems I: Cohesion and adaptability dimensions, family types, and clinical applications. Family Process, 18, 3-28.

Patterson, J. (1989). A family stress model: The family adjustment and adaptation response. In C. Ramsely Jr. (Ed), Family Systems in Medicine (pp. 95-118). New York, NY: Guilford Press.

Pence, E. & Paymar, M., (1993). Education Groups for Men Who Batter: The Duluth Model. Springer Publishing Company: New York

Retzlaff, R. (2007). Families of children with Rett syndrome: Stories of coherence and resilience. Families, Systems, & Health, 25(3), 246-262. doi: 10.1037/1091-7527.25.3.246

Richardson, G. (2002). The metatheory of resilience and resiliency. Journal of Clinical Psychology, 58(3). 307-321. doi: 10.1002/jclp.10020

Van Der Kolk, B., (1989). The compulsion to repeat the trauma. Pediatric Clinics of North America, 12(2). 389-411.

Acknowledgments

First and foremost, I wish to acknowledge my husband, Captain Robert (Bob) Hain, MC, (USN Retired), who is strong enough, self-assured enough, and loves me enough to be unconcerned how this book's publication will ultimately affect his life. He has encouraged me to grow, to be myself, and to love myself, without concern for what others may think. Knowing my husband's love is not contingent upon my possessing society's approval has been paramount to my healing. I would have continued to hide my pain if he wasn't the unselfish and loving husband he has proven himself to be. No wonder I love him so much.

My journey has also been documented for my children. Long before I ever considered publicly exposing intimate details and secrets, they often asked me to write a book. I know now, as adults, that they can understand love relationships, and my human failures, having experienced some of those things in their own lives. They are now my dear friends as well as my adult children. I pray this book helps with their healing.

To my many former co-workers at Fleet and Family Support Center, Naval Air Station Pensacola, Florida, I want to thank you for contributing to my healing. There is nothing like working every day with a group of social workers, clinicians, counselors, and marriage and family therapists. Through good times and bad, they have always been there to listen, normalize, and offer support. Working with them made me feel almost as if I had been in group therapy for eight years. Working with these caring people was such a pleasure, and I thank each of them for the life's work they have chosen.

The silence of shame empowers the abuser. Holding that belief, I decided to start the slow and arduous path of documenting my travels through this life. I thank you for walking along with me. Because I knew you would be by my side, the tough parts were easier. In the end, I am stronger for breaking my silence, and it will all be worthwhile if after reading my story, you are stronger too.

—Phyllis Hain, March 2013

My Special Thanks to...

Sylvia Starling, LMHC

Sylvia, a co-worker at Fleet and Family Support Center, graciously volunteered untold hours to work as my first proof reader and "editor-in-chief." She helped me prepare my manuscript for submission to publishers. Even though she "bled" red commas all over my first draft, she gave me encouragement that my ability as a fledgling writer conveyed heartfelt truth and engaging literary promise.

Bryan Glazier, Ph.D., LMFT, LMHC

Bryan, another co-worker, was the first person to read my completed first draft. He wrote an insightful clinical commentary and collaborated with Sylvia and me as we determined how I could use my story to best serve other victims, especially the ones suffering in the silence of shame.

AND, to Bruce L. Bortz, Esq., Publisher, Bancroft Press

My sincere appreciation to Mr. Bruce Bortz, my publisher and editor. Finding Bruce had to be fate because he was willing to vet my manuscript and use his expertise to guide me on the long path of bringing my first book to print. He was able to see value in sharing my life with others, and he intuitively gave me what I needed most—someone to truly hear and preserve my voice. His innate sense recognized that lives can start the journey to change when their voices are met with empathy and kindness. I deeply appreciate his gentle guidance in keeping my focus, not on myself but on the bigger goal of helping victims of abuse.

About the Author

Photo by: Robert Hain

Phyllis Hain was born in Alabama and grew up in the Gulf Coast city of Pensacola, Florida. She considers herself an accomplished graduate of the "School of Very Hard Knocks," though she points with pride to the fact that, despite being a teenage mother forced her to drop out of high school, she somehow managed, in her thirties, to earn a college degree in communications and at age 47, a B.S. in Management of Human Resources from Faulkner University in Montgomery, Alabama.

She worked for over twenty-one years for the Department of the Navy. For five and a half years, she was a Navy Sexual Assault Response Coordinator (SARC), and spent four years as a Family Advocacy Educator, during which time she taught well over 20,000 students. Working alongside military and community law enforcement, she helped educate first-responders on how to properly document incidents and how to provide sensitive, effective support to victims of sexual assault. She provided response to hundreds of victims in crisis—all during a career in which she received hundreds of hours of training in the field of domestic violence, child abuse, child sexual abuse, sexual assault and victim intervention, and the correlation between animal abuse and domestic violence.

Highlights of Phyllis's DoD service include: working on the National Joint Task Force in Washington DC, which studied the problem of sexual assault in the military; working with the National Organization for Victims' Assistance; serving as Vice President of Northwest Florida's Victim Coalition; and being selected NASP's Civilian of the Year for her contributions to the Sexual Assault Victim Intervention Program.

Inspired by interviewing, and responding to, many courageous victims and survivors of abuse, she decided to undergo what turned out to be the multi-year ordeal of writing an autobiography about her own tumultuous life as the victim of child abuse, child sexual abuse, sexual assault, and spousal abuse. The resulting *Diamond in the Dark* is a Southern girl's true story of growing up in the midst of jealousy and family violence—the gripping, unceasingly honest account of a blond, green-eyed child of a beautiful farmer's daughter and a Marine sent home from WWII suffering from acute brain trauma.

Phyllis survived devastating domestic violence and abuse by creating two personas—one for the darkness of home, the other constantly seeking the brilliance of life. Persistence, and a winning smile, opened a path for her to escape, and gave her strength to confront both the demons of her past and the darkness of truth. But it also led her to love, money, betrayal, murder, celebrated court trials, and prison, all taking place in what she calls the "oxymoronic world of Southern justice."

In time, Phyllis crossed paths with a handsome Navy doctor. She and Captain Robert Hain, Medical Corps (USN Ret), have been happily married for more than eighteen years. The two are now enjoying retirement together in the very place she spent her formative years—Pensacola, Florida.